# THE CONTINENTAL SHELF DELIMITATION BEYOND 200 NAUTICAL MILES

*The Continental Shelf Delimitation Beyond 200 Nautical Miles* provides an up-to-date and informed analysis of the now fast developing, yet confusing, field of the law of maritime delimitation. It examines the procedural matters in relation to the competence of international courts and tribunals in the light of the institutional framework of the United Nations Convention on the Law of the Sea and discusses the methodological questions arising out of the delimitation process. The book engages with the key concepts of maritime entitlement, delineation and delimitation with a view to developing a coherent and consistent approach to the delimitation of the continental shelf beyond 200 nautical miles. Essentially, it argues that the delimitation of the continental shelf will be unified with existing maritime delimitation, and a common approach to maritime boundary-making within and beyond 200 nautical miles is likely to emerge.

XUEXIA LIAO is an assistant professor at Peking University Law School. She completed her doctoral studies in International Law at the Graduate Institute of International and Development Studies, Geneva and was awarded the Diploma of the Hague Academy of International Law (2016). She was also the winner of the Writing Prize of International Cable Protection Committee in 2018.

# THE CONTINENTAL SHELF DELIMITATION BEYOND 200 NAUTICAL MILES

## Towards A Common Approach to Maritime Boundary-Making

XUEXIA LIAO
*Peking University Law School*

CAMBRIDGE
UNIVERSITY PRESS

CAMBRIDGE
UNIVERSITY PRESS

Shaftesbury Road, Cambridge CB2 8EA, United Kingdom

One Liberty Plaza, 20th Floor, New York, NY 10006, USA

477 Williamstown Road, Port Melbourne, VIC 3207, Australia

314–321, 3rd Floor, Plot 3, Splendor Forum, Jasola District Centre, New Delhi – 110025, India

103 Penang Road, #05–06/07, Visioncrest Commercial, Singapore 238467

Cambridge University Press is part of Cambridge University Press & Assessment,
a department of the University of Cambridge.

We share the University's mission to contribute to society through the pursuit of education, learning and research at the highest international levels of excellence.

www.cambridge.org
Information on this title: www.cambridge.org/9781108821650

DOI: 10.1017/9781108909112



First published 2022
First paperback edition 2026

*A catalogue record for this publication is available from the British Library*

*Library of Congress Cataloging-in-Publication data*
Names: Liao, Xuexia, 1989- author.
Title: The continental shelf delimitation beyond 200 nautical miles : towards a common approach to maritime boundary-making / Xuexia Liao, Peking University Law School, China.
Description: Cambridge, United Kingdom ; New York, NY : Cambridge University Press, 2021. | Includes bibliographical references and index.
Identifiers: LCCN 2021006958 (print) | LCCN 2021006959 (ebook) | ISBN 9781108830133 (hardback) | ISBN 9781108821650 (paperback) | ISBN 9781108909112 (epub)
Subjects: LCSH: Continental shelf–Law and legislation. | Maritime boundaries. | Territorial waters. | Maritime law.
Classification: LCC KZA1660 .L53 2021 (print) | LCC KZA1660 (ebook) | DDC 341.4/48–dc23
LC record available at https://lccn.loc.gov/2021006958
LC ebook record available at https://lccn.loc.gov/2021006959

ISBN 978-1-108-83013-3 Hardback
ISBN 978-1-108-82165-0 Paperback

# CONTENTS

# FIGURES

# TABLE OF CASES
*(in chronological order by jurisdiction)*

## International Court of Justice

Interpretation of Peace Treaties with Bulgaria, Hungary and Romania (Advisory Opinion) (First Phase) [1950] ICJ Rep 65

Fisheries case (United Kingdom *v.* Norway) [1951] ICJ Rep 116

Case of the Monetary Gold removed from Rome in 1943 (Preliminary Objections) [1954] ICJ Rep 19

South West Africa (Ethiopia *v.* South Africa; Liberia *v.* South Africa), Preliminary Objections [1962] ICJ Rep 319

North Sea Continental Shelf Cases (Federal Republic of Germany/Denmark; Federal Republic of Germany/Netherlands) [1969] ICJ Rep 3.

Aegean Sea Continental Shelf (Greece *v.* Turkey) [1978] ICJ Rep 3

Continental Shelf (Tunisia/Libyan Arab Jamahiriya) [1982] ICJ Rep 18

Delimitation of the Maritime Boundary in the Gulf of Maine Area (Canada/United States of America) [1984] ICJ Rep 246

Continental Shelf (Libyan Arab Jamahiriya/Malta) [1985] ICJ Rep 13

Military and Paramilitary Activities in and against Nicaragua (Nicaragua *v.* United States of America) (Merits) [1986] ICJ Rep 14

Frontier Dispute (Burkina Faso/Mali) [1986] ICJ Rep 554

Maritime Delimitation in the Area between Greenland and Jan Mayen (Denmark *v.* Norway) [1993] ICJ Rep 38

Legality of the Threat or Use of Nuclear Weapons, Advisory Opinion [1996] ICJ Rep 226

Maritime Delimitation and Territorial Questions (Qatar *v.* Bahrain) (Merits) [2001] ICJ Rep 40

Land and Maritime Boundary between Cameroon and Nigeria (Cameroon *v.* Nigeria: Equatorial Guinea intervening) [2002] ICJ Rep 303

Territorial and Maritime Dispute between Nicaragua and Honduras in the Caribbean Sea (Nicaragua *v.* Honduras) [2007] ICJ Rep 659

Application of the Convention on the Prevention and Punishment of the Crime of Genocide (Croatia *v.* Serbia) (Preliminary Objections) [2008] ICJ Rep 412

Maritime Delimitation in the Black Sea (Romania *v.* Ukraine) [2009] ICJ Rep 61

Dispute Regarding Navigational and Related Rights (Costa Rica *v.* Nicaragua) [2009] ICJ Rep 213

Pulp Mills on the River Uruguay (Argentina *v.* Uruguay) [2010] ICJ Rep 14

Jurisdictional Immunities of the State (Germany *v.* Italy: Greece intervening) [2012] ICJ Rep 99

Territorial and Maritime Dispute (Nicaragua *v.* Colombia) [2012] ICJ Rep 624

Maritime Dispute (Peru *v.* Chile) [2014] ICJ Rep 3

Whaling in the Antarctic (Australia *v.* Japan: New Zealand intervening) [2014] ICJ Rep 226

Question of the Delimitation of the Continental Shelf between Nicaragua and Colombia beyond 200 Nautical Miles from the Nicaraguan Coast (Nicaragua *v.* Colombia) (Preliminary Objections) [2016] ICJ Rep 100

Obligations concerning Negotiations relating to Cessation of the Nuclear Arms Race and to Nuclear Disarmament (Marshall Islands *v.* United Kingdom), Preliminary Objections [2016] ICJ Rep 833

Maritime Delimitation in the Indian Ocean (Somalia *v.* Kenya) (Preliminary Objections) [2017] ICJ Rep 3

Maritime Delimitation in the Caribbean Sea and the Pacific Ocean (Costa Rica *v.* Nicaragua) (Judgment) [2018] ICJ Rep 139

## Permanent Court of International Justice

Mavrommatis Palestine Concessions (Greece *v.* United Kingdom), Judgment on Jurisdiction [1924] PCIJ Rep, Series A.

## International Tribunal for the Law of the Sea

Southern Bluefin Tuna (New Zealand *v.* Japan; Australia *v.* Japan), Provisional Order of August 27, 1999, [1999] ITLOS Rep 280

Delimitation of the maritime boundary in the Bay of Bengal (Bangladesh/Myanmar), [2012] ITLOS Rep 4

Delimitation of the Maritime Boundary in the Atlantic Ocean (Ghana/Côte d'Ivoire), [2017] ITLOS Rep 4

## Arbitral Tribunals constituted under Annex VII UNCLOS

Maritime Boundary Arbitration (Barbados *v.* Trinidad and Tobago) (2006) XXVII RIAA 147

Maritime Boundary Arbitration (Guyana *v.* Suriname) (2007) XXX RIAA 1

Bay of Bengal Bay of Bengal Maritime Boundary Arbitration (Bangladesh *v.* India) (2014) 167 ILR 1

Chagos Marine Protected Area Arbitration (Mauritius *v.* United Kingdom), (2015) XXXI RIAA 359
South China Sea Arbitration (Philippines *v.* China) (Merits) (2016) 170 ILR 180

## Conciliation under Annex V UNCLOS

Timor Sea Conciliation (Timor-Leste *v.* Australia), Commission Report and Recommendations of September 19, 2016

## Ad hoc Arbitral Tribunals

Island of Palmas case (Netherlands/USA), (1926) II RIAA 829
Continental Shelf (France/UK) (1977) XVIII RIAA 3
Delimitation of the Maritime Boundary between Guinea and Guinea-Bissau (Guinea/Guinea-Bissau) (1985) XIX RIAA 149
Case concerning the Arbitral Award of July 31, 1989 (Guinea-Bissau/Senegal), (1990) 83 ILR 1
Decision in Case concerning Delimitation of Maritime Areas (St. Pierre and Miquelon), (1992) 31 ILM 1145
Second Stage of the Proceedings between Eritrea and Yemen (Maritime Delimitation) (Eritrea/Yemen) (1999) XXII RIAA 335
Arbitration between Newfoundland and Labrador and Nova Scotia (Newfoundland and Labrador/Nova Scotia) (Second Phase) (2002) 128 ILR 504
Arbitration between Croatia and Slovenia under the Arbitration Agreement of 4 November 2009 (Croatia/Slovenia), Award of 29 June 2017

# TABLE OF TREATIES

## Multilateral Treaties

*(in chronological order by date of adoption)*

Convention on the Continental Shelf (April 29, 1958), 499 UNTS 311

Vienna Convention on the Law of Treaties (May 23, 1969), 1155 UNTS 331

United Nations Convention on the Law of the Sea (December 10, 1982), 1833 UNTS

## Bilateral Treaties

*(in chronological order by date of conclusion)*

Agreement between the Government of the Commonwealth of Australia and the Government of the Republic of Indonesia Establishing Certain Seabed Boundaries in the Area of the Timor and Arafura Seas Supplementary to the Agreement of 18 May 1971 (October 9, 1972), 974 UNTS 319

Treaty between Australia and the Independent State of Papua New Guinea Concerning Sovereignty and Maritime Boundaries in the Area between the Two Countries, including the Area known as Torres Strait, and Related Matters (December 18, 1978), 1429 UNTS 207

1982 Agreement on Maritime Delimitation between the Government of Australia and the Government of the French Republic (January 4, 1982), 1329 UNTS 107

Agreement between the Government of Solomon Islands and the Government of Australia establishing certain sea and seabed boundaries (September 13, 1988), (1988) 12 LoSB 19

Agreement between the Republic of Ireland and the United Kingdom of Great Britain and Northern Ireland Concerning the Delimitation of the Continental Shelf between the Two Countries (November 7, 1988), 1765 UNTS 421

Treaty between the Republic of Trinidad and Tobago and the Republic of Venezuela on the Delimitation of Marine and Submarine Areas (April 18, 1990), in JI Charney and LM Alexander (eds.), *International Maritime Boundaries*, Vol. I (Martinus Nijhoff 1993) 657

Agreement between the United States of America and the Union of Soviet Socialist Republics on the maritime boundary (June 1, 1990), (1991) 17 LoSB 15.

Treaty between Australia and Indonesia Establishing an Exclusive Economic Zone Boundary and Certain Seabed Boundaries (March 14, 1997), (1997) 36 ILM 1053

Agreement between the Government of the Kingdom of Denmark along with the Local Government of Greenland on the one hand and the Government of the Republic of Iceland on the other hand on the Delimitation of the Continental Shelf and Fishery Zone in the Area between Greenland and Iceland (November 11, 1997), (1999) 39 LoSB 35

Treaty between Mexico and the United States on the Delimitation of the Continental Shelf in the Western Gulf of Mexico beyond 200 Nautical Miles (June 9, 2000), (2001) 44 LoSB 71

Treaty between Australia and New Zealand Establishing certain Exclusive Economic Zone and Continental Shelf Boundaries (July 25, 2004), 2441 UNTS 235 117

Agreement between the United Republic of Tanzania and the Republic of Kenya on the Delimitation of the Maritime Boundary of the Exclusive Economic Zone and the Continental Shelf (June 23, 2009), 2603 UNTS 37

Agreement between the Government of Barbados and the Government of the French Republic on the Delimitation of the Maritime Space between Barbados and France (October 15, 2009), 2663 UNTS 163

Treaty between the Republic of Trinidad and Tobago and Grenada on the Delimitation of Marine and Submarine Areas (April 21, 2010), (2010) 73 LoSB 43

Treaty between the Kingdom of Norway and the Russian Federation concerning Maritime Delimitation and Cooperation in the Barents Sea and the Arctic Ocean (September 15, 2010), 2791 UNTS 3

Agreement between the Commonwealth of The Bahamas and the Republic of Cuba for the Delimiting Line between their Maritime Zones (October 3, 2011), (2013) 79 LoSB 19

Agreement between the Government of the Cook Islands and the Government of the Republic of Kiribati concerning the Delimitation of the Maritime Boundaries between the Cook Islands and the Republic of Kiribati (August 29, 2012), (2015) 85 LoSB 35

Agreement between Ireland and the United Kingdom of Great Britain and Northern Ireland Establishing a Single Maritime Boundary between the Exclusive Economic Zone of the two Countries and Parts of their Continental Shelves (March 28, 2013), UKTS No. 21 (2014)

Agreement on Maritime Delimitation between the Government of the French Republic and the Government of the Republic of Suriname (November 8, 2017), Official Gazette of the French Republic (December 16, 2018), NOR: EAEJ1831584D

Treaty between Australia and the Democratic Republic of Timor-Leste Establishing Their Maritime Boundaries in the Timor Sea (March 6, 2018), ATS [2019] 16

# FOREWORD

The book I have the great pleasure to introduce is a version of the PhD thesis defended by its author at the Graduate Institute of International and Development Studies of Geneva in 2018. I also had the pleasure to be the PhD supervisor of Liao Xuexia during the years of research and preparation of this work.

The subject chosen is timely and its analysis necessary. The candidate has chosen to focus on a specific problem that has arisen as a result of the opportunity for coastal States to extend their continental shelf beyond 200 nautical miles: the delimitation of the continental shelf when at least one of the States concerned invokes the existence in its favor of an extended one. The submissions made by States to the Commission on the Limits of the Continental Shelf (CLCS) and the reaction of third States thereto in some cases – the, sometimes, contradictory manner in which the relevant issues have been addressed by judges or arbitrators and the pending cases waiting for adjudication – underscore the importance of this in-depth study.

Dr. Liao performed an outstanding research. She has extensively and carefully studied the relevant instruments and their preparatory works, the case law, the work of the CLCS, the practice of States, including their national legislation, and doctrine. The outcome is an excellent piece and an extraordinary contribution to the better understanding of the problems existing in the delimitation of the continental shelf going beyond 200 nm. The author has not only highlighted the difficulties, she has also made concrete proposals to overcome them.

The book is well written and clearly articulated. It is divided into two parts, preceded by an introductory chapter. Each part is composed of four chapters. The first part examines the questions of overlapping entitlements to the continental shelf beyond 200nm, through the evolution of the legal notion of continental shelf, the analysis of Article 76 of the UNCLOS (United Nations Convention on the Law of the Sea), the different possible scenarios of overlapping entitlements and the relationship between delineation and delimitation, with particular emphasis on the work of the CLCS. The second part determines the methodology for the delimitation of the continental shelf beyond 200 nm. It highlights the difficulties of applying the now common three-steps method of maritime delimitation to this particular case. In an original manner, the volume aims at decrypting the specificities of these delimitations. It goes against the common belief that coastal geography has less impact than in other maritime delimitations and that the major factors are geological. The text is complemented by very useful tables and figures. The Bibliography, although mainly containing English publications, also contains references in French.

The reader may have different views with regard to some of the author's analysis. This can be particularly true with regard to the possibility of having a valid claim of an extended continental shelf within 200 nm of another State. In the same manner, one can share (or not) a particular interpretation of the relevant rules of UNCLOS and the case law or the manner in which State practice is evaluated. I am thinking in particular of the interpretation of the trend in coastal States' submissions to the CLCS that avoids encroaching the 200-nm limits of other States. Even the reader disagreeing with Dr. Liao will find her analysis sound, meticulous and useful.

This is in my view the most comprehensive and reasoned production in its field. I am persuaded that *The Continental Shelf Delimitation beyond 200 Nautical Miles: Towards a Common Approach to Maritime Boundary-Making* is an indispensable reference book on the matter, and an extremely useful tool for practitioners and scholars.

Marcelo G. Kohen
Professor of International Law
Graduate Institute of International and Development Studies

# PREFACE

The last two decades have witnessed a burgeoning interest in the continental shelf beyond 200 nautical miles (nm). The number of submissions concerning the delineation of the outer limits of the continental shelf to the Commission on the Limits of the Continental Shelf (CLCS) far exceeds the original anticipation of the Third United Nations Convention on the Law of the Sea (UNCLOS III), and coastal States increasingly request international courts and tribunals to delimit the continental shelf beyond 200 nm in addition to maritime zones within 200 nm. The *Bangladesh/Myanmar* case decided by the International Tribunal for the Law of the Sea (ITLOS) inaugurated the judicial process of delimiting the continental shelf beyond 200 nm, and in the following years cases concerning the continental shelf beyond 200 nm were launched before the International Court of Justice (ICJ) and Annex VII tribunals under the United Nations Convention on the Law of the Sea (UNCLOS) as well.

The surge in continental shelf delimitation beyond 200 nm disputes across jurisprudence raises concerns as much as interest. First and foremost, it revives the debate over the applicability of the delimitation methodology developed primarily in the single maritime delimitation of the continental shelf and the exclusive economic zone (EEZ) in the extended area of the continental shelf. The discussion has acquired new dimensions due to the gradual consolidation of the three-stage approach in the jurisprudence, which was formulated by the ICJ in the 2009 *Black Sea* case and subsequently employed by other international tribunals. Whether and how the specific attributes of the continental shelf beyond 200 nm play out in the choice, formulation, and application of delimitation methodology are questions that test the robustness of the delimitation methodology and the integrity of the jurisprudence. Challenge is, however, not limited to the actual delimitation process. Questions arise as to whether international courts and tribunals should and, to a lesser degree, can exercise jurisdiction over a dispute concerning the continental shelf beyond 200 nm in the light of the function and mandate of CLCS, to which the jurisprudence has yet to reach a uniform response due to the variety of factual and procedural circumstances. Needless to say, international courts and tribunals' approaches to these questions would inevitably have implications for the future development of the law of maritime delimitation.

The search for a coherent and consistent approach to the delimitation of the continental shelf beyond 200 nm is therefore the impetus for the present study. It is aimed at the clarification of a rule-based approach to the delimitation of the continental shelf beyond 200 nm that reconciles the existing law of maritime delimitation and the factors or circumstances inherent in the continental shelf beyond 200 nm. The study sets out from the premise that the delimitation of the continental shelf beyond 200 nm shares the same constructive and creative nature of any maritime boundary-making and consequently should be examined as an integral part – rather than a separate problem – of the maritime delimitation process. The research is primarily concerned with the practices of international courts and tribunals, which are the main actors in developing the law of maritime delimitation. Nevertheless, it also delves into the practice of the CLCS and coastal States to elucidate issues such as the interaction between delineation and delimitation of the continental shelf beyond 200 nm and the relationship between maritime delimitation within and beyond 200 nm.

This book is a revised version of my doctoral thesis submitted to the Graduate Institute of International and Development Studies, Geneva, in 2018. I am deeply grateful to my thesis supervisor Professor Marcelo G. Kohen for his guidance and generous support both during and after my PhD studies. I am also thankful to the other members of the jury, Professor Zachary Douglas of the Graduate Institute, Geneva, and Professor Sir Malcolm D. Evans of the University of Bristol, for their invaluable comments and critiques. Professor Alex G. Oude Elferink of the Netherlands Institute for the Law of the Sea read several draft chapters of my thesis and gave me many constructive suggestions that continued to inspire my thoughts during the preparation of this book. In addition, I owe a debt of gratitude to Professor Yao Huang of Sun Yat-Sen University, who supervised me between 2011 and 2014 and introduced me to international law studies.

My special thanks go to a number of people who inspired, helped, and supported me in various ways when this book was being written. I would like to thank Mihaela Barnes, Gor Movsisyan, Janina Barkholdt, Yang

Xie, Alfredo Crosato, Ana Luisa Bernardino, Rong Dai, Charalampos Giannakopoulos, Defne Gönenç, Najib Messihi, Lorenzo Palestini, Alberto Ulises Quero, Aliki Semertzi, Weiwei Shang, Yilin Wang, Umut Yüksel, Chuxiao Yu, and Yongji Zheng.

I am grateful to Tom Randall and Jane Bowbrick of Cambridge University Press. Tom guided me through the preparation and production processes with efficiency and expertise, always patiently responding to my questions and fixing the problems. I should also like to thank Dhanuja Ragunathan, Denise Bannerman, and Birgitte Necessary for their professional work and support in the production process.

Finally, I would like to express my deepest gratitude to my parents, Liyan Zou and Xiaofei Liao, for their love and encouragement.

**Xuexia Liao**

# ABBREVIATIONS

| | |
|---|---|
| AFDI | Annuaire Français de Droit International |
| *African JICL* | *African Journal of International and Comparative Law* |
| *AJIL* | *American Journal of International Law* |
| *Australian JIL* | *Australian Journal of International Law* |
| *Austrian RIEL* | *Austrian Review of International and European Law* |
| ATS | Australian Treaty Series |
| BIILC | British Institute of International and Comparative Law |
| BYIL | British Yearbook of International Law |
| *Canadian JIL* | *Canadian Journal of International Law* |
| *Chinese JIL* | *Chinese Journal of International Law* |
| *CJICL* | *Cambridge Journal of International and Comparative Law* |
| *EJIL* | *European Journal of International Law* |
| *Finnish YIL* | *Finnish Yearbook of International Law* |
| GYIL | German Yearbook of International Law |
| *ICLQ* | *International and Comparative Law Quarterly* |
| *IJMCL* | *International Journal of Marine and Coastal Law* |
| ILC | International Law Commission |
| ILM | International Legal Materials |
| ILR | International Law Reports |
| *JENRL* | *Journal of Energy and Natural Resources Law* |
| *JIDS* | *Journal of International Dispute Settlement* |
| *LJIL* | *Leiden Journal of International Law* |
| *LoSB* | *Law of the Sea Bulletin* |
| *LPICT* | *Law and Practice of International Courts and Tribunals* |
| *MLR* | *Modern Law Review* |
| *Nordic JIL* | *Nordic Journal of International Law* |
| *ODIL* | *Ocean Development and International Law* |
| *RBDI* | *Revue Belgique de Droit International* |
| *RIAA* | *Reports of International Arbitral Awards* |
| *San Diego LR* | *San Diego Law Review* |
| UNTS | United Nations Treaty Series |
| *Vanderbilt JTL* | *Vanderbilt Journal of Transnational Law* |

# 1

# Legal Uncertainties in the Continental Shelf Delimitation beyond 200 NM

## I Seaward Extension and its Unfolding Challenges

The legal regime of the continental shelf has existed for more than seven decades. In the aftermath of World War II, driven by the desire to exploit and conserve oil or gas and other non-living resources discovered in the continental shelf, the United States first affirmed its jurisdiction and control over these resources,[1] which inaugurated a period of history known as the "territorial temptation."[2] The rationalization of the legal regime of the continental shelf, which drew on the tremendous efforts of lawyers, naturally followed this development.

In the almost four decades following the Truman Proclamation, although being developed rapidly and having huge impacts on the landscape of the law of the sea, the legal definition of the continental shelf, in particular, its seaward limits, was subject to great uncertainty. The Convention on the Continental Shelf, which concluded in 1958, essentially divorced the legal continental shelf from its geographical counterpart by introducing the "exploitability criterion" into the definition of the continental shelf, which may entail unlimited extension of a coastal State's continental shelf.[3] It was not until the conclusion of the United Nations Convention on the Law of the Sea (UNCLOS or "the Convention") that the seaward limits of the continental shelf were eventually settled.[4] Article 76 of the Convention defines the continental shelf by reference to two criteria, namely, the 200-nautical-mile (nm)

[1] See the Presidential Proclamation No. 2667, concerning the policy of the United States with respect to the Natural Resources of the Subsoil and Sea Bed of the Continental Shelf, September 28, 1945 (the Truman Proclamation), in United Nations (ed.), *Laws and Regulations on the Regime of the High Seas* (United Nations 1951) 39.

[2] B. H. Oxman, "The Territorial Temptation: A Siren Song at Sea" (2006) 100 *AJIL* 830, 831–832.

[3] Article 1 of the Convention on the Continental Shelf (April 29, 1958), 499 UNTS 311.

[4] United Nations Convention on the Law of the Sea (December 10, 1982), 1833 UNTS.

distance criterion and the outer edge of the continental margin criterion, which extends beyond that distance.

Under UNCLOS, the continental shelf beyond 200 nm differs from the continental shelf up to the 200 nm limit in several aspects. First, in terms of substance, the entitlement to a continental shelf beyond 200 nm is established on the basis of geomorphological or geological elements in accordance with Article 76. Second, under Article 76(8), State parties of UNCLOS are under an obligation to submit information to the Commission on the Limits of the Continental Shelf (CLCS or "the Commission"), a scientific and technical body established by UNCLOS[5] in order to establish States' outer limits of the continental shelf. Only on the basis of the recommendations of the CLCS are coastal States' outer limits of the continental shelf final and binding. Therefore, the establishment of the outer limits beyond 200 nm involves a procedural and institutional aspect. Third, as part of the compromises reached during the Third United Nations Conference on the Law of the Sea (UNCLOS III), coastal States shall make payments or contributions in kind in respect of the exploitation of the non-living resources of the continental shelf beyond 200 nm.[6] The payments and contributions shall be made through and distributed by the International Seabed Authority (ISA), an international organization established by UNCLOS to supervise activities in the areas beyond national jurisdiction – the Common Heritage of Mankind (or "the Area").[7] Whereas the ISA has no role in the establishment of the outer limits of the continental shelf, the geographical scope of its mandate is sometimes subject to the Article 76 process because the outer limits of the continental shelf beyond 200 nm may serve as the boundary between the areas within national jurisdiction and those beyond. As a result, notwithstanding coastal States' exclusive jurisdiction over the continental shelf beyond 200 nm,[8] there is an international dimension in this extended area in which other parties to UNCLOS may be said to have an interest.[9]

[5] See Annex II to UNCLOS.

[6] Article 82(1) of UNCLOS.

[7] Article 136, Articles 156, and 157 of UNCLOS.

[8] Article 77(2) of UNCLOS.

[9] See T. Treves, "Remarks on Submissions to the Commission on the Limits of the Continental Shelf in Response to Judge Marotta's Report" (2006) 21 *IJMCL* 363, 365; LDM Nelson, "The Settlement of Disputes Arising from Conflicting Outer Continental Shelf Claims" (2009) 24 *IJMCL* 409, 421.

The procedural, institutional, as well as the international dimensions of the continental shelf beyond 200 nm introduce a great measure of uncertainty into the delimitation of the extended maritime area. A first and important question is whether the continental shelf beyond 200 nm can be delimited before the outer limits are established with certainty and finality through the Article 76 process. To be sure, delineation of the outer limits of the continental shelf is conceptually distinct from the delimitation of the continental shelves. Whereas the former is in essence a unilateral act to be conducted by coastal States,[10] the latter involves the lateral relationship between two or more coastal States and must be based on agreement of the relevant parties.[11] States certainly can delimit the continental shelf beyond 200 nm before establishing their outer limits of the shelf, as long as they are agreed on the existence of overlapping entitlements beyond 200 nm. In fact, some States have done so.[12] But the absence of established outer limits of the continental shelf or recommendations from the CLCS may call into question the precision of the spatial scope of the continental shelves that have been delimited, and there is a risk of States including areas that subsequently prove to be not within their jurisdiction. States are aware of this problem and it is not uncommon that they make specific arrangements about potential adjustment of the delimitation line in case of disagreement of the CLCS.[13]

Things are more complicated, however, if States intend to resort to a third-party forum to settle their disputes concerning the continental shelf beyond 200 nm. First, international courts and tribunals not only have to rule on jurisdiction over the continental shelf beyond 200 nm, but must also examine the propriety of exercising jurisdiction if the parties' outer limits of the continental shelf have not been established through the CLCS. It was exactly because of consideration of the interests of the international community that the *St. Pierre and Miquelon* case declined jurisdiction to entertain France's claim to delimit the continental shelf beyond 200 nm.[14] Second, the complexity arising out of the geomorphological and geological elements of Article 76 of UNCLOS also poses challenges to the judicial capacity to delimit the continental shelf beyond

[10] *Fisheries case (United Kingdom v. Norway) [1951] ICJ Rep 116*, 132.

[11] *Delimitation of the Maritime Boundary in the Gulf of Maine Area (Canada/United States of America) [1984] ICJ Rep 246, 292* [87–89].

[12] Chapter 4, Section II.B.

[13] Chapter 4, Section II.A.

[14] See *Decision in Case concerning Delimitation of Maritime Areas (St. Pierre and Miquelon), (1992) 31 ILM 1145, 1171–1172* [75–79].

200 nm in the absence of recommendations from the CLCS. Third and more profoundly, how and to what extent does the law of maritime delimitation, which has been developed primarily through the jurisprudence concerning maritime delimitation within 200 nm from territorial baselines, govern the delimitation of the continental shelf beyond 200 nm? There is no doubt that Article 83 of UNCLOS, the rule governing the delimitation of the continental shelf, applies to the continental shelf delimitation beyond 200 nm as a formal source of law, because Article 83 as such does not distinguish the continental shelf beyond 200 nm from that within 200 nm.[15] This, however, says very little about the applicable principles, relevant circumstances to be taken account of, and specific delimitation methods that can be employed in the delimitation process, because in Article 83(1) (as well as Article 74(1) concerning the delimitation of the exclusive economic zone) "any indication of a specific criterion which could give guidance to the interested States in their effort to achieve an equitable solution has been excluded."[16] Hence details of the delimitation methodology for the continental shelf beyond 200 nm are still in a stage of fluidity and in want of further refinement.

These legal uncertainties are exacerbated because of two unexpected developments. First, the actual workload of the CLCS has far surpassed the initial estimations about the volume of submissions made during UNCLOS III.[17] To date, the Commission has received 85 submissions,[18] and it is now commonly believed that this number will rise to more than 100.[19] In contrast, only 32 recommendations have been issued by the Commission. Decades more are required before all coastal States making a claim to the continental shelf beyond 200 nm can establish their outer limits in a definitive manner.

The other underestimated issue is the potentially large number of overlapping claims to the continental shelf beyond 200 nm. Coastal

15 See *Delimitation of the Maritime Boundary in the Bay of Bengal (Bangladesh/Myanmar) (Judgment) [2012] ITLOS Rep 4, 117* [454].

16 *Continental Shelf (Tunisia/Libyan Arab Jamahiriya) [1982] ICJ Rep 18, 49* [50].

17 Letter dated April 5, 2019 from the Chair of the CLCS addressed to the President of the ninth SPLOS (UN Doc. SPLOS/29/6, April 8, 2019) [9–10].

18 Executive summaries of coastal States' submissions are available on the CLCS website: www.un.org/Depts/los/clcs_new/commission_submissions.htm, last accessed on 30 August 2020.

19 See L. Parson, "Observations on the Article 76 Process: Coastal States' Submissions and the Work Outstanding for the Commission on the Limits of the Continental Shelf," in J. Barrett and R. Barnes (eds.), *Law of the Sea: UNCLOS as a Living Treaty* (BIILC 2016) 125.

States' submissions to the CLCS, together with the diplomatic notes sent by other interested States, provide one of the contemporary sources where one could identify the existing or potential overlapping claims. To date, only 8 out of 85 submissions are not subject to the claim of a third party to the same area of the continental shelf beyond 200 nm.[20] This list is not complete, for there are States that have not yet presented a full submission, but reserved their procedural right to do so by submitting preliminary information;[21] States that have only submitted partial submissions while preparing for submissions concerning other areas at a later stage; and States which are not parties to UNCLOS but indicate their claims to a continental shelf beyond 200 nm nevertheless.[22]

In contrast with the large number of submissions and potential overlap of continental shelves beyond 200 nm, the actual practice concerning delimitation is quite limited. Around 15 maritime boundary agreements concluded between coastal States deal with the continental shelf beyond 200 nm.[23] Therefore, the certainty and stability attached to permanent maritime boundaries beyond this distance are lacking for most coastal States. This is detrimental because a permanent maritime boundary provides strong incentives for private actors to invest in the exploration and exploitation of the natural resources on the continental shelf, which is the primary objective of the legal regime. Coastal States threatened by sea-level rise have every incentive to press for the establishment of the outer limits of the continental shelf – given the "final and binding" nature of such seaward limits – as well as a maritime boundary with their neighbors in order to strengthen or at least preserve their legal position.[24]

[20] See Appendix 2.

[21] Article 4 of Annex II to UNCLOS requires the submission to be made to the CLCS within 10 years of entry into force of the Convention for a State party. In 2008, the Meetings of States Parties to UNCLOS decided that the 10-year deadline could be met by a State submitting preliminary information indicative of its outer limits of the continental shelf. See Decision regarding the workload of the CLCS and the ability of States, particularly developing States, to fulfil the requirements of article 4 of annex II to UNCLOS, as well as the decision contained in SPLOS/72, paragraph (a) (UN Doc. SPLOS/183, 20 June 2008).

[22] See Note Verbale of the United States dated 30 June 2009, in response to the submission of Cuba (1 June 2009), available at www.un.org/Depts/los/clcs_new/submissions_files/cub51_09/usa_re_cuba_2009.pdf; Note Verbale of Venezuela dated September 17, 2008, in response to Barbados's submission (May 8, 2008), available at www.un.org/Depts/los/clcs_new/submissions_files/brb08/ven_sept_2008.pdf.

[23] See Chapter 9, Section III.A.

[24] See, for instance, comments of Maldives (2019 UN/N/50, 31 December 2019) and the Federated States of Micronesia (FSMUN 058-2019, 27 December 2019) submitted in response to the call for submission of information and examples of State practice on "Sea-

The absence of a maritime boundary dividing continental shelves beyond 200 nm may also undermine the effective operation of the revenue-sharing obligation under Article 82 because the spatial scope of the application of the obligation remains undefined before the relevant States establish their maritime boundary.

The law of maritime delimitation governing the continental shelf beyond 200 nm is thus of great importance to provide guidance for coastal States in the pursuit of the stability and certainty of maritime boundaries. As the law of maritime delimitation is essentially a body of "judge-made" law,[25] it is natural to look to the jurisprudence for solutions to delimitation beyond this distance. Nonetheless, the jurisprudence is developing with twists and turns and in itself forms part of the uncertainties arising out of the delimitation of the continental shelf beyond 200 nm.

## II Uncertainties in the Current Development of the Jurisprudence

After the hesitations reflected in the *St. Pierre and Miquelon* and the *Barbados* v. *Trinidad and Tobago* cases, only in 2012 did the International Tribunal for the Law of the Sea (ITLOS or "the Tribunal") break new ground by delimiting the continental shelves beyond 200 nm for the first time in the *Bangladesh/Myanmar* case.[26] Subsequently, an arbitral tribunal constituted in accordance with Annex VII to UNCLOS and a special chamber of ITLOS delimited the continental shelves beyond 200 nm in the *Bangladesh* v. *India* case and the *Ghana/Côte d'Ivoire* case respectively.[27] The International Court of Justice (ICJ or "the Court"), for its part, has two pending cases concerning delimitation beyond this distance, i.e., *Maritime delimitation in the Indian Ocean (Somalia* v. *Kenya)*, and *Question of the Delimitation of the*

level Rise in relation to International Law" by ILC. See Analytical Guide to the Work of the ILC on "Sea-level Rise in relation to International Law," available at legal.un.org/ilc/guide/8_9.shtml.

25 See P. Weil, *The Law of Maritime Delimitation: Reflections* (Grotius 1989) 6–8; A. G. Oude Elferink et al., 'The Judiciary and the Law of Maritime Delimitation: Setting the Stage' in A. G. Oude Elferink et al. (eds.), *Maritime Boundary Delimitation: The Case Law: Is It Consistent and Predictable?* (Cambridge University Press 2018), 3.

26 *Bangladesh/Myanmar* (n 15) 103 [394].

27 *Bay of Bengal Maritime Boundary Arbitration (*Bangladesh *v.* India*) (2014) 167 ILR 1; Delimitation of the Maritime Boundary in the Atlantic Ocean (Ghana/Côte d'Ivoire), [2017] ITLOS Rep 4.*

*Continental Shelf between Nicaragua and Colombia beyond 200 Nautical Miles from the Nicaraguan Coast (Nicaragua* v. *Colombia)* ("*Nicaragua* v. *Colombia II* case").

The decisions are, however, not entirely consistent with regard to the competence of a court or tribunal to delimit the continental shelf beyond 200 nm. Whereas the *Bay of Bengal* cases and the *Ghana/Côte d'Ivoire* case adopted essentially the same approach to the procedural questions, the practices of the ICJ are less coherent.[28] In particular, the finding of the ICJ in the *Nicaragua* v. *Colombia II* case that Nicaragua was under an obligation to submit information to the CLCS "as a prerequisite for the delimitation of the continental shelf beyond 200 nautical miles by the Court" is highly controversial in legal terms.[29]

Another challenging question encountered by the judiciary concerns the relationship between the two criteria of entitlement to the continental shelf under Article 76(1). As maritime delimitation presupposes an area of overlapping entitlements,[30] prior to the exercise of maritime delimitation the scope of the area of overlapping entitlements must be specified. When the distance criterion and the outer edge of the continental margin criterion are invoked by two parties to a dispute of maritime delimitation, is it legally permissible for the areas encompassed by the two criteria to overlap? Alternatively, does the former take precedence over the latter so that no delimitation issues would arise? This problem underlies the disputes of the *Nicaragua* v. *Colombia* cases and remains to be clarified by the ICJ.

Most importantly, many questions regarding the delimitation methodology for the continental shelf beyond 200 nm have been raised but few answers are given. For example, will the entitlement have implications for the choice and application of the delimitation methodology? It has long been argued in academic circles that in the delimitation beyond 200 nm, "geological and geomorphological factors will not merely be important; they will be of the essence."[31] Is it inevitable that

28 Chapter 4, Section III.B.

29 *Question of the Delimitation of the Continental Shelf between Nicaragua and Colombia beyond 200 Nautical Miles from the Nicaraguan Coast (Nicaragua v. Colombia) (Preliminary Objections) [2016] ICJ Rep 100, 136* [105].

30 *Bangladesh/Myanmar* (n 15) 105 [397].

31 K. Highet, "The Use of Geophysical Factors in the Delimitation of Maritime Boundaries," in J. I. Charney and L. M. Alexander (eds.), *International Maritime Boundaries, Volume I* (Martinus Nijhoff Publishers 1993), 196.

geophysical factors, which have been excluded from maritime delimitation within 200 nm,[32] will assume importance in the delimitation of the continental shelf beyond that distance? Between adjacent coasts, will the boundary line within the 200 nm be adjusted when it is extended beyond 200 nm in order to account for circumstances exclusively relevant beyond that distance? As to opposite coasts, will a delimitation that is solely concerned with the continental shelf beyond 200 nm take into account geographical circumstances at all, since the latter are predominantly attached to delimitation of the Exclusive Economic Zone (EEZ) and the continental shelf within 200 nm?

Far from settling all these questions, the current jurisprudence is limited in its contribution to the clarification of the delimitation methodology for the continental shelf beyond 200 nm. To some extent it is inevitable, because the decisions that have delimited beyond 200 nm are confined to one particular geographical situation, namely between States with an *adjacent* coastal relationship. International courts and tribunals have not decided on a case solely concerning the continental shelf beyond 200 nm, or a case between two States with opposite coasts.

Issues of delimitation methodology beyond 200 nm may be considered in the light of the recent development of the delimitation methodology for maritime delimitation within 200 nm. The *Black Sea* case, as the high-water mark of the trend towards a refined delimitation methodology, establishes a three-stage approach to maritime delimitation: first, a provisional equidistance method is constructed; second, relevant circumstances are examined in order to determine if the provisional line should be adjusted or shifted in order to achieve an equitable solution; and third, a disproportionality test that compares the ratios of coastal lengths and the ratios of attributed maritime areas checks the equity of the delimitation result in a final stage.[33] The three-stage approach of delimitation methodology has been an orthodox approach in the jurisprudence ever since the *Black Sea* case, including in the delimitation of the continental shelf beyond 200 nm.[34] However, some recent judicial decisions cast doubt on the purported separation of stages in the application of the three-stage approach and the manner of the application of the

[32] See *Continental Shelf (Libyan Arab Jamahiriya/Malta) [1985] ICJ Rep 13, 35* [39].

[33] *Maritime Delimitation in the Black Sea (Romania* v. *Ukraine) [2009] ICJ Rep 61, 101–103* [115–122].

[34] See Chapter 5, Section III A.

delimitation methodology.[35] Therefore, whether the three-stage approach provides a proper framework applicable in the delimitation of the continental shelf beyond 200 nm is in itself a question to be analyzed separately. Indeed, whether the three-stage approach is adequate to address all the methodological questions and how the three-stage approach can be further refined to accommodate the special character of the continental shelf beyond 200 nm are crucial for the future development of the law of maritime delimitation.

## III Structure of the Book

This book responds to the legal uncertainties arising out of the now fast-developing, yet confusing field of the continental shelf delimitation beyond 200 nm. It endeavors to develop a coherent and consistent approach to delimiting the continental shelf beyond 200 nm that is firmly founded on the existing law of maritime delimitation, which is of great importance to guide coastal States in reaching equitable solutions to maritime boundary-making, to check on excessive claims to the continental shelf beyond 200 nm, and to discourage uncompromising positions that may accentuate conflicts between coastal States. Much of the attention will be devoted to third-party dispute settlement, for the obvious reason that the procedural and substantive questions primarily arise in this context. That said, the book will also explore the relevant State practice and the practices of the CLCS with a view to informing the interpretative exercises with regard to Article 76 of UNCLOS, rules governing maritime delimitation, and, more broadly, the perception of the continental shelf delimitation beyond 200 nm vis-à-vis maritime delimitation within 200 nm.

This book is divided into two parts. Part I (Chapter 2 to Chapter 4) addresses the questions of overlapping entitlements to the continental shelf beyond 200 nm, while Part II (Chapter 5 to Chapter 9) is dedicated to the delimitation methodology. The division conforms to the basic tenet of the law of maritime delimitation, namely, "the task of

[35] See M. D. Evans, 'Relevant Circumstances' in A. G. Oude Elferink et al. (eds.), *Maritime Boundary Delimitation: The Case Law: Is It Consistent and Predictable?* (Cambridge University Press 2018) 232–243; Y. Tanaka, *Predictability and Flexibility in the Law of Maritime Delimitation* (2nd ed., Hart 2019), 458–468.

delimitation consists in resolving the overlapping claims by drawing a line of separation of the maritime areas concerned."[36]

Chapter 2 discusses the establishment of the entitlement to the continental shelf beyond 200 nm under Article 76 of UNCLOS. The notion of natural prolongation is a critical concept in this respect, whose meaning, scope, as well as contemporary relevance under UNCLOS calls for articulation. Other elements constitutive of the entitlement to the continental shelf beyond 200 nm include the foot of the continental slope (FOS), the outer limits of the continental shelf and the coast.

Chapter 3 moves to the precondition to maritime delimitation, namely the existence of overlapping entitlements. This Chapter first summarizes the factors that contextualize the determination of overlapping entitlements to the continental shelf beyond 200 nm on the basis of a survey of relevant State practice. This exercise contributes to understanding the interaction between delineation and delimitation with reference to concrete geographical contexts. In addition, two special scenarios wherein the existence of overlapping entitlements is open to question are also examined. One scenario concerns the invocation of the two criteria of entitlement to the continental shelf by two parties to a dispute. The other scenario deals with the "zone-locked" problem, namely a situation where a State is closed off by a previously determined maritime boundary but still intends to claim a continental shelf beyond 200 nm beyond that boundary.

Chapter 4 studies the interaction between delineation and delimitation of the continental shelf beyond 200 nm. It first surveys how coastal States coordinate the two procedures in order to avoid a deadlock in the delineation procedure, which results from other interested States' objection to the consideration of a submission by the CLCS. Next it assesses the progress and problems in the jurisprudence in terms of the competence of international courts and tribunals to delimit the continental shelf beyond 200 nm in the absence of recommendations from the CLCS. On that basis, factors underlying the decision (not) to delimit the continental shelf beyond 200 nm will be analyzed. This Chapter also argues that resolving the deadlock in the delineation procedure requires a check on the unconstrained veto power enjoyed by States to block the consideration of other States' submissions under the Rules of Procedure of the CLCS.

Chapter 5, as an opening chapter of Part II, sets out the conceptual framework for subsequent discussion. In particular, it identifies the

[36] *Black Sea* (n 33) 89 [77].

elements and formulations of the delimitation methodology, with a view to clarifying the methodological questions to be addressed in the context of the continental shelf beyond 200 nm. Following that, Chapter 6 discusses the determination of overlapping entitlements.

Chapter 7 and Chapter 8 focus on the relevant circumstances in the delimitation of the continental shelf beyond 200 nm. Chapter 7 examines geomorphological and geological factors and Chapter 8 addresses geographical ones. Chapter 9 explores the broader question of whether the delimitation beyond 200 nm should differ from maritime delimitation within 200 nm because an equitable solution for the continental shelf may differ from that for the EEZ. Chapter 9 concludes that the law of maritime delimitation is likely to develop to embrace a common approach to maritime delimitation within and beyond 200 nm, which is based on the unification of the relevant circumstances, the continuing relevance of underlying principles of maritime delimitation, and the trend towards a single exercise of maritime delimitation within and beyond 200 nm.

# PART I

# Overlapping Entitlements to the Continental Shelf beyond 200 Nautical Miles

# 2

# Establishing the Entitlement to the Continental Shelf beyond 200 NM

## I Definitions of the Continental Shelf: Between Science and Law

The contemporary definition of the continental shelf beyond 200 nautical miles (nm) is found in Article 76 of the 1982 United Nations Convention on the Law of the Sea (UNCLOS or "the Convention").[1] Establishing the entitlement to the continental shelf beyond 200 nm is therefore a matter of interpreting and applying Article 76. As Article 76 is one of the most complex articles of UNCLOS due to its incorporation of a significant amount of technical criteria drawn from natural science, it is inevitable that "its appropriate interpretation and application requires both legal and scientific expertise".[2] Before undertaking this task, it is essential, first of all, to understand how the legal concept of the continental shelf emerges out of, but distinguishes from the physical fact of the continental shelf as understood in science. This exercise is crucial for assigning proper weight to the scientific and natural elements in Article 76 in relation to the continental shelf beyond 200 nm in the treaty interpretation.

The history of how the legal definition of the continental shelf evolves over time is well known,[3] and the present section solely focuses on the "taming" of the natural fact for legal, political, and societal purposes. "Continental shelf" first emerged as a scientific concept, and, as observed

[1] 1833 UNTS 3.

[2] *Delimitation of the Maritime Boundary in the Bay of Bengal (Bangladesh/Myanmar) (Judgment) [2012] ITLOS Rep 4, 107* [411].

[3] S. N. Nandan and S. Rosenne (eds.), *United Nations Convention on the Law of the Sea 1982: A Commentary, Volume II* (Martinus Nijhoff 1993) 837–883; R. R. Churchill and A. V. Lowe, *The Law of the Sea* (3rd ed., Manchester University Press, 1999), 142–157; S. V. Suarez, *The Outer Limits of the Continental Shelf: Legal Aspects of Their Establishment* (Springer 2008), 21–74; Ø. Jensen, *The Commission on the Limits of the Continental Shelf: Law and Legitimacy* (Martinus Nijhoff Publishers 2014), 8–44; T. L. McDorman, "The Continental Shelf," in D. R. Rothwell et al. (eds.), *The Oxford Handbook of the Law of the Sea* (Oxford University Press 2015), 189–195.

by the International Court of Justice (ICJ or "the Court"), it is, "by definition, an area physically extending the territory of most coastal States into a species of platform which has attracted the attention first of geographers and hydrographers and then of jurists."[4] Coastal States started to expand national jurisdiction over the submarine areas after World War II.[5] It is customary to view the Truman Proclamation issued on September 28, 1945 as the starting point of this process,[6] which provoked a chain of claims over natural resources and the submarine areas.[7] Although made within a short period of time, there are significant differences between these claims.[8] Many proclamations and enactments claim the entire continental shelf without defining its scope or extent,[9] which seems to suggest that the term "continental shelf" was understood and used in its originally geographical sense.[10] Others, notwithstanding claiming the geographical continental shelf, seek to break the confines of nature by setting a numeratical outer limit of the claimed area (e.g., Peru[11] and Chile[12]) where the existence of a physical continental shelf seems doubtful. As pointed out by Sir Hersch Lauterpacht, "the expression 'continental shelf' has become no more than a convenient formula covering a diversity of titles or claims to the sea-bed and its subsoil adjacent to the territorial waters of the State."[13] Although it was

4 *North Sea Continental Shelf Cases (Federal Republic of Germany/Denmark; Federal Republic of Germany/Netherlands) [1969] ICJ Rep 3, 51* [95].

5 Churchill and Lowe (n 3), 141; M. W. Mouton, "The Continental Shelf" (1954) *85 Recueil des Cours* 354; D. N. Hutchinson, "The Seaward Limit to Continental Shelf Jurisdiction in Customary International Law" (1986), 56 *BYIL* 111, 112–115.

6 Nonetheless, the Treaty on the Gulf of Paria between the United Kingdom and Venezuela in 1942 in effect delimited the continental shelf before the legal concept of the continental shelf was established. See Churchill and Lowe (n 3) 143.

7 See S. Oda, "The Continental Shelf [1955]," *Fifty Years of the Law of the Sea: with a Special Section on The International Court of Justice: Selected Writings* (Kluwer Law International, 2003) 18–23; A. R. Maggio, "Article 77," in A. Proelss (ed.), *The United Nations Convention on the Law of the Sea: A Commentary* (Hart 2017), 608.

8 See H. Lauterpacht, "Sovereignty over Submarine Areas" (1950) 27 *BYIL* 376, 382.

9 See, for example, regulations and declarations of Iceland, Mexico, Costa Rica, Guatemala, and Honduras. United Nations (ed.), *Laws and Regulations on the Regime of the High Seas* (United Nations 1951), 9–14.

10 See Lauterpacht (n 8) 383.

11 Peru established a 200 nm zone of control and protection of natural resources from its coasts in its Presidential Decree No.781. United Nations (n 9), 16–17.

12 Chile claimed a 200 nm zone of protection and control for whaling and deep-sea fishery from its coasts. Ibid., 7.

13 Lauterpacht (n 8), 383; C. H. M. Waldock, "The Legal Basis of Claims to the Continental Shelf" (1950) 36 *Transactions of the Grotius Society* 115, 140.

considered that these States practices "constituted a starting point for the formulation of positive law,"[14] the reliance on a geographical concept inevitably left the spatial scope of continental shelf rights indeterminate, for a geographical continental shelf may extend to a very great or limited distance, or may not exist at all.[15] Accordingly, at this initial stage of developing the legal institution, the concept and spatial scope of the continental shelf was deeply marked by its origin in nature.

The International Law Commission (ILC) made a determinant step in divorcing the legal continental shelf from the geographical one during its work between 1950 and 1956. Early on in the ILC sessions, the members agreed on an exploitation-oriented approach to rationalizing the legal regime on the continental shelf,[16] which left a marked influence on the definition of the area and its seaward limits (should there be any) under the 1958 Convention on the Continental Shelf (CCS).[17] Indeed, the ILC started from the premise that the right to the continental shelf should not necessarily depend on the existence of a continental shelf.[18] Thus there was a preference of "widening of the concept for legal purposes," which "eventually embrace[d] any sea-bed area possessing a particular relationship with the coastline of a neighboring State, whether or not such area presented the specific characteristics" of a geographical continental shelf.[19]

In consequence, the definition under Article 1 of the CCS is clearly a legal fiction, as the term "continental shelf" refers to the seabed and subsoil to "a depth of 200 metres or, beyond that limit, to where the depth of the superjacent waters admits of the exploitation of the natural resources of the said areas." The exploitability test was intended to overcome the natural limits of the geographical continental shelf, as its purpose was "to let the territorial extension of the exercise of the powers given the coastal State depend on the practical possibilities of

[14] Summary Records of the Second Session (June 5–July 29, 1950), *ILC* Yearbook (1950), Vol. I, 215 (François).
[15] See Lauterpacht (n 8) 384.
[16] Summary Records of the Third Session (May 16 –27 July 27, 1951), ILC Yearbook (1951), Vol.I, 272 [78] (Kerno).
[17] 499 UNTS 311.
[18] Report of the International Law Commission on Its Second Session, UN Doc. A/1316 (5 June to 29 July 1950) ILC Yearbook (1950), Vol.II, 384.
[19] *Continental Shelf (Tunisia/Libyan Arab Jamahiriya) [1982] ICJ Rep 18, 45* [41].

exploitation."[20] The 200-meter-depth criterion, on the other hand, took into account the consideration that this limit was then the approximate maximum depth at which exploitation would prove possible,[21] and it often conforms to the natural and physical limit of the continental shelf in a geographical sense.[22] Nonetheless, this geographical fact was merely one of the many factors that contributed to the formalization of the legal concept of the continental shelf, and apparently not a major one.[23] This initial attempt to define the legal continental shelf in the CCS was therefore largely indifferent to the physical components of the continental shelf. As commented by the ICJ, "the legal concept, while it derived from the natural phenomenon, pursued its own development."[24]

The CCS entered into force in 1964. However, the definition provided in Article 1 soon became incompatible with the reality, primarily because of the advancement of technology that made the exploitation of resources at a depth of several thousand meters a foreseeable possibility,[25] thus rendering the 200-meter-depth criterion obsolete. In addition, the exploitability criterion aroused suspicion that all submarine areas might be subject to coastal States' exclusive control.[26] As the natural resources in the deep seabed attracted the attention of States – coastal or land-locked, developed or developing – it gave rise to proposals of internationalization of deep-sea resources. A historic event in this regard was the adoption of Resolution 2749 (XXV) by the General Assembly on December 12, 1970, according to which the seabed and ocean floor, and the subsoil thereof, beyond the limits of national jurisdiction were regarded as the Common Heritage of Mankind ("the Area"), and no State shall claim or exercise sovereignty or sovereign rights over any part of the Area.[27] It was thus imperative to

[20] Report of the International Law Commission Covering the Work of Its Fifth Session, UN Doc. A/2456 (June 1–August 14), ILC Yearbook (1953), Vol.II, 213.

[21] Report of the Special Rapporteur François on the Regime of the High Seas (UN Doc. A/CN.4/17), ILC Yearbook (1950), Vol.II, 51.

[22] ILC Yearbook (1953), Vol. II (n 20) 213.

[23] See Hutchinson (n 5) 138–140; Mouton (n 5) 40–41.

[24] *Tunisia/Libya* (n 19) 45–46 [42].

[25] J.-F. Pulvenis, "The Continental Shelf Definition and Rules Applicable to Resources," in R.-J. Dupuy and D. Vignes (eds.), *A Handbook on the New Law of the Sea* (Martinus Nijhoff 1991), 329.

[26] See S. Oda, "Proposals for Revising the Convention on the Continental Shelf," *Fifty Years of the Law of the Sea: with a Special Section on the International Court of Justice: Selected Writings* (Kluwer Law International 2003) 265; I. Brownlie, *Principles of Public International Law* (7th ed., Oxford University Press, 2008) 211–212.

[27] UN Doc. A/RES/2749(XXV) (December 17, 1970).

define the continental shelf with precise outer limits, which is another proof that the legal construction of the area fulfils the prevailing needs of human societies.

With this general background in mind, three more specific issues contributed to the normative development of the concept of the continental shelf under UNCLOS. The first was the emergence of the concept of the exclusive economic zone (EEZ) on the basis of 200 nm distance.[28] The widespread support for the EEZ concept not only challenged the very *raison d'être* of the continental shelf regime,[29] but also had a huge impact on the seaward limits of the continental shelf. Countries with narrow continental margins also gave their support to a continental shelf up to 200 nm.[30] The distance criterion was practical and straightforward and it may also preserve a meaningfully large deep seabed area for the Area. The distance criterion for measuring the continental shelf thus emerged from State practice concerning the EEZ and it is unrelated to the physical continental shelf.[31]

Second, the *North Sea* cases played a significant role in the normative development of the continental shelf definition for giving weight to the notion of natural prolongation. In the ICJ's view, what "entertains the most fundamental of all the rules of law relating to the continental shelf" is:

> [T]he rights of the coastal States in respect of the area of continental shelf that constitutes a natural prolongation of its land territory into and under the sea exist *ipso facto* and *ab initio*, by virtue of its sovereignty over the land, and as an extension of it in an exercise of sovereign rights for the purpose of exploring the seabed and exploiting its natural resources. In short, there is here an inherent right.[32]

[28] See G. Apollis, *Les Frontières Maritimes en Droit International: Mutations et Perspectives* (Faculté de droit et des sciences économiques, 1979) 24–26; D. J. Attard, *The Exclusive Economic Zone in International Law* (Oxford University Press, 1987) 14–21.

[29] UN Doc. A/CONF.62/C.2/SR.16 (July 26, 1974), *Official Records of the Third United Nations Conference on the Law of the Sea, Vol.II*, 144–145 (Honduras and Paraguay); UN Doc. A/CONF.62/C.2/SR.17 (26 July 1974), ibid., 148–149 (Lebanon); UN Doc. A/CONF.62/C.2/SR.18 (29 July 1974), ibid., 151 (Singapore and Uganda), 153–154 (Egypt and Pakistan); UN Doc. A/CONF.62/C.2/SR.19 (30 July 1974), ibid., 157 (Switzerland); UN Doc. A/CONF.62/C.2/SR.20 (30 July 1974), ibid., 160 (The Gambia), 161 (Kenya), 163 (Tunisia), 165 (Ghana), 166–167 (Mali), 168 (Malta).

[30] See Pulvenis (n 25) 341.

[31] Attard (n 28) 133.

[32] *North Sea* (n 4) 22 [19].

This paragraph seeks to explain the legal basis of coastal States' entitlement to the continental shelf, which is in accordance with the CCS, although the Court seemed to treat it as a customary rule independent of the treaty rule.[33] While it is common to regard the *North Sea* cases as the point from which the notion of natural prolongation came to thrive,[34] the meaning of the notion was quite vague, as the ICJ neither defined it nor took a position as to how it could be identified.[35] Nonetheless, the notion of natural prolongation was quickly endorsed by other judicial decisions.[36] During the Third United Nations Conference on the Law of the Sea (UNCLOS III), the notion of natural prolongation became a powerful rhetoric that lent support for a more scientifically precise definition of the continental shelf.[37]

Third, in the light of the popular support for a distance-based continental shelf, whether coastal States' continental shelf rights may extend beyond the 200 nm became a debated issue.[38] By 1970, knowledge of the continental slope and the continental rise had expanded enormously and technology had made the exploitation of continental slope and continental rise feasible.[39] The notion of natural prolongation as developed in the *North Sea* cases also strengthened this claim.[40] Coastal States with broad continental margins were thus reluctant to be confined to a continental shelf up to 200 nm and to give up large parts of their continental margin.[41]

33 Ibid.

34 *Tunisia/Libya* (n 19) 46 [43].

35 J.-H. Paik, "The Origin of the Principle of Natural Prolongation: North Sea Continental Shelf Cases Revisited," in L. del Castillo (ed.), *Law of the Sea, From Grotius to the International Tribunal for the Law of the Sea: Liber Amicorum Judge Hugo Caminos* (Brill Nijhoff Publishers 2015) 588.

36 Section II A below.

37 See Pulvenis (n 25) 349; L. Parson, "Article 76," in A. Proelss (ed.), *The United Nations Convention on the Law of the Sea: A Commentary* (Hart 2017), 593.

38 See Nandan and Rosenne (n 3) 845.

39 See R. Y. Jennings, "The Limits of Continental Shelf Jurisdiction: Some Possible Implications of the North Sea Case Judgment" (1969) 18 ICLQ 819, 830. K. O. Emery, "Geological Limits of the Continental Shelf" (1981) 10 ODIL 1, 2.

40 See Jennings (n 39) 826–830. See also UN Doc. A/CONF.62/C.2/SR.17 (July 26, 1974), *Official Records of UNCLOS III, Vol. II* (n 29) 147 (Australia), 148 (Republic of Korea); UN Doc. A/CONF.62/C.2/SR.18 (July 29, 1974), ibid., 149 (El Salvador), 150 (Argentina), and 152 (Venezuela).

41 Churchill and Lowe (n 3), 148.

The eventual outcome of these conflicting ideas and propositions, exacerbated by the protracted negotiations of UNCLOS III,[42] is that the continental shelf definition under UNCLOS is part of an indivisible package that accommodated both legal and political demands.[43] Coastal States' entitlement beyond 200 nm is accepted as part of the continental shelf regime, together with its exclusive and inherent nature.[44] Political compromises are expressed in the complex technical criteria as well as in the institutional and procedural obligations. On the substantive level, the outer limits of the continental shelf beyond 200 nm are subject to technical criteria that draw heavily on the natural components of the physical continental margin, such as "the thickness of sedimentary rocks," "the foot of the continental slope," "submarine ridges," and "submarine elevations," etc. The incorporation of these geomorphological and geological features, though to a certain extent scientifically based, may nevertheless cause definitional difficulties in the application of Article 76 to a given situation.[45] The Commission on the Limits of the Continental Shelf (CLCS or "the Commission"), a scientific body comprised of 21 experts on geology, geophysics, or hydrography,[46] is established to give recommendations for coastal States in respect of the outer limits of the continental shelf.[47] These procedural and institutional arrangements by no means suggest that the establishment of the entitlement to the area beyond 200 nm, or the outer limits of the continental shelf, is a straightforward technical exercise that can be outsourced to scientific experts, because "the Convention makes use of scientific terms in a legal context which at times departs significantly from accepted scientific definitions and terminology."[48] Accordingly, establishing the entitlement to the continental shelf beyond 200 nm requires both scientific and legal input. To substantiate its existence and extent, proof has to be ascertained from geomorphology and geology, a legal process that is exclusively governed by Article 76 of UNCLOS.[49]

42 Nandan and Rosenne (n 3), 837–883.
43 Ibid., 854–856.
44 See Article 77 of UNCLOS.
45 McDorman (n 3), 195.
46 Article 21(1) of Annex II to UNCLOS.
47 Article 76(8) of UNCLOS.
48 Scientific and Technical Guidelines of the Commission on the Limits of the Continental Shelf (May 13, 1999, Doc. CLCS/11), [1.3].
49 This is certainly the case for States parties to UNCLOS. Whether the Article 76 process (including the procedure involving the CLCS) is applicable to non-parties, is contentious. See Chapter 4, Section III B.4.

Before embarking on the details of the establishment of the entitlement to the continental shelf beyond 200 nm, a word on terminology is needed. There is a nuanced distinction between "entitlement to the continental shelf beyond 200 nm" and "claim to the continental shelf beyond 200 nm." Kunoy argues that coastal States' rights over the continental shelf exist *ipso facto* and *ab initio*, rendering the reference to a "claim to the continental shelf" incorrect.[50] However, the procedure to establish the outer limits beyond 200 nm under Article 76 places on coastal States an obligation to demonstrate and prove the existence of their entitlement. This should be distinguished from the legal nature of the rights prescribed in Article 77. As will become apparent soon, a claim to a continental shelf beyond 200 nm may not be confirmed by the CLCS in the process of establishing the outer limits. Therefore, "entitlement" refers to coastal States' right to the continental shelf in accordance with international law, and it also connotes a sense of factual certainty of the existence of such a right. "Claim," for its part, is used as a neutral word to describe a State's view of its legal entitlement and its act to assert its right.

## II The Notion of Natural Prolongation

Article 76(1) defines the continental shelf as

> the seabed and subsoil of the submarine areas that extend beyond its territorial sea throughout the natural prolongation of its land territory to the outer edge of the continental margin, or to a distance of 200 nautical miles from the baselines from which the breadth of the territorial sea is measured where the outer edge of the continental margin does not extend up to that distance.

The text is clear that if a coastal State is entitled to a continental shelf beyond 200 nm, its entitlement is not measured from the 200 nm limits, but rather from the outer limits of the territorial sea, and the continental shelf beyond 200 nm extends all the way throughout the natural prolongation of a coastal State's land territory. The 200 nm distance criterion and the natural prolongation to the outer edge of the continental margin criterion are thus two alternative definitions of the legal continental shelf.

[50] See B. Kunoy, "Admissibility of a Plea to an International Adjudicative Forum to Delimit the Outer Continental Shelf Prior to the Adoption of Final Recommendations by the Commission on the Limits of the Continental Shelf" (2010) 25 *IJMCL* 237, 241.

Article 76(3) defines the concept of the continental margin as comprising the shelf, the slope, and the rise, excluding the deep ocean floor with its oceanic ridges or the subsoil thereof. Article 76(4) provides two formulae for the measurement of the outer edge of the continental margin, which are conveniently known as the Gardiner formula and the Hedberg formula.[51] Whereas the former relies on geological information about the thickness of the sedimentary rocks of the continental margin, the latter adopts a simple geodetic measurement of 60 nm from the foot of the continental slope (FOS).[52] Article 76(2) further requires that, no matter where the outer edge of the continental margin lies, the extent of the continental shelf must not exceed certain limits in accordance with Article 76(4)–(6). As a result, the eventual outer limits of the continental shelf may not coincide with the outer edge of the continental margin. In other words, for a given coastal State, its legal continental shelf may not extend to the outer edge of the continental margin as defined by Article 76(4). That is the methodology that establishes the entitlement and the extent of the continental shelf beyond 200 nm. What role does the notion of natural prolongation under Article 76(1) play?

As a legacy of the *North Sea* cases, the meaning and role of the notion of natural prolongation are to some extent nebulous, yet States from time to time resort to this notion, not only for establishing the entitlement to the continental shelf beyond 200 nm,[53] but also for its delimitation beyond 200 nm.[54] To understand the notion of natural prolongation properly, two sources are relevant: first, the judicial decisions prior to the entry into force of UNCLOS, and, second, the interpretation and application of natural prolongation in the context of UNCLOS. The meanings attached to the notion are not necessarily identical under the two sources.

[51] The Gardiner formula was named after the Irish geologist Piers Gardiner, and the Hedberg formula was named after Hollis D. Hedberg, an American geologist. See Nandan and Rosenne (n 3), 878–879.

[52] Article 76(4)(a) of UNCLOS: "4. (a) For the purposes of this Convention, the coastal State shall establish the outer edge of the continental margin wherever the margin extends beyond 200 nautical miles from the baselines from which the breadth of the territorial sea is measured, by either: (i) a line delineated in accordance with paragraph 7 by reference to the outermost fixed points at each of which the thickness of sedimentary rocks is at least 1 per cent of the shortest distance from such point to the foot of the continental slope; or (ii) a line delineated in accordance with paragraph 7 by reference to fixed points not more than 60 nautical miles from the foot of the continental slope."

[53] See Section II B. 1 below.

[54] See Section II B. 2 below.

### A *Natural Prolongation in Judicial Decisions Prior to the Entry into Force of UNCLOS*

Starting from the *North Sea* cases of 1969, the notion of natural prolongation has been used by international courts and tribunals in different circumstances with multiple meanings.[55] The fact that this notion was used both in the context of the law conferring entitlement and that of the law governing maritime delimitation further accentuates its fluidity, because the two bodies of law are not identical.[56] Therefore, being aware of the context that the notion of natural prolongation is used is of particular importance in order not to give the notion meanings which it was not supposed to have.[57] Notwithstanding the risk of oversimplification, judicial decisions referred to natural prolongation either in a legal sense or in a physical sense. The differentiation does not imply that natural prolongation in the legal sense is deprived of a physical entity, nor does it suggest that natural prolongation in the physical sense has no legal relevance. Quite modestly, the legal/physical distinction serves a descriptive tool to navigate through the jurisprudence, which is not always explicit as to the specific meaning attributed to natural prolongation on a particular occasion.

#### 1 Natural Prolongation in the Legal Sense

As a legal concept, the first and foremost role of natural prolongation is to justify the appurtenance of continental shelf rights to coastal States. Natural prolongation explains why coastal States are entitled to the continental shelf, and it concerns "the rules governing the existence, '*ipso jure* and *ab initio*', and the exercise of sovereign rights of the coastal State over areas of continental shelf situate off its coasts."[58] The *North Sea* cases used natural prolongation in this connection at various instances.[59] The underlying idea of this aspect of natural prolongation is "an extension of something already possessed," which is, in the opinion of the Court, determinant.[60] As elaborated in the judgment:

[55] See D. N. Hutchinson, "The Concept of Natural Prolongation in the Jurisprudence Concerning Delimitation of Continental Shelf Areas" (1985) 55 *BYIL* 133.
[56] *Tunisia/Libya* (n 19), 46–47 [44].
[57] Paik (n 35), 585.
[58] *Continental Shelf (Libyan Arab Jamahiriya/Malta) [1985] ICJ Rep 13, 29–30* [27].
[59] See *North Sea* (n 4) 22 [19] and 29 [39].
[60] Ibid., 31 [43].

> What confers the *ipso jure* title which international law attributes to the coastal State in respect of its continental shelf, is the fact that the submarine areas concerned may be deemed to be actually part of the territory over which the coastal State already has dominion, – in the sense that, although covered with water, they are a prolongation or continuation of that territory, an extension of it under the sea.[61]

Natural prolongation as the basis of the entitlement to the continental shelf was endorsed by subsequent judicial decisions as well. In the *Anglo-French Arbitration* case, the Court of Arbitration agreed that natural prolongation underlies the fundamental rule in respect of coastal States' right to the continental shelf.[62] In the *Aegean Sea Continental Shelf* case, the ICJ reaffirmed that the continental shelf rights derived from the State's sovereignty over the land territory as captured by the notion of natural prolongation.[63] The judgment of the ICJ in the *Tunisia/Libya* case considered that "[w]hile the term 'natural prolongation' may have been novel in 1969, the idea to which it gave expression was already a part of existing customary law as the basis of the title of the coastal State."[64] In this sense, natural prolongation conveys the quality of continental shelf rights, namely, sovereign rights derived from coastal States' sovereignty over the land.[65] Accordingly, natural prolongation not only signifies the physical continuation of the area with the land territory, but more importantly the conceptual continuation between the continental shelf rights and the territorial sovereignty.

A second use of natural prolongation in the legal sense is the reference to the spatial scope of continental shelf rights. As put by the ICJ, "the idea of the natural prolongation of the land territory defined, in general terms, the physical object or location of the rights of the coastal State."[66] Hence natural prolongation was a synonym of the legal concept of continental shelf. This idea was clearly expressed by the ICJ in the *Libya/Malta* case. Discussing the relationship between natural prolongation and the distance criteria of Article 76(1) of UNCLOS, the Court observed that "where the continental margin does not extend as far as 200 miles from

61 Ibid.

62 See *Delimitation of the Continental Shelf between the United Kingdom of Great Britain and Northern Ireland, and the French Republic (United Kingdom/France) (1978) 18 RIAA 3, 48-49* [77–79].

63 See *Aegean Sea Continental Shelf (Greece v. Turkey) [1978] ICJ Rep 3, 36* [86].

64 *Tunisia/Libya* (n 19), 46 [43].

65 See *North Sea* (n 4), 51 [96]; *Aegean Sea* (n 63), 36 [86].

66 *Tunisia/Libya* (n 19), 46 [43].

the shore, natural prolongation [. . .] is *in part* defined by distance from the shore."[67] This observation would have been incomprehensible if the term was not referred to as the legal concept of continental shelf as such. This understanding was supported by Judge Mbaye. According to him, "[t]he principle of natural prolongation in Article 76 of the 1982 Convention is a purely legal concept,"[68] and it "can be applied in two ways: either by means of the rule of the 'outer edge of the continental margin', or by means of the '200-mile' rule."[69] Recalling that before the adoption of UNCLOS, the legal concept of continental shelf was in a state of flux, natural prolongation was thus "a term of art" that captured the juridical concept.[70]

### 2 Natural Prolongation in the Physical Sense

Natural prolongation in the physical sense was frequently resorted to in connection with identification of natural prolongations as a method for the delimitation of the continental shelf. The *North Sea* cases are responsible for having nurtured this idea:

> [W]henever a given submarine area does not constitute a natural – or the most natural – extension of the land territory of a coastal State, even though that area may be closer to it than it is to the territory of any other State, it cannot be regarded as appertaining to that State; – or at least it cannot be so regarded in the face of a competing claim by a State of whose land territory the submarine area concerned is to be regarded as a natural extension, even if it is less close to it.[71]

That natural prolongations can be identified as facts of nature was further strengthened when the Court stated that "the continental shelf of any State must be the natural prolongation of its land territory and must not encroach upon what is the natural prolongation of the territory of another State."[72] Nonetheless, the judgments of the *North Sea* cases are less clear about whether natural prolongation was understood in a geographical sense or in a geomorphological or geological sense, which is however crucial for its identification. While the former entails "the

[67] *Libya/Malta* (n 58), 33–34 [34] (emphasis added).
[68] Ibid., 97 (Separate Opinion of Judge Mbaye).
[69] Ibid., 99 (Separate Opinion of Judge Mbaye).
[70] Hutchinson (n 5), 150.
[71] *North Sea* (n 4) 31 [43].
[72] Ibid., 47 [85(c)].

continuation or extension seawards of each State's coastal front,"[73] the latter refers to the characteristics or structures of the seabed and subsoil. A geological understanding was explicitly mentioned when the Court was considering factors to be taken into account during negotiations of the continental shelf delimitation:

> [I]t can be useful to consider the geology of that shelf in order to find out whether the direction taken by certain configurational features should influence delimitation because, in certain localities, they point-up the whole notion of the appurtenance of the continental shelf to the State whose territory it does in fact prolong.[74]

The impression that the Court had a geological natural prolongation in mind was shared by some judges as well as scholars.[75] Should this be the case, the identification of natural prolongations would turn on fact-finding of geological or geomorphological discontinuities in the seabed.

On the other hand, a geographical concept of natural prolongation was also readily visible in the judgments of the *North Sea* cases. A general context to be borne in mind is that the seabed of the North Sea disputed by the parties consists of a common continental shelf at a depth of less than 200 meters.[76] It therefore seems unnecessary for the Court to pronounce on the geology of the continental shelf.[77] Moreover, the crux of the *North Sea* cases is the applicability of equidistance to the concave coasts of the Federal Republic of Germany, which is a problem arising out of coastal geography.[78] It becomes more apparent that natural prolongation was understood as a geographical concept when the Court compared the effects of equidistance applied to opposite coasts and adjacent coasts:

> [W]hereas a median line divides equally between the two opposite countries areas that can be regarded as being the natural prolongation of the

[73] *Tunisia/Libya* (n 19), 116 [58] (Separate Opinion of Judge Jiménez de Aréchaga).

[74] *North Sea* (n 4), 51 [95].

[75] Ibid., 116 [16] (Separate Opinion of Judge Ammoun); ibid., 59 [4] (Separate Opinion of President JL Bustamante Y Rivero). See also Pulvenis (n 25), 339–340; D. P. O'Connell, *The International Law of the Sea, Volume I* (I. A. Shearer ed., Oxford University Press 1982), 491; M. D. Evans, *Relevant Circumstances and Maritime Delimitation* (Oxford University Press 1989), 101–103.

[76] See *North Sea* (n 4), 13–14 [4].

[77] M. B. Feldman, "The Tunisia-Libya Continental Shelf Case: Geographic Justice or Judicial Compromise?" (1983), 77 *AJIL* 219, 227.

[78] *North Sea* (n 4), 23–24 [24]. See also H. Thirlway, "The Law and Procedure of the International Court of Justice 1960–1989 Part Five" (1994), 64 *BYIL* 1, 20–24.

> territory of each of them, a lateral equidistance line often leaves to one of the States concerned areas that are a natural prolongation of the territory of the other.[79]

In this statement the Court was apparently not concerned with the structure or the characteristics of the seabed and subsoil of the continental shelf, but with the effects produced by coastal geography. Indeed, given that the Court had already asserted that Articles 1 to 3 of the CCS were "reflecting, or as crystallizing, received or at least emergent rules of customary international law relative to the continental shelf,"[80] the Court would have contradicted itself if it introduced a geomorphologically or geologically based concept.[81] As mentioned earlier, the definition of the continental shelf under the CCS was intentionally divorced from the physical continental shelf.[82] In fact, the subsequent negotiations between Denmark, the Netherlands, and the Federal Republic of Germany were premised on overlapping natural prolongations defined as projections of the parties' coastal fronts.[83] That the notion of natural prolongation was used in a geographical sense in the *North Sea* cases was also acknowledged by the *Anglo-French Arbitration* case.[84]

Nonetheless, a geomorphological or geological concept of natural prolongation was taken up by parties to subsequent continental shelf delimitation cases. In the *Tunisia/Libya* case, Libya contended that natural prolongation was determinable as a matter of scientific fact by the application of geological criteria, and that the delimitation should give effect to the identification of natural prolongations.[85] Tunisia, invoking geomorphological and bathymetric evidence, argued that the limits of physical natural prolongations of the parties can be determined.[86] The

[79] *North Sea* (n 4), 37 [58].

[80] Ibid., 38–39 [63].

[81] *Tunisia/Libya* (n 19), 112 [46] (Separate Opinion of Judge Jiménez de Aréchaga). For an opposite view, see Pulvenis (n 25), 339.

[82] Section I above.

[83] See A. G. Oude Elferink, *The Delimitation of the Continental Shelf between Denmark, Germany and the Netherlands: Arguing Law, Practicing Politics?* (Cambridge University Press 2013), 330–331, 345.

[84] The Court of Arbitration considered that "[t]he problem of delimitation arises precisely because in situations where the territories of two or more States abut on a single continuous area of continental shelf, it may be said geographically to constitute a natural prolongation of the territory of each of the States concerned." *Anglo-French Arbitration* (n 62), 49 [79].

[85] See *Tunisia/Libya* (n 19), 44 [39].

[86] See ibid., 56 [64].

Court did not refute the use of natural prolongation in this manner. In fact, the Court engaged with evaluating the scientific evidence provided by Tunisia and Libya and eventually found that the disputed submarine area constituted a common continental shelf without identifiable distinct or separate continental shelves.[87] As a result, the Court decided that the delimitation should be "governed by criteria of international law other than those taken from physical feature."[88] That said, the Court nevertheless acknowledged that a delimitation could be justified on the basis of its identification as the division between areas of natural prolongation if a submarine feature "were such as to disrupt the essential unity of the continental shelf."[89]

Natural prolongation in a physical sense is thus part of the vocabulary of international courts and tribunals. The Chamber of the *Gulf of Maine* case observed that the shelf subject to dispute "is a single continuous, uniform and uninterrupted physiographical structure," and can be defined as "the natural prolongation of the land mass around the Gulf of Maine."[90] The *Guinea/Guinea-Bissau* case stated that "the rule of natural prolongation can be effectively invoked for purposes of delimitation only where there is a separation of continental shelves."[91]

In the *Libya/Malta* case, whereas Libya again relied on identifying natural prolongation on a geological ground as the method for delimitation, the ICJ, applying the distance criterion as the basis of entitlement,[92] declared that:

> [I]n so far as those areas are situated at a distance of under 200 miles from the coasts in question, title depends solely on the distance from the coasts of the claimant States of any areas of sea-bed claimed by way of continental shelf, and the geological or geomorphological characteristics of those areas are completely immaterial.[93]

The *Libya/Malta* case therefore rules out geomorphological and geological factors from the continental shelf delimitation within 200 nm.[94]

[87] See ibid., 57–58 [66–67].

[88] Ibid., 58 [67].

[89] Ibid., 64 [80].

[90] *Delimitation of the Maritime Boundary in the Gulf of Maine Area (Canada/United States of America) [1984] ICJ Rep 246, 273–274* [45].

[91] *Delimitation of the Maritime Boundary between Guinea and Guinea-Bissau (Guinea/Guinea-Bissau) (1985) XIX RIAA 149* [116].

[92] *Libya/Malta* (n 58), 33–34 [34].

[93] Ibid., 35 [39].

[94] Ibid., 35 [39]

However, the Court indirectly recognized the relevance of geomorphological or geological factors in relation to the notion of natural prolongation in the continental shelf beyond 200 nm,[95] but it is silent as to how this exercise is to be conducted. Notwithstanding the judicial pronouncements, the meaning of natural prolongation has been significantly transformed in the context of the Article 76 process.

### B *Natural Prolongation in the Context of UNCLOS*

UNCLOS modifies the definition of the continental shelf, and the interpretation of natural prolongation should keep in mind this conceptual shift. Under UNCLOS, natural prolongation has been applied by coastal States and the CLCS in the procedure of establishing the outer limits of the continental shelf and interpreted by the *Bangladesh/Myanmar* case in the delimitation of the area beyond 200 nm.

#### 1 Natural Prolongation in the Application of Article 76

The Scientific and Technical Guidelines ("the Guidelines") adopted by the Commission provide instructions for States to implement Article 76. Although not legally binding, the Guidelines aim to "clarify the scope and depth of admissible scientific and technical evidence to be examined by the Commission" and "to clarify its interpretation of scientific, technical and legal terms contained in the Convention."[96] The Guidelines formulate the process of delineating the outer limits of the continental shelf as comprising two stages. In the first stage, the coastal State's entitlement beyond 200 nm has to be demonstrated, which is called the "test of appurtenance."[97] Only after the fulfilment of the test are coastal States able to delineate their outer limits. The Guidelines make a distinction between the "basis for entitlement to delineate the outer limits of an extended continental shelf" and "the methods to be applied in this delineation," because "it is clear that the positive proof of the former precedes the implementation of the latter."[98] Following this distinction, the Guidelines provide that:

> If a State is able to demonstrate to the Commission that the natural prolongation of its submerged land territory to the outer edge of its

95 Ibid., 55–56 [77].
96 The Guidelines (n 48), [1.2] and [1.3].
97 See the Guidelines (n 48), Section 2.2.
98 Ibid., [2.2.1].

> continental margin extends beyond the 200-nautical-mile distance criterion, the outer limit of its continental shelf can be delineated by means of the application of the complex set of rules described in paragraphs 4 to 10.[99]

This paragraph seems to suggest that the demonstration of the natural prolongation of a coastal State is a separate and independent procedure preceding the establishment of the outer limits of the continental shelf. However, when it comes to the formulation of the test of appurtenance in the Guidelines, it becomes clear that it is in effect implemented by locating the outer edge of the continental margin in accordance with Article 76(4).[100] Accordingly, under the Guidelines, Article 76(4) serves two purposes: first, to determine the existence of the entitlement to the continental shelf beyond 200 nm as the test of appurtenance, and second, to determine the location of the outer edge of the continental margin as a step of establishing the outer limits of the continental shelf. Consequently, natural prolongation is substantiated through the search for the outer edge of the continental margin by applying Article 76(4).[101]

The practice of coastal States does not shed much light on the substance of natural prolongation. For one thing, the main body of coastal States' submissions is not available to the public; only executive summaries are accessible, which are brief in substance. For another, the notion of natural prolongation is either not used at all, or its use is confined to a succinct statement that the natural prolongation has been demonstrated.[102] This

99 Ibid., [2.2.3].

100 According to the Guidelines: "The formulation of the test of appurtenance can be described as follows: If either the line delineated at a distance of 60 nautical miles from the foot of the continental slope, or the line delineated at a distance where the thickness of sedimentary rocks is at least 1 per cent of the shortest distance from such point to the foot of the slope, or both, extend beyond 200 nautical miles from the baselines from which the breadth of the territorial sea is measured, then a coastal State is entitled to delineate the outer limits of the continental shelf as prescribed by the provisions contained in article 76, paragraphs 4 to 10." Ibid., [2.2.8].

101 For an opposite view, A. Serdy, "Interpretation of UNCLOS Article 76 and the Negative Recommendation of the Commission on the Limits of the Continental Shelf on Ascension Island: Is the United Kingdom Stuck with It?" (2013) 2 *CJICL* 591, 602–604.

102 For example, the executive summary of the Philippines' submission states that "[a]nalysis of all the data and information collected clearly demonstrated a natural prolongation and geomorphological continuity between the Philippine Island of Luzon and Benham Rise." "Executive summary of the Philippines's Submission (8 April 2009)," 14, available at www.un.org/Depts/los/clcs_new/submissions_files/phl22_09/phl_esummary.pdf. The conjunction of "natural prolongation" and "geomorphological continuity" seems to suggest that the two are not identical.

appears to be a standard statement. The Commission, for its part, has not discussed to any extent the concept or the significance of natural prolongation, and has rarely referred to it in the summaries of their recommendations to coastal States.[103] Instead, the Commission consistently determines the entitlement to the continental shelf beyond 200 nm by applying Article 76(4), adhering to the formulation of the test of appurtenance of the Guidelines.[104]

Only on two occasions was the notion of natural prolongation elaborated by the CLCS. First, in respect of the UK submission for Ascension Island, the Commission outlined the subcommission's view on natural prolongation and the delineation of the outer edge of the continental margin as follows:

(i) The "natural prolongation of [the] land territory" is based on the physical extent of the continental margin to its "outer edge" (article 76, paragraph 1), i.e., "the submerged prolongation of the land mass..." (article 76, paragraph 3);
(ii) The outer edge of the continental margin in the sense of article 76, paragraph 3, is established by applying the provisions of article 76, paragraph 4, through measurements from the FOS.[105]

The Commission thus treated the natural prolongation and continental margin as synonymous with each other and did not assign to natural prolongation an autonomous role in determining the entitlement to the continental shelf beyond 200 nm. The United Kingdom, however, disagreed with the Commission's interpretation of natural prolongation. The United Kingdom argued that "[b]y jumping immediately to the formulae in Article 76(4) in this way the Subcommission overlooks the requirement in Article 76(1) to first determine the extent of natural prolongation of the land territory,"[106] and it did not consider that natural

[103] See Parson (n 37), 593.

[104] To give some examples, see summaries of the recommendations to Australia (April 9, 2008), Norway (March 27, 2009), France (September 2, 2009), Mexico (March 31, 2009), and Barbados (April 15, 2020), available at www.un.org/Depts/los/clcs_new/commission_submissions.htm.

[105] "Summary of the recommendations in respect of Ascension Island adopted (15 April 2010)," [22], available at www.un.org/Depts/los/clcs_new/submissions_files/gbr08/gbr_asc_isl_rec_summ.pdf.

[106] "Paper Summarising the Presentation by the United Kingdom of Great Britain and Northern Ireland to the Commission on the Limits of the Continental Shelf on Points of Legal Interpretation made on 12 April 2010," [22], available at www.un.org/Depts/los/clcs_new/submissions_files/gbr08/gbr_nv_11jan2011.pdf.

prolongation, "an inherent property of any landmass, can be defined by applying Article 76(4)."[107] Instead, whether there is any natural prolongation "can only be established by an assessment of all of the available geoscientific data as a whole."[108] In plain words, the United Kingdom argued that the identification of natural prolongation is a separate exercise other than the application of Article 76(4), and it asked for consideration of geology in the determination of natural prolongation.[109] Notwithstanding the challenge of the United Kingdom, it is arguable that the CLCS adhered to its consistent practice in terms of establishing the entitlement to the continental shelf beyond 200 nm by first locating the FOS, from which the outer edge of the continental margin is measured.[110]

On a second and more recent occasion, the practice of the CLCS, however, tends to disturb the consistency of the approach adopted so far. In recommendations to the Cook Islands in respect of the Manihiki Plateau, the Commission seemed to indicate that natural prolongation does have a separate existence. One of the key questions relating to the natural prolongation was raised: "Can the natural prolongation be ensured morphologically and geologically from the islands to the base of the continental slope proposed in the Submission?"[111] This question frames natural prolongation as extending to the base of the continental slope, in contradiction to the CLCS's previous understanding that natural prolongation was "based on the physical extent of the continental margin to its 'outer edge'."[112] Although it has been suggested that many geologists would accept the line of the FOS as the limit of natural prolongation based on geological and geomorphological knowledge of the continental margin,[113] this interpretation of natural prolongation lacks textual support from Article 76(1), which defines the continental shelf as extending throughout the natural prolongation of the land territory *to the outer edge of the continental margin*. The physical scope of natural

107 Ibid., [23].

108 See ibid., [23] and [25].

109 Ibid., [26–27].

110 See "Summary of Recommendations in respect of Ascension Island" (n 105), [28] and [50].

111 "Summary of Recommendations to the Cook Islands adopted on 19 August 2016," [52], available at www.un.org/Depts/los/clcs_new/submissions_files/cok23_09/2016_08_19_com_sumrec_cok.pdf.

112 "Summary of Recommendations in respect of Ascension Island" (n 105), [22].

113 Parson (n 37), 594.

prolongation should therefore coincide with that of the continental margin. It is also on the basis of this understanding that the approach to identifying natural prolongation through application of Article 76(4) can be sustained.

Despite this particular occasion, the practice of the Commission demonstrates a high degree of consistency regarding the meaning and role of natural prolongation. Although neither the interpretation nor the recommendations of the CLCS are binding on States parties, the work of the CLCS is not deprived of normative value. Several observations are in order.

First, a distinction must be made between the interpretation by the CLCS and that by States parties to UNCLOS, and only the latter constitutes the authentic interpretation of UNCLOS.[114] Nonetheless, as the function of the CLCS consists of "mak[ing] recommendations in accordance with article 76 and the Statement of Understanding adopted on 29 August 1980 by the Third United Nations Conference on the Law of the Sea,"[115] the Commission "has to be presumed to be competent to deal with issues concerning the interpretation or application of article 76 or other relevant articles of the Convention to the extent this is required to carry out the functions which are explicitly assigned to it."[116] The Commission is clear about this interpretative function, as the Guidelines justify its own *raison d'être* by pointing out that "various terms in the Convention might be left open to several possible and equally acceptable interpretations."[117]

Second, since the CLCS is a treaty body, its practice cannot, therefore, be considered as subsequent practice within the meaning of Article 31(3)(b) of the Vienna Convention on the Law of Treaties (VCLT),[118] because the practice as such is not attributed to States parties.[119] However, the

114 International Law Association, "Report of Committee on Legal Issues of the Outer Continental Shelf," ILA Report of the Seventy-First Conference (Berlin, 2004) 779.

115 Article 3(1)(a) of Annex II to UNCLOS.

116 ILA, "First Report (Berlin, 2004)" (n 114), 778. See also E. Jarmache, "La pratique de la commission des limites du plateau continental" (2008) 54 *AFDI* 429, 433; B. Kunoy, "The Terms of Reference of the Commission on the Limits of the Continental Shelf: A Creeping Legal Mandate" (2012) 25 *LJIL* 109, 110–111; D. Roughton and C. Trehearne, "The Continental Shelf," in D. Attard et al. (eds.), *The IMLI Manual on International Maritime Law, Volume I: The Law of the Sea* (Oxford University Press 2014), 161–162.

117 The Guidelines (n 48), [1.3].

118 Vienna Convention on the Law of Treaties (May 23, 1969), 1155 UNTS 331.

119 G. Nolte, "Fourth report on subsequent agreements and subsequent practice in relation to the interpretation of treaties" (UN Doc. A/CN.4/694, March 7, 2016), 7-8.

normative value of the practice of the CLCS would increase if its interpretation is endorsed by States parties in their submissions, which would qualify as subsequent practice of the parties. Furthermore, States may have a strong incentive to follow the approaches adopted by the CLCS in its recommendations in order to smoothen the process of establishing the outer limits of the continental shelf,[120] which is due to the stability and legitimacy attached to the outer limits recommended by the Commission, the limited procedural options available to States faced with negative recommendations, and the time-consuming procedure. Therefore, the authority of the interpretation by the CLCS is to be ascertained in its interaction with States parties.[121]

### 2 Interpretation of Natural Prolongation in the *Bangladesh/Myanmar* Case

The *Bangladesh/Myanmar* case concerning maritime boundary delimitation in the Bay of Bengal was the first delimitation case decided by the International Tribunal for the Law of the Sea (ITLOS or "the Tribunal"), and it was the first case in which the continental shelf beyond 200 nm was actually delimited. The meaning of natural prolongation under Article 76 was one of the most disputed points in this case, and ITLOS interpreted it in order to determine the parties' entitlements to the continental shelf beyond 200 nm.

Bangladesh argued that "[n]atural prolongation beyond 200 [nm] is, at root, a physical concept [and] must be established by both geological and geomorphological evidence."[122] Bangladesh made considerable efforts to describe the geological evolution of the Bay of Bengal and its geophysical

120 This is clearly seen in the practice of coastal States in the choice of the 2,500-meter-isobath. See B. Kunoy et al., "Appraisal of Applicable Depth Constraint for the Purpose of Establishing the Outer Limits of the Continental Shelf" (2010) 41 *ODIL* 357, 358–359.

121 The ILC suggests that "a pronouncement of an expert treaty body may give rise to, or refer to, a subsequent agreement and subsequent practice by parties under article 31, paragraph 3, or other subsequent practice under article 32." Conclusion 13 of the Draft Conclusions on Subsequent Agreements and Subsequent Practice in relation to Interpretation of Treaties (A/73/10), Report of the ILC on the work of its seventieth session (April 30–June 1 and July 2–August 10, 2018). See also E. Jarmache, "A propos de la Commission des Limites du Plateau Continental" (2006) XI *Annuaire du Droit de la Mer* 51, 55. G. Taft, "The United Nations Convention on the Law of the Sea: The Commission on the Limits of the Continental Shelf – A Force for Enhancing Stability in the Oceans (or Not)" (2010), *24 Ocean Yearbook* 151, 157; Kunoy, "The Terms of Reference of the Commission on the Limits of the Continental Shelf" (n 116), 116.

122 *Bangladesh/Myanmar* (n 2), 111[426].

characteristics, and pointed out that a subduction zone which resulted from the collision between the Indian plate and the adjacent Burma plate "represents the most fundamental geological discontinuity in the Bay of Bengal."[123] In the view of Bangladesh, because of this geological discontinuity, Myanmar is not entitled to a continental shelf beyond 200 nm. Myanmar, on the other hand, contended that "natural prolongation is a legal term employed in the specific context of defining the continental shelf and carries no scientific connotation," and that the controlling concept is the outer edge of the continental margin.[124] In essence, the two parties diverged on the question of whether natural prolongation has to be demonstrated separately from the determination of the outer edge of the continental margin, and, in particular, whether this exercise requires evidence of geological continuity.

ITLOS started from the text of Article 76(1) and found that "[w]hile the term 'natural prolongation' is mentioned in this paragraph, it is clear from its language that the notion of 'the outer edge of the continental margin' is an essential element in determining the extent of the continental shelf."[125] The Tribunal observed that the notion of the outer edge of the continental margin is further elaborated in Article 76(3)–(4), and that by applying Article 76(4), the precise location of the outer edge of the continental margin can be identified.[126] On the contrary, the notion of natural prolongation was not endorsed in subsequent paragraphs. From the history of UNCLOS III, the Tribunal found that natural prolongation was "a concept to lend support to the trend towards expanding national jurisdiction over the continental margin."[127] After highlighting that the notion of continental margin and the notion of natural prolongation refer to the same area, and emphasizing the principal objects and purposes of Article 76 to define the precise outer limits of the continental shelf, the Tribunal concluded that it was "difficult to accept that natural prolongation referred to in article 76, paragraph 1, constitutes a separate and independent criterion a coastal State must satisfy in order to be entitled to a continental shelf beyond 200 nm."[128] Referring to relevant parts of the Guidelines of the CLCS,[129] the Tribunal determined that the

[123] Ibid., 110 [424].
[124] Ibid., 111 [427].
[125] Ibid., 112 [429].
[126] See ibid., 113 [431].
[127] Ibid., 113 [433].
[128] Ibid., 113 [435].
[129] The Guidelines (n 48), [2.2.8].

notion of natural prolongation should be understood in light of the subsequent provisions of Article 76 defining the continental shelf and the continental margin,[130] and the entitlement should be determined "by reference to the outer edge of the continental margin, to be ascertained in accordance with article 76, paragraph 4."[131]

In effect, the Tribunal was aligned with the CLCS in the approach of establishing the entitlement to the continental shelf beyond 200 nm. While the interpretation correctly clarifies the relationship between natural prolongation and the continental margin under Article 76, it nonetheless might be criticized as depriving the notion of natural prolongation of any meaning, either in a physical sense or in a legal sense, because the focus was placed, perhaps unduly, on the extent or the outer limits of the continental shelf.[132] Notwithstanding the principal purpose and objective to establish precise outer limits of the area, the overall objective of Article 76 is to define the legal continental shelf, as suggested by the title of this article. Therefore, the notion of natural prolongation should be interpreted with this overall objective in mind. Whereas the Tribunal treats the notion of natural prolongation as synonymous with that of the continental margin, a more accurate reading is that natural prolongation refers to the legal continental shelf itself. The text of Article 76(1) is clear in this respect, as it provides that the continental shelf extends throughout the natural prolongation of its land territory "to the outer edge of the continental margin" or "to a distance of 200 nautical miles." The word "or" indicates that natural prolongation is spelled out by the two alternative criteria. In addition, according to Article 76(2), the spatial scope of natural prolongation is subject to the maximum outer limits of the continental shelf. In this regard, Myanmar was correct to point out that "natural prolongation is not the criterion, but the (legal) outcome."[133] This interpretation is in line with the use of natural prolongation in the legal sense in the jurisprudence.[134] The meaning and

130 *Bangladesh/Myanmar* (n 2), 113–114 [436–437].

131 Ibid., 114 [437].

132 See Ø. Jensen, "Maritime Boundary Delimitation Beyond 200 Nautical Miles: The International Judiciary and the Commission on the Limits of the Continental Shelf" (2015) 84 *Nordic JIL* 580, 603.

133 *Bangladesh/Myanmar*, Counter-memorial of Myanmar, Volume I (1 December 2010), [A.10].

134 See Section II.A.1 above.

role of natural prolongation is thus conceptual and definitional, rather than functional or operative.[135]

Therefore, it would probably be more effective to interpret the notion of natural prolongation as synonymous with the legal concept of the continental shelf.[136] What follows is that the outer edge of the continental margin does not replace or prevail over the notion of natural prolongation, but rather substantiates the notion of natural prolongation. This interpretation would satisfy the requirement to interpret Article 76 as a whole rather than in isolation,[137] and preserve both the definitional and functional aspects of Article 76, which could give Article 76 the maximum effect.

To summarize, notwithstanding the significant or even fundamental value assigned to the notion of natural prolongation in early jurisprudence, Article 76 of UNCLOS has modified the legal concept of the continental shelf, and, as a result, transformed the notion of natural prolongation into a concept that finds substance in the process of establishing the outer edge of the continental margin in accordance with Article 76(4). ITLOS made a significant contribution to clarifying the normatively obscure concept of natural prolongation, though it could have maintained the use of natural prolongation in the legal sense in order to give it effect as a treaty term.

## III The Outer Limits of the Continental Shelf

With the meaning and role of natural prolongation clarified, the establishment of the entitlement to the continental shelf beyond 200 nm becomes a straightforward exercise, namely, searching for the outer edge

135 See Evans (n 75) 118; L. H. Legault and B. Hankey, "From Sea to Seabed: The Single Maritime Boundary in the Gulf of Maine Case" (1985) 79 *AJIL* 961, 982; H.-J. Kim, "Natural Prolongation: A Living Myth in the Regime of the Continental Shelf?" (2014) 45 *ODIL* 374, 383–384; Thirlway (n 78), 30.

136 Although the maxim *res magis valeat quam pereat* is not explicitly laid out in the interpretation rule of the VCLT, it has been suggested that "[w]hen a treaty is open to two interpretations one of which does and the other does not enable the treaty to have appropriate effects, good faith and the objects and purpose of the treaty demand that the former interpretation should be adopted." Reports of the International Law Commission on the Second Part of Its Seventeenth Session and on Its Eighteenth Session (A/CN.4/SER.A/1966/Add.1), ILC Yearbook (1966), Vol. II, 219.

137 See *Bangladesh/Myanmar* (n 2) 225–226 [89–91] (Separate Opinion of Judge Gao); ibid., 273–274 (Dissenting Opinion of Judge Lucky).

of the continental margin in accordance with Article 76(4) of UNCLOS. However, it is not the end of the Article 76 process because the precise extent of the continental shelf beyond 200 nm has to be specified in the procedure establishing the outer limits. Three issues merit consideration in this process, namely, the role of FOS in establishing the outer limits, the delineation of the outer limits, and the relationship between the entitlement and the outer limits of the continental shelf.

### A The Role of the FOS

The incorporation of the FOS into the legal definition of the continental shelf is an example that the law seeks to regulate the subject by taking into account the scientific reality.[138] It is recalled that the Hedberg formula and the Gardiner formula achieved widespread support during UNCLOS III because both of them are built on the FOS, which is a scientifically reliable feature that marks the salient characteristics of the seabed and subsoil and may serve to indicate the scope of the continental margin.[139]

Article 76(4)(b) provides that "in the absence of evidence to the contrary, the foot of the continental slope shall be determined as the point of maximum change in the gradient at its base." This provision contains two key elements for the determination of the FOS: one of "evidence to the contrary" and the other of "maximum change in the gradient at its base." Although the interpretation of the sequence to apply the two elements varies,[140] the Guidelines adopted by the CLCS interpret the provision as consisting of a general rule (the point of maximum change in the gradient at its base) and an exception (the evidence to the contrary), and emphasizes the primacy of the general rule.[141] The application of the general rule involves two steps: identification of the region defined as the base of the continental slope, and determination of the location of the point of maximum change in the gradient at the base of the continental slope.[142] The first step is necessary in order to confine

[138] See O'Connell (n 75) 440.

[139] H. D. Hedberg, "Ocean Floor Boundaries" (1979) 204 *Science* 135, 135.

[140] See Parson (n 37) 596; International Law Association, "Second Report of Committee on Legal Issues of the Outer Continental Shelf," *Report of the Seventy-Second Conference* (2006, Toronto) 223.

[141] See the Guidelines (n 48), [6.1.1] and [6.1.2].

[142] See the Guidelines (n 48), [5.1.3].

the FOS to the region where the continental slope merges with the continental rise.[143] In the recommendations to coastal States, the Commission is consistent in finding the base of the continental slope before identifying the FOS, though occasionally specific approaches for this purpose are not consistent.[144] As to the "evidence to the contrary" exception, although it introduces a certain degree of uncertainty in terms of interpretation,[145] in practice the Commission sets a very high standard to apply the "evidence to the contrary" rule, and only on rare occasions do coastal States invoke the "evidence to the contrary" rule, and in even fewer cases does the CLCS accept their approach.[146]

Because of its significance in determining the outer edge of the continental margin, some scholars have argued that it is the FOS, rather than the coast, which serves as the reference baseline for the measurement of the extent of the entitlement to the continental shelf beyond 200 nm.[147] This argument has implications for the delimitation beyond 200 nm as well.[148] For the moment suffice it to say that it is the FOS that makes the Article 76 process work, because, without the scientifically identifiable submarine feature that serves legal clarity and certainty, there would be no viable method to establish the outer edge of the continental margin. In this sense the FOS is central to the legal definition of the continental shelf beyond 200 nm and its location, as well its identification, is crucial for coastal States' entitlement to the continental shelf beyond 200 nm.

143 See the Guidelines (n 48), [5.4.5].

144 F. Mørk, "Identification of the Base of the Continental Slope on Sedimentary Fans" (2016) 47 *ODIL* 131, 132–138.

145 See S. T. Gudlaugsson, "Natural Prolongation and the Concept of the Continental Margin for the Purposes of Article 76," in M. H. Nordquist et al. (eds.), *Legal and Scientific Aspects of Continental Shelf Limits* (Martinus Nijhoff 2004), 82–86.

146 See Parson (n 37), 597.

147 See C. M. Carleton et al., "The Practical Realisation of the Continental Shelf Limit," in P. J. Cook and C. M. Carleton (eds.), *Continental Shelf Limits: The Scientific and Legal Interface* (Oxford University Press 2000), 271; B. Kunoy, "Admissibility of a Plea to an International Adjudicative Forum to Delimit the Outer Continental Shelf Prior to the Adoption of Final Recommendations by the Commission on the Limits of the Continental Shelf" (2010) 25 *IJMCL* 237, 268; B. Kunoy, "The Delimitation of an Indicative Area of Overlapping Entitlement to the Outer Continental Shelf" (2013) 83 *BYIL* 61, 72; B. M. Magnússon, "The Rejection of a Theoretical Beauty: The Foot of the Continental Slope in Maritime Boundary Delimitations beyond 200 Nautical Miles" (2014) 45 *ODIL* 41, 45.

148 See Chapter 6, Section III.C.

### B The Procedure to Delineate the Outer Limits of the Continental Shelf

Article 76(5) prescribes two maximum limits, or the so-called "constraints," on the outer edge of the continental margin: one is 350 nm from the territorial baselines, and the other is 100 nm plus 2,500-meter isobaths. Article 76(6) further specifies the application of the two constraints by distinguishing submarine ridges and submarine elevations.[149] Article 76 (7) requires States to draw straight lines not exceeding 60 nm that connect the fixed points of the outer limits of the continental shelf. Accordingly, the eventual extent and shape of the continental shelf entitlement beyond 200 nm is the outcome of applying Articles 76(5)–(7).

In addition to these substantive rules governing the establishment of the entitlement to the continental shelf beyond 200 nm, Article 76(8) sets out the procedural obligation imposed on coastal States:

> Information on the limits of the continental shelf beyond 200 nautical miles from the baselines from which the breadth of the territorial sea is measured shall be submitted by the coastal State to the Commission on the Limits of the Continental Shelf set up under Annex II on the basis of equitable geographical representation. The Commission shall make recommendations to coastal States on matters related to the establishment of the outer limits of their continental shelf. The limits of the shelf established by a coastal State on the basis of these recommendations shall be final and binding.

Coastal States shall submit information to the CLCS and the CLCS shall make recommendations with regard to the establishment of the outer limits of the continental shelf. As mentioned earlier, the CLCS is a scientific and technical body established in accordance with Annex II of UNCLOS, and its mandate includes giving recommendations to coastal States in respect of the outer limits of the continental shelf and providing scientific and technical assistance upon request of coastal States for preparing submissions.[150] If the CLCS does not agree with a submission made by the coastal State, the State will be recommended to submit a revised or a new submission. Because of the theoretical

[149] Article 76(6) provides: "Notwithstanding the provisions of paragraph 5, on submarine ridges, the outer limit of the continental shelf shall not exceed 350 nautical miles from the baselines from which the breadth of the territorial sea is measured. This paragraph does not apply to submarine elevations that are natural components of the continental margin, such as its plateaux, rises, caps, banks and spurs."

[150] Article 3(1) of Annex II to UNCLOS.

possibility of an indefinite dialogue between the coastal State and the CLCS, this procedure is characterized as a "ping-pong" process.[151]

However, what "on the basis of" actually means and what "final and binding"' entail are questions of considerable debate. It is well known that the wording "on the basis of" was a delicate choice to replace "taking into account" during UNCLOS III, which clearly illustrates the intention of the parties to restrict the freedom of coastal States to reject the recommendations of the CLCS.[152] On the other hand, it is also agreed that "on the basis of" allows the coastal State certain flexibility when it proceeds to establish its outer limits with the recommendations of the CLCS.[153] Accordingly, the interpretation of "on the basis of" has to be undertaken with these two parameters in mind. Arguably, whether a coastal State has established the outer limits of the continental shelf on the basis of the recommendations of the CLCS has to be assessed in its particular context. In reality, however, this may turn out to be a difficult task given the confidentiality of the main body of the recommendations and the lack of publicly available supportive information when the coastal State deposits the information of its outer limits in accordance with Article 76(9).[154]

The meaning of "final and binding" is even more ambiguous. For whom are the outer limits established on the basis of the

[151] See R. W. Smith and G. Taft, "Legal Aspects of the Continental Shelf," in P. J. Cook and C. M. Carleton (eds.), *Continental Shelf Limits: The Scientific and Legal Interface* (Oxford University Press 2000) 20; T. L. McDorman, "The Role of the Commission on the Limits of the Continental Shelf: A Technical Body in a Political World" (2002) 17 *IJMCL* 301, 306.

[152] See Nandan and Rosenne (n 3), 862–869; ILA, "First Report (Berlin, 2004)" (n 114), 802.

[153] See A. de Marffy Mantuano, "La Fixation des Dernières Limites Maritimes: La Rôle de la Commission des Limites du Plateau Continental," in V. Coussirat-Coustère (ed.), *La mer et son droit: mélanges offerts à Laurent Lucchini et Jean-Pierre Quéneudec* (Pedone 2003) 407; ILA, "First Report (Berlin, 2004)" (n 114), 803; Roughton and Trehearne (n 116), 162–163.

[154] Article 76(9) provides that "the coastal State shall deposit with the Secretary-General of the United Nations charts and relevant information, including geodetic data, permanently describing the outer limits of its continental shelf. The Secretary-General shall give due publicity thereto." However, it does not require coastal States to disclose the detailed contents in their submissions to any party other than the Secretary-General. There is also no provision for disclosure of the full content of the recommendations issued by the CLCS. See R. Macnab, "The Case for Transparency in the Delimitation of the Outer Continental Shelf in Accordance with UNCLOS Article 76" (2004) 35 *ODIL* 1, 11–12; M. A. Namountougou, "La commission des limites du plateau continental: problèmes de statut juridique et attributions" (2008) *RBDI* 292, 326–327.

recommendations final and binding? For the submitting coastal State only,[155] or for the States parties to UNCLOS,[156] or for the international community as a whole?[157] What are the effects entailed by "final and binding"?[158] Does the "final and binding" effect preclude any possibility to modify the outer limits of the continental shelf already established, even if the basis of the entitlement beyond 200 nm (e.g., a mid-ocean island) has disappeared because of the rising sea level?[159] ITLOS seems to interpret "final and binding" as the effect of opposability upon other States:

> Although [the delineation of outer limits] is a unilateral act, the opposability with regard to other States of the limits thus established depends upon satisfaction of the requirements specified in article 76, in particular compliance by the coastal State with the obligation to submit to the Commission information on the limits of the continental shelf beyond 200 nm and issuance by the Commission of relevant recommendations in this regard. It is only after the limits are established by the coastal State on the basis of the recommendations of the Commission that these limits become "final and binding."[160]

The Tribunal, however, did not specify whether by "other States," it referred to States parties to UNCLOS or to all the States of the international community.

[155] See McDorman (n 151), 315.

[156] See R. Wolfrum, "The Role of International Dispute Settlement Institutions in the Delimitation of the Outer Continental Shelf," in R. Lagoni and D. Vignes (eds.), *Maritime Delimitation* (Martinus Nijhoff 2006) 24–25; T. H. Heidar, "Legal Aspects of Continental Shelf Limits," in M. H. Nordquist et al. (eds.), *Legal and Scientific Aspects of Continental Shelf Limits* (Martinus Nijhoff 2004), 32.

[157] Nelson argues that the established outer limits of the continental shelf become *erga omnes* for the international community as a whole. See L. D. M. Nelson, "The Settlement of Disputes Arising from Conflicting Outer Continental Shelf Claims" (2009) 24 *IJMCL* 409, 418–419. See also Kunoy, "The Terms of Reference of the CLCS" (n 116), 112.

[158] It is not clear if by "final and binding" it means that the coastal State should not change the outer limits of the continental shelf already established, or it also excludes the possibility for other States (parties or non-parties) to challenge the established outer limits. See Wolfrum (n 156), 24.

[159] This hypothesis is explored by, for example, L. Mayer, "The Continental Shelf and Changing Sea Level," in M. H. Nordquist and J. N. Moore (eds.), *Maritime Border Diplomacy* (Martinus Nijhoff Publishers 2012) 204–211; M. Hayashi, "Sea Level Rise and the Law of the Sea: How Can the Affected States Be Better Protected?," in C. Schofield et al. (eds.), *The Limits of Maritime Jurisdiction* (Martinus Nijhoff Publishers 2014), 614–615.

[160] *Bangladesh/Myanmar* (n 2), 106–107 [407].

The ICJ has not yet interpreted the meaning of "final and binding", though it considered the "final and binding" effect to be upon the States parties to UNCLOS.[161] Therefore, most of the questions concerning the "final and binding" effect remain unsettled as the case law stands at the moment.

Notwithstanding the controversies relating to the interpretation of Article 76(8), it is clear that, once fulfilled, the procedure provided for in this provision has a "legitimizing effect" on the outer limits of the continental shelf of a coastal State.[162] The outer limits of the continental shelf established on the basis of the recommendations of the Commission would thus secure a considerable degree of certainty and stability with respect to the precise extent of the continental shelf entitlement beyond 200 nm.

### *C The Relationship between the Entitlement and the Outer Limits of the Continental Shelf*

As a matter of legal interpretation, delineation of the outer limits of the continental shelf is different from entitlement beyond 200 nm, because the latter is demonstrated by applying Article 76(4) while the former has to satisfy the requirements of Article 76(5)–(7) as well. They involve the application of different paragraphs of Article 76 and therefore should not be treated as identical. The distinction between them is recognized by ITLOS in the *Bangladesh/Myanmar* case:

> A coastal State's entitlement to the continental shelf exists by the sole fact that the basis of entitlement, namely, sovereignty over the land territory, is present. It does not require the establishment of outer limits. Article 77, paragraph 3, of the Convention confirms that the existence of entitlement does not depend on the establishment of the outer limits of the continental shelf by the coastal State.[163]

161 *Question of the Delimitation of the Continental Shelf between Nicaragua and Colombia beyond 200 Nautical Miles from the Nicaraguan Coast (Nicaragua v. Colombia) (Preliminary Objections) [2016] ICJ Rep 100, 136* [108].

162 See R. Wolfrum, "The Delimitation of the Outer Continental Shelf: Procedural Considerations," in *liber amicorum Jean-Pierre Cot: Le procès international* (Bruylant 2009); T. L. McDorman, "The Continental Shelf beyond 200 NM: A First Look at the Bay of Bengal (Bangladesh/Myanmar) Case," in M. H. Nordquist et al. (eds.), *The Regulation of Continental Shelf Development: Rethinking International Standards* (Martinus Nijhoff Publishers 2013), 99.

163 *Bangladesh/Myanmar* (n 2), 107 [409].

Apparently, the Tribunal's position finds support from the inherency of continental shelf rights. However, it is submitted that the relationship between the entitlement and the outer limits of the continental shelf should not be mingled with the inherency of continental shelf rights, as the latter is solely concerned with the legal nature of continental shelf rights and cannot be resorted to for ascertaining the factual existence or spatial scope of the continental shelf beyond 200 nm.

To some eyes there appears to be tension between the procedure to establish the outer limits of the continental shelf and the inherency of continental shelf rights.[164] Since the outer limits of the continental shelf are integral to the definition of the continental shelf,[165] to create a special procedure for delineation and to entrust the work of verification to a particular institution, Article 76 separates the delineation procedure from the definition of the continental shelf, which seems to challenge the traditional rule that "no special legal process has to be gone through, nor have any special legal acts to be performed" for coastal States' entitlement to the continental shelf.[166]

However, the procedure of establishing the outer limits of the continental shelf is not a procedure of proclamation. Rather, it is a procedure of proof. As the definition of the continental shelf beyond 200 nm makes use of geomorphology and geology for legal purposes, the existence and the extent of the entitlement must be demonstrated from the geomorphological and geological facts in accordance with the legal rules.[167] The burden on coastal States to prove their entitlement does not interfere with the nature of continental shelf rights, which exist *ab initio* and *ipso facto*.[168] As long as the continental shelf beyond 200 nm exists, coastal States are entitled to exercise its jurisdiction to the extent that the area beyond 200 nm is physically known to them, subject to the maximum limits under Article 76(5).[169] For instance, Canada has for a long time

164 See V. J. M. Tassin, *Les défis de l'extension du plateau continental: la consécration d'un nouveau rapport de l'État à son territoire* (Pedone 2013) 230–239.

165 O'Connell (n 75) 492.

166 *North Sea* (n 4), 22 [19].

167 See G. Eiriksson, "The Case of Disagreement between the Coastal State and the Commission on the Limits of the Continental Shelf," in M. H. Nordquist et al. (eds.), *Legal and Scientific Aspects of Continental Shelf Limits* (Martinus Nijhoff Publishers 2004), 258.

168 *North Sea* (n 4), 22 [19].

169 See G. Taft, "Applying the Law of the Sea Convention and the Role of the Scientific Community Relating to Establishing the Outer Limits of the Continental Shelf Where It Extends Beyond the 200 Mile Limit," in M. H. Nordquist et al. (eds.), *Law, Science &*

exercised jurisdiction over hydrocarbon development and sedentary species beyond 200 nm.[170] There are also a number of delimitation agreements concerning the continental shelf beyond 200 nm concluded before the delineation of the outer limits.[171] These are clear instances where the absence of established outer limits of the continental shelf does not cast doubt on the entitlement beyond 200 nm, nor challenge the inherent nature of continental shelf rights.

Nevertheless, the fact that the entitlement to the continental shelf beyond 200 nm has to be proved with geophysical evidence implies that not only its extent, but also its *existence* has to be ascertained on a case-by-case basis, and neither can be presumed. In practice there are widely acknowledged continental margins extending well beyond 200 nm, therefore the existence of the entitlement is in no doubt,[172] but in other geomorphological or geological contexts the matter is less clear. Sometimes the existence of the entitlement is clear, but the scope of the entitlement is utterly obscure. For instance, the CLCS agreed that the Cook Islands were entitled to the continental shelf beyond 200 nm but was unable to recommend their precise outer limits.[173] This instance illustrates that determining the precise extent of the area beyond 200 nm can be factually challenging, even for the scientific and technical body. The distinction made by Article 76(5)–(6) between submarine ridges and submarine elevations introduces an additional dimension of complexity, and the size of the continental shelf beyond 200 nm may vary significantly given the characterization of the submarine feature.[174] Accordingly, a neat distinction between the existence of the entitlement and its seaward extent is hardly sustainable, because the verification of

*Ocean Management* (Martinus Nijhoff Publishers 2007), 473–474; F. M. Armas-Pfirter, "Submissions on the Outer Limit of the Continental Shelf: Practice to Date and Some Issues of Debate," in D. Vidas (ed.), *Law, Technology and Science for Oceans in Globalisation: IUU Fishing, Oil Pollution, Bioprospecting, Outer Continental Shelf* (Martinus Nijhoff Publishers 2010), 493.

170 See McDorman (n 3), 191.

171 See B. M. Magnússon, "Outer Continental Shelf Boundary Agreements," (2013) 62 *ICLQ* 345, 350–368.

172 See V. Prescott and C. H. Schofield, *The Maritime Political Boundaries of the World* (2nd ed., Martinus Nijhoff Publishers 2005), 187.

173 "Summary of Recommendations to the Cook Islands" (n 111), [61] and [79].

174 See H. Brekke and P. Symonds, "Submarine Ridges and Elevations of Article 76 in Light of Published Summaries of Recommendations of the Commission on the Limits of the Continental Shelf" (2011) 42 *ODIL* 289, 302–303; J. Gao, "The Seafloor High Issue in Article 76 of the LOS Convention: Some Views from the Perspective of Legal Interpretation" (2012) 43 *ODIL* 119, 121.

the latter inevitably involves the ascertainment of the former, as illustrated by the practices of the CLCS that the "test of appurtenance" precedes the determination of the outer limits of the continental shelf. It is also not impossible that the very existence of the entitlement to the continental shelf beyond 200 nm is denied during the delineation procedure, as shown by the case of Ascension Island.[175]

Therefore, without prejudice to the inherency of continental shelf rights, the task of establishing the outer limits is not confined to defining the precise limits of the continental shelf beyond 200 nm; the ascertainment of the existence of the entitlement is also integral to this procedure. While proving the existence of entitlement beyond 200 nm does not require the fulfillment of the delineation procedure formally, the absence of the latter is bound to raise doubts over the exact extent of the entitlement.[176] As a result, although distinct in a procedural sense, the determination of the entitlement and the establishment of the outer limits of the continental shelf are, in fact, inextricable and cannot be considered in isolation from each other.

## IV The Coast

The coast is the most fundamental element that underlies continental shelf rights, as "[t]he juridical link between the State's territorial sovereignty and its rights to certain adjacent maritime expanses is established by means of its coast,"[177] which is derived from the principle that "the land dominates the sea."[178] As the continental shelf beyond 200 nm is part of the continental shelf that extends throughout the natural prolongation of the land territory, there is little doubt that the fundamental principle continues to govern the area beyond 200 nm in that rights beyond this distance derive from a land territory possessing a coast.

As a preliminary remark, there is no hierarchy between coasts inasmuch as coasts are capable of generating the same rights to maritime zones, whether they are coasts of a continent or those of an island. In the *Qatar* v. *Bahrain* case, the Court declared Article 121(2) of UNCLOS a

[175] Section II.B.1 above.
[176] See ILA, "First Report (Berlin, 2004)" (n 114), 793.
[177] *Libya/Malta* (n 58), 40–41 [49].
[178] *Fisheries case (United Kingdom v. Norway) [1951] ICJ Rep 116*, 133; *North Sea* (n 4), 51 [96]; *Aegean Sea* (n 63), 36 [86].

customary rule,[179] and observed that "islands, regardless of their size, in this respect enjoy the same status, and therefore generate the same maritime rights, as other land territory."[180] The effect of any coast in the delimitation process, on the other hand, is an issue to be considered under the law of maritime delimitation.[181]

Under Article 76 of UNCLOS, either the 200 nm continental shelf or the outer edge of the continental margin are measured from the coast,[182] or, to be more specific, the territorial baselines.[183] The spatial scope of the continental shelf within 200 nm is geometrically defined by reference to the coasts, but the mere existence of the coasts cannot guarantee either the existence of the entitlement beyond 200 nm or the extent of such entitlement. While ITLOS stated in the *Bangladesh/Myanmar* case that "[a] coastal State's entitlement to the continental shelf exists by the sole fact that the basis of entitlement, namely, sovereignty over the land territory, is present,"[184] it qualified this observation by mentioning that "[n]ot every coast generates entitlements to a continental shelf extending beyond 200 nm."[185] This statement, consequently, confirms that the coast is necessary but not sufficient for establishing the entitlement to the continental shelf beyond 200 nm, which is further conditioned on the location of the outer edge of the continental margin.

However, it would be incorrect to deny in a general fashion the relevance of the coast with the entitlement to the continental shelf beyond 200 nm. According to Article 76(5), one of the maximum limits of the continental shelf is found at 350 nm from the territorial baselines. Should a coastal State apply the 350 nm limit, the outer limits of its continental shelf would be parallel to its territorial baselines and reflect

[179] Article 121(2) of UNCLOS provides: "Except as provided for in paragraph 3, the territorial sea, the contiguous zone, the exclusive economic zone and the continental shelf of an island are determined in accordance with the provisions of this Convention applicable to other land territory."

[180] *Maritime Delimitation and Territorial Questions (Qatar v. Bahrain) (Merits) [2001] ICJ Rep 40, 97* [185].

[181] See S. D. Murphy, "International Law Relating to Islands" (2016) 386 *Recueil des Cours* 9, 221–276; M. Lando, *Maritime Delimitation as a Judicial Process* (Cambridge University Press 2018), 178–192; Y. Tanaka, *Predictability and Flexibility in the Law of Maritime Delimitation* (2nd ed., Hart 2019), 242–275.

[182] See ILA, "Second Report (Toronto, 2006)" (n 140) 28.

[183] As a general rule, "the drawing of base-lines must not depart to any appreciable extent from the general direction of the coast." *Fisheries* (n 178) 133.

[184] *Bangladesh/Myanmar* (n 2) 107 [409].

[185] Ibid., 114 [439].

the general configuration of its coast. This is the case for Pakistan in the establishment of its outer limits.[186]

That said, the loosened relationship between the coast and the entitlement to the continental shelf beyond 200 nm leads to a less direct correlation between relevant coasts and relevant areas, two key terms for the purpose of maritime delimitation.[187] In maritime delimitation within 200 nm, the relevant area is identified by referring to the overlapping projections generated by relevant coasts.[188] This exercise may not be viable in the context of the delimitation of the continental shelf beyond 200 nm, for the extent of the entitlement is subject to the outer limits of the area. Therefore, identification of relevant coasts and relevant areas in the delimitation of the continental shelf beyond 200 nm requires further reflection.

## V The Legal Process Reaffirmed

Establishing the entitlement to the continental shelf beyond 200 nm is a legal process, whether under treaty law or customary international law. It would thus be incorrect to state that the continental shelf beyond 200 nm is purely a geomorphological or geological fact. In a different yet relevant context, the Chamber in the *Gulf of Maine* case stated that "international law confers on the coastal State a legal title to an *adjacent* continental shelf or to a maritime zone *adjacent* to its coasts," rather than "the mere natural fact of adjacency produced legal consequences" upon coastal States' maritime entitlements.[189] In a similar vein, every reference to geomorphological or geological facts has been assigned its legal relevance and value under Article 76 of UNCLOS, making the establishment of the entitlement to the continental shelf beyond 200 nm a legal process. The notion of natural prolongation, though historically significant yet mysterious, has been transformed under Article 76 of UNCLOS, and it is not an independent or separate apparatus for continental shelf entitlement. As a result, the notion of natural prolongation can no longer be invoked to justify a more or less stringent standard to ascertain the entitlement

[186] See "Summary of Recommendations to Pakistan adopted on 13 March 2015," 15, available at www.un.org/Depts/los/clcs_new/submissions_files/pak29_09/2015_03_13_SC_PAK.pdf.

[187] Chapter 6, Section I.

[188] *Tunisia/Libya* (n 19), 61–62 [75]; *Maritime Delimitation in the Black Sea (Romania v. Ukraine) [2009] ICJ Rep 61, 96–97* [99].

[189] *The Gulf of Maine* (n 90), 296 [103] (emphasis in the original).

beyond 200 nm or to justify the introduction of factors extraneous to Article 76 into the delineation procedure. The legal process to establish the entitlement to the continental shelf beyond 200 nm is exclusively governed by Article 76 of UNCLOS, which consists of, first, discovering the outer edge of the continental margin by applying Article 76(4) – which should be located beyond 200 nm from the territorial baselines of a coastal State – and, second, specifying the extent of such entitlement in accordance with Article 76(5)–(7). The coast remains the conceptual and legal reference line for measuring the continental shelf beyond 200 nm, though it is not sufficient for ascertaining the existence or extent of the entitlement.

# 3

# Defining Overlapping Entitlements to the Continental Shelf beyond 200 NM

## I The Significance of Overlapping Entitlements

Maritime delimitation presupposes an area of overlapping entitlements.[1] This stands in contrast with land delimitation, the objective of which is to determine which State has the territorial title.[2] While the essence of territorial title is its validity against other claims to territorial sovereignty,[3] the entitlement to maritime zones does not preclude the co-existence of other equally valid maritime entitlements.[4]

Determination of overlapping entitlements is important in maritime delimitation because, first, it contributes to determining the relevant area subject to maritime delimitation. The area of overlapping entitlements is deemed to be part of the relevant area.[5] In the delimitation of the continental shelf beyond 200 nm, the exercise of identifying the relevant area must take into account the new dimension introduced by the entitlement to the continental shelf beyond this distance.[6]

The significance of overlapping entitlements lies, second, in its influence on the choice and application of delimitation methods. Any maritime delimitation takes place in a given geographical context, to which the area of overlapping entitlements constitutes an integral part. The importance of the geographical context or geographical circumstances

1 *Maritime Delimitation in the Black Sea (Romania v. Ukraine) [2009] ICJ Rep 61, 89* [77]; *Delimitation of the Maritime Boundary in the Bay of Bengal (Bangladesh/Myanmar) (Judgment) [2012] ITLOS Rep 4, 105* [397].

2 See P. Weil, "Délimitation Maritime et Délimitation Terrestre," in M. Tabory and Y. Dinstein (eds.), *International Law at a Time of Perplexity: Essays in Honour of Shabtai Rosenne* (Martinus Nijhoff Publishers 1989), 1121–1126.

3 I. Brownlie, *Principles of Public International Law* (7th ed., Oxford University Press 2008), 119.

4 See N. Marques Antunes, *Towards the Conceptualisation of Maritime Delimitation: Legal and Technical Aspects of a Political Process* (Martinus Nijhoff Publishers 2003), 128–132.

5 See *Black Sea* (n 1), 100 [114].

6 Chapter 2, Section IV.

cannot be overemphasized because "the appropriateness – the equitable character – of the method is always a function of the particular geographical situation,"[7] and "[t]here can never be any question of completely refashioning nature."[8] Fundamentally, maritime delimitation must consider how the area of overlapping entitlements should be delimited in a manner that is "faithful to the actual geographical situation."[9]

Different hypotheses have been raised about the determination of the overlapping entitlements to the continental shelf beyond 200 nm as well as its implications for the delimitation process. Whereas these propositions focus on the geomorphological or geological elements in the entitlement to the continental shelf beyond 200 nm,[10] the present chapter is aimed at highlighting the varieties in the actual geographical contexts, since as with any maritime delimitation, delimitation of the continental shelf beyond 200 nm does not take place in a vacuum. Factors within a geographical context, such as coastal configuration, the coastal relationship between the relevant States, the presence of third States' claims or interests, etc., interact with the determination of overlapping entitlements and inform the delimitation process. A study of these factors in relation to the overlapping entitlements to the continental shelf beyond 200 nm is conducive to thinking about the delimitation of the continental shelf beyond 200 nm *in concreto* rather than *in abstracto*.

Since the existence of overlapping entitlements constitutes the precondition to maritime delimitation, its absence entails that no delimitation will arise. In this respect, two special scenarios are worthy of attention. One concerns whether one party's claimed continental shelf beyond 200 nm can overlap with the other party's 200 nm continental shelf, a

[7] *Delimitation of the Continental Shelf between the United Kingdom of Great Britain and Northern Ireland, and the French Republic (United Kingdom/France) (1978) 18 RIAA 3, 51* [84].

[8] *North Sea Continental Shelf Cases (Federal Republic of Germany/Denmark; Federal Republic of Germany/Netherlands) [1969] ICJ Rep,3*, 49–50 [91].

[9] *Continental Shelf (Libyan Arab Jamahiriya/Malta) [1985] ICJ Rep,13,44–45* [57].

[10] See K. Highet, 'The Use of Geophysical Factors in the Delimitation of Maritime Boundaries' in J. I. Charney and L. M. Alexander (eds.), *International Maritime Boundaries, Volume I* (Martinus Nijhoff 1993), 196; D. Colson, 'The Delimitation of the Outer Continental Shelf between Neighboring States' (2003) 97 *AJIL* 91, 102–107; B. Kunoy, "A Geometric Variable Scope of Delimitations: The Impact of a Geological and Geomorphologic Title to the Outer Continental Shelf" (2006), 11 *Austrian RIEL* 49, 67–70; S. Fietta and R. Cleverly, *A Practitioner's Guide to Maritime Boundary Delimitation* (Oxford University Press 2016), 615.

question underlying the pending *Question of the Delimitation of the Continental Shelf between Nicaragua and Colombia beyond 200 nautical miles from the Nicaraguan Coast (Nicaragua* v. *Colombia II)* case before the ICJ.[11] The other is the so-called "zone-locked" scenario, in which one State is prevented from accessing its continental shelf beyond 200 nm as a result of maritime delimitation within 200 nm. This latter scenario provokes the question of whether the "zone-locked" State can still claim a continental shelf beyond 200 nm.

Section II sets out the factors that contextualize overlapping entitlements to the continental shelf beyond 200 nm on the basis of a survey of relevant State practice. Section III examines the question of overlapping entitlements based on different criteria and Section IV analyzes the origin of the "zone-locked" problem.

## II Contextualizing Overlapping Entitlements to the Continental Shelf beyond 200 NM

### *A Outer Limits of the Continental Shelf beyond 200 NM*

There is a definitional distinction between the delimitation of the continental shelf under Article 83 of UNCLOS and the delineation of the outer limits of the continental shelf under Article 76.[12] Although the two are subject to different rules, in practice, "the two operations may impact upon one another."[13] As the outer limits of the continental shelf constitute the precise seaward extent of the entitlement beyond 200 nm, a question naturally arises as to whether determination of the overlapping entitlements beyond 200 nm requires established outer limits. A review of State practice demonstrates that this question can only be answered in a case-specific fashion.

In some circumstances, the establishment of the outer limits of the continental shelf may be unnecessary at all. Where there exists a common continental margin shared by the relevant coastal States, the parties could proceed to delimit the continental shelf beyond 200 nm

[11] *Question of the Delimitation of the Continental Shelf between Nicaragua and Colombia beyond 200 Nautical Miles from the Nicaraguan Coast (Nicaragua* v. *Colombia)*, available at www.icj-cij.org/en/case/154.

[12] *Bangladesh/Myanmar* (n 1) 99 [376]; *Question of the Delimitation of the Continental Shelf between Nicaragua and Colombia beyond 200 Nautical Miles from the Nicaraguan Coast (Nicaragua v. Colombia) (Preliminary Objections) [2016] ICJ Rep 100,137* [112].

[13] *Nicaragua* v. *Colombia II (Preliminary Objections)* (n 12), 137 [113].

without ascertaining the exact extent of each other's entitlement. For instance, Mexico and the United States delimited the western polygon area of the Gulf of Mexico prior to establishing the outer limits of the continental shelf,[14] and this boundary eventually became Mexico's outer limits of the continental shelf in this region.[15] Similarly, in the recommendations to Norway in respect of the Loop Hole, the CLCS recognized that the entire Loop Hole forms part of the continental shelf of Norway and Russia and recommended that "only a bilateral delimitation between [the two countries] remains to be carried out to delineate the extent of each coastal State's continental shelf in the Loop Hole."[16] In such situations, the outer limits of the continental shelf are not a requisite for determining overlapping entitlements, and the delimitation line serves the dual function of the outer limits of the continental shelf of each State and the maritime boundary between the two States.

The outer limits of the continental shelf may well be indispensable for defining the precise endpoint of the maritime boundary. For instance, Norway and Russia delimited most of their continental shelves beyond 200 nm in the Arctic Ocean and agreed upon a formula according to which the terminus can be established after the establishment of the outer limits of both States.[17] Alternatively, coastal States might define the terminus but explicitly agree that the terminus is subject to adjustment after the parties' outer limits of the continental shelf are established with the recommendations of the CLCS.[18] These practices show that the outer limits of the continental shelf are not a precondition to the

[14] Treaty between Mexico and the United States on the Delimitation of the Continental Shelf in the Western Gulf of Mexico beyond 200 Nautical Miles (June 9, 2000), (2001) 44 LoSB 71.

[15] See "Recommendations to Mexico adopted on 31 March 2009" [49], available at www.un.org/Depts/los/clcs_new/submissions_files/mex07/mex_rec.pdf.

[16] "Recommendations to Norway in respect of Areas in the Arctic Ocean, the Barents Sea and the Norwegian sea adopted on 27 March 2009," [21–22], available at www.un.org/Depts/los/clcs_new/submissions_files/nor06/nor_rec_summ.pdf.

[17] Article 1 of the Treaty between the Kingdom of Norway and the Russian Federation concerning Maritime Delimitation and Cooperation in the Barents Sea and the Arctic Ocean (September 15, 2010), 2791 UNTS 3.

[18] For instance, the 1982 Agreement on Maritime Delimitation between the Government of Australia and the Government of the French Republic (January 4, 1982, 1329 UNTS 107) defines the termini of the boundary between the Australian Heard/McDonald Islands and the French Kerguelen Islands and agrees that the line could be extended subject to the agreement of the parties. See also B. M. Magnússon, "Outer Continental Shelf Boundary Agreements" (2013), 62 *ICLQ* 345, 370–371.

delimitation process as such, but they are necessary components of a complete course of the maritime boundary.

It is equally likely that there are occasions upon which the determination of the outer limits of the continental shelf beyond 200 nm – at least approximately – is necessary *before* the delimitation takes place. It is because in these circumstances the outer limits of the continental shelf are critical to ascertain the exact scope of the overlapping entitlements of the parties. Should the outer limits of the continental shelf remain uncertain, coastal States may be reluctant to delimit the continental shelf beyond 200 nm for fear of losing the part that should have been its own. The Agreed Minutes on the Delimitation of the Continental Shelf beyond 200 Nautical Miles between Greenland and Iceland in the Irminger Sea ("2013 Denmark (Greenland)–Iceland Agreed Minutes") is an example in point, as the "area of interest" subject to delimitation in this agreement is defined by reference to the overlap of the two countries' outer limits of the continental shelf.[19]

The relevance of outer limits of the continental shelf with the determination of overlapping entitlements is thus case-specific, and should not be generalized without due regard to the variety of geographical, geomorphological or geological particularities.

### B Maritime Delimitation within 200 NM

Frequently in State practice, coastal States have maritime delimitation issues within and beyond 200 nm. A typical situation is between adjacent States that share a common land frontier at the coast. Among the States that claim a continental shelf beyond 200 nm, coastal States with adjacent coasts either have pre-existing boundaries up to 200 nm,[20] or have to delimit all the relevant maritime zones including the continental shelf beyond 200 nm. In fact, the delimitation of the continental shelf beyond 200 nm between adjacent States underlies most cases where there are overlapping entitlements to the continental shelf beyond 200 nm.[21]

[19] See paragraph 2 of the 2013 Denmark (Greenland)–Iceland Agreed Minutes, reproduced in B. M. Magnússon, "Denmark (Greenland)–Iceland, Report Number 9-22 (2)," in C. G. Lathrop (ed.), *International Maritime Boundaries, Vol. VII* (Brill Nijhoff 2016), 5269.

[20] For instance, Brazil and Uruguay have delimited their boundary with an all-purpose line up to 200 nm and needs to extend their boundary to delimit the continental shelf beyond 200 nm. See Magnússon (n 18) 367–368.

[21] See T. L. McDorman, "The Continental Shelf beyond 200 NM: A First Look at the Bay of Bengal (Bangladesh/Myanmar) Case," in M. H. Nordquist et al. (eds.), *The Regulation of*

It is self-evident that for a pre-existing boundary up to the 200 nm limit between the parties, its terminus must coincide with the point of departure for the delimitation of the continental shelf beyond 200 nm.[22] An example from State practice can be found in the 2013 Denmark (Greenland)–Iceland Agreed Minutes.[23] In the jurisprudence, it is also not unusual for a court or tribunal to delimit a maritime boundary from a point which was the terminus point of a previous maritime boundary agreement,[24] or a point specially agreed by the parties that means to preclude the jurisdiction of the court or the tribunal over a particular area.[25] The terminus point of a pre-existing maritime boundary up to the 200 nm limit is therefore a potentially relevant circumstance in the delimitation of the continental shelf beyond 200 nm. An analogy with the land frontier that meets the coast can be made in this respect.[26]

If, on the other hand, coastal States have overlapping entitlements to the continental shelf within and beyond 200 nm but they have not concluded maritime boundary agreements within 200 nm, they may settle the delimitation issue in a complete package.[27] Again, this scenario is most common among adjacent coastal States, though other States also have delimitation issues within and beyond 200 nm even if their coastal relationship cannot be classified in "adjacent" or "opposite" terms.[28] All the judicial decisions that delimited the continental shelf beyond 200 nm so far, namely the *Bay of Bengal* cases and the *Ghana/Côte d'Ivoire* case are concerned with adjacent coastal States. The pending

*Continental Shelf Development: Rethinking International Standards* (Martinus Nijhoff 2013), 100.

22 See J. Lilje-Jensen and M. Thamsborg, "The Role of Natural Prolongation in Relation to Shelf Delimitation beyond 200 Nautical Miles" (1995), 64 *Nordic JIL* 619, 643.

23 The starting point of the 2013 Agreed Minutes is "an updated version of the intersection point of the EEZs of the Parties (point Q of the 1997 Agreement between Iceland and Denmark/Greenland on the Delimitation of the Continental Shelf and the Fishery Zones in the Area between Iceland and Greenland)," Magnússon (n 19) 5265.

24 See *Land and Maritime Boundary between Cameroon and Nigeria (Cameroon v. Nigeria: Equatorial Guinea intervening) [2002] ICJ Rep 303, 431–432* [268–269]. *Black Sea* (n 1) 130 [218]; *Maritime Dispute (Peru v. Chile) [2014] ICJ Rep 3, 66* [183].

25 See *Delimitation of the Maritime Boundary in the Gulf of Maine Area (Canada/United States of America) [1984] ICJ Rep 246, 332–333* [212].

26 *Continental Shelf (Tunisia/Libyan Arab Jamahiriya) [1982] ICJ Rep 18, 65* [82].

27 For instance, see Agreement between the United Republic of Tanzania and the Republic of Kenya on the Delimitation of the Maritime Boundary of the Exclusive Economic Zone and the Continental Shelf (June 23, 2009), 2603 UNTS 37.

28 Coastal relationship may not be determined with accuracy. See *Maritime Boundary Arbitration (Barbados v. Trinidad and Tobago) (2006) XXVII RIAA 147* [121–124].

*Kenya* v. *Somalia* case before the ICJ also raises the issue of drawing a single line that delimits all the relevant maritime zones between two adjacent States, the continental shelf beyond 200 nm included.[29]

As a result, when coastal States have overlapping entitlements both within and beyond 200 nm, the delimitation of the continental shelf beyond 200 nm is better considered as part of the entire delimitation process rather than an isolated exercise. Where there exist maritime boundary agreements between the parties, the delimitation of the continental shelf beyond 200 nm is restricted by the pre-existing boundary line as a matter of determining the point of departure. That the delimitation process involves maritime areas within and beyond 200 nm is also critical for examining the relevant circumstances: will the factors relevant in maritime delimitation within 200 nm continue to influence the course of the boundary beyond 200 nm? Alternatively, will the factors relevant only to the continental shelf beyond 200 nm take over and call for the shift of the maritime boundary? These questions will be addressed in connection with the delimitation methodology for the continental shelf beyond 200 nm.[30]

### *C Multiple Claims to the Same Area of Continental Shelf beyond 200 NM*

In many geographical contexts, three or more States have overlapping entitlements or lay claims to the same area of continental shelf beyond 200 nm. Strictly speaking, this is not a situation unique to the continental shelf beyond 200 nm, as coastal States bordering an enclosed or semi-enclosed sea may have the same problem with respect to maritime delimitation within 200 nm.[31] However, several factors complicate the scenario in which the continental shelf beyond 200 nm is claimed by three or more States.

First, while all the coastal States claim the same continental shelf beyond 200 nm, not all of them have delimitation issues within 200 nm. This can produce different layers of disagreement between the coastal States. It is possible for State A and State B to have delimitation issues within and beyond 200 nm, whereas for State B and State C only

[29] *Maritime Delimitation in the Indian Ocean (Somalia v. Kenya) (Preliminary Objections) [2017] ICJ Rep* 3, 10–11[12].

[30] See Chapter 7, Section II, Chapter 8, and Chapter 9, Section II.

[31] See *Libya/Malta* (n 9) 40 [47].

the delimitation of the continental shelf beyond 200 nm is at stake. This situation can be found among the coastal States bordering the Arctic Ocean. Canada, Denmark (Greenland), Norway, Russia, and the United States claim the continental shelf beyond 200 nm of the Arctic Ocean to different extents.[32] While Russia and the United States have to delimit their maritime zones within 200 nm as well as the continental shelf beyond 200 nm,[33] Russia and Denmark (Greenland) have overlapping claims to the continental shelf beyond 200 nm only.[34]

Second, it is also possible that one or more States do not recognize the claims made by other coastal States to the same area of the continental shelf beyond 200 nm. Should a coastal State deny the existence of overlapping entitlements to the continental shelf beyond 200 nm, it may invoke Article 76(10) and Article 9 of Annex II to UNCLOS, as well as Rule 46 of the Rules of Procedure of the CLCS to block the Commission's consideration of the submissions made by other coastal States.[35] As a result, the delineation of the outer limits of the continental shelf and the delimitation in the same area may end up in a stalemate. In the Bay of Bengal, Bangladesh, Myanmar, and India had overlapping claims to the continental shelf beyond 200 nm, and Bangladesh availed itself of the opportunity to block the Commission's examination of Myanmar and India's submissions.[36] Accordingly, coordination between delineation and delimitation is of particular importance in a regional context.

Third, the absence of definite outer limits of the continental shelf might cast doubt on the exact extent of each coastal State's entitlement to the continental shelf beyond 200 nm in the same area, and may therefore widen the disagreement among coastal States to settle delimitation issues. A more complicated situation arises if a coastal State claims the continental shelf beyond 200 nm where other coastal States have

32 See A. G. Oude Elferink, "The Delimitation of the Continental Shelf Beyond 200 Nautical Miles in the Arctic Ocean: Recent Developments, Applicable Law and Possible Outcomes," in R. Long et al. (eds.), *Challenges of the Changing Arctic* (Brill 2016) 55–68. B. Kunoy, "Assertions of Entitlement to the Outer Continental Shelf in the Central Arctic Ocean" (2017) 66 *ICLQ* 367, 367–371.

33 See Maritime Boundary Agreement Between the United States of America and the Union of the Soviet Socialist Republics (June 1, 1990), (1991) 17 LoSB 15.

34 See "Executive Summary of Russia's partial revised submission (3 August 2015)," 9, www.un.org/Depts/los/clcs_new/submissions_files/submission_rus_rev1.htm.

35 Chapter 4, Section I and IV.

36 See *Bangladesh/Myanmar* (n 1) 101 [387]; *Bay of Bengal Maritime Boundary Arbitration (Bangladesh v. India) (2014) 167 ILR 1, 32–33* [81].

already concluded a delimitation agreement. For example, New Zealand and Australia delimited their continental shelves beyond 200 nm in the Three Kings Ridge area, which was subsequently claimed by France in its submission in respect of New Caledonia.[37] This raises the issue of third States' interest in continental shelf delimitation beyond 200 nm. From the review of the submissions to the CLCS, it has been identified that there are nine occasions where three States have overlapping continental shelf claims beyond 200 nm and seven occasions where more than four States make a claim to the same continental shelf beyond 200 nm.[38] The complexities underlying multiple claims to the same continental shelf beyond 200 nm highlight the importance of addressing the delimitation issue with an inclusive and multilateral approach instead of a strictly bilateral one.

Based on the above-mentioned factors, two scenarios of overlapping entitlements to the continental shelf beyond 200 nm can be identified. One concerns a "pure" continental shelf delimitation beyond 200 nm and the other occurs where coastal States have overlapping entitlements within and beyond 200 nm. The classification helps to examine the legal issues that are of different degrees of relevance with each of the scenarios, without implying any normative distinction between the two.

The "pure" continental shelf delimitation beyond 200 nm scenario provides an ideal framework to consider if there are any circumstances exclusively relevant to the continental shelf beyond 200 nm, as no maritime delimitation within 200 nm is involved. Furthermore, this scenario may test the relevance of the opposite coastal relationship in the continental shelf delimitation beyond 200 nm. As envisaged by Judge Evensen in the *Tunisia/Libya* case, "The definition given in Article 76, paragraph 3, may have a bearing on the delimitation of the continental shelves of neighboring countries. This is obvious with regard to 'opposite' States. It is not so obvious that the definition of paragraph 3 will have equal practical bearing on the lateral delimitation of the shelves of adjacent States."[39]

37 See "France's Executive Summary of Submission (22 May 2007)" and Note Verbale of New Zealand dated August 15, 2007, available at www.un.org/Depts/los/clcs_new/submissions_files/submission_fra.htm.

38 See B. J. Van Pay, "Disputed Areas Beyond 200 Nautical Miles: How Many and Will Geophysical Characteristics Matter in Their Resolution?," in M. H. Nordquist and J. N. Moore (eds.), *Maritime Border Diplomacy* (Martinus Nijhoff Publishers 2012), 67 (Appendix III and IV).

39 *Tunisia/Libya* (n 26) 290 [11] (Dissenting Opinion of Judge Evensen).

In contrast, where coastal States have overlapping entitlements both within and beyond 200 nm, the delimitation of the continental shelf beyond 200 nm is better considered as integral to the overall delimitation process. The classification of "adjacency" or "oppositeness" is not decisive, though delimitation of the continental shelf beyond 200 nm between two adjacent coasts is the principal example falling within this scenario. This scenario helps the analysis of two questions: first, the relevance of the outer limits of the continental shelf with the delimitation process, and, second, the influence of coastal geography over the delimitation of the continental shelf beyond 200 nm.

## III Overlapping Entitlements Based on Different Criteria: A Question of Priority?

Logically speaking, when two States base their continental shelf rights on the two different criteria of entitlement under Article 76, one first has to ascertain whether it is legally permissible for the two criteria of entitlement to overlap; otherwise there would be no question of overlap nor delimitation.[40] If it is not legally possible, then it may be asked which criterion takes precedence over the other. To be sure, this scenario only arises between coastal States with opposite coasts, and only when one of them claims the continental shelf beyond 200 nm. Adjacent States do not encounter this problem because even if one claims a continental shelf beyond 200 nm while the other does not, the area of overlapping entitlements ceases to exist when it reaches the 200 nm limit from the relevant coasts.

In this scenario there are two variations in accordance with the distance between the opposite coasts. One is where the distance between the two coasts is greater than 400 nm, and one State claims a continental shelf beyond 200 nm that intrudes into the 200 nm limit of the other State. In this situation, delimitation issues would not arise should both States base their entitlements solely on distance. This is the situation in the *Nicaragua v. Colombia II* case (Figure 3.1). The other situation is where the distance between the opposite coasts is less than 400 nm, but one State still claims a continental shelf beyond 200 nm. In this latter situation, even without the continental shelf beyond 200 nm claim, there is a need for maritime

[40] Section III is an adapted and updated version of an article first published as X. Liao, "Is There a Hierarchical Relationship between Natural Prolongation and Distance in the Continental Shelf Delimitation?" (2018), 33 *IJMCL* 79. The author is grateful to the publishers Brill Nijhoff for permission to reproduce some of the text here.

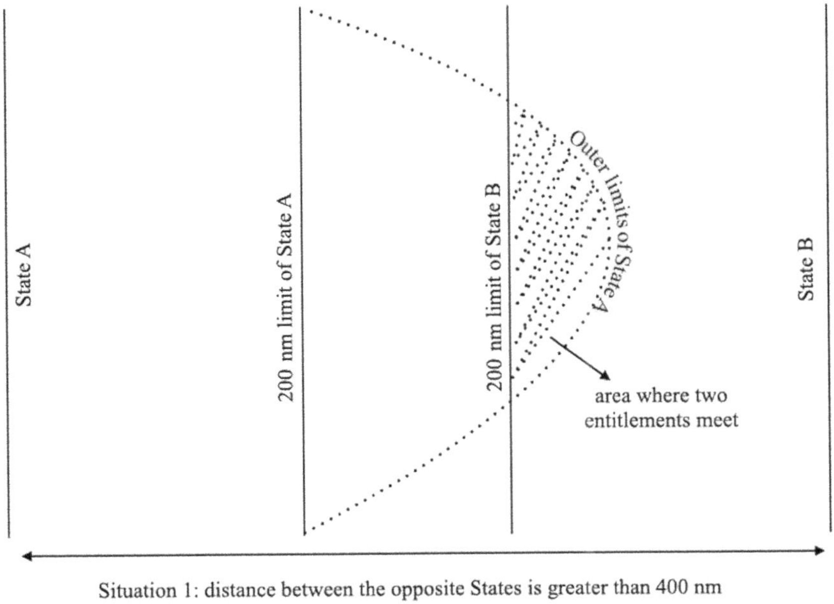


**Figure 3.1** Overlap of the two continental shelf criteria under Article 76 of UNCLOS: Situation 1

delimitation. This situation occurs between China and Japan, and between Korea and Japan in the East China Sea (Figure 3.2).[41]

In both situations, the States whose 200 nm shelf was intruded upon claim that the continental shelf beyond 200 nm cannot encroach upon their 200 nm limits. Colombia argued that natural prolongation cannot take precedence over distance if they come into conflict,[42] while Japan contended that where the distance between two opposite States is less than 400 nm, there should be no claim of continental shelf beyond 200 nm.[43] Either argument hinges on the question of whether the distance criterion prevails over the outer edge of the continental margin criterion. If such a hierarchical relationship is established, Colombia could therefore enjoy its

[41] See J. Gao, "The Okinawa Trough Issue in the Continental Shelf Delimitation Disputes within the East China Sea" (2010), 9 *Chinese JIL* 143.

[42] *Nicaragua* v. *Colombia I*, Rejoinder of Colombia, vol. I (June 18, 2010), 149 [4.60].

[43] See Note Verbale of Japan dated December 28, 2012, available at www.un.org/Depts/los/clcs_new/submissions_files/chn63_12/jpn_re_chn_28_12_2012.pdf; Note Verbale of Japan dated January 11, 2013, available at www.un.org/Depts/los/clcs_new/submissions_files/kor65_12/jpn_re_kor_11_01_2013.pdf.

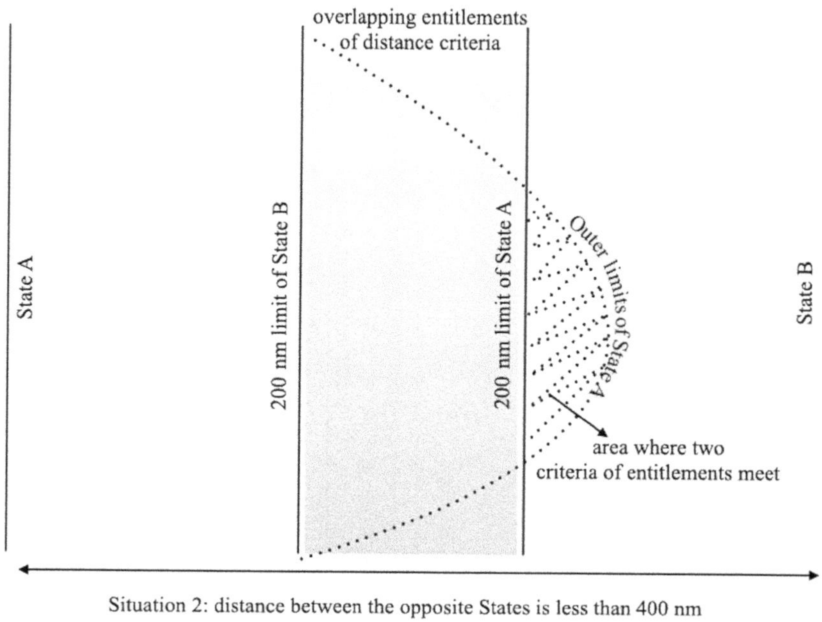


**Figure 3.2** Overlap of the two continental shelf criteria under Article 76 of UNCLOS: Situation 2

continental shelf up to 200 nm, while between China, Korea, and Japan, the outstanding delimitation issues would only concern their maritime entitlements based on the distance criterion. On the other hand, if no priority exists between the two criteria and both criteria are equally valid, there would be an area of overlap that calls for a delimitation.

Whether there is a hierarchical relationship between the two criteria is first a question of interpreting Article 76(1). It is also necessary to examine the relevant judicial decisions, State practice, as well as the relationship between the regimes of the continental shelf and the EEZ to ascertain if there exists an international rule that permits the overlap of the two or a rule that recognizes the priority of the distance criterion over the outer edge of the continental margin criterion.

## A *Interpretation of Article 76(1)*

The text of Article 76(1) of UNCLOS is clear that there are two alternative criteria of entitlement, one of natural prolongation to the outer edge of the continental margin, and the other of the 200 nm distance if the outer edge of the continental margin does not reach that distance. Article 76 as a whole is silent on the question of the relationship between the two criteria if they are invoked by different parties in a single case.

One may argue that the 200 nm distance criterion is given as a minimum extent of the continental shelf.[44] Every coastal State is entitled to a 200 nm continental shelf, but only those coastal States bordering on a wide continental margin that extends beyond 200 nm are entitled to a continental shelf beyond 200 nm. It follows that the minimum extent of the continental shelf should be secured against a continental shelf beyond 200 nm if they are invoked by two opposite States in a confined maritime area. In the situation between coastal States with a distance greater than 400 nm apart, it sounds counterintuitive to argue that coastal State A, which is already entitled to a continental shelf up to 200 nm, can extend its continental shelf further into the 200 nm limits of coastal State B. This leads to the seemingly inequitable result that State A enjoys a full 200 nm continental shelf plus some area beyond 200 nm, whereas State B could not even reach its 200 nm limits.

However, instead of providing a minimum extent of the continental shelf, the text of Article 76(1) is open to an interpretation that, in a logical sequence, the distance criterion applies "where the outer edge of the continental margin does not extend up to that distance," which suggests that the 200 nm shelf is the legal outcome of applying Article 76(1) in its entirety.[45] Indeed, the text is open to be interpreted as "only if a State's natural continental margin is narrower than 200 miles does the distance criteria come into operation."[46] This interpretation resonates with the ICJ's reading of Article 76 in the, then, draft convention on the law of the sea in the *Tunisia/Libya* case:

> That definition consists of two parts, employing different criteria. According to the first part of paragraph 1 the natural prolongation of the land territory is the main criterion. In the second part of the paragraph, the distance of 200 nautical miles is *in certain circumstances* the basis of the title of a coastal State.[47]

[44] T. Treves, "La limite extérieure du plateau continental: Evolution récente de la pratique" (1989), 35 *AFDI* 724, 725.

[45] See J. I. Charney, "International Maritime Boundaries for the Continental Shelf: The Relevance of Natural Prolongation," in N. Ando et al. (eds.), *Liber Amicorum Judge Shigeru Oda, Volume II*, (Kluwer Law International 2002), 1024.

[46] S. Lloyd, "Natural Prolongation: Have the Rumours Its Demise Been Greatly Exaggerated" (1991), 3 *African JICL* 558, 570.

[47] *Tunisia/Libya* (n 26) 48 [47] (emphasis added).

The cautious manner in which the ICJ treats the distance criterion in this judgment may seem like an understatement today, as the distance criterion provides the basis of entitlement for a majority of coastal States.[48] However, it accurately sets out the logical sequence followed by the text of Article 76(1). It is recalled that the order of the two criteria of continental shelf entitlement as they appeared in the current text was a delicate choice during UNCLOS III. Originally there were proposals that put the distance criterion before the outer edge of the continental margin criterion,[49] but the current order of the text was preferred because it established a separateness between the continental shelf and the EEZ and even gave the criterion of natural prolongation a certain primacy.[50] As international courts and tribunals have acknowledged, natural prolongation and the distance criteria are complementary in the definition of the continental shelf, and "both remain essential elements in the juridical concept of the continental shelf."[51] To say that the 200 nm shelf is the minimum extent of the continental shelf misjudges the textual relationship of the two criteria.

Still, one may argue that the differences derived out of the continental shelf within and beyond 200 nm may attest to the priority of the former over the latter. These differences are mainly concerned with the procedure establishing the outer limits of the continental shelf,[52] the revenue-sharing system imposed on the exploitation of the shelf beyond 200 nm,[53] and the restriction on coastal States' discretion to withhold consent to scientific research on the continental shelf beyond 200 nm.[54] It has

[48] See D. Anderson, "Some Recent Developments in the Law Relating to the Continental Shelf"(1988), 6 *JENRL* 95, 96–97.

[49] For instance, the Informal Group of Judicial Experts in the Tentative Draft Articles for a Convention on the Law of the Sea (August 5, 1974) suggested that "the continental shelf of a coastal State extends beyond its territorial sea up to a distance of 200 miles or, beyond that distance, throughout the natural prolongation of the land territory of the coastal State (including the continental margin)." Text reproduced in R. Platzöder (ed.), *Third United Nations Conference on the Law of the Sea: Documents, Volume XI* (Oceana Publications Inc. 1982), 406.

[50] International Law Association, "The Relationship between the Exclusive Economic Zone and the Continental Shelf," *Report of the Sixty-Second Conference* (Seoul, 1987), 329–330.

[51] See *Libya/Malta* (n 9) 33 [34]; *Barbados* v. *Trinidad and Tobago* (n 28) [225].

[52] Article 76(8) of UNCLOS.

[53] Article 82 of UNCLOS.

[54] Article 246(6) states: "Notwithstanding the provisions of paragraph 5, coastal States may not exercise their discretion to withhold consent under subparagraph (a) of that paragraph in respect of marine scientific research projects to be undertaken in accordance with the provisions of this Part on the continental shelf, beyond 200 nautical miles from the baselines from which the breadth of the territorial sea is measured, outside those specific areas which coastal States may at any time publicly designate as areas in which

been suggested that these differences undermine the exclusivity of continental shelf rights in the area beyond 200 nm.[55]

The differences between the two criteria of entitlements have to be evaluated in the context of Article 76(1) and in the light of its object and purpose.[56] To start with, one cannot disregard the exclusive and inherent nature of continental shelf rights embedded in Article 77(2)–(3), which does not distinguish between the continental shelf within or beyond 200 nm. Above all, in law there is a single continental shelf, rather than an inner continental shelf and a separate outer continental shelf by reference to the 200 nm limit.[57] The entitlement to the continental shelf beyond 200 nm is measured from the territorial baselines, which confirms that the area of the continental shelf beyond 200 nm is not something extra or surplus, but is integral to a coastal State's continental shelf entitlement. Notwithstanding the operational implications derived from the differences between the two criteria of entitlements,[58] the continental shelf based on the outer edge of the continental margin criterion and that on the distance criterion are equal in terms of the legal nature of continental shelf rights. Therefore, it would be against the legal nature of the continental shelf to argue that one criterion would prevail over the other. Furthermore, the international aspect of the continental shelf beyond 200 nm does not deprive the primacy of coastal States' rights and jurisdiction over the resources of this part of continental shelf.[59] Article 142(2) of UNCLOS provides, *inter alia*, that: "In cases where activities in the Area may result in the exploitation of resources lying within national jurisdiction, the prior consent of the coastal State concerned shall be required." This provision reiterates the exclusivity of coastal States' rights over resources of the continental shelf, even in the light of the interest of the international community in the continental shelf beyond 200 nm.

exploitation or detailed exploratory operations focused on those areas are occurring or will occur within a reasonable period of time."

55 See B. Kwiatkowska, *The 200 Mile Exclusive Economic Zone in the New Law of the Sea* (Martinus Nijhoff Publishers 1989), 18.

56 Article 31(1) of the Vienna Convention on the Law of Treaties (May 23, 1969), 1155 UNTS 331.

57 See *Barbados* v. *Trinidad and Tobago* (n 28) [213]; *Bangladesh* v. *India* (n 36) 31–32 [77]; *Delimitation of the Maritime Boundary in the Atlantic Ocean (Ghana/Côte d'Ivoire), [2017] ITLOS Rep 4* [490].

58 M. D. Evans, "Maritime Boundary Delimitation: Whatever Next?," in J. Barrett and R. Barnes (eds.), *Law of the Sea: UNCLOS as a Living Treaty* (BIILC 2016), 75.

59 See S. N. Nandan and S. Rosenne (eds.), *United Nations Convention on the Law of the Sea 1982: A Commentary, Volume II* (Martinus Nijhoff Publishers 1993), 947.

Moreover, the differences between the two criteria of entitlement to the continental shelf cannot be appreciated without taking into account their origin, namely, the compromises reached during UNCLOS III.[60] The negotiations on the definition of the continental shelf were profoundly influenced by three trends in the development of the law of the sea at that time, including the popular support for the 200 nm EEZ regime, the concept of the Common Heritage of Mankind, and the trend to expand the legal continental shelf to include the continental margin.[61] The last trend highlights two things: first, the idea that the legal continental shelf should extend beyond 200 nm was not a novel creation of UNCLOS III;[62] second, coastal States' rights to a continental shelf beyond 200 nm were widely recognized, even though its precise limits were subject to intense discussion.

Even before the commencement of UNCLOS III, State practice concerning the granting of licenses has been extended to the continental slope.[63] Arguably this practice had its legal basis in the exploitability test of the 1958 Convention on the Continental Shelf (CCS). But it gave rise to the need to include the continental slope and even the continental rise in the legal concept of the continental shelf. By 1973, the Sea-bed Committee received many proposals to define the continental shelf by referring to geological criteria. For instance, the draft articles submitted by Colombia, Mexico, and Venezuela define the continental shelf as "the sea-bed and subsoil of the submarine areas adjacent to the coast, but outside the area of the territorial sea, to the outer limits of the continental rise bordering on the ocean basin or abyssal floor."[64] During UNCLOS III, for many coastal States, the notion of natural prolongation provides the legal basis for the extension of the legal continental shelf to the outer edge of the continental margin,[65] which lent support for the idea that coastal States' rights to the

[60] See T. L. McDorman, "The Continental Shelf," in D. R. Rothwell et al. (eds.), *The Oxford Handbook of the Law of the Sea* (Oxford University Press 2015), 195.

[61] Chapter 2, Section I.

[62] Colson (n 10), 102.

[63] See R. Y. Jennings, "The Limits of Continental Shelf Jurisdiction: Some Possible Implications of the North Sea Case Judgment" (1969) 18 *ICLQ* 819, 830.

[64] Doc. A/AC.138/SC.II/L.21 (April 2, 1973) in *Report of the Committee on the Peaceful Uses of the Sea-Bed and the Ocean Floor beyond the Limits of National Jurisdiction* (United Nations 1973), 21.

[65] Doc. A/CONF.62/C.2/SR.17 (26 July 1974), *Official Records of the Third United Nations Conference on the Law of the Sea, vol.II* (United Nations 1975) 147 (Australia) and 148 (Korea); Doc. A/CONF.62/C.2/SR.18 (July 26, 1974), ibid., 150 (Argentina), 152 (Venezuela), 154 (Trinidad and Tobago) and 155 (Burma); Doc. A/CIBF.62/C.2/SR.19

continental margin that extends beyond 200 nm were *existing rights*. As put by Australia, "it was necessary to respect existing sovereign rights of coastal States over the resources of the natural prolongation of their land territories," and "there was no reason of equity why a coastal State should be deprived of an area over which it had existing rights, while the area under the jurisdiction of other States was being maintained or even extended [by the 200-nm distance criterion]."[66]

The idea that coastal States' existing rights to the continental shelf beyond 200 nm should be preserved was also respected by other coastal States whose continental shelf cannot extend beyond 200 nm. Peru expressed that its position was based on "respect for the sovereign rights of other States over their respective adjacent seas and over the submerged prolongations of their territories, even if they exceeded 200 miles."[67] Even countries that argued for the replacement of the continental shelf with the EEZ believed that coastal States' existing rights to the continental shelf beyond 200 nm should be preserved. Ghana, for instance, stated that "there was no need to maintain the concept of the continental shelf if the Conference decided to establish an economic zone beyond the territorial sea," but that "there was no means of compelling those States to relinquish their hold on those areas of the continental shelf outside the proposed 200-mile limit."[68] The respect for existing rights to the continental shelf beyond 200 nm highlights that the new continental shelf rights based on the 200 nm distance criterion cannot overturn the existing continental shelf rights based on natural prolongation.

As a result, what is new in the continental shelf regime of UNCLOS is the methodology to establish the outer limits of the continental shelf, not the right to the continental shelf beyond 200 nm as such. The compromises underlying the continental shelf beyond 200 nm are not meant to undermine the integrity of the continental shelf regime, much less the exclusive and inherent nature of continental shelf rights. The intention of Article 76(1) cannot thus be interpreted to create or secure a minimum extent of continental shelf for all coastal States – this simply leaves the considerations of

(July 30, 1974), ibid., 160 (Thailand); Doc. A/CONF.62/C.2/SR.20 (July 30, 1974), ibid., 163 (Mauritius); Doc. A/CIBF,62/C.2/SR.21 (July 31, 1974), ibid., 170 (New Zealand).

66 Doc. A/CONF.62/C.2/SR.17 (July 26, 1974), ibid., 147 (Australia); Doc. A/CONF,62/C.2/SR.19 (July 30, 1974), ibid., 153 (Ecuador) and 158 (Uruguay).

67 Doc. A/CONF.62/C.2/SR.16 (July 26, 1974), ibid., 145 (Peru); Doc. A/CONF.62/C.2/SR.17 (July, 26 1974), ibid., 149 (El Salvador).

68 Doc. A/CONF.62/C.2/SR.20 (July 30, 1974), ibid., 165 (Ghana). See also Doc. A/CONF.62/C.2/SR.18 (July 29, 1974), ibid., 154 (Pakistan) and 159 (Iceland).

existing rights to the continental shelf beyond 200 nm out of the general picture. On the contrary, the *travaux préparatoires* demonstrate that interests of different groups of States were acknowledged and accommodated. As aptly put by Judge Oda, "It should be crystal clear that Article 76 of the draft convention is essentially a product of compromise – not consensus – between the conflicting positions of various groups which have different, and sometimes opposite, interests in the use of sea-bed areas."[69]

Given the single regime of the continental shelf, Article 76(1) is more appropriately interpreted as a combination of two criteria of entitlement to the continental shelf without providing for the priority of either. The equality of the two criteria was endorsed by the *Guinea/Guinea-Bissau* case, which observed that both natural prolongation and distance are rules of entitlement included in Article 76, and that the distance rule, "without derogating from the rule of natural prolongation, reduces its scope by substituting it in certain circumstances."[70] The Arbitral Tribunal continued that "[t]here are therefore two rules between which there is neither priority nor precedence."[71]

It is thus futile to infer from Article 76(1) any priority between the distance criterion and the outer edge of the continental margin criterion. It is fundamental not to confuse the rule of entitlement with the rule of maritime delimitation.[72] Where the same criterion of the continental shelf entitlement is invoked by two parties to the maritime boundary dispute, neither State is entitled to a maximum extent of its continental shelf entitlement.[73] Under the law of maritime delimitation, to allow the two criteria of continental shelf to overlap is consistent with the non-absolute nature of maritime entitlements.

In consequence, Article 76(1), as a rule of entitlement, cannot be interpreted to suggest a hierarchical relationship between the two criteria of entitlement.

### B *From* Libya/Malta *to* Nicaragua *v.* Colombia

It is thus necessary to inquire into the judicial decisions in which the two criteria were invoked by two States in the context of maritime

69 *Tunisia/Libya* (n 26) 220 [104] (Dissenting Opinion of Judge Oda).

70 *Delimitation of the Maritime Boundary between Guinea and Guinea-Bissau (Guinea/Guinea-Bissau) (1985) XIX RIAA 149* [115].

71 Ibid., [116].

72 Colson (n 10), 104–105.

73 *Bangladesh* v. *India* (n 36), 160–161 [469].

delimitation. In the *Libya/Malta* case, the ICJ made certain observations regarding the role of geophysical factors in determining the continental shelf entitlement and in the delimitation process. The Court started with the observation that within 200 nm, geophysical factors do not have a role "either in verifying the legal title of the States concerned or in proceeding to a delimitation as between their claims," and therefore "the geological or geomorphological characteristics of those areas are completely immaterial."[74] What followed was the statement that:

> [S]ince the distance between the coasts of the Parties is less than 400 miles, so that no geophysical feature can lie more than 200 miles from each coast, the feature referred to as the "rift zone" cannot constitute a fundamental discontinuity terminating the southward extension of the Maltese shelf and the northward extension of the Libyan as if it were some natural boundary.[75]

In the *Nicaragua* v. *Colombia I* case, Nicaragua argued that it had a continental shelf beyond 200 nm which overlapped with the 200 nm shelf of Colombia and requested a delimitation in the overlapping areas of the two entitlements. Nicaragua adopted two different approaches to the delimitation issue during the course of the proceedings. Nicaragua first contended that the delimitation be an equal division of the overlapping continental margins of Nicaragua and Colombia,[76] and next it shifted to a position that the delimitation should be a "median line between the outer limit of Nicaragua's continental margin and the outer limit of Colombia's 200-nautical-mile continental shelf."[77] The former position was premised on the idea of overlapping entitlements of the same kind, but it is difficult to maintain, as Colombia is entitled to a 200 nm continental shelf even if its outer edge of the continental margin does not extend up to that distance. As the ICJ declared in *Nicaragua* v. *Colombia I*, "the definition of the continental shelf set out in Article 76, paragraph 1, of UNCLOS forms part of customary international law."[78]

Colombia invoked the passage of the *Libya/Malta* case quoted above and contended that "the geological or geophysical characteristics of the continental shelf within 200 nautical miles of a State's coast are completely immaterial to issues of entitlement and delimitation," and that its

[74] *Libya/Malta* (n 9), 35 [39].
[75] Ibid.
[76] *Nicaragua* v. *Colombia I*, Reply of Nicaragua, Volume I (September 18, 2009) [3.46].
[77] *Nicaragua* v. *Colombia I*, Verbatim record, CR 2012/9 (April 24, 2012) [75].
[78] *Territorial and Maritime Dispute (Nicaragua v. Colombia) [2012] ICJ Rep 624*, 666 [118].

entitlement to the 200 nm limit is not affected by any such geophysical factors.[79] Colombia interpreted the *Libya/Malta* case as sanctioning the irrelevance of geophysical factors located within the 200 nm limit of a coastal State, irrespective of the distance between the two opposite States.[80] What is entailed by this interpretation is the superiority of a 200 nm shelf over a continental shelf beyond 200 nm, since no geophysical factors located within one State's 200 nm limits can be invoked to justify the other State's continental shelf entitlement beyond 200 nm.[81] Nicaragua, for its part, distinguished the present case from the *Libya/Malta* case and argued that the *Libya/Malta* case was silent about the situation where two opposite States invoked the two continental shelf criteria under Article 76 of UNCLOS and the distance between the two countries was more than 400 nm.[82]

The Court found that there was no need to address any arguments "as to whether a delimitation of overlapping entitlements which involves an extended continental shelf of one party can affect a 200-nautical-mile entitlement to the continental shelf of another party,"[83] because Nicaragua "has not established that it has a continental margin that extends far enough to overlap with Colombia's 200-nautical-mile entitlement to the continental shelf, measured from Colombia's mainland coast,"[84] However, since the *Nicaragua* v. *Colombia II* case is now pending before the ICJ, it seems inevitable for the Court to appreciate the relevance of the *Libya/Malta* case for purposes of clarifying the relationship between the two criteria of continental shelf entitlements when they are invoked by two different parties.

Read in the context of the *Libya/Malta* case, the Court was merely stating the obvious. Since the distance between Libya and Malta is less than 200 nm,[85] no geophysical feature could possibly lie more than 200 miles from each coast, and the "rift zone" claimed by Libya was thus too close to the coasts to be relevant. Nevertheless, it is questionable

[79] See *Nicaragua* v. *Colombia I*, Rejoinder of Colombia (n 42) [4.58].

[80] See *Nicaragua* v. *Colombia I*, Verbatim record, CR 2012/11 (April 26, 2012), [34].

[81] See Y. Tanaka, *Predictability and Flexibility in the Law of Maritime Delimitation* (2nd ed., Hart 2019), 304–305; Charney (n 45), 1028–1029; R. Kolb, *Case Law on Equitable Maritime Delimitation: Digest and Commentaries* (Martinus Nijhoff Publishers 2003), 333.

[82] See *Nicaragua* v. *Colombia I*, Verbatim record, CR 2012/9 (April 24, 2012), [45–47].

[83] *Nicaragua* v. *Colombia I* (n 78), 669–670 [130].

[84] Ibid., 669 [129].

[85] *Libya/Malta* (n 9), 20 [16].

whether the passage has such broad implications as to preclude an overlap between a continental shelf beyond 200 nm and a continental shelf up to 200 nm. For one thing, the factual circumstances of the *Libya/Malta* case and the *Nicaragua* v. *Colombia* cases are essentially different, as the former does not involve a continental margin which extends beyond 200 nm. It is based on this factual consideration that the Court observed that "in so far as those areas are situated at a distance of under 200 miles from the coasts in question, title depends solely on the distance from the coasts of the claimant States."[86] Therefore, it might be difficult to infer from a factual statement a general rule that, between two opposite States, geophysical factors are irrelevant for entitlement and delimitation whether the distance between the two is within or beyond 400 nm. In fact, the ICJ itself interpreted the observation in a restrictive manner. As the Court put it in the *Nicaragua* v. *Colombia I* case, citing the *Libya/Malta* case, "It has repeatedly made clear that geological and geomorphological considerations are not relevant to the delimitation of overlapping entitlements *within 200 nautical miles* of the coasts of States."[87]

More importantly, the passage of the *Libya/Malta* case was not intended to address the priority of the distance criterion over the natural prolongation criterion. Instead, the Court was considering which criterion was applicable as the basis of entitlement for *both* States. The applicable law between Libya and Malta was customary international law, as Libya was not a party to the CCS and UNCLOS was not in force.[88] The Court did not pronounce on the status of the distance criterion in Article 76(1) of UNCLOS. Rather, the Court determined the applicability of the distance criterion by linking the continental shelf regime with the EEZ regime. The Court emphasized that:

> As the 1982 Convention demonstrates, the two institutions – continental shelf and exclusive economic zone – are linked together in modern law. Since the rights enjoyed by a State over its continental shelf would also be possessed by it over the sea-bed and subsoil of any exclusive economic zone which it might proclaim, one of the relevant circumstances to be taken into account for the delimitation of the continental shelf of a State is the legally permissible extent of the exclusive economic zone appertaining to that same State. This does not mean that the concept of the continental

[86] Ibid., 35 [39].
[87] *Nicaragua* v. *Colombia I* (n 78), 703 [214] (emphasis added).
[88] See *Libya/Malta* (n 9), 29 [26].

> shelf has been absorbed by that of the exclusive economic zone; it does however signify that greater importance must be attributed to elements, such as distance from the coast, which are common to both concepts.[89]

Following this observation, the Court stated that "[a]lthough there can be a continental shelf where there is no exclusive economic zone, there cannot be an exclusive economic zone without a corresponding continental shelf."[90] Taking into account the geographical relationship between Libya and Malta, the Court decided that "title depends solely on the distance from the coasts of the claimant States of any areas of sea-bed claimed by way of continental shelf."[91] In other words, the practical effect of these observations was to apply the distance criterion to the ascertainment of entitlement as well as to the delimitation process, while excluding geomorphological and geological factors from both processes.

However, the transportation of the distance criterion of the EEZ to a continental shelf delimitation is legally precarious, because there is a logical gap to claim that the distance criterion of the EEZ, a customary rule,[92] should also be applied to the continental shelf under Article 76 of UNCLOS, unless the Court considered there to be a merger of the two institutions, which was however rejected by the Court. As the Court saw it, the two regimes are "different and distinct."[93] In any event, neither Libya nor Malta by that time proclaimed an EEZ.[94] The statement that "there cannot be an exclusive economic zone without a corresponding continental shelf" would only make sense under UNCLOS, which was not applicable between Libya and Malta.[95]

Despite the questionable application of the distance criterion in the *Libya/Malta* case, the Court explicitly confined the irrelevance of geomorphological or geological factors to the continental shelf within 200 nm, showing an awareness of not prejudicing a situation where a continental margin is involved:

> [I]n a geographical situation like that with which the present case is concerned, where a single continental shelf falls to be delimited between

89 Ibid., 33 [33].
90 Ibid., [34].
91 Ibid., 35 [39].
92 See ibid., 33 [34].
93 Ibid.
94 See ibid., 70 (Separate Opinion of Vice-President Sette-Camara).
95 M. D. Evans, *Relevant Circumstances and Maritime Delimitation* (Oxford University Press 1989), 51–53.

> two opposite States, so that *no question arises as between those States, of delimitation by reference to a continental margin extending beyond 200 miles from the baselines* round the coast of either State, the legal concept of natural prolongation does not attribute any relevance to geological or geophysical factors either as basis of entitlement or as criterion for delimitation.[96]

In fact, even Judge Oda, who appended a dissenting opinion in which he considered that the Court failed to grasp the importance of the distance criterion, doubted whether the Court had gone as far as to imply that "*whenever* dealing with claims in regard to combined distances between coasts of less than 400 miles, 'there is no longer any reason to ascribe any role to geological or geophysical factors." '[97] Judge Oda pointed out the potential challenge to the Court's approach "had the sea-bed in the present case featured, not a rift zone, but the outer edge of a continental margin," and, in that case, the Court would have to "weigh the merits of two convincing claims invoking the sense of Article 76, the one based on geomorphology, the other relying on distance."[98] The concurrent invocation of the two continental shelf criteria by two different parties envisioned by Judge Oda is exactly the situation underlying the *Nicaragua* v. *Colombia II* case.

Having clarified the specific factual circumstances and the legal issues of the *Libya/Malta* case, it is more appropriate to say that the *Nicaragua* v. *Colombia* cases are the first judicial cases where one party relies on the outer edge of the continental margin criterion while the other relies on the distance criterion in maritime delimitation. The ICJ has to decide whether the overlap of the two criteria of entitlements under Article 76 (1) is legally possible. The value of the *Libya/Malta* case as a precedent in this respect seems limited.

### *C State Practice in the Application of Article 76*

When coastal States submit information to the CLCS in accordance with the procedural obligation under Article 76(8) of UNCLOS, it is not uncommon that the areas included in their submissions overlap with their neighbors' claims in the same area. Within this body of practice,

96 *Libya/Malta* (n 9), 55–56 [77] (emphasis added).
97 Ibid., 157 [61] (Dissenting Opinion of Judge Oda) (emphasis in the original).
98 Ibid.

there is a discernible tendency of coastal States to refrain from encroaching upon neighboring States' 200 nm limits.

Among the 85 submissions made to the CLCS,[99] 30 individual submissions made by 24 States[100] clearly demonstrate self-constraint in avoiding encroaching upon neighboring States' 200 nm limits. Two methods are adopted by States to this end. First, the submitting State deliberately avoids touching upon the 200 nm limit of another State when they propose the outer limits of the continental shelf. Mexico in its submission states that "[t]he endpoints of this outer limit of the continental shelf remain deliberately short of the outer limit of the exclusive economic zones of other States in the region."[101] Other coastal States which adopt this method include the United Kingdom (in respect of the Hatton-Rockall region), Ghana, and Iceland (in the Ægir Basin area and in the western and southern parts of Reykjanes Ridge).[102] Second, a more popular method is to locate fixed points of their proposed outer limits on the 200 nm limit of another State. For example, in Canada's submission in respect of the Atlantic Ocean, its outer limits in the Labrador Sea region are defined by combination of the fixed points in accordance with the formulae and constraints of Article 76 of UNCLOS and "a point on the intersection of the line delineating the outer edge of the continental margin and the 200 M limit of the Kingdom of Denmark."[103] Such practices are found in all 25 individual submissions, including those of Somalia, Tonga, and Pakistan, to name a few. A full account of individual submissions in which States refrain from encroaching upon neighboring States' 200 nm limits can be found in Appendix 1 of this volume.

In addition to individual submissions, joint submissions made by a group of States also demonstrate the same self-constraint in respect of

99 The Executive Summaries of coastal States' Submissions and the Summaries of Recommendations are available at www.un.org/Depts/los/clcs_new/commission_submissions.htm, last accessed on August 30, 2020. Revised submissions made by Russia, Brazil, Barbados, and Argentina are not counted repeatedly.

100 Denmark submitted five partial submissions, while Tonga and Canada respectively submitted two partial submissions, making a total number of 30 individual submissions.

101 "Executive summary of Mexico's submission (13 December 2017)," 13, available at www.un.org/Depts/los/clcs_new/submissions_files/mex58_11/01_Executive_Summary.pdf.

102 See Executive summaries of submissions of the United Kingdom in respect of Hatton-Rockall region (March 31, 2009), Ghana (April 28, 2009), and Iceland in the Ægir Basin area and in the western and southern parts of Reykjanes Ridge (April 29, 2009).

103 "Executive summary of Canada's submission (6 December 2013)," 6–7, available at www.un.org/Depts/los/clcs_new/submissions_files/can70_13/es_can_en.pdf.

other States' 200 nm limits. The areas included in the joint submissions are usually confined to the areas beyond the 200 nm of each State making up the joint submission. The joint submission made by France, Ireland, Spain, and the United Kingdom is a case in point.[104] Similarly, joint submissions also adopt the method of locating fixed points on the 200 nm limits of other States. For instance, the joint submission made by the Federated States of Micronesia, Papua New Guinea, and the Solomon Islands places end points on the intersection of the proposed outer limits of the continental shelf and the 200 nm limits of Nauru and Tuvalu.[105] The practice is of considerable consistency throughout the joint submissions submitted by States so far.[106]

Nevertheless, six individual submissions depart from this body of practice. Three of them are made by China,[107] Korea,[108] and Nicaragua,[109] and they intentionally lay claims to the continental shelf that is situated within their neighbors' 200 nm continental shelf. The other three submissions are of a somewhat different nature. France's submission in respect of St. Pierre and Miquelon overlaps with the 200 nm continental shelf of Canada. This submission involves the question of whether a "zone-locked" coastal State can still claim a continental shelf beyond 200 nm.[110] Vietnam and Malaysia's partial submissions in respect of the South China Sea overlap with the 200 nm continental shelf claimed by China on the basis of the Spratly Islands.[111] However, these

[104] "Joint submission by France, Ireland, Spain, and the United Kingdom (19 May 2006)," available at www.un.org/Depts/los/clcs_new/submissions_files/submission_frgbires.htm.

[105] See "Joint submission by the Federated States of Micronesia, Papua New Guinea and Solomon Islands (5 May 2009)," 10–11, available at www.un.org/Depts/los/clcs_new/submissions_files/fmpgsb32_09/exsumdocs/fmpgsb2009executivesummary.pdf.

[106] See the joint submission by Mauritius and Seychelles (December 1, 2008), joint submission by France and South Africa (May 6, 2009), joint submission by Tuvalu, France, and New Zealand (Tokelau) (December 7, 2012), and joint submission by Benin and the Togolese Republic (September 21, 1028).

[107] See "Executive summary of China's submission (December 6, 2012)," available at www.un.org/Depts/los/clcs_new/submissions_files/submission_chn_63_2012.htm.

[108] See "Executive summary of Korea's submission (December 26, 2012)," available at www.un.org/Depts/los/clcs_new/submissions_files/submission_kor_65_2012.htm.

[109] See "Executive summary of Nicaragua's submission (June 24, 2013)," available at www.un.org/Depts/los/clcs_new/submissions_files/submission_nic_66_2013.htm.

[110] Section IV below.

[111] See Note Verbale of China dated 7 May 2009 in reaction to Vietnam's partial submission (May 7, 2009), available at www.un.org/Depts/los/clcs_new/submissions_files/vnm37_09/chn_2009re_vnm.pdf; Note Verbale of China dated December 12, 2019 in reaction to

two submissions reflect the submitting States' challenge to the validity of another State's maritime entitlements as such,[112] thus they do not add to the practices that encroach upon neighboring countries' 200 nm limits.

In spite of these exceptions, the tendency to avoid intruding into neighboring States' 200 nm continental shelf is evidently strong. Although only 30 individual submissions out of 85 take the position not to encroach upon other States' 200 nm limit, none of the remaining 39 submissions (8 joint submissions, 6 exceptions, and 2 irrelevant ones[113] excluded from the remaining 55 submissions) has the possibility of encroaching upon neighboring States' 200 nm limit because of two circumstances. First and foremost, the adjacent or lateral coastal relationship between the submitting State and its neighbors makes it impossible for the proposed outer limits of the continental shelf to encroach upon its neighbor's 200 nm limit. Twenty-four submissions fall within this category.[114] Second, the location of the

Malaysia's partial submission (December 12, 2019), available at www.un.org/Depts/los/clcs_new/submissions_files/mys85_2019/CML_14_2019_E.pdf.

112 In reaction to Malaysia's partial submission (December 12, 2019), China reiterated in its Note Verbale (December 12, 2019) its sovereignty over Nanhai Zhudao (Islands in the South China Sea), its rights to internal waters, territorial sea and contiguous zone, EEZ and continental shelf on the basis of Nanhai Zhudao, as well as its historic rights in the South China Sea. The Philippines, Vietnam, Indonesia, United States of America, Australia, and Malaysia each sent a diplomatic note to protest China's territorial and/or maritime claims. For instance, Malaysia stated that "the Peoples' Republic of China's claim to the maritime features in the South China Sea has no basis under international law." Note Verbale of dated July 29, 2020, available at www.un.org/Depts/los/clcs_new/submissions_files/submission_mys_12_12_2019.html. The same disputes over the basis of maritime entitlements also arise out of the joint submission made by Malaysia and Vietnam (May 6, 2009), available at www.un.org/Depts/los/clcs_new/submissions_files/submission_mysvnm_33_2009.htm.

113 Two submissions are identified as irrelevant for the purposes of the present study. They are the submissions made by Cuba and the United Kingdom (in respect of the Falkland Islands, and of South Georgia and the South Sandwich Islands). The endpoints of the outer limits of the continental shelf claimed by Cuba are located on the intersection of the 200-nautical-mile limits of Cuba and the United States, and intersection of that of Cuba and Mexico respectively, which signifies more of awareness of outstanding delimitation issues than of entitlement. The submission made by the United Kingdom is excluded because it covers the same area claimed by Argentina in its submission due to territorial disputes between the two States.

114 These submissions are made, in a chronological order of submission, by Brazil, Ireland, Barbados, Indonesia (North West of Sumatra Island), Suriname, Myanmar, Yemen, Uruguay, Argentina, South Africa, Kenya, Nigeria, Cote d'Ivoire, India, Trinidad and Tobago, Namibia, Bangladesh, Guyana, Gabon, Kiribati, Angola, Bahamas, Spain (in respect of area west of the Canary Islands), and Liberia.

area claimed in the submissions is far away from any other State's 200 nm limit. There are 12 submissions in total in this category.[115] The remaining three individual submissions, namely, Mexico's partial submission concerning the western polygon of the Gulf of Mexico, Ireland's partial submission concerning the Hatton-Rockall Area, and Spain's partial submission concerning the area of Galicia, do not touch upon other States' 200 nm limits for different reasons. Mexico proposed its maritime boundary with the United States to be the outer limits of the continental shelf,[116] while the partial submission of Ireland places a fixed point on the maritime boundary between Ireland and the United Kingdom.[117] Accordingly, there is no question of engaging neighboring States' 200 nm limits in these two submissions because of pre-existing boundary lines. Spain's partial submission places a fixed point on the proposed outer limits of the continental shelf in the joint submission made by France, Ireland, Spain, and the United Kingdom, which serves to connect the claimed areas of continental shelf of Spain in these two submissions.[118]

It is therefore evident that the majority of States intentionally take the position not to encroach upon their neighbors' 200 nm limit. What is the relevance of this body of State practice for the interpretation of Article 76? One may consider that the State practice falls within the meaning of subsequent practice under Article 31(3)(b) of the Vienna Convention on the Law of Treaties (VCLT) and therefore contributes to the interpretation of Article 76.[119] According to Article 31(3)(b) of the VCLT, together with the context, treaty interpretation should take into account "any subsequent practice in the application of the treaty which establishes the agreement of the parties regarding its interpretation." As part of the general rule of interpretation, once established, subsequent practice

[115] These submissions are made by, in a chronological order of submission, Russia, the United Kingdom (Ascension Island), France (Antilles and Kerguelen Islands), the Philippines (in the Benham Rise region), Fiji, Norway (in respect of Bouvetøya and Dronning Maud Land), Mauritius (in respect of the Region of Rodrigues Island), Seychelles, France (in respect of La Réunion Island and Saint-Paul and Amsterdam Islands), Madagascar, France (in respect of Polynesia), and Mauritius (in respect of the Southern Chagos Archipelago region).

[116] See "Executive summary of Mexico's submission (22 May 2007)," 4, available at www.un.org/Depts/los/clcs_new/submissions_files/mex07/part_i_executive_summary.pdf.

[117] See "Executive summary of Ireland's submission (31 March 2009)," 7, available at www.un.org/Depts/los/clcs_new/submissions_files/irl09/irl09_exsum.pdf.

[118] See "Executive summary of Spain's submission (11 May 2009)," 8, available at www.un.org/Depts/los/clcs_new/submissions_files/esp47_09/esp_2009_summary_english.pdf.

[119] Vienna Convention on the Law of Treaties (May 23, 1969), 1155 UNTS 331.

is an authentic means of interpretation,[120] and it could contribute to "a clarification of the meaning of a treaty in the sense of a specification (narrowing down) of different possible meanings of a particular term or provision."[121] In addition, as observed by the ICJ, "the subsequent practice of the parties, within the meaning of Article 31(3)(b) of the Vienna Convention, can result in a departure from the original intent on the basis of a tacit agreement between the parties."[122] It is also crucial to bear in mind that only when the practice establishes the agreement among the parties to the treaty can it be regarded as the subsequent practice for purposes of treaty interpretation.

Although the above-mentioned State practice is clearly the practice of the States parties in the application of Article 76 of UNCLOS, it seems unable to satisfy the requirement of establishing the agreement of the parties due to the submissions made by China, Korea, and Nicaragua. Whereas Article 31(3)(b) of the VCLT does not require that every party must individually have engaged in the practice, it nevertheless demands an agreement being reached among the "parties as a whole."[123] Disagreement of one or several parties may militate against the establishment of agreement. The ICJ adopted a stringent standard in this regard. In the *Whaling* case, the Court considered the legal significance of the International Whaling Commission (IWC) Resolutions on treaty interpretation and observed that:

> [M]any IWC resolutions were adopted without the support of all States parties to the Convention and, in particular, without the concurrence of Japan. Thus, such instruments cannot be regarded as subsequent agreement to an interpretation of Article VIII, nor as subsequent practice establishing an agreement of the parties regarding the interpretation of the treaty within the meaning of [Article 31(3)(a)-(b) of the VCLT].[124]

Failing to achieve agreement of the parties to UNCLOS, this body of practice may nevertheless contribute to the interpretation of Article 76(1)

[120] Draft Articles on the Law of Treaties with Commentaries 1966, ILC Yearbook (1966), vol. II, 222.

[121] G. Nolte, Second Report on Subsequent Agreements and Subsequent Practice in Relation to the Interpretation of Treaties (A/CN.4/671, March 26, 2014), International Law Commission Sixty-sixth session (May 5–June 6 and July 7–August 8, 2014), 11.

[122] *Dispute regarding Navigational and Related Rights (Costa Rica v. Nicaragua) [2009] ICJ Rep 213, 242* [64].

[123] Draft Articles on the Law of Treaties with Commentaries 1966 (n 120), 222.

[124] *Whaling in the Antarctic (Australia v. Japan: New Zealand intervening) [2014] ICJ Rep 226, 257* [83].

as supplementary means of interpretation through the application of Article 32 of the VCLT,[125] the text of which does not make an exhaustive list of all supplementary means of interpretation. Accordingly, subsequent practice of States parties, though having not established agreement among the parties, might be considered as part of the supplementary means of interpretation.[126] The considerably large number of submissions adopting a self-constraint approach might be given weight together with the ordinary meaning, the context, as well as the object and purpose of Article 76. It is noteworthy that this body of practice represents coastal States' understanding and implementation of the notion of natural prolongation under Article 76,[127] and its relevance with interpretation of the relationship between the two continental shelf criteria under Article 76(1) may outweigh earlier judicial decisions that were delivered before the entry into force of UNCLOS.

In addition to the potential effect on treaty interpretation, another issue worthy of inquiry is whether State practice could contribute to the formation of a customary rule on the non-encroachment of the 200 nm limits of another State.

Before analyzing this possibility, one first has to distinguish this issue from that of a treaty rule passing into the *corpus* of customary international law. The latter was considered in the *North Sea* cases, in which Denmark and the Netherlands argued that Article 6 of the CCS had become a customary rule "partly because of its own impact, partly on the basis of subsequent State practice."[128] Although this argument was not accepted by the ICJ, the Court acknowledged that "this process is perfectly possible," and "it constitutes indeed one of the recognized methods

[125] Article 32 of the VCLT reads: "Recourse may be had to supplementary means of interpretation, including the preparatory work of the treaty and the circumstances of its conclusion, in order to confirm the meaning resulting from the application of article 31, or to determine the meaning when the interpretation according to article 31: (a) Leaves the meaning ambiguous or obscure; or (b) Leads to a result which is manifestly absurd or unreasonable."

[126] It has been suggested that "a subsequent practice as a supplementary means of interpretation under article 32 consists of conduct by one or more parties in the application of the treaty, after its conclusion." Conclusion 4(3) of the Draft Conclusions on Subsequent Agreements and Subsequent Practice in relation to Interpretation of Treaties (A/73/10), Report of the ILC on the work of its seventieth session (April 30–June 1 and July 2–August 10, 2018). See also L. Sbolci, "Supplementary Means of Interpretation," in E. Cannizzaro (ed.), *The Law of Treaties Beyond the Vienna Convention* (Oxford University Press 2011), 160.

[127] See Chapter 2, Section II.B.1.

[128] *North Sea* (n 8), 41[70].

by which new rules of customary international law may be found."[129] The Court thus formulated the conditions to be satisfied by this process.[130] The State practice of self-constraint towards their neighbors' 200 nm limit is, however, not an application of an existing treaty rule, because the relevant State practice concerns the application of Article 76 (2)–(8), whereas the self-constraint approach that emerges out of this practice reflects coastal States' understanding of Article 76(1), the latter not imposing on coastal States an obligation to refrain from encroaching other States' 200 nm limits of the continental shelf.

It is common knowledge that "the existence of a rule of customary international law requires that there be a settled practice together with *opinio juris*."[131] The State practice under examination is arguably uniform and consistent, in particular considering that almost all the States take this position when their neighbors' 200 nm limits are located close to their proposed outer limits of the continental shelf. Furthermore, from Appendix 1 it is obvious that such practice is representative in terms of geographical distribution and different socio-economic systems, and no doubt that the States taking this position are those "whose interests were specially affected."[132] Notably, the approach of not encroaching upon the 200 nm limit of neighboring States is not limited to States parties to UNCLOS, but also maintained by States parties vis-à-vis non-parties. For example, Japan, the Cook Islands, and Mexico deliberately refrain from encroaching upon the 200 nm limit of the United States.[133]

At this moment one has to consider the effect of the submissions made by China, Korea, and Nicaragua on the formation of the customary international rule. To take a balanced view, for the formation of customary international law the State practice need not be universal,[134] and the persistent objector rule is applicable as long as the conditions are met.[135]

[129] Ibid., [71].

[130] See ibid., [72–79].

[131] *Jurisdictional Immunities of the State (Germany v. Italy: Greece intervening) [2012] ICJ Rep 99, 122* [55].

[132] *North Sea* (n 8), 42 [73].

[133] See Executive Summaries of Submission of Japan (November 12, 2008), the Cook Islands (April 16, 2009), and Mexico in respect of the eastern polygon in the Gulf of Mexico (December 19, 2022).

[134] See M. E. Villiger, *Customary International Law and Treaties: A Study of Their Interactions and Interrelations with Special Consideration of the 1969 Vienna Convention on the Law of Treaties* (Martinus Nijhoff Publishers 1985), 13.

[135] *Fisheries case (United Kingdom v. Norway) [1951] ICJ Rep 116,* 131 and 138.

Nevertheless, the existence of conflicting State practice might undermine the normative value of the State practice.[136]

The *opinio juris* is, however, difficult to establish. For one thing, it is unclear whether coastal States refrain from intruding into neighboring States' 200 nm shelves because of the belief that "this practice is rendered obligatory by the existence of a rule of law requiring it."[137] In fact, it is probable that non-legal reasons play a role. Coastal States may have a strong incentive to avoid encroaching upon their neighbors' 200 nm shelf for fear of objections made to their submissions, which may result in blocking the delineation procedure.[138] Alternatively, States might be carrying out this practice on a reciprocal basis, which is highly relevant in a regional context.[139] In addition, States could be simply following an already discernible pattern of practice. Unless more convincing evidence regarding the binding nature of States' behavior is available, it is difficult to establish the *opinio juris* that is necessary for the formation of customary international law.

Moreover, there is a significant factual difference between the submissions made by the majority of States and those made by China, Korea, and Nicaragua. In the majority's case, the same area of the continental shelf beyond 200 nm is subject to claims of their neighbors, and the submitting State is aware of the existence of overlapping entitlements or claims.[140] As a result, there is no point to intruding into the 200 nm limits of their neighbors for there is already potential for overlap in the area beyond 200 nm. In contrast, the areas claimed by China, Korea, and Nicaragua are not subject to the claim to a continental shelf beyond 200 nm of the State whose 200 nm limits are encroached. Factual differences can be an important aspect of ascertaining the existence of a customary international rule.[141]

136 See S. Talmon, "Determining Customary International Law: The ICJ's Methodology between Induction, Deduction and Assertion" (2015), 26 *EJIL* 417, 421–422.

137 *North Sea* (n 8), 44 [77].

138 See Rule 46 of Annex I to the Rules of Procedure of the CLCS.

139 See Chapter 4, Section II. E.

140 The awareness of neighboring States' claims to the same continental shelf beyond 200 nm is reflected by the acknowledgement of the potential or existing overlapping claims to the same area. See Chapter 4, Section II. F.

141 For example, the *North Sea* cases distinguished the boundary agreements concluded between opposite States and lateral States in assessing the customary nature of the equidistance method under Article 6 of the CCS, and found that "[i]n only one situation discussed by the Parties does there appear to have been a geographical configuration which to some extent resembles the present one." *North Sea* (n 8), 45 [79].

Even though one cannot affirm the existence of a customary rule with respect to the non-encroachment of the 200 nm limit of neighboring States, the gradual cumulative State practice over time might make coastal States reluctant to depart from this consistent body of practice. Together with other factors, it may enable the "gradual hardening of practice into law" over time.[142] International courts and tribunals, though bound to apply existing law,[143] might make efforts to harmonize *lex lata* with *lex ferenda*, in particular considering that the existing law is not conclusive. Besides, sometimes the ICJ declares the existence of a customary rule not based on an inducive approach to State practice and *opinio juris*, but rather on techniques of deduction or analogy.[144] Therefore, it is possible for the Court to take a more relaxed approach to assessing the existence of customary international law in certain circumstances.

To sum up, the legal significance of State practice not to encroach upon neighboring States' 200 nm limits cannot be underestimated because of its influence on treaty interpretation as well as the formation of a rule of customary international law. At the same time, to be informed about the current status of law, one must also keep in mind the legal implications of the exceptions to State practice in the application of Article 76.

### *D Relationship between the Continental Shelf and the EEZ*

The question of whether there exists priority between the two criteria of continental shelf entitlements may also be considered from the perspective of the relationship between the continental shelf and the EEZ. As the distance criterion applies for both the continental shelf up to the 200 nm limits and the EEZ and the legal regime of EEZ confers on coastal States "sovereign rights for the purpose of exploring and exploiting, conserving and managing the natural resources, whether living or non-living ... of the seabed and its subsoil" under Article 56(1) of UNCLOS, the two regimes are inevitably "linked together in modern law."[145] The crucial

[142] Villiger (n 134), 29–30.

[143] See *Legality of the Threat or Use of Nuclear Weapons, Advisory Opinion [1996] ICJ Rep 226, 237* [18].

[144] See P. Tomka, "Custom and the International Court of Justice" (2013) 12 *LPICT* 195, 215.

[145] *Libya/Malta* (n 9), 33 [33].

question is, nevertheless, how to perceive this link as well as its consequences for appreciating the question of priority under analysis. During the oral proceedings in the *Nicaragua* v. *Colombia I* case, Colombia argued that "if the natural prolongation of another State's continental shelf beyond 200 nm intrudes into another State's shelf entitlement as defined by the width of its EEZ then the former must give way to the latter."[146] This argument seems to suggest that coastal States' right to the EEZ is absolute wherever the area concerned is situated within the limits of the EEZ of that State.

It is however difficult to accept that coastal States' rights to the EEZ are absolute and take precedence over the rights to the continental shelf. The EEZ and the continental shelf are two separate regimes, as established by UNCLOS and confirmed in international jurisprudence as well as State practice. The Arbitral Tribunal of the *Barbados* v. *Trinidad and Tobago* case stated that "the continental shelf and the EEZ coexist as separate institutions, as the latter has not absorbed the former [...] and as the former does not displace the latter."[147] This is a position consistently held in the jurisprudence.[148] The separation of the two regimes derives from the different legal nature of the two regimes. A continental shelf exists *ipso facto* and *ab initio*, whereas an EEZ has to be proclaimed by a coastal State. What follows is that, although coastal States have sovereign rights in respect of non-living resources according to the EEZ regime, the inherent right to these non-living resources and to the seabed and subsoil can only be derived from the continental shelf rights.[149] Accordingly, when a coastal State proclaims an EEZ, it makes no difference to its right to the seabed and the non-living resources thereof, as the latter has already been part of its inherent continental shelf rights.

One may argue that the common distance criterion for both the continental shelf and the EEZ regimes renders the distinction between the two regimes less meaningful.[150] Judge Oda suggested that within the 200 nm limit there is "a single homogeneous maritime

146 *Nicaragua* v. *Colombia I*, Verbatim record, CR 2012/17 (May 24, 2012), 34.

147 *Barbados* v. *Trinidad and Tobago* (n 28), [234].

148 See *The Gulf of Maine* (n 25), 267 [27]; *Maritime Delimitation in the Area between Greenland and Jan Mayen (Denmark v. Norway) [1993] ICJ Rep 38,* 57–59[42–48]; *Bangladesh/Myanmar* (n 1), 121 [475].

149 See J. I. Charney, "The Exclusive Economic Zone and Public International Law" (1985), 15 *ODIL* 233, 246–247.

150 See M. Lando, *Maritime Delimitation as a Judicial Process* (Cambridge University Press 2018), 109–121.

area."[151] By combining the two regimes, the "single homogeneous maritime area" is legally stronger than that of a continental shelf beyond 200 nm. This argument is, however, inconsistent with the conceptual separation between the continental shelf and the EEZ. Inasmuch as the EEZ and the continental shelf are essentially two regimes, and as long as the continental shelf regime comprises the continental shelf within and beyond 200 nm, the arguments that the common distance criterion creates an absolute maritime area up to 200 nm denies the integrity of the continental shelf regime.

If there was a *de facto* merging of the EEZ and the continental shelf within 200 nm in the practice of maritime delimitation, one might expect that the delimitation of the EEZ automatically involves the delimitation of the continental shelf.[152] This is, however, not how coastal States perceive the relationship between the two regimes. For example, the Indonesia–Philippines agreement, which is concerned with the delimitation of the EEZ, explicitly provides that "this agreement shall not prejudice any rights or positions of the Contracting Parties with regard to the delimitation of the Continental Shelf boundary."[153] In fact, when coastal States negotiate single maritime boundaries within 200 nm, they make clear that their maritime boundaries delimit both the continental shelf and the EEZ, which confirms the separate existence of the two regimes.[154] Indeed, although the trend of single maritime delimitation of

[151] See *Libya/Malta* (n 9), 157–158 [61–62] (Dissenting Opinion of Judge Oda). Similarly, Proelss interprets Article 56(3) as to mean "if and to the extent to which the coastal State has claimed and established an EEZ above its continental shelf, the two zones form part of an integral regime." A. Proelss, "Article 56" in A. Proelss (ed.), *The United Nations Convention on the Law of the Sea: A Commentary* (Hart 2017), 436.

[152] See D. Attard, *The Exclusive Economic Zone in International Law* (Oxford University Press 1987), 215; F. Orrego Vicuña, *The Exclusive Economic Zone: Regime and Legal Nature under International Law* (Cambridge University Press 1989) 198.

[153] See Article I (3) of the Agreement between the Government of the Republic of the Philippines and the Government of the Republic of Indonesia Concerning the Delimitation of the Exclusive Economic Zone Boundary, text reproduced in C. Scofield and I. M. A Arsana, "Indonesia–Philippines, Report Number 5-41," in C. G. Lathrop (ed.), *International Maritime Boundaries, Vol.VII* (Brill Nijhoff Publishers 2016), 4960.

[154] See, for instance, Treaty between the Republic of Trinidad and Tobago and Grenada on the Delimitation of Marine and Submarine Areas (April 21, 2010, (2010) 73 LoSB 43); Agreement between the Commonwealth of The Bahamas and the Republic of Cuba for the Delimiting Line between their Maritime Zones (October 3, 2011, (2013) 79 LoSB 19); Agreement between the United Republic of Tanzania and the Republic of Kenya on the Delimitation of the Maritime Boundary of the Exclusive Economic Zone and the Continental Shelf (June 23, 2009), 2603 UNTS 37; Agreement between the

the continental shelf and the EEZ prevails in practice, which may be partially attributed to the common distance criterion of the two regimes, it by no means suggests that a merger of the two regimes is taking place. A single maritime boundary delimiting both the continental shelf and the EEZ originates from the common will of the coastal States concerned, not from a requirement in law.[155] As carefully examined by Evans, there seems to be inconsistency between the perception of the separation of the two regimes and the practice of the single maritime boundary.[156] This phenomenon might be explained by the prevailing desire for practical convenience when States negotiate their maritime boundaries.

As it is established that conceptually and practically, the legal regimes of the continental shelf and the EEZ are separate, the key question is: can State A's continental shelf co-exist with State B's EEZ vertically over the same maritime space? Key to this question is the proper interpretation of Article 56(3) of UNCLOS, which provides that "the rights set out in this article with respect to the seabed and subsoil shall be exercised in accordance with Part VI." While some consider it to imply that the EEZ trumps the continental shelf up to 200 nm for practical purposes,[157] others interpret this provision to mean that it is the continental shelf regime that applies to the seabed and subsoil within 200 nm of the EEZ.[158]

It is submitted that the latter view is more consistent with the separation of the two regimes as well as their harmonization. For one thing, the idea that within 200 nm the continental shelf is "trumped" by the EEZ simply goes against the legal nature of the two regimes and the concept of a single continental shelf. The text of Article 56(3) is a clear

Government of the Cook Islands and the Government of the Republic of Kiribati concerning the Delimitation of the Maritime Boundaries between the Cook Islands and the Republic of Kiribati (August 29, 2012, (2015) 85 LoSB 35).

155 *Maritime Delimitation and Territorial Questions (Qatar v. Bahrain) (Merits) [2001] ICJ Rep 40, 93* [173].

156 See M. D. Evans, "Delimitation and the Common Maritime Boundary" (1994) 64 *BYIL* 283, 298–329.

157 P. Allott, "Power Sharing in the Law of the Sea" (1983) 77 *AJIL* 1, 14; F. Orrego Vicuña, "La limite intérieure de la limite extérieure: Le chevauchement de revendications et la délimitation du plateau continental étendu," in R. C. Raigón and G. Cataldi (eds.), *L'évolution et l'état actuel du droit international de la mer: mélanges de droit de la mer offerts à Daniel Vignes* (Bruylant 2009), 703.

158 See Attard (n 152), 139; J.-F. Pulvenis, "The Continental Shelf Definition and Rules Applicable to Resources," in R.-J. Dupuy and D. Vignes (eds.), *A Handbook on the New Law of the Sea* (Martinus Nijhoff Publishers 1991), 353.

indication of the applicable law in terms of the seabed and subsoil and the effect is to separate the water column from the seabed and its subsoil within the EEZ regime.[159] The reference to the continental shelf regime under Article 56(3) might stem from the consideration that the continental shelf and the EEZ are essentially dealing with different natural resources. From the inception of the continental shelf regime, it was concerned with the exploration and exploitation of the non-living resources and sedentary resources in the seabed and subsoil, whereas the EEZ emerged out of coastal States' will to exercise exclusive jurisdiction over living resources in the water column, in particular fisheries.[160] It is therefore in line with the functional purposes of the two regimes if the continental shelf regime applies to the seabed and subsoil, even if the area is also part of the subject of the EEZ. In addition, the historical records of UNCLOS III reveal that Article 56(3) was meant to safeguard the independence of the regime of the continental shelf, and that its practical effect is, therefore, that the continental shelf regime prevails over the EEZ (as applicable law) when it comes to the seabed and subsoil, including the resources.[161] Article 68 of UNCLOS further illustrates this point, as it provides that Part V of UNCLOS does not apply to the sedentary species defined in Article 77(4).[162] In other words, Article 56(3) takes away what Article 56(1) gives. Indeed, in the 21 articles of Part V concerning the legal regime of the EEZ, there is no other article that deals with the seabed or its non-living resources other than Article 56.[163]

This interpretation leads to the conclusion that, as far as the seabed and subsoil are concerned, it is the continental shelf regime that applies. Consequently, the presence of the EEZ should not have a bearing upon the question of overlap of a continental shelf beyond 200 nm and a

159 See A. G. Oude Elferink, "Does Undisputed Title to a Maritime Zone Always Exclude Its Delimitation: The Grey Area Issue" (1998), 13 *IJLMC* 143, 173.

160 See J. C. Phillips, "The Exclusive Economic Zone as a Concept in International Law" (1977), 26 *ICLQ* 585, 600; L. Caflisch, "Les zones maritimes sous juridiction nationale, leurs limites et leur délimitation," in D. Bardonnet and M. Virally (eds.), *Le nouveau droit international de la mer* (Pedone 1983), 81; Attard (n 152), 137.

161 See Orrego Vicuña (n 152), 69–70; International Law Association (n 50), 331; P. Weil, *The Law of Maritime Delimitation: Reflections* (Grotius 1989), 129–130; S. Kaye, "The Use of Multiple Boundaries in Maritime Boundary Delimitation: Law and Practice" (1998), 19 *Australian YIL* 9, 51.

162 See Orrego Vicuña (n 152), 70.

163 In fact, even Article 73, which concerns "enforcement of laws and regulations of the coastal State," explicitly recognizes that enforcement measures are applicable when coastal States exercise sovereign rights with respect to *living resources* in the EEZ.

continental shelf within 200 nm, as the latter only concerns the seabed and subsoil.

The *Bay of Bengal* cases confirmed this interpretation and acknowledged that one State's continental shelf beyond 200 nm can co-exist with another State's EEZ with regard to the superjacent water column. This is reflected in the consideration of the grey area problem in the two cases. In the *Bangladesh/Myanmar* case, the adjustment of the equidistance line resulted in an area of limited size which is beyond the 200 nm of Bangladesh but within 200 nm of Myanmar, yet on Bangladesh's side of the delimitation line.[164] ITLOS noted that "the boundary delimiting the area beyond 200 nm from Bangladesh but within 200 nm of Myanmar is a boundary delimiting the continental shelves of the Parties, since in this area only their continental shelves overlap."[165] According to ITLOS, "the maritime boundary delimits the Parties' rights with respect to the seabed and subsoil of the continental shelf but does not otherwise limit Myanmar's rights with respect to the [EEZ], notably those with respect to the superjacent waters."[166] Given the co-existence of Bangladesh's continental shelf beyond 200 nm and Myanmar's EEZ, ITLOS proposed that "each coastal State must exercise its rights and perform its duties with due regard to the rights and duties of the other."[167] Judge Lucky, in his academic writing, put forward that "[i]t seemed to me that continental shelf rights in the special circumstances of [the Bangladesh/Myanmar case] had priority over EEZ rights. As a result, I would have allocated the 'grey area' to Bangladesh." This suggestion thus subordinates the EEZ jurisdiction to the continental shelf jurisdiction on the basis of "a wide and generous interpretation of article 56, paragraph 3."[168] However, to say that the continental shelf regime takes precedence over the EEZ regime is untenable, because, in any event, the continental shelf regime does not govern the living resources nor the water column. Bangladesh does not have any right to the water column superjacent to the seabed and subsoil in the grey area created by the *Bangladesh/Myanmar* case. The interpretation of Article 56(3) leads to the conclusion that Bangladesh enjoys continental shelf rights over the

164 See *Bangladesh/Myanmar* (n 1), 119 [463].

165 Ibid.,120 [471].

166 Ibid., 121 [474].

167 Ibid., [475].

168 A. Lucky, "The Issues Concerning the Continental Shelf: Reflections" (2015) 17 *ICLR* 95, 108–111.

seabed and subsoil, whereas Myanmar's EEZ rights are confined to the water column over the same area.[169] Nothing more can be inferred from this solution to the grey area problem.

In terms of the grey area in the *Bangladesh* v. *India* case, the Arbitral Tribunal adopted the same approach and suggested that the parties should employ cooperative measures in the area.[170] Notably, the Arbitral Tribunal observed that:

> [I]n the grey area, the exclusive economic zone to which India is entitled includes rights to the seabed and subsoil pursuant to article 56(1)(a) of the Convention that also fall within the regime for the continental shelf. In practice, however, the Convention distinguishes between the rights that arise under multiple regimes and those that pertain only to the exclusive economic zone. Article 56(3) provides that rights with respect to the seabed and subsoil in the exclusive economic zone are to be exercised in accordance with the regime for the continental shelf. Article 68 excludes sedentary species from the provisions relating to the exclusive economic zone altogether.[171]

This observation explains why the seabed and subsoil fall within the continental shelf regime rather than the EEZ regime. It is also because of this understanding that a continental shelf beyond 200 nm and a continental shelf up to 200 nm can overlap, as both concern the seabed and subsoil only. It has been suggested that the *Bay of Bengal* cases illustrate that "[p]riority was given in certain areas to the outer continental shelf entitlement of Bangladesh over the continental shelf entitlement within 200 nm of Myanmar and India."[172] However, as pointed out earlier, the solution to the grey area problem was found through the delimitation of the overlap of the continental shelves rather than by establishing a hierarchy between the two entitlements. Nonetheless, it is also noteworthy that the *Bay of Bengal* cases did not try to avoid the creation of grey areas in the delimitation process. In other words, the relationship between the EEZ and the continental shelf was not predominantly a factor that influenced the delimitation of the continental shelf beyond

169 See Oude Elferink (n 159), 173–175.

170 See *Bangladesh* v. *India* (n 36), [498–508].

171 Ibid., [504].

172 N. Marques Antunes and V. Becker-Weinberg, "Entitlement to Maritime Zones and Their Delimitation: In the Doldrums of Uncertainty and Unpredictability," in A. G. Oude Elferink et al. (eds.), *Maritime Boundary Delimitation: The Case Law: Is It Consistent and Predictable?* (Cambridge University Press 2018), 88.

200 nm (or the overall delimitation within and beyond 200 nm) in the views of the tribunals.[173]

Dr. P. S. Rao, an arbitrator in the *Bangladesh* v. *India* case, criticized the creation of the grey area in his concurring and dissenting opinion. Not only did he consider the "EEZ as one single, common maritime zone within 200 nm which effectively incorporates the regime of the continental shelf within it,"[174] he also thought that "the entitlement to the EEZ takes priority over the entitlement to the continental shelf beyond 200 nm,"[175] because "[t]his complicated method to calculate the outer limits of the continental shelf suggests that the entitlement to the continental shelf beyond 200 nm depends on different factors and is not as absolute as the entitlement to the EEZ."[176] However, his arguments lack support from UNCLOS or customary international law, in particular viewed against Article 77 of UNCLOS.[177] More importantly, the arguments confuse the simplicity of establishing the entitlement to the EEZ with the absoluteness of such rights. As explained earlier, there is nothing absolute about coastal States' EEZ rights.[178]

The preceding analysis demonstrates that, legally, coastal State A's continental shelf may co-exist with coastal State B's EEZ over the same maritime space. A second issue is whether such an overlap is practically desirable. In reality, there are, so far, two situations that may give rise to this scenario. The first is where two coastal States delimit their continental shelf and EEZ with different boundary lines. The 1997 Australia–Indonesia agreement is an example in point.[179] The two countries agreed that in the areas of overlapping jurisdiction, the State with rights to the EEZ after the delimitation may exercise EEZ sovereign rights in relation

173 See Ø. Jensen, "The Delimitation of the Continental Shelf beyond 200 Nm: Substantive Issues," in A. G. Oude Elferink et al. (eds.), *Maritime Boundary Delimitation: The Case Law: Is It Consistent and Predictable?* (Cambridge University Press 2018), 373.

174 *Bangladesh* v. *India* (n 36), 199 [24] (Concurring and Dissenting Opinion of Dr. P. S. Rao).

175 Ibid., 207 [40].

176 Ibid.

177 See Evans (n 58), 79.

178 Article 69 and Article 70 of UNCLOS, respectively, provide for rights of land-locked States and geographically disadvantaged States to access the surplus of living resources in coastal States' EEZ.

179 Treaty between Australia and Indonesia Establishing an Exclusive Economic Zone Boundary and Certain Seabed Boundaries (March 14, 1997), (1997) 36 ILM 1053.

to the water column, whereas the other State may exercise continental shelf rights in relation to the seabed.[180]

The second situation where State A's continental shelf overlaps with State B's EEZ is the grey area situation. In State practice, coastal States tend to transfer or exchange the sovereign rights to maritime areas so that each State has a complete set of rights to the EEZ and the continental shelf vertically over the same maritime space. Three agreements using this method can be identified, namely, the 1990 United States–USSR agreement,[181] the 2010 Norway–Russia agreement,[182] and the 2013 Ireland–United Kingdom agreement.[183] In the 1990 United States–USSR agreement, several grey areas were created, and the parties defined these grey areas as "eastern special area" and "western special area" in accordance with their relative location to the maritime boundary. "Eastern special area" refers to any area lying east of the maritime boundary, which is located within the Soviet Union's 200 nm limits but beyond the United States' 200 nm limits, while "western special area" refers to the area lying west of the maritime boundary, within the 200 nm limits of the United States and beyond the 200 nm limits of the Soviet Union. The two parties agreed to transfer their EEZ rights to the other party so that each party "may exercise the sovereign rights and jurisdiction derived from exclusive economic zone jurisdiction that [the other party] would otherwise be entitled to exercise under international law in the absence of the agreement of the Parties on the maritime boundary."[184] As a result, the transfer of the sovereign rights and jurisdiction ensures that each party exercises jurisdiction in all maritime areas within its 200 nm continental shelf.[185] In the 2010 Norway–Russia agreement, the two parties agree to transfer the EEZ rights of Norway to Russia in the one grey area, though

[180] See Article 7 of the 1997 Australia–Indonesia agreement.

[181] Agreement between the United States of America and the Union of Soviet Socialist Republics on the maritime boundary (June 1, 1990), (1991) 17 LoSB 15.

[182] Treaty between the Kingdom of Norway and the Russian Federation concerning Maritime Delimitation and Cooperation in the Barents Sea and the Arctic Ocean (September 15, 2010), 2791 UNTS 3.

[183] Agreement between Ireland and the United Kingdom of Great Britain and Northern Ireland Establishing a Single Maritime Boundary between the Exclusive Economic Zone of the two Countries and Parts of their Continental Shelves (March 28, 2013), UKTS No. 21 (2014).

[184] Article 3(1) and (2) of the 1990 United States–USSR agreement.

[185] E. G. Verville, "United States–Soviet Union, Report Number 1-6," in I. L. Charney and L. M. Alexander (eds.), *International Maritime Boundaries, Vol.I* (Martinus Nijhoff Publishers 1993), 447.

it is important to note that the overall delimitation results in an equal division of the disputed area between the parties.[186] The 2013 Ireland–United Kingdom agreement amends the 1988 agreement that delimits the continental shelf of the two parties.[187] During negotiations the two governments agreed in principle that the continental shelf and the EEZ boundaries should be aligned in a single maritime boundary. However, because the 1988 agreement did not delimit the continental shelf boundary with equidistant lines, there were two small areas of Irish continental shelf lying beyond 200 nm from Irish baselines but within 200 nm of the United Kingdom. The 2013 agreement transfers these two small areas to the United Kingdom and, in exchange, small areas of the United Kingdom continental shelf of equal size and equivalent exploitability are transferred to Ireland as well.[188] The State practice, though of limited numbers, illustrates coastal States' willingness to have a complete set of continental shelf and EEZ rights vertically. Nevertheless, it is doubtful if a court or a tribunal has competence to order *proprio motu* the exchange or transfer of EEZ rights to avoid the creation of grey areas in the context of delimitation of the continental shelf beyond 200 nm.

Accordingly, if not avoiding the issue at all, the co-existence of one State's continental shelf and the other State's EEZ is only possible if the EEZ rights are reduced to sovereign rights in respect of living resources in the water column. Legally speaking this is in line with Article 56(3). However, practical difficulties may ensue. Under Article 56(2), coastal States have jurisdiction over marine scientific research, protection of the marine environment, and artificial islands, installations, and structures. Coastal States have the same jurisdiction over these three issues with respect to their continental shelf.[189] In consequence, the exercise of these jurisdictions may come into conflict if coastal State A's continental shelf overlaps with coastal State B's EEZ. For instance, coastal State A's installations for drilling the seabed in order to exploit oil and gas resources may undermine coastal State B's marine environment protection measures, or

186 Article 3(1) of the 2010 Norway–Russia agreement. See R. E. Fife, "Norway–Russia Federation, Report Number 9-6(3)," in C. G. Lathrop (ed.), *International Maritime Boundaries, Vol. VII* (Brill Nijhoff Publishers 2016), 5191.

187 The Agreement between the Republic of Ireland and the United Kingdom of Great Britain and Northern Ireland Concerning the Delimitation of the Continental Shelf between the Two Countries (November 7, 1988), 1765 UNTS 421.

188 See D. Anderson, "Ireland–United Kingdom, Report Number 9-5(3)," in C. G. Lathrop (ed.), *International Maritime Boundaries, Vol. VII* (Brill Nijhoff Publishers 2016), 5153.

189 See Articles 80, 194, and 246 of UNCLOS.

interfere with coastal State B's fishing activities.[190] When an entity intends to conduct marine scientific research in the area of the overlapping continental shelf and EEZ of the two coastal States and requests the consent of the two States, what if one States grants its consent while the other does not? In consequence, the co-existence of a continental shelf of one State and an EEZ of another State may open a door for future frictions between the States in their exercise of maritime jurisdiction. These practical difficulties may be considered from the perspective of the public order in the sea. It is recalled that in the *Nicaragua* v. *Colombia I* case, the ICJ did not find enclaving the Colombian islands to be a proper solution to the maritime delimitation, because the enclave method would, *inter alia*, "produce a disorderly pattern of several distinct Colombian enclaves within a maritime space which otherwise pertained to Nicaragua with unfortunate consequences for the orderly management of maritime resources, policing and the public order of the oceans in general."[191]

To conclude, Article 56(3) has to be understood in the light of the separation of the continental shelf regime and the EEZ regime, and it is the continental shelf regime that applies to the seabed and subsoil. Following this conclusion, one State's continental shelf beyond 200 nm can overlap with another State's continental shelf within 200 nm regardless of the existence of the latter State's EEZ, as confirmed by the *Bay of Bengal* cases.

### E *Customary Status of Article 76(2)-(7) in* Nicaragua *v.* Colombia II

As mentioned at the beginning, the question of whether a continental shelf beyond 200 nm and a 200 nm continental shelf can overlap in a confined maritime area underlies the dispute in the *Nicaragua* v. *Colombia II* case. This case is, however, subject to a second complexity; that is, since Colombia is not a party to UNCLOS, unless the ICJ decides that the distance criterion prevails over the outer edge of the continental margin criterion, the question of the customary status of Article 76(2)–(7) will arise as a matter of applicable law for the delimitation to proceed. Any decision on this point, however, may impact on other aspects of the legal regime of the continental shelf as well, therefore it is necessary to consider this issue as part of the potential implications of the decision on the relationship between the distance criterion and the outer edge of the continental margin criterion.

[190] See Kaye (n 161), 54–55.

[191] *Nicaragua* v. *Colombia I* (n 78), 708 [230].

It seems, first of all, that Article 76(2)–(7) is neither a codification of existing customary international law nor a crystallization of emerging customary rule.[192] Therefore, it is necessary to determine if they acquire customary status due to the generation of customary international law from UNCLOS. The criteria for this process are authoritatively set out by the *North Sea* cases. To start with, the provision at stake should be "of a fundamentally norm-creating character such as could be regarded as forming the basis of a general rule of law."[193] Second, there should be "a settled practice" with respect to the provision invoked in that the State practice, "including that of States whose interests are specially affected, should have been both extensive and virtually uniform."[194] Finally, the State practice must be carried out with *opinio juris* – that is, "a general recognition that a rule of law or legal obligation is involved."[195]

So far, there is no practice of non-States parties establishing their outer limits of the continental shelf beyond 200 nm, and little evidence that non-States parties incorporate the rules of Article 76(2)–(7) into their domestic legislation.[196] It seems that the United States tends to acknowledge the customary status of all the provisions of Article 76,[197] which may contribute to the determination of *opinio juris*, if such a belief is shared by other non-States parties as well. Nonetheless, in terms of the State practice capable of giving rise to a customary rule, it may be concluded that the State practice concerning Article 76(2)–(7) has not reached that stage.[198]

However, the ICJ declared the customary status of Article 76(1) in the *Nicaragua* v. *Colombia I* case,[199] which may circumscribe the determination of the customary status of the other provisions of Article 76. For one thing, Article 76(1) contains the crucial element that determines the outer limits of the continental shelf, namely, the outer edge of the continental margin. It follows that Article 76(3)–(4) has to be considered as customary rules because they elaborate on the determination of the outer edge of the

[192] See Chapter 2, Section I.
[193] *North Sea* (n 8), 42 [72].
[194] Ibid., 43 [74].
[195] Ibid.
[196] See the written applies of Nicaragua and Colombia to Judge Bennuna's question, available at www.icj-cij.org/en/case/124/other-documents.
[197] See B. M. Magnússon, "Can the United States Establish the Outer Limits of Its Extended Continental Shelf Under International Law?" (2017) 48 *ODIL* 1, 5.
[198] T. Treves, "UNCLOS and Non-Party States before the International Court of Justice," in Carlo Espósito et al. (eds.), *Oceans Law and Policy: 20 Years under UNCLOS* (Brill Nijhoff Publishers 2016), 373.
[199] *Nicaragua* v. *Colombia I* (n 78), 666 [118].

continental margin, otherwise the definition of the continental shelf under Article 76(1) would be deprived of substance. Another important, and perhaps, inevitable consideration is that there is no alternative definition of the outer edge of the continental margin or the outer limits of the continental shelf beyond 200 nm.[200] This latter consideration strengthens the point that Article 76(1)–(7) has to be considered as a united whole. In consequence, by deduction, one can argue that if Article 76(1) is customary international law, then all the elements that contribute to determining the continental shelf beyond 200 nm should also be customary international law. It is not impossible for the ICJ to determine the existence of a customary international rule on the basis of the textual and logical linkage between the provisions. In fact, in the *Nicaragua* v. *Colombia I* case, the ICJ found Article 121(3) of UNCLOS to form part of customary international law because it was part of an 'indivisible régime'.[201]

However, the conclusion that Article 76(1)–(7) are customary rules prompts at least two problems. First, would the outer limits of the continental shelf established by non-States parties without resorting to the procedure under Article 76(8) have the same effect of opposability? A relevant, and prior question is, is the CLCS open to non-States parties to UNCLOS?[202] Apparently, the CLCS and the procedure to establish the outer limits of the continental shelf beyond 200 nm are creatures of UNCLOS, and are not easily amenable to becoming customary rules.[203] There are no conclusive answers to these questions for the moment.[204]

The second problem is whether non-States parties are obliged to undertake the revenue-sharing obligation under Article 82. It is recalled

200 See J. Crawford, *Change, Order, Chance: The Course of International Law*, vol. 365 (Martinus Nijhoff Publishers 2013), 103.

201 *Nicaragua* v. *Colombia I* (n 78), 674 [139].

202 See discussion in Chapter 4, Section III.B.4.

203 See Treves, "UNCLOS and Non-Party States before the International Court of Justice" (n 198), 374.

204 Some argue that non-States parties are either under a legal obligation to cooperate and take into account the Article 76 process, or it is of their interest to voluntarily accept the procedure and related obligations. See T. L. McDorman, "The Entry into Force of the 1982 LOS Convention and the Article 76 Outer Continental Shelf Regime" (1995), 10 *IJMCL* 165, 179–183; V. I. J. M. Tassin, *Les défis de l'extension du plateau continental: la consécration d'un nouveau rapport de l'État à son territoire* (Pedone 2013), 22–23. Others contend that the Article 76 procedure and the CLCS are not open to non-States parties. See T. Treves, "Remarks on Submissions to the Commission on the Limits of the Continental Shelf in Response to Judge Marotta's Report" (2006) 21 *IJMCL* 363, 363–364. See also UN Doc. A/CONF.62/SR.193 (December 10, 1982), *Official Records of the Third United Nations Conference on the Law of the Sea, Volume XVII* (United Nations 1982), 136 (Koh).

that the revenue-sharing obligation in respect of exploitation of resources in the continental shelf beyond 200 nm was the *sine qua non* of the package-deal in relation to the outer limits of the continental shelf.[205] Once the Court declared Article 76(1) a customary rule, the issue of whether non-parties are under the same obligation of revenue-sharing is deemed to arise. Similar to Article 76(8), Article 82 also contains treaty-specific arrangements that are unlikely to be open to non-parties, for "the payments or contributions shall be made through the Authority, which shall distribute them to States Parties to this Convention."[206] The explicit mention of "States Parties" further casts doubt on the applicability of Article 82 outside of the UNCLOS regime.

Although it is beyond the scope of the present study to pursue these legal issues further, the fact that Article 76 – including its procedural and substantive rules – and Article 82 form a package-deal may turn out to be a strong argument that the whole idea of the continental shelf beyond 200 nm should be confined to the treaty regime of UNCLOS. Is there not a case to be argued that the inextricable links between these rules prove that the whole regime of the continental shelf beyond 200 nm is, in fact, a contractual one that is intended to apply only among the parties to UNCLOS? They are not norm-creating.[207] Thus the very basis for the regime of the continental shelf beyond 200 nm to form part of customary international law seems to be questionable. Nevertheless, this argument may be difficult to maintain in the light of the ICJ's finding that Article 76(1) is already part of customary international law.

To sum up, although the customary status of Article 76(2)–(7) is not the primary problem in the *Nicaragua* v. *Colombia II* case, a conclusion on the equality of the two continental shelf criteria has to be followed by a decision on the status of Article 76(2)–(7) in order to effect maritime delimitation between Nicaragua and Colombia. The latter may prove to be a difficult task given its potential impacts on the legal regime of the continental shelf.

### *F A Tentative Conclusion*

A tentative conclusion drawn from the analysis above is, perhaps frustratingly, that the existing international law is not decisively

[205] See Nandan and Rosenne (n 59), 846.

[206] See Article 82(4).

[207] For "norm-creating" rule, see G. G. Fitzmaurice, "Some Problems Regarding the Formal Sources of International Law," *Symbolae Verzijl* (Martinus Nijhoff Publishers 1958).

conclusive as to the question of priority between the two continental shelf entitlements. The combination of the two continental shelf entitlements under Article 76(1), in the light of the *travaux préparatoires* of UNCLOS III, is better understood as a balance and reconciliation between pre-existing continental shelf rights based on natural prolongation and the newly developed rights based on distance, thus no hierarchy can be inferred from the text. Early judicial cases, in particular the *Libya/Malta* case, are too different in factual and legal circumstances to offer a solution to a situation where two parties invoke different continental shelf criteria that confront each other. State practice, on the other hand, demonstrates a strong tendency of self-constraint in avoiding encroaching on other States' 200 nm limit, though its legal relevance in terms of treaty interpretation and customary international law might be circumscribed by the notable exceptions that depart from general practice. The presence of an EEZ may not prevent the overlap of continental shelves based on the two criteria, as it is the continental shelf regime that applies to the seabed and subsoil even in areas within the 200 nm limit of a coastal State. It seems that divergent conclusions could be drawn by reading these international law materials.

Given the indeterminacy of international law governing the relationship between the two continental shelf entitlements, it remains to be seen what direction the ICJ will point to in the *Nicaragua* v. *Colombia II* case: the equality of two entitlements or the hierarchy of the distance over the outer edge of the continental margin? It is hoped that the judgment of this case could clear up the controversies that have been lingering so far.

As a final remark, even if the equality of the two continental shelf criteria was established, the delimitation process has to take into account all the relevant circumstances in a given context. For opposite States between which the distance is less than 400 nm, relevant circumstances such as coastal geography might have a significant role, as in most maritime delimitation cases. As for opposite States between which the distance is greater than 400 nm, it is not impossible that a delimitation line corresponds to the 200 nm limit of one State – not as a result of a hierarchical relationship between the two criteria of Article 76(1), but of the relevant circumstances of the particular case in the pursuit of an equitable solution.[208]

[208] This prospect was acknowledged by Nicaragua's counsel during the oral proceedings of the *Nicaragua* v. *Colombia I* case. See *Nicaragua* v. *Colombia I*, Verbatim record, CR 2012/9 (24 April 2012), [67].

## IV A "Zone-Locked" Problem

Another scenario that casts doubt on the existence of overlapping entitlements is where two coastal States share the common continental margin, but, due to their relative locations, State A cannot reach the continental shelf beyond 200 nm without trespassing on the 200 nm shelf of State B. In other words, part of the continental shelf beyond 200 nm of State A overlaps with the continental shelf within 200 nm of State B. Moreover, State A is closed off by the maritime boundary with State B. This is the situation between Canada and France's St. Pierre and Miquelon Islands, and between Barbados and Trinidad and Tobago.

In the *St. Pierre and Miquelon Arbitration*, France requested the Court of Arbitration to delimit the continental shelf of the parties beyond 200 nm, and to prolong the delimitation lines at least as far as the Canadian 200 nm lines, otherwise it would "result in denying France right to a broad continental shelf extending as far as the outer edge of the continental margin."[209] The Court of Arbitration did not consider itself competent to delimit the continental shelf beyond 200 nm, and confined itself to the task of delimiting the continental shelf within 200 nm of both States.[210] To the south of St. Pierre and Miquelon, the Court of Arbitration accorded France a corridor with a width of 10.5 nm up to its 200 nm limits, and the boundary line closes at the 200 nm limits to the south of St. Pierre and Miquelon, which is some distance short of reaching Canada's 200 nm limit.

Subsequent to the delimitation, both Canada and France submitted information to the CLCS concerning the establishment of the outer limits of the continental shelf in this area. Canada, however, rejects France's claim because it considered that the 1992 decision of the Court of Arbitration had settled the maritime boundaries and a claim by France "to an area of extended continental shelf off St. Pierre and Miquelon simply cannot arise."[211] France, on the other hand, considered that the Court of Arbitration "did not include a determination on the merits of French claims to the continental shelf beyond 200 nautical miles from

209 *Decision in Case concerning Delimitation of Maritime Areas (St. Pierre and Miquelon), 31 ILM 1145 (1992)* 1171 [75].
210 Ibid., 1172 [78].
211 Note Verbale of Canada dated September 3, 2014, available at www.un.org/Depts/los/clcs_new/submissions_files/fra72_14/2014_09_03_can_nv_un_001.pdf.

Saint Pierre and Miquelon" and its claims "have a scientific basis clearly established in the documents supporting the French submission."[212]

In the Arbitration between Barbados and Trinidad and Tobago, Trinidad and Tobago argued that part of its continental shelf beyond 200 nm is located within the 200 nm zone of Barbados. It further contended that in this area Barbados has the EEZ rights and the two parties have overlapping continental shelf entitlements.[213] The Arbitral Tribunal, while considering that it had jurisdiction to delimit the continental shelf beyond 200 nm, refrained from extending the maritime boundary line beyond 200 nm and took no question on the substance of the arguments advanced by Trinidad and Tobago.[214] The boundary line drawn by the Tribunal terminates at the junction of Trinidad and Tobago's 200 nm EEZ limit and its southern maritime boundary with Venezuela.[215] Trinidad and Tobago was thus "zone-locked" within 200 nm by its boundary lines with Barbados and Venezuela.

Barbados believed that the Arbitral Award had determined the respective maritime entitlement as between itself and Trinidad and Tobago when it submitted information to the CLCS,[216] implying that no question of overlapping entitlements to the continental shelf beyond 200 nm should arise. Trinidad and Tobago did not agree,[217] and informed the CLCS in its submission that "this Submission covers maritime space over which the Arbitral Tribunal in its 2006 Award exercised no jurisdiction and accordingly made no award."[218]

In the *St. Pierre and Miquelon Arbitration* and the *Barbados* v. *Trinidad and Tobago* case, the fact that one State is "zone-locked" makes it unclear whether it could still claim a continental shelf beyond 200 nm. This is primarily a question of ascertaining the *res judicata* of each

[212] Note Verbale of France dated on December 17, 2014, available at www.un.org/Depts/los/clcs_new/submissions_files/can70_13/1467831E.pdf.

[213] See *Barbados* v. *Trinidad and Tobago*, Counter-Memorial of Trinidad and Tobago, Volume 1(1) (March 30, 2005), 100.

[214] *Barbados* v. *Trinidad and Tobago* (n 28), [368].

[215] Ibid., [382].

[216] See "Executive Summary of Barbados's of Submission (8 May 2008)," 4, available at www.un.org/Depts/los/clcs_new/submissions_files/brb08/brb08_executive_summary.pdf.

[217] See Note Verbale of Trinidad and Tobago dated August 11, 2008, available at www.un.org/Depts/los/clcs_new/submissions_files/submission_brb.htm.

[218] See "Executive Summary of Trinidad and Tobago's of Submission (12 May 2009)," 17, available at www.un.org/Depts/los/clcs_new/submissions_files/tto49_09/tto2009executive_summary.pdf.

decision.[219] If it were determined that the delimitation of the continental shelf beyond 200 nm was beyond the *res judicata*, it would be necessary to consider whether a zone-locked State A can claim a continental shelf beyond 200 nm within the area of a 200 nm continental shelf of State B. Two theoretical solutions are possible. First, the continental shelf beyond 200 nm of State A overlaps with the continental shelf within 200 nm of State B, and their overlapping entitlements continue into the area that is beyond 200 nm of both States. Findings of Section III above show that the legal viability of this solution under existing international law is unclear.

The second solution is based on the idea that the two criteria of entitlement cannot overlap. As a result, zone-locked State A cannot claim any right in the area within the 200 nm shelf of State B, and only beyond the 200 nm limit of State B can the question of overlapping entitlements to the continental shelf beyond 200 nm of both States arise. However, such a resolution would go against the notion of natural prolongation under Article 76(1), as State B's continental shelf within 200 nm interrupts State A's entitlement that extends throughout the natural prolongation to its outer edge of the continental margin. There is thus no continuity between the continental shelf beyond 200 nm and the continental shelf within 200 nm for zone-locked State A. In his dissenting opinion appended to the *St. Pierre and Miquelon Arbitration*, Mr. Allan E. Gotlieb believed that "[t]he issue of a French claim to a continental shelf beyond its 200 mile limit therefore cannot arise" after St. Pierre and Miquelon had been "zone-locked" by the Award.[220] In his view, Canada had full rights to the seabed and subsoil by reference to the EEZ under customary international law, and a French claim has to travel through Canada's 200 nm zone to generate a claim to the physical shelf beyond Canada's 200 nm zone.[221] Notwithstanding the relationship between the EEZ and the continental shelf, Mr. Gotlieb pointed out the problem of cutting off the natural prolongation of State A and the consequential difficulty for State A to establish its entitlement to the continental shelf beyond 200 nm.

219 Chapter 4, Section III.B.1 and 2.

220 *St. Pierre and Miquelon Arbitration* (n 209), [63] (Dissenting Opinion of Mr. Gotlieb).

221 Ibid.

# 4

# Interaction between Delineation and Delimitation of the Continental Shelf beyond 200 NM

## I The Dynamic between Delineation and Delimitation

Conceptually, delineation and delimitation are two different processes. The former is concerned with the establishment of the seaward limits of a coastal State, while the latter with the lateral relationship between two or more neighboring States. Article 76(10) of the United Convention on the Law of the Sea (UNCLOS or "the Convention") provides that the definitions of the continental shelf, including the establishment of the outer limits of the continental shelf, "are without prejudice to the question of delimitation of the continental shelf between States with opposite or adjacent coasts." Notwithstanding the separateness of the two processes, in practice delineation and delimitation of the continental shelf beyond 200 nm interact with each other in a more dynamic way. As State practice shows, whether delineation and delimitation can be undertaken independently from each other is a case-specific issue.[1]

Delineation and delimitation of the continental shelf beyond 200 nm may also be entangled due to the procedural rights and obligations of States in the process of establishing the outer limits of the continental shelf. While Article 76(10) ensures that the outer limits of the continental shelf established on the basis of the recommendations of the CLCS cannot be considered final and binding if a neighboring State also has a continental shelf entitlement beyond 200 nm in the same area,[2] Article 9 of Annex II to UNCLOS requires that the actions of the Commission shall not prejudice matters relating to delimitation of boundaries between States. This latter provision differs from Article 76(10) in that it "places

[1] Chapter 3, Section II.A.

[2] See A. G. Oude Elferink and C. Johnson, "Outer Limits of the Continental Shelf and 'Disputed Areas': State Practice Concerning Article 76(10) of the LOS Convention" (2006) 21 *IJMCL* 461, 461–487.

on the Commission a responsibility to prevent prejudicial actions from occurring," shifting from a passive wording to a positive one.[3] Article 9 of Annex II may thus be interpreted as the justification for the CLCS to adopt its own rules to govern its actions regarding the questions of delimitation between States.[4] The Rules of Procedure adopted are, however, more expansive in scope than Article 76(10) and Article 9 of Annex II.[5] Rule 46 and Annex I to the Rules of Procedure provide rules governing coastal States' submissions in case of a dispute between States with opposite or adjacent coasts or in other cases of unresolved land or maritime disputes. Submitting States have to inform the CLCS of the disputes related to the submission, and assure the CLCS that the submission will not prejudice matters relating to the delimitation of boundaries between States.[6] Moreover, paragraph 5(a) of Annex I to the Rules of Procedure provides that "in cases where a land or maritime dispute exists, the Commission shall not consider and qualify a submission made by any of the States concerned in the dispute" without prior consent given by all the parties to the dispute.[7]

The practical result of these rules is that other States are in a position to block the consideration of a coastal State's submission should there be any dispute or, indeed, mere difference of opinion concerning maritime delimitation or other unresolved land or maritime issues.[8] The practice of the CLCS is to defer the consideration of the submission (or the part of the submission which is being objected to) until such time as the submissions are next in line for consideration as queued in the order they were received. In practice, States have invoked Rule 46 and paragraph 5(a) of Annex I of the Rules of Procedure and requested the

[3] T. L. McDorman, "Revisiting the Commission on the Limits of the Continental Shelf: 'A Technical Body in a Political World,'" in M. H. Nordquist et al. (eds.), *Legal Order in the World's Oceans: UN Convention on the Law of the Sea* (Brill Nijhoff Publishers 2017), 294.

[4] See A. G. Oude Elferink, "Submissions of Coastal States to the CLCS in Cases of Unresolved Land or Maritime Disputes," in M. H. Nordquist et al. (eds.), *Legal and Scientific Aspects of Continental Shelf Limits* (Martinus Nijhoff Publishers 2004), 264–265; McDorman (n 3), 294.

[5] See Oude Elferink and Johnson (n 2), 465–466.

[6] Paragraph 2 of Annex I to the Rules of Procedure of the CLCS.

[7] Paragraph 5(a) of Annex I to the Rules of Procedure of the CLCS.

[8] See C. G. Lathrop, "Continental Shelf Delimitation Beyond 200 Nautical Miles: Approaches Taken by Coastal States before the Commission on the Limits of the Continental Shelf," in R. W. Smith and D. A. Colson (eds.), *International Maritime Boundaries, Volume VI* (Martinus Nijhoff Publishers 2011), 4145; S. V. Busch, *Establishing Continental Shelf Limits beyond 200 Nautical Miles by the Coastal State: A Right of Involvement for Other States?* (Brill Nijhoff Publishers 2016), 134–140.

Commission not to consider a submission by another State for various reasons in addition to maritime delimitation disputes.[9]

Given the potential use of veto and lack of procedural remedies for the submitting State, it is vital for coastal States to coordinate delineation and delimitation in order to secure their respective positions and to move through the delineation procedure before the CLCS smoothly. Section II introduces the approaches taken by coastal States to coordinate and even integrate delineation and delimitation in their practice. As will be highlighted, any successful coordination shares the common ground that the relevant parties acknowledge the overlapping entitlements of all the relevant parties, or at least recognize the overlapping claims to the same area of the continental shelf beyond 200 nm.

Where bilateral efforts to coordinate delineation and delimitation fail, coastal States may resort to third-party dispute settlement and request an international court or tribunal to settle the maritime delimitation dispute prior to the establishment of the outer limits of the continental shelf. This raises the question of the competence of international courts and tribunals to delimit the continental shelf beyond 200 nm in the absence of recommendations from the CLCS. The interaction between delineation and delimitation, as well as the institutional relationship between the CLCS and international courts or tribunals, are part of the issues that have puzzled the jurisprudence in recent years. Both progress and confusion are evident in the international jurisprudence. Section III attempts to chart the course of the development in the jurisprudence and summarize the factors underlying a court or tribunal's decision (not) to proceed with delimitation without recommendations of the CLCS.

To request international courts or tribunals to delimit the continental shelf beyond 200 nm is, nevertheless, not an option for many coastal States due to the unwillingness of States to submit disputes to third-party dispute settlement. In addition, as Section III will elaborate, delimitation of the continental shelf beyond 200 nm by a court or tribunal is not always plausible without recommendations of the CLCS. In the latter situations, the deadlock between delineation and delimitation cannot be resolved by international courts or tribunals. Instead, the key to the impasse lies in the veto power enjoyed by States under the Rules of Procedure of the CLCS. Section IV argues that, in cases of maritime

[9] See Busch (n 8), 214–219, 227–241.

delimitation, the veto power runs the risk of impeding the effective operation of UNCLOS and its use should be restricted.

## II Coordinating Delineation and Delimitation in State Practice

The survey of State practice shows that, as long as the relevant parties proceed on the basis of mutual acknowledgment of each other's entitlement or claim to the same continental shelf beyond 200 nm, a range of approaches are available for them to coordinate delineation and delimitation in the spirit of cooperation. The approaches taken by States to coordinate delineation and delimitation have been discussed by several authors.[10] The present section intends to highlight one aspect of these practices, namely, the degree of integration between delineation and delimitation, as well as the methods to balance the delimitation process with the function of the CLCS. Note that a single submission may involve more than one approach discussed below, because a submitting State may adopt different approaches if the same area is subject to the claims of multiple States. Similarly, a State may cooperate with some of the interested States but not all of them, which may elicit objections from the other interested parties. A comprehensive account of the approaches adopted by States to coordinate delineation and delimitation is provided in Appendix 2.

### *A Provisional Delimitation of the Continental Shelf beyond 200 NM*

It is within a regional setting that a sophisticated integrated approach to delineation and delimitation was first adopted. Since it was employed between Nordic countries, this approach was also called a "Nordic Model."[11] The *Agreed Minutes on the Delimitation of the Continental*

[10] See Lathrop (n 8), 4139; L. D. M. Nelson, "The Commission on the Limits of the Continental Shelf and Coastal States' Submissions," in H. P. Hestermeyer et al. (eds.), *Coexistence, Cooperation and Solidarity: Liber Amicorum Rüdiger Wolfrum, Volume II* (Martinus Nijhoff Publishers 2012), 976–979; B. M. Magnússon, *The Continental Shelf beyond 200 Nautical Miles: Delineation, Delimitation and Dispute Settlement* (Brill Nijhoff Publishers 2015), 107–116.

[11] T. H. Heidar, "Delimitation of the Continental Shelf and Determination of the Outer Limits of the Continental Shelf beyond 200 Nautical Miles in Areas of Overlapping Claims: The Nordic Model," in M. W. Lodge and M. H. Nordquist (eds.), *Peaceful Order in the World's Oceans: Essays in Honor of Satya N. Nandan* (Brill Nijhoff Publishers 2014), 156.

*Shelf beyond 200 Nautical Miles between the Faroe Islands, Iceland and Norway in the Southern Part of the Banana Hole of the Northeast Atlantic* ("the 2006 Agreed Minutes") delimits the continental shelf beyond 200 nm provisionally, while at the same time preserving the functions of the CLCS with regard to delineation of the outer limits of the continental shelf.[12] It is a politically binding agreement rather than a treaty, with a model agreement on maritime delimitation appending to it. According to the 2006 Agreed Minutes, three parallel bilateral delimitation agreements are to be finalized no later than three months after the procedure of Article 76(8) has been concluded.[13]

The 2006 Agreed Minutes set out on the assumption that the whole area concerned consists of a continuous continental shelf.[14] It allows the adjustment of the boundary lines in accordance with the recommendations of the CLCS with a formula of adjustment if any of the parties fails to document the area of continental shelf of a minimum size.[15] This flexible approach accommodates the uncertainty in the scope of the entitlement to the continental shelf beyond 200 nm before receiving the recommendations of the CLCS and it avoids the potential risk of including an area which turns out to be not within the entitlement of any party.[16] In fact, under the 2006 Agreed Minutes the parties would submit their proposed outer limits of the continental shelf to the CLCS, which

[12] See ibid.

[13] Paragraph 9 and Appendix II of the 2006 Agreed Minutes, text reproduced in R. E. Fife, "Denmark/The Faroes–Iceland–Norway, Report Number 9-26," in D. A. Colson and R. W. Smith (eds.), *International Maritime Boundaries, Vol.VI* (Martinus Nijhoff Publishers 2011), 4548. The CLCS issued recommendations in respect of the areas contained in the 2006 Agreed Minutes to Norway in 2009, to Iceland in 2014, and to Denmark in 2016. The three States have finalized the maritime delimitation agreements on October 30, 2019. See "Norway signed maritime delimitation agreements with Iceland and Denmark/the Faroe Islands, Press release dated 30 October 2019," available at www.regjeringen.no/en/aktuelt/norge-undertegnet-maritime-avgrensningsavtaler-med-island-og-danmarkfaroyene/id2675744/.

[14] Fife (n 13), 4547.

[15] For instance, Paragraph 8 of the 2006 Agreed Minutes provides that if Iceland fails to document an area of continental shelf beyond 200 nautical miles of at least 29 000 km$^2$, the excess area will be shared between Denmark/the Faroe Islands (40 percent) and Norway (60 percent). Ibid., 4548.

[16] For instance, a small area on Australia's side of its boundary with New Zealand in accordance with their 2004 agreement delimiting part of their continental shelf beyond 200 nm, which was submitted to the CLCS as part of the Macquarie Ridge region, was not recommended by the CLCS as forming part of Australia's continental shelf. See A. Serdy, "Delineation of the Outer Limits of Canada's Arctic Ocean Continental Shelf and Its Delimitation with Neighboring States: Does It Matter Which Comes First?," in S. Lalonde

differs from the practice that States submit their maritime boundary beyond 200 nm as their proposed outer limits.[17] The inclusive and efficient aspects of this approach may be attractive for coastal States bordering a region.

Provisional delimitation has also been agreed upon bilaterally by Denmark/Greenland and Iceland. The 2013 Denmark (Greenland)–Iceland Agreed Minutes models upon the 2006 Agreed Minutes,[18] and it provisionally delimits the area of interest of Denmark and Iceland in the continental shelf beyond 200 nm. It also presupposes that the area concerned is the continental shelf of each State. Importantly, "the area of interest" is defined as the area in which the outer limits of the continental shelves of Greenland and Iceland overlap.[19] The dividing line is based on a defined apportioning ratio, which shares out the area of interest according to a ratio of 53 percent to Denmark (Greenland) and 47 percent to Iceland.[20] If the scope of the area of interest is adjusted by way of the recommendations of the CLCS, the relevant area appertaining to the parties will be divided according to the same apportioning ratio.[21] The dividing line in the 2013 Denmark (Greenland)–Iceland Agreed Minutes starts from the point where it intersects with the boundary line that delimited the continental shelf and the fishery zone of Denmark and Iceland in 1997.[22] Therefore, it provides a useful approach for coastal States with delimitation issues within and beyond 200 nm.

Together with the provisional delimitation, the two Agreed Minutes also require each party to supply a no-objection declaration to the Secretary-General of the United Nations that it does not object to the consideration and qualification of a submission made by another party.[23] This approach thus reflects a high degree of integration between delineation and delimitation.

and T. L. McDorman (eds.), *International Law and Politics of the Arctic Ocean: Essays in Honor of Donat Pharand* (Brill Nijhoff Publishers 2015), 428.

17 See Chapter 3, Section II.A.

18 See B. M. Magnússon, "Denmark (Greenland)–Iceland, Report Number 9-22 (2)," in C. G. Lathrop (ed.), *International Maritime Boundaries, Vol. VII* (Brill Nijhoff Publishers 2016), 5260.

19 Paragraph 2 of the 2013 Agreed Minutes, ibid., 5269.

20 Paragraphs 2 and 3 of the 2013 Agreed Minutes, ibid., 5269–5270.

21 Paragraph 3 of the 2013 Agreed Minutes, ibid.

22 Ibid.

23 Paragraph 7 of the 2006 Agreed Minutes, Fife (n 13), 4547; Paragraph 7 of the 2013 Agreed Minutes, Magnússon (n 18), 5270.

### B Delimitation Prior to Delineation through Negotiations

Coastal States can delimit their continental shelves beyond 200 nm partially or completely before they make submissions to the CLCS. This approach is only possible where all the relevant parties recognize the existence of overlapping entitlements and it allows coastal States to settle their maritime boundaries before going through the delineation procedure. So far it is undertaken by coastal States with delimitation issues within and beyond 200 nm.

For coastal States having pre-existing maritime boundaries, they could conclude a new agreement that extends the previous boundary to the outer limits of the continental shelf to be recommended by the CLCS. Kenya and Tanzania in their 2009 agreement adopt this approach by formally defining their maritime boundary in respect of the EEZ and the continental shelf and extend the maritime boundary to the "outermost limits of national jurisdiction as may be determined by international law."[24]

Coastal States could also delimit part of the continental shelves beyond 200 nm and they acknowledge the possibility to extend the boundary in accordance with the recommendations of the CLCS in the future. The 1982 agreement between France (Kerguelen Islands) and Australia (Heard/McDonald Islands) delimits the parties' continental shelves beyond 200 nm to a large extent, and provides that "[i]f it becomes necessary to extend a line of delimitation [. . .] for the purpose of further delimiting the continental shelf adjacent to Australian and French territory, that line shall be extended by agreement between the two Governments in accordance with international law."[25]

In other circumstances, coastal States may delimit a substantial part of their continental shelf beyond 200 nm and predetermine a formula that allows the terminus of the boundary to be specified after receiving the recommendations from the CLCS. The 2010 Norway–Russia agreement is an example in point.[26]

[24] Article 2 of Agreement between the United Republic of Tanzania and the Republic of Kenya on the Delimitation of the Maritime Boundary of the Exclusive Economic Zone and the Continental Shelf (June 23, 2009), 2603 UNTS 37.

[25] Article 3(2) of Agreement on Marine Delimitation between the Government of Australia and the Government of the French Republic (January 4, 1982), 1329 UNTS 107.

[26] Article 1(1) of Treaty between the Kingdom of Norway and the Russian Federation concerning Maritime Delimitation and Cooperation in the Barents Sea and the Arctic Ocean (September 15, 2010), 2791 UNTS 3.

### C Joint Submission

The Rules of Procedure of the CLCS suggest the use of a joint submission in case of a dispute between States with opposite or adjacent coasts or in other cases of unresolved land or maritime disputes.[27] With this approach, relevant States can internalize the issue of delimitation within the group of submitting States.[28] The cooperation entailed by a joint submission can be significant. For instance, the joint submission made by seven West African States (Cabo Verde, The Gambia, Guinea, Guinea-Bissau, Mauritania, Senegal, and Sierra Leone) comprises a single set of documents and data prepared collectively and collaboratively.[29] The sub-regional cooperation is extensive, as it "grew to include several regional agreements, national commissions, regular joint technical workshops, a Liaison Committee of Government officials, as well as joint acquisition of seismic and bathymetric data."[30]

A joint submission could be useful for multiple coastal States making claims to the same area where the existence of overlapping entitlements is relatively straightforward. As demonstrated by the joint submission made by France, Ireland, Spain, and the United Kingdom in respect of the area of the Celtic Sea and the Bay of Biscay, the area concerned could be the natural prolongation of the landmasses of two or more of them viewed in isolation.[31]

Two neighboring States with delimitation issues within and beyond 200 nm may also coordinate through joint submission. Mauritius and the Seychelles delimited their EEZs in 2008 and they made a joint submission

27 Paragraph 4 of Annex I to the Rules of Procedure of the CLCS. Partial submission is also one method suggested by the Rules of Procedure for coastal States to exclude the area in dispute from their submissions. Partial submission is not discussed in the present section because it in fact requires no efforts to coordinate delineation and delimitation with neighboring States.

28 See Lathrop (n 8), 4147.

29 "Executive summary of Joint Submission in Respect of Areas in the Atlantic Ocean Adjacent to the Coast of West Africa (25 September 2014)," 4, available at www.un.org/Depts/los/clcs_new/commission_submissions.htm.

30 "Speech given by M. F. Tveiten (Director General) at the lodgement ceremony for the West African Joint submission at the New United Nations (New York, September 25, 2014)," in K. Thygesen and E. Baker, *The Shelf Programme: A Decade of Successfully Helping to Secure the Maritime Rights of Developing Coastal States* (GRID–Arendal 2015), 27.

31 See A. Serdy, "The Commission on the Limits of the Continental Shelf and Its Disturbing Propensity to Legislate" (2011), 26 *IJMCL* 355, 369–370.

to the CLCS in the same year.[32] Without objections being raised by other States, Mauritius and Seychelles received recommendations from the CLCS in 2011. The two States subsequently reached agreements on the joint development of the area (referred to as the "joint management area") of the continental shelf beyond 200 nm in 2012, which is an unprecedented example of State practice for putative joint development of natural resources within their overlapping continental shelf areas beyond 200 nm.[33]

Accordingly, joint submission is an approach which may accelerate the delineation process through the CLCS and contributes to ascertaining the overlapping entitlements as between the parties without prejudicing the subsequent delimitation between the parties. With all these advantages in mind, it should be noted that a joint submission is procedural in nature; it cannot and should not alter the substance of the rights of an individual State.[34] As expressed in one Statement of the Chairman of the CLCS, "in any joint submission, each coastal State has to establish its own set of criteria for the feet of the continental slope, applied formulas, constraints and respective outer limits" in order to ensure that the total area of the continental shelf reflected in a joint submission would not be in excess of the individual area of the continental shelf as proposed in a separate submission.[35]

### D Self-Restraint in the Light of Potential Delimitation

Where coastal States with delimitation issues within and beyond 200 nm have not coordinated between delimitation and delineation using the above-mentioned approaches, they may use several techniques to show self-restraint in the submissions to the CLCS in order not to provoke their neighbors. This is particularly the case between States with adjacent costs.

32 See V. Prescott and G. Triggs, "Mauritius-Syechelles, Report Number 6-22," in D. A. Colson and R. W. Smith (eds.), *International Maritime Boundaries, Vol. VI* (Martinus Nijhoff Publishers 2011), 4391.

33 See D. M. Ong, "Delimitation of the Outer Continental Shelf and Prospects for Revenue Sharing Between States and the International Community," in J. Barrett and R. Barnes (eds.), *Law of the Sea: UNCLOS as a Living Treaty* (BIILC 2016), 96–102.

34 See Statement by the Chairman of the Commission on the Limits of the Continental Shelf on the progress of the work in the Commission – Twentieth session (CLCS/56, October 4, 2007) [27].

35 Ibid., [28].

Where no delimitation agreement has been concluded, a notional boundary line might be indicated to circumscribe the proposed outer limits of the continental shelf. For instance, South Africa has not delimited its maritime boundaries with its neighbors, i.e., Mozambique in the east and Namibia in the west. In its submission, South Africa draws two provisional median lines between itself and its two neighbors, and its proposed outer limits of the continental shelf do not extend beyond the provisional median line.[36] Namibia also indicated a provisional equidistance line in its submission and clarified that this line is subject to negotiations between itself and South Africa.[37] This method shows the awareness of the delimitation issue with their neighbors and avoids extending the proposed outer limits of the continental shelf to areas lying directly in front of their neighbors.

As to coastal States where there have been delimitation agreements in place within 200 nm, they may use an equidistant point or an equidistance line to limit their proposed outer limits of the continental shelf. Uruguay adopted a fixed point FP 01 (the southernmost point in its proposed outer limits) which is "equidistance from Punta Médenos in Argentina [. . .] and Cabo Santa María in Uruguay."[38] While it is certain that such unilateral moves to extend a pre-existing boundary through an indicative equidistance line cannot prejudice the positions of the parties on the delimitation of the continental shelf beyond 200 nm, they reflect the submitting States' respect for their pre-existing maritime boundary by restraining the scope of the proposed outer limits of the continental shelf. Sometimes, coastal States may separately extend their pre-existing boundary to the same direction in their individual submissions. For instance, Brazil and Uruguay, respectively, extended their boundary line concluded in 1972 to their proposed outer limits of the continental shelf. This gives rise to the question of whether an agreement has in fact been reached between the parties to extend their maritime boundary in the manner indicated in their submissions.[39] In any event, it should be borne

[36] "Executive summary of South Africa's submission (5 May 2009)," 4, available at www.un.org/Depts/los/clcs_new/submissions_files/zaf31_09/zaf2009executive_summary.pdf.

[37] "Executive summary of Namibia's submission (12 May 2009)," 4, available at www.un.org/Depts/los/clcs_new/submissions_files/nam50_09/nam2009executivesummary.pdf.

[38] "Executive summary of Uruguay's submission (7 April 2009)," 11, available at www.un.org/Depts/los/clcs_new/submissions_files/ury09/ury_esummary.pdf.

[39] See B. M. Magnússon, "Outer Continental Shelf Boundary Agreements" (2013), 62 *ICLQ* 345, 367–368.

in mind that "[t]he establishment of a permanent maritime boundary is a matter of grave importance and agreement is not easily to be presumed."[40] Consequently, whether Brazil and Uruguay have delimited their continental shelf beyond 200 nm has to be considered in light of their future practice.

### E No-Objection Agreement

Coastal States may reach a formal or informal no-objection agreement prior to filing the submission in order to enable the delineation procedure to proceed before the CLCS.

This approach is typical in the practice of coastal States bordering the Arctic Ocean. Most parts of the seabed and subsoil of the Central Arctic is claimed by the five Arctic States, namely, Canada, Denmark, Norway, Russia, and the United States.[41] To date, all these claimants, except the United States, have submitted information to the CLCS with regard to the Arctic Ocean. The United States made no objection to the consideration of these submissions.[42] Among the other four Arctic States, they ensure no objection between each other by agreement or by reciprocity. For instance, Denmark (with the government of Greenland) and Russia entered into an understanding by exchange of notes on March 27, 2014 which provides, *inter alia*, that "one state will not raise an objection against the Commission considering the submission of the other State and making recommendations on it."[43] Another no-objection agreement of identical wording is found between Canada and Russia.[44] Between Norway and Denmark, although no such understanding is known to the public, it is clear from the submission of Denmark as well as the

[40] *Territorial and Maritime Dispute between Nicaragua and Honduras in the Caribbean Sea (Nicaragua v. Honduras) [2007] ICJ Rep 659, 735* [253].

[41] See B. Kunoy, "Assertions of Entitlement to the Outer Continental Shelf in the Central Arctic Ocean" (2017), 66 *ICLQ* 367, 367.

[42] See Note Verbale of the United States dated October 30, 2015, available at www.un.org/Depts/los/clcs_new/submissions_files/rus01_rev15/2015_11_02_US_NV_RUS_001_en.pdf.

[43] See "Executive summary of Denmark submission (Greenland) (December 15, 2014)," 18, available at www.un.org/Depts/los/clcs_new/submissions_files/dnk76_14/dnk2014_es.pdf.

[44] See Understanding reached between Canada and Russia, reproduced in "Executive summary of Russia's revised submission (3 August 2015)," 11, available at www.un.org/Depts/los/clcs_new/submissions_files/rus01_rev15/2015_08_03_Exec_Summary_English.pdf.

communication from Norway that they do not object to the consideration of each other's submission on a reciprocal basis.[45] Therefore, the no-objection agreement concluded among the Arctic States demonstrates a high degree of coordination because they have been in close communication with each other and have obtained no-objection assurance before making submissions to the CLCS.[46]

The employment of a no-objection agreement is, of course, one option for States to bilaterally coordinate delineation and delimitation as well. One example is the Agreed Minutes signed by Madagascar and Mozambique on the harmonization of the continental shelf between the two States.[47]

In cases where no formal no-objection agreement is concluded, coastal States may still try to obtain assurance from their neighbors that they would not object to the consideration of the coastal States' submissions through bilateral consultations. For example, Canada indicated in its submission in respect of the Atlantic Ocean that regular consultations between Canada and the United States were held during the preparation of its submission, and that the United States would not object to the consideration of Canada's submission.[48] On the contrary, Yemen did not consent to the consideration of Somalia's submission because at the time of Somalia filing its submission, there had not been agreement or understanding between the two States that would allow the CLCS to make recommendations.[49] Consultations with neighboring States before filing the submission to the CLCS are thus vital to ensure no-objection.

[45] See Note Verbale of Denmark dated January 24, 2007, available at www.un.org/Depts/los/clcs_new/submissions_files/submission_nor.htm; Note Verbale of Norway dated December 17, 2014, available at www.un.org/Depts/los/clcs_new/submissions_files/submission_nor.htm.

[46] H. Brekke, "Defining and Recognizing the Outer Limits of the Continental Shelf in the Polar Regions," in R. C. Powell and K. Dodds (eds.), *Polar Geopolitics? Knowledges, Resources and Legal Regimes* (Edward Elgar 2014), 45.

[47] See the Agreed Minutes on the Harmonization of the Extended Continental Shelf between Madagascar and Mozambique (Antananarivo, January 30, 2009), reproduced in "Executive Summary of Madagascar's submission (29 April 2011)," 69, available at www.un.org/Depts/los/clcs_new/submissions_files/submission_mgd_56_2011.htm.

[48] See "Executive summary of Canada's submission in respect of the Atlantic Ocean (6 December 2013)," 8, available at www.un.org/Depts/los/clcs_new/submissions_files/can70_13/es_can_en.pdf.

[49] See "Executive summary of Somalia's submission (21 July 2014)," 9; Note Verbale of Yemen dated December 10, 2014, available at www.un.org/Depts/los/clcs_new/submissions_files/submission_som_74_2014.htm.

Two conclusions can be drawn from the preceding discussion about coordinating delineation and delimitation. First, a range of approaches are available to coastal States to ensure that their submissions to the CLCS do not meet with objections raised by other States. The degree of integration between delineation and delimitation may vary, from the least coordinated method of acknowledging the potential of overlap to the most sophisticated one of provisional delimitation. Among these approaches, the mutual acknowledgment of the existence or the potential of overlapping entitlements or claims constitutes the basis for cooperative arrangements that would allow the delineation to proceed through the CLCS. Even if one cannot identify from the submissions of coastal States any specific approach discussed above, the submitting State almost always assures the CLCS that consideration of the submission would not prejudice the right of other interested States to establish the outer limits of the continental shelf or prejudice the delimitation issue between the relevant parties. The interested parties, for their part, often avail themselves of the opportunities to communicate with the CLCS about their position with regard to the submission and reiterate that the recommendations of the Commission are without prejudice to the future submission of their own submission or to the delimitation issues.[50]

Second, the review of coastal States' practice demonstrates that most States can coordinate between delineation and delimitation with each other in a spirit of cooperation. The above-mentioned approaches are widely adopted, as can be seen in Appendix 2, and a majority of the submissions are not objected to by other States.

Where bilateral efforts fail to achieve cooperative approaches to coordinating delineation and delimitation, objections may be raised against the consideration of the submission by a relevant State. If the parties cannot make progress in the negotiations on their delimitation issues, there might be a deadlock in the delineation and delimitation. Under such circumstances, States may resort to third-party dispute settlement mechanisms for settling their maritime delimitation disputes. However, without recommendations from the CLCS, international courts and tribunals must assess the appropriateness of exercising jurisdiction over the continental shelf delimitation beyond 200 nm in the light of the function of the CLCS. It is this problem that Section III will turn to.

[50] See Appendix 2.

## III The Competence of International Courts and Tribunals to Delimit the Continental Shelf beyond 200 NM

### *A A Note on Terminology*

The term "competence" is used here to capture both the jurisdiction of a court or tribunal over the delimitation of the continental shelf beyond 200 nm and the admissibility of such claims.[51] Jurisdiction derives from the consent of the parties to submit their dispute to an international court and tribunal.[52] So far, only on eight occasions has an international court or tribunal been requested to delimit a continental shelf beyond 200 nm.[53] Given the variety of the jurisdictional bases invoked for these proceedings, the preconditions to jurisdiction of a particular case may be subject to different, and treaty-specific requirements. For instance, whether an Annex VII arbitral tribunal constituted under UNCLOS has jurisdiction to hear a case submitted unilaterally by one party is a matter to be appreciated under Part XV of UNCLOS, whereas the jurisdiction of a dispute submitted to the ICJ on the basis of the optional clause under Article 36(2) of the Statute of the ICJ has to be analyzed accordingly. Nevertheless, regardless of the judicial forum, the crux of establishing the jurisdiction of a court or a tribunal is the ascertainment of the mutual consent of the parties. Admissibility, on the other hand, concerns whether "there exists a legal reason, even when there is jurisdiction, why the Court should decline to hear the case, or more usually, a specific claim therein."[54]

The conceptual distinction between jurisdiction and admissibility is introduced in the following discussion, because, first, international courts and tribunals have addressed the competence to delimit the continental shelf beyond 200 nm on these two conceptual levels, and sometimes they reached different conclusions either in terms of jurisdiction or admissibility. These inconsistencies have to be appreciated in

51 S. Rosenne, *The Law and Practice of the International Court* (AW Sijthoff-Leyden 1965), 302.

52 *Application of the Convention on the Prevention and Punishment of the Crime of Genocide (Croatia v. Serbia) (Preliminary Objections) [2008] ICJ Rep 412, 456–457* [120].

53 This list does not include the *Newfoundland and Labrador/Nova Scotia* case since it is not an interstate proceeding. Nevertheless, some of its findings are relevant for the legal analysis of the delimitation of the continental shelf beyond 200 nm, both procedurally and substantively. *Newfoundland and Labrador/Nova Scotia (Award of the Tribunal in the Second Phase) [2002] 128 ILR 504.*

54 *Croatia* v. *Serbia (Preliminary Objections)* (n 52), 456–457 [120].

the light of the specific procedural rules of each case, for different jurisdictional bases or different characterizations of the problem may have an impact on the court or tribunal's decisions. Second, international courts and tribunals have so far considered various factors for upholding or declining a request to delimit the continental shelf beyond 200 nm, and these factors, depending upon their nature, may find more relevance with issues of jurisdiction than admissibility, or vice versa. For example, whether the delimitation of the continental shelf beyond 200 nm has been part of the dispute existent between the parties is an issue of jurisdiction,[55] while the relationship between delineation and delimitation tends to be more frequently characterized as an issue of admissibility.

Therefore, the following discussion will clarify, whenever available, on what conceptual level (jurisdiction or admissibility) an international court or tribunal makes its decision to proceed or not with the delimitation of the continental shelf beyond 200 nm, and what factors are relevant on which level. Understanding the nuances of the procedural contexts is crucial in order not to overgeneralize or oversimplify the relevant factors underlying the judiciary's decision.

Finally, a word of caution. Notwithstanding the clarity of the conceptual distinction between jurisdiction and admissibility, in practice their distinction may be difficult to maintain in each and every case. For example, the ICJ has not always categorized the parties' preliminary objections in line with the distinction between jurisdiction and admissibility in its practice.[56] Indeed, the Court may provide the most direct and conclusive answer to whether it has jurisdiction and whether it should exercise it without following a schematic course in examining preliminary objections, and it may even reject an application for lack of admissibility before having addressed all issues relating to jurisdiction.[57] Consequently, the fall-back term "competence" has the benefit of convenience to indicate the power of a court or tribunal to decide the merits of an application to delimit the continental shelf beyond 200 nm.

[55] See H. Thirlway, *The International Court of Justice* (Oxford University Press 2016), 53–55.

[56] See C. Tomuschat, "Article 36," in A. Zimmermann et al. (eds.), *The Statute of the International Court of Justice: A Commentary* (3rd ed., Oxford University Press 2019), 784.

[57] Ibid.

### B Progress and Confusion in the Jurisprudence

#### 1 St. Pierre and Miquelon Arbitration

In the *St. Pierre and Miquelon Arbitration*, the parties requested the Court of Arbitration to "carry out the delimitation as between the Parties of the maritime areas appertaining to France and of those appertaining to Canada" in the area south of Canadian Newfoundland and the French islands of St. Pierre and Miquelon, and to "establish a single delimitation which shall govern all rights and jurisdiction which the Parties may exercise under international law in these maritime areas."[58] Whereas both States were parties to the 1958 Convention on the Continental Shelf (CCS), the Court of Arbitration found that to the effect of a single or all-purpose delimitation operation, Article 6 of the CCS was not applicable.[59] UNCLOS was not in force at that time. As a result, the applicable law in the case was customary international law.[60]

France requested that the Court of Arbitration prolonged the delimitation line at least as far as the Canadian 200 nm limit in order to preserve its claim to a continental margin.[61] Canada, while acknowledging that the continental margin off Newfoundland generally extends beyond 200 nm, contended that France did not know the exact location of the outer edge of the continental margin, which, in its opinion, was fundamental to the French claim.[62] The Court of Arbitration found itself not competent to declare on the question of the continental shelf beyond 200 nm, because "[t]his Court is not competent to carry out a delimitation which affects the rights of a Party which is not before it,"[63] and

> Any decision by this Court recognizing or rejecting any rights of the parties over the continental shelf beyond 200 nautical miles, would constitute a pronouncement involving a delimitation, not "between the Parties" but between each one of them and the international community, represented by organs entrusted with the administration and protection of the international sea-bed Area.[64]

58 *Decision in Case concerning Delimitation of Maritime Areas (St. Pierre and Miquelon), 31 ILM 1145 (1992)* Court of Arbitration, 1152 [1].
59 Ibid., 1163 [40]. Convention on the Continental Shelf (April 29, 1958), 499 UNTS 311.
60 See ibid., 1163 [38].
61 See ibid., 1171 [75].
62 See ibid., 1171–1172 [76].
63 Ibid., 1172 [79].
64 Ibid., [78].

These observations, echoing the language of the *Monetary Gold* case,[65] seem to decline jurisdiction over the delimitation of the area beyond 200 nm for fear of affecting the interests of an indispensable party, i.e., the international community. However, this line of reasoning is problematic because the Court of Arbitration seems to have treated all the provisions of Article 76 of UNCLOS as customary international law.[66] Furthermore, neither the CLCS nor the International Seabed Authority (ISA), even if they were existent at the time of the case, would have standing to appear before international courts or tribunals in disputes concerning the continental shelf delimitation beyond 200 nm.[67]

The Court of Arbitration supported its decision to decline jurisdiction with two additional considerations. Pointing out the lack of elucidation of the factual situation concerning the geological and geomorphological data, the Court of Arbitration found that "[t]his deficiency strengthens the Court's decision to abstain from pronouncing on the substance of the matter," and "[i]t is not possible for a tribunal to reach a decision by assuming hypothetically the eventuality that such rights will in fact exist."[68] In addition, the Court of Arbitration emphasized that its task was to effect a delimitation as far as 200 nm because the parties requested to "establish a single delimitation," which was "a single boundary line that would apply both to the sea-bed and the superjacent waters in the area subject to the delimitation."[69] Apparently, the interpretation of the scope of the Arbitration Agreement to mean a delimitation to be effected simultaneously to the continental shelf and the EEZ played a significant role in limiting the jurisdiction of the Court of Arbitration.[70]

[65] See *Case of the Monetary Gold removed from Rome in 1943 (Preliminary Objections) [1954] ICJ Rep 19*, 32.

[66] See *St. Pierre and Miquelon Arbitration* (n 58), 1215 [42] (Dissenting opinion of Mr Weil). See also L. de La Fayette, "The Award in the Canada-France Maritime Boundary Arbitration" (1993) 8 *IJMCL* 77, 101; T. L. McDorman, "The Entry into Force of the 1982 LOS Convention and the Article 76 Outer Continental Shelf Regime" (1995) 10 *IJMCL* 165, 168.

[67] See B. M. Magnússon, "Is There a Temporal Relationship between the Delineation and the Delimitation of the Continental Shelf beyond 200 Nautical Miles?" (2013), 28 *IJMCL* 465, 473.

[68] *St. Pierre and Miquelon Arbitration* (n 58), 1172 [81].

[69] See ibid., [82].

[70] See K. Highet, "St. Pierre and Miquelon Arbitration", *Max Planck Encyclopedia of Public International Law [MPEPIL]* (June 2009), available at opil.ouplaw.com/view/10.1093/law:epil/9780199231690/law-9780199231690-e213?rskey=cOoyFe&result=1&prd=MPIL.

However, it is not obvious that "a single delimitation" should be interpreted to mean a delimitation applicable simultaneously to the area where the continental shelf and the EEZ co-exist. Instead, a single maritime delimitation can be understood simply as a single maritime boundary dividing multiple maritime areas, which is in effect more accurate where a single line divides the territorial sea, the EEZ, and the continental shelf between two coastal States.[71] It is clear that such a single delimitation does not require that all the maritime zones co-exist vertically over the same space. Should the latter interpretation prevail, the continental shelf beyond 200 nm could also be considered as "maritime areas appertaining to" the parties. A necessary component to this line of argumentation is, however, the applicability of Article 76 to the parties and the factual certainty of the existence of continental shelf beyond 200 nm.[72]

The Court of Arbitration stated explicitly that a denial of a pronouncement on the French claim "cannot signify nor may be interpreted as prejudging, accepting or refusing the rights that may be claimed by France, or by Canada, to a continental shelf beyond 200 nautical miles."[73] However, the fact that France is "zone-locked" led members of the Court of the Arbitration and commentators to reach different conclusions as to the feasibility of a French claim to the continental shelf beyond 200 nm in this area.[74] Nonetheless, as the Court of Arbitration declined jurisdiction over the claim to the continental shelf beyond 200 nm, it is sensible to argue that the legal status of the entitlement to the continental shelf beyond 200 nm of both parties is not affected by the Award. France is thus not precluded from claiming a continental shelf beyond 200 nm in this area, though the question of overlapping entitlements based on different criteria of entitlement would emerge with the French claim.[75]

### 2 *Barbados* v. *Trinidad and Tobago* Case

In 2004, Barbados initiated arbitration proceedings against Trinidad and Tobago under Annex VII to UNCLOS, which related to "the delimitation

71 *Maritime Delimitation and Territorial Questions (Qatar v. Bahrain) (Merits) [2001] ICJ Rep 40*, 93 [173].

72 *St. Pierre and Miquelon Arbitration* (n 58), 1215 [42] (Dissenting opinion of Mr. Weil).

73 Ibid., 1172 [80].

74 See ibid., 1215 [42] (Dissenting opinion of Mr. Weil); ibid., 1195–1196 [63] (Dissenting opinion of Mr Gotlieb). M. D. Evans, "Less than an Ocean Apart: The St Pierre and Miquelon and Jan Mayen Islands and the Delimitation of Maritime Zones" (1994) 43 *ICLQ* 678, 689.

75 Chapter 3, Section IV.

of a single maritime boundary between the exclusive economic zones and the continental shelves appertaining to Barbados and Trinidad and Tobago respectively."[76] Trinidad and Tobago argued that the Arbitral Tribunal lacked jurisdiction over the dispute, but that if it did have jurisdiction, the dispute should also involve the continental shelf boundary between the two States beyond 200 nm.[77] Trinidad and Tobago argued that it had a substantial continental shelf extending beyond 200 nm, some of which lay within the 200 nm limit of Barbados. Therefore, the continental shelves of the two States overlap and call for delimitation.[78] Barbados, on the other hand, did not consider that the jurisdiction of the Arbitral Tribunal should include the continental shelf delimitation beyond the 200 nm limit.[79]

The Arbitral Tribunal approached the issue differently from the Court of Arbitration in the *St. Pierre and Miquelon Arbitration* because it started from the point of the existence and scope of the dispute between the parties. In its view, the dispute to be dealt with included the continental shelf beyond 200 nm ("the outer continental shelf," as the Arbitral Tribunal put it), since:

(i) it either forms part of, or is sufficiently closely related to, the dispute submitted by Barbados,
(ii) the record of the negotiations shows that it was part of the subject-matter on the table during those negotiations, and
(iii) in any event there is in law only a single "continental shelf" rather than an inner continental shelf and a separate extended or outer continental shelf.[80]

The Arbitral Tribunal thus confirmed its jurisdiction over the continental shelf beyond 200 nm. In terms of delimitation, Barbados argued for an equidistance line as the boundary line in the eastern segment. Trinidad and Tobago, for its part, contended that the boundary line should be a constant azimuth running eastwards at 88 degrees from the eastern end of the central segment of the boundary to the outer limits of its continental shelf as determined in accordance with international law.[81] The

[76] *Maritime Boundary Arbitration (Barbados v. Trinidad and Tobago) (2006) XXVII RIAA 147* [1].
[77] Ibid., [190].
[78] *Barbados* v. *Trinidad and Tobago*, Counter-Memorial of Trinidad and Tobago, Volume 1 (1) (March 30, 2005), 91–94.
[79] See *Barbados* v. *Trinidad and Tobago* (n 76), [189].
[80] Ibid., [213].
[81] Ibid., [187].

effect of this line of loxodrome is that, beyond the 200 nm limits of Trinidad and Tobago and within the 200 nm limits of Barbados, there would be a "grey area" in which Trinidad and Tobago's continental shelf co-exists with Barbados's EEZ. Eventually, the Arbitral Tribunal observed that "[a]s will become apparent, however, the single maritime boundary which the Tribunal has determined is such that, as between Barbados and Trinidad and Tobago, there is no single maritime boundary beyond 200 nm,"[82] and the boundary line stops at the point of intersection of Trinidad and Tobago's 200 nm limit with its southern maritime boundary with Venezuela,[83] and no issue of "grey area" arises.

It is not entirely clear from this outcome whether the Arbitral Tribunal exercised its jurisdiction to delimit the continental shelf beyond 200 nm or not. On the one hand, it can be argued that it did not. First, the boundary line does not extend beyond the 200 nm limits of either State. Second, the statement that "there is no single maritime boundary beyond 200 nm" may entail that the delimitation of the continental shelf beyond 200 nm is beyond the task of the Arbitral Tribunal,[84] resonating the interpretation of "a single delimitation" of the *St. Pierre and Miquelon* case. Third, the Tribunal did not engage with the examination of the existence or extent of Trinidad and Tobago's entitlement to the continental shelf beyond 200 nm. This interpretation will enable Trinidad and Tobago to claim a continental shelf beyond 200 nm beyond the boundary decided by the Award.

On the other hand, the Award could also be interpreted as having delimited all the maritime areas appertaining to Barbados and Trinidad and Tobago with the latter's entitlement to the continental shelf beyond 200 nm being rejected. The final result is what the Arbitral Tribunal deemed an equitable solution.[85] The statement that "as between Barbados and Trinidad and Tobago, there is no single maritime boundary beyond 200 nm" could imply that only Barbados has a continental

82 Ibid., [368].
83 Ibid., [374].
84 See C. Carleton et al., "Current Issues Regarding the Delimitation of the Outer Continental Shelf: A Panel Discussion in the International Tribunal for the Law of the Sea (30 September 2012)," in J. Basedow et al. (eds.), *The Hamburg Lectures on Maritime Affairs 2011–2013* (Springer 2015), 164; Magnússon (n 67), 474.
85 See *Barbados* v. *Trinidad and Tobago* (n 76), [376–380]. See also R. Volterra, "Problems Arising from Submissions by States to the CLCS in Relation to Disputed Areas: A Selective Survey of State Practice to Date," in C. R. Symmons (ed.), *Selected Contemporary Issues in the Law of the Sea* (Martinus Nijhoff Publishers 2011), 278.

shelf beyond 200 nm, while Trinidad and Tobago does not. There is no single maritime boundary beyond 200 nm between them because no overlapping entitlements beyond that distance exist.[86] Furthermore, to say that the Arbitral Tribunal did not exercise the jurisdiction over the continental shelf beyond 200 nm is contradictory to the *dispositif*, which stated that the jurisdiction "includes the delimitation of the maritime boundary in relation to that part of the continental shelf extending beyond 200 nm," and that "[c]laims of the Parties inconsistent with this Boundary are not accepted."[87] It is therefore more convincing that the Arbitral Tribunal had settled the two States' maritime boundary disputes in a comprehensive manner, with Trinidad and Tobago's claim to a continental shelf beyond 200 nm being rejected.[88] Trinidad and Tobago's claim to a continental shelf beyond 200 nm, which extends beyond the current boundary, will not be opposable to Barbados due to the principle of *res judicata*.

Although the *Barbados* v. *Trinidad and Tobago* case reached different conclusions from the *St. Pierre and Miquelon Arbitration*, it must be pointed out that the two started out from very different premises. For one thing, Article 76 is applicable between Barbados and Trinidad and Tobago as both are parties to UNCLOS. For another, the reasoning of the Arbitral Tribunal was marked by the need to ascertain the existence and scope of the dispute, which was the precondition to its jurisdiction. It is in this respect that the Arbitral Tribunal resorted to the concept of a single continental shelf under Article 76, as a supplementary to the record of negotiations of the parties.[89] However, as will be elaborated below, the *Bay of Bengal* cases and the *Ghana/Côte d'Ivoire* case applied the concept of a single continental shelf to establish the jurisdiction over the continental shelf beyond 200 nm in a more general fashion, even though the underlying procedural context is significantly different.

[86] See R. Churchill, "Bangladesh/Myanmar Case: Continuity and Novelty in the Law of Maritime Boundary Delimitation" (2012), 1 *CJICL* 137, 148.

[87] *Barbados* v. *Trinidad and Tobago* (n 76), [384(ii) and 385(2)].

[88] See A. G. Oude Elferink, "The Establishment of Outer Limits of the Continental Shelf beyond 200 Nautical Miles by the Coastal State: The Possibilities of Other States to Have an Impact on the Process" (2009), 24 *IJMCL* 535, 545. The same author also argues that the Tribunal may not be prepared to face the legal complexities in the delimitation of the continental shelf beyond 200 nm. A. G. Oude Elferink, "International Law and Negotiated and Adjudicated Maritime Boundaries: A Complex Relationship" (2015), 58 *GYIL* 231, 258–259.

[89] *Barbados* v. *Trinidad and Tobago* (n 76), [212–214].

### 3 *Bay of Bengal* Cases and *Ghana/Côte d'Ivoire* Case

By declarations made under Article 287 of UNCLOS, Bangladesh and Myanmar submitted their dispute relating to the delimitation of their maritime boundary in the Bay of Bengal to ITLOS with mutual consent.[90] Bangladesh initiated arbitral proceedings against India pursuant to Article 287, and requested an Annex VII Arbitral Tribunal to delimit the maritime boundary between them in the Bay of Bengal.[91] By a special agreement, Ghana and Côte d'Ivoire submitted their dispute of maritime boundary in the Atlantic Ocean to a special chamber of ITLOS.[92] These three judicial cases delimited the continental shelf beyond 200 nm of the relevant parties, and they adopted essentially the same approach to the jurisdictional and admissibility issues concerning the continental shelf beyond 200 nm, thus it is preferable to discuss the three cases in relation to each other.

It was ITLOS in the *Bangladesh/Myanmar* case that first undertook a thorough discussion of the competence of international courts and tribunals to delimit the continental shelf beyond 200 nm in the absence of the recommendations from the CLCS. It first endorsed the concept of the single continental shelf and affirmed its jurisdiction over the delimitation of the continental shelf beyond 200 nm,[93] even though the parties were agreed on the Tribunal's jurisdiction in this respect.[94] What was disputed between the parties was whether the Tribunal should exercise its jurisdiction to delimit the continental shelf beyond 200 nm, and the crux was whether a delimitation of the continental shelf beyond 200 nm should await the recommendations of the CLCS on the existence and the seaward limits of the entitlement to the continental shelf beyond this distance.[95] It is from this point onward that the relationship between the CLCS and international courts and tribunals, as well as the relationship between delineation and delimitation, are more frequently characterized as that of admissibility.[96]

[90] See *Delimitation of the Maritime Boundary in the Bay of Bengal (Bangladesh/Myanmar) (Judgment) [2012] ITLOS Rep 4* [2].

[91] *Bay of Bengal Maritime Boundary Arbitration (Bangladesh v. India) (2014) 167 ILR 1* [1].

[92] See *Delimitation of the Maritime Boundary in the Atlantic Ocean (Ghana/Côte d'Ivoire), [2017] ITLOS Rep 4* [4].

[93] *Bangladesh/Myanmar* (n 90), 96–97 [361–363].

[94] Ibid., 93 [348].

[95] See ibid., 92–93 [345–349].

[96] See S. V. Busch, "The Delimitation of the Continental Shelf Beyond 200 Nm: Procedural Issues," in A. G. Oude Elferink et al. (eds.), *Maritime Boundary Delimitation: The Case Law: Is It Consistent and Predictable?* (Cambridge University Press 2018), 331.

The Tribunal did not consider that it should refrain from exercising jurisdiction to delimit the continental shelf beyond 200 nm. To support its position, the Tribunal built upon two sets of conceptual distinctions, one between delineation and delimitation and the other between entitlement and delineation. The Tribunal started from the institutional framework set up by UNCLOS, which includes ITLOS, the CLCS, and the ISA. According to ITLOS, "[a]ctivities of these bodies are complementary to each other so as to ensure coherent and efficient implementation of the Convention."[97] The Tribunal further found that "[t]here is a clear distinction between the delimitation of the continental shelf under article 83 and the delineation of its outer limits under article 76."[98] Based on this distinction, and drawing from the State practices that concluded continental shelf delimitation agreements beyond 200 nm prior to making submissions to the CLCS, the Tribunal observed that the function of the CLCS regarding the delineation and the function of the dispute settlement would not prejudice each other.[99]

Whereas ITLOS sanctioned the distinction between delineation and delimitation in a general and conceptual level, it should however be emphasized that the specific geographical context of the *Bangladesh/ Myanmar* case was a crucial factor that substantiated such distinction. The adjacent coastal relationship between Bangladesh and Myanmar allows ITLOS to determine the direction of the seaward segment of a maritime boundary without indicating its precise terminus.[100] Consequently, the mandate of the CLCS to examine the submissions of the parties is not prejudiced nor precluded, as the delimitation only concerns the lateral relationship between the parties.[101]

The second set of the conceptual distinctions relates to the distinction between entitlement and delineation. Although the Tribunal did not consider the determination of the entitlement to the continental shelf beyond 200 nm in connection with its competence, the former was indeed related to the latter, for the Tribunal observed that "it would be dealing with a hypothetical question" if it did not address whether the parties have overlapping entitlements to the continental shelf beyond 200

97 *Bangladesh/Myanmar* (n 90), 98 [373].
98 Ibid., 99 [376].
99 See ibid., 99–100 [376–380].
100 See ibid., 97 [367].
101 The *Newfoundland and Labrador and Nova Scotia* Arbitration also considered this to be one of the reasons for it to delimit the continental shelf beyond 200 nm. *Newfoundland and Labrador and Nova Scotia Arbitration* (n 53), [2.31].

nm.[102] ITLOS distinguished the notion of entitlement to the continental shelf beyond 200 nm from that of the outer limits of the continental shelf,[103] and considered that "[a] coastal State's entitlement to the continental shelf exists by the sole fact that the basis of entitlement, namely, sovereignty over the land territory, is present. It does not require the establishment of outer limits."[104] As a result, the Tribunal did not find that it should refrain from determining the existence of entitlement to the continental shelf or delimiting the continental shelf due to the absence of established outer limits.[105]

That said, as a matter of applying Article 76 for the purpose of establishing the entitlement to the continental shelf beyond 200 nm, the determination of the existence of entitlements to the continental shelf beyond 200 nm requires positive proof of geomorphological or geological evidence. As admitted by ITLOS, the proper interpretation and application of Article 76 "requires both legal and scientific expertise."[106] Although ITLOS is competent to interpret Article 76 because "the entitlement to a continental shelf beyond 200 nm raises issues that are predominantly legal in nature,"[107] it is not without doubt that ITLOS, or any other international court or tribunal, is capable of evaluating scientific and technical data evidence regarding the entitlement to the continental shelf beyond 200 nm.[108] In addition, such tasks are essentially the same as those entrusted to the CLCS, for the ascertainment of the existence of the entitlement to the continental shelf beyond 200 nm is integral to the delineation procedure.[109] Therefore, it may call into question the separateness between entitlement and delineation.

In fact, the solution to determining overlapping entitlements to the continental shelf beyond 200 nm found by ITLOS in the *Bangladesh/Myanmar* case was rather the uncontested scientific evidence, the unique situation of the Bay of Bengal, and the reference to the submissions made by Bangladesh and Myanmar.[110] The Tribunal affirmed that it can

102 *Bangladesh/Myanmar* (n 90), 105 [399].
103 Ibid., 106 [406].
104 Ibid., 107 [409].
105 Ibid., [410].
106 Ibid., 107 [411].
107 Ibid., 108 [413].
108 See J. Noyes, "Judicial and Arbitral Proceedings and the Outer Limits of the Continental Shelf" (2009), 42 *Vanderbilt JTL* 1211, 1251–1252.
109 See Chapter 2, Section III.C.
110 See *Bangladesh/Myanmar* (n 90), 115–116 [444–449].

interpret and apply Article 76, which may include "dealing with uncontested scientific materials or require recourse to experts,"[111] and it concluded that "there is a continuous and substantial layer of sedimentary rocks extending from Myanmar's coast to the area beyond 200 nm."[112] The Tribunal further acknowledged that it "would have been hesitant to proceed with the delimitation of the area beyond 200 nm had it concluded that there was significant uncertainty as to the existence of a continental margin in the area in question."[113] This latter statement further confirmed that the Tribunal treated the existence of overlapping entitlement as an issue relating to its competence to delimit the continental shelf beyond 200 nm.

In addition to the two sets of conceptual distinction, the Tribunal also highlighted the existing impasse in the delineation procedure of the two parties, and observed that "[a] decision by the Tribunal not to exercise its jurisdiction over the dispute relating to the continental shelf beyond 200 nm would not only fail to resolve a long-standing dispute, but also would not be conducive to the efficient operation of the Convention."[114] Other factual circumstances that contributed to the decision to exercise jurisdiction include the location of the area under dispute, which would not prejudice the rights of third parties or the rights of the international community.[115]

The *Bangladesh* v. *India* case in essence followed the same line of reasoning with regard to the jurisdiction and admissibility of the continental shelf delimitation beyond 200 nm. The Arbitral Tribunal maintained the observations concerning the concept of a single continental shelf, the distinction between delineation and delimitation, and the complementary functions of the CLCS and international courts and tribunals, as well as the practical impasse in the delineation and delimitation.[116] The Arbitral Tribunal more explicitly addressed the existence of overlapping entitlements as one of the considerations relating to the jurisdiction over the continental shelf beyond 200 nm. According to the Tribunal, "Both Parties agree that they have entitlements, and neither Party denies that there is a continental shelf beyond

111 Ibid., 107 [411].
112 Ibid., 115 [446].
113 Ibid., [443].
114 Ibid., 102 [391].
115 Ibid., 97 [367–368].
116 See *Bangladesh* v. *India* (n 91), 31–33 [76–82].

200 nm in the Bay of Bengal."[117] Similar to the *Bangladesh/Myanmar* case, Bangladesh and India are adjacent States, and the delimitation of maritime zones only concerns their lateral relationship without prejudicing the location of their respective outer limits.

In the *Ghana/Côte d'Ivoire* case, neither the jurisdiction of the Special Chamber nor the admissibility of the claim to delimit the continental shelf beyond 200 nm was contested. Nevertheless, the Special Chamber stated that it had to "decide on its jurisdiction *proprio motu* and whether the submissions of the Parties concerning the continental shelf beyond 200 nm are admissible."[118] To establish its jurisdiction, the Special Chamber reiterated the concept of a single continental shelf in law.[119] It also emphasized that it "can delimit the continental shelf beyond 200 nm only if such a continental shelf exists."[120] Here the Special Chamber seems to have taken the existence of the entitlement as a precondition to the jurisdiction. Different from the *Bay of Bengal* cases and, in fact, from all the previous cases concerning a continental shelf beyond 200 nm, Ghana had received recommendations from the CLCS. Whereas Côte d'Ivoire had yet to receive the recommendations, the Special Chamber had no doubt of its entitlement, because "its geological situation is identical to that of Ghana, for which affirmative recommendations of the CLCS exist."[121] Accordingly, the *Ghana/Côte d'Ivoire* case is the only one, so far, where the factual certainty of the existence of overlapping entitlements to the continental shelf beyond 200 nm has been underwritten by the CLCS, although only partially.

In terms of admissibility, the Special Chamber endorsed the reasoning of ITLOS in the *Bangladesh/Myanmar* case on the distinction between delineation and delimitation as well.[122] It is noted that the parties also share an adjacent coastal relationship, and the Special Chamber determines the boundary line without a specific endpoint, which will extend until it reaches the outer limits of the continental shelf.[123]

The *Bay of Bengal* cases and the *Ghana/Côte d'Ivoire* case thus firmly established an approach to the jurisdiction and admissibility of the continental shelf beyond 200 nm, which is built upon the conceptual

[117] Ibid., 32 [78].
[118] *Ghana/Côte d'Ivoire* (n 92), [489].
[119] See ibid., [490].
[120] Ibid., [491].
[121] Ibid.
[122] See ibid., [493–494].
[123] *Ghana/Côte d'Ivoire* (n 92), [660(3)].

distinction between delineation and delimitation and between entitlement and delineation. Nevertheless, what substantiated the distinction between delineation and delimitation in these three cases was the adjacent coastal relationship between the relevant parties. Nor should the factual certainty of the overlapping entitlements to the continental shelf beyond 200 nm escape the reader's attention, which, explicitly or implicitly, underlies the tribunal's decision to proceed with the delimitation.

### 4 *Nicaragua* v. *Colombia* Cases

In contrast with the consistent approach to the delimitation of the continental shelf beyond 200 nm in the *Bay of Bengal* cases and the *Ghana/Côte d'Ivoire* case, the jurisprudence of the ICJ concerning the continental shelf beyond 200 nm witnesses more twists and turns. The starting point of analyzing the approach of the ICJ is, however, a case where the issue of delimiting the continental shelf beyond 200 nm did not arise. In the *Nicaragua* v. *Honduras* case, the Court delimited the maritime boundary without specifying a precise endpoint and stated that the boundary extends beyond the 82nd meridian without affecting third-State rights. The Court added that,

> It should also be noted in this regard that in no case may the line be interpreted as extending more than 200 nautical miles from the baselines from which the breadth of the territorial sea is measured; any claim of continental shelf rights beyond 200 miles must be in accordance with Article 76 of UNCLOS and reviewed by the Commission on the Limits of the Continental Shelf established thereunder.[124]

As the ICJ referred to "any claim of continental shelf rights beyond 200 miles," it could be understood that not only the extent of such a claim, but also the very existence of such a claim should be reviewed by the CLCS. This observation provoked much debate among scholars as to its implications for international courts and tribunals to delimit the continental shelf beyond 200 nm before the CLCS issues recommendations to the parties.[125] It is submitted that the statement has to be understood in its own context, primarily as an *obiter dictum*, since it does not constitute

[124] *Nicaragua* v. *Honduras* (n 40), 759 [319].

[125] See B. Kunoy, "Admissibility of a Plea to an International Adjudicative Forum to Delimit the Outer Continental Shelf Prior to the Adoption of Final Recommendations by the Commission on the Limits of the Continental Shelf" (2010), 25 *IJMCL* 237, 262; Magnússon (n 10), 252.

part of the rationale for the Court's decision.[126] Moreover, neither Nicaragua nor Honduras claimed that the jurisdiction of the Court included the delimitation of the continental shelf beyond 200 nm. Therefore, what the Court stated was to clarify the scope of the boundary line between the parties in the light of the scope of jurisdiction of the case.

In the *Nicaragua* v. *Colombia I* case, in its final submission I(3), Nicaragua asked the Court to define "a continental shelf boundary dividing by equal parts the overlapping entitlements to a continental shelf of both Parties."[127] Colombia argued that the new continental shelf claim was not admissible because it was "a new claim which changes the subject-matter of the dispute originally submitted."[128]

The Court addressed the admissibility of Nicaragua's claim to the delimitation of the continental shelf beyond 200 nm from its mainland coasts mainly as a question of the admissibility of a new claim. Invoking and applying the tests of the relevant jurisprudence, the Court decided that Nicaragua's claim was admissible because "the claim to an extended continental shelf falls within the dispute between the Parties relating to maritime delimitation and cannot be said to transform the subject-matter of that dispute."[129]

The ICJ then turned to the request in Nicaragua's final submission I(3). As Colombia is not a party to UNCLOS, only customary law may apply in respect of the maritime delimitation requested by Nicaragua.[130] The Court declared the customary status of Article 76(1), but refrained from determining the customary status of other provisions of Article 76.[131] Nicaragua submitted preliminary information to the CLCS but had not made a full submission. Colombia argued that the preliminary information could not fulfil the requirements for the Commission to make recommendations, and that Nicaragua could not merely assume that it possesses such rights in this case or to ask the Court to effect a delimitation "based on rudimentary and incomplete technical information."[132]

The Court first noted that the jurisprudence referred to by Nicaragua to support its claim "involves no case in which a court or a tribunal was

126 See Busch (n 96), 328.
127 *Territorial and Maritime Dispute (Nicaragua v. Colombia) [2012] ICJ Rep 624, 664* [106].
128 Ibid., 664 [107].
129 Ibid., 665 [111].
130 Ibid., 666 [114].
131 Ibid., [118].
132 See ibid., 667 [122].

requested to determine the outer limits of a continental shelf beyond 200 nautical miles."[133] The Court distinguished the *Bangladesh/Myanmar* case from the present one, taking note of the unique situation of the Bay of Bengal. The Court also emphasized that:

> [B]oth parties in the Bay of Bengal case were States parties to UNCLOS and had made full submissions to the Commission and that the Tribunal's ruling on the delimitation of the continental shelf in accordance with Article 83 of UNCLOS does not preclude any recommendation by the Commission as to the outer limits of the continental shelf in accordance with Article 76, paragraph 8, of the Convention.[134]

The Court then invoked the *obiter dictum* in the *Nicaragua* v. *Honduras* case and recalled the Preamble of UNCLOS, highlighting its object and purpose to establish a legal order for the seas and oceans, and observed that the fact that Colombia is not a party to UNCLOS does not relieve Nicaragua of its obligations under Article 76.[135] The Court further considered that the preliminary information submitted by Nicaragua "by its own admission, falls short of meeting the requirements for information on the limits of the continental shelf beyond 200 nautical miles."[136] Finally, the Court determined that Nicaragua "has not established that it has a continental margin that extends far enough to overlap with Colombia's 200-nautical-mile entitlement to the continental shelf," and thus "the Court is not in a position to delimit the continental shelf boundary between Nicaragua and Colombia."[137] The Court, unanimously, found that it could not uphold Nicaragua's claim contained in its final submission I(3).[138]

Inherent ambiguity is found in the Court's reasoning. The Court might have either dismissed Nicaragua's claim because Nicaragua did not satisfy the burden of proof to demonstrate that it had an entitlement to the continental shelf beyond 200 nm. Alternatively, the Court might have subtly suggested that it could not proceed to the delimitation because Nicaragua had not made a submission to the CLCS. Due to the ambiguity of the judgment, several judges felt obliged to clarify their reasoning for their vote. Judge Donoghue criticized the judgment because it "alludes to

[133] Ibid., 668 [125].
[134] Ibid.
[135] Ibid., 668–669 [126].
[136] Ibid., 669 [127].
[137] Ibid., [129].
[138] Ibid., 670 [131] and 719 [251(3)].

legal and institutional reasons for rejecting Nicaragua's submission I(3)," and she could not agree "[t]o the extent that the Judgment suggests a more general bar on the delimitation of entitlements to continental shelf in areas beyond 200 nautical miles of coastal baselines."[139] Judge Donoghue voted for the operative clause because Nicaragua did not provide a sufficient factual basis to permit the Court to proceed to delimitation.[140] This view was shared by Judge ad hoc Mensah, who believed that the Court could not proceed because "the evidence submitted by Nicaragua to the Court was considered to be inadequate, not because the required information has not been submitted to the [CLCS], or because the Commission has not made recommendations pursuant to Article 76, paragraph 8, of UNCLOS."[141] He also expressed the concern that the present judgment might be interpreted to suggest "that a court or tribunal should, in every case, automatically rule that it is not able to decide on a dispute relating to the delimitation of the continental shelf beyond 200 nautical miles whenever one of the Parties to the dispute has not followed" the procedure under Article 76.[142] On the other hand, Judge Owada dissented on the point of the admissibility of Nicaragua's new claim. For him, the new claim in fact replaced the original claim not only in formulation but also in substance in terms of the relevant legal issues.[143] Pointing out the differences in law entailed by Nicaragua's new claim and the legal nature of the claim, Judge Owada believed that the Court "did not proceed to dispose of this Nicaraguan submission I(3) by simply rejecting it on the basis of inadequacy of evidence produced by Nicaragua."[144]

The observation that Nicaragua had an obligation under Article 76 even in relation to Colombia, a non-party to UNCLOS, was also criticized by several judges.[145] This is particularly problematic because Article 76(8) creates institutional and procedural mechanisms, which, under the law of treaties, should be only available to parties to UNCLOS.[146] As expressed by Judge ad hoc Cot, "It is difficult to regard

139 Ibid., 756 [18] (Separate opinion of Judge Donoghue).
140 Ibid., 751 [1] (Separate opinion of Judge Donoghue).
141 Ibid., 765 [9] (Declaration of Judge ad hoc Mensah).
142 Ibid., 766 [12] (Declaration of Judge ad hoc Mensah).
143 Ibid., 727–728 [21] (Dissenting opinion of Judge Owada).
144 Ibid., [24] (Dissenting opinion of Judge Owada).
145 Ibid., 770–771 [17–19] (Declaration of Judge ad hoc Cot); ibid., 762–765 [2–8] (Declaration of Judge ad hoc Mensah).
146 Ibid., 764 [8] (Declaration of Judge ad hoc Mensah). See also T. Treves, "UNCLOS and Non-Party States before the International Court of Justice," in Carlo Espósito et al.

paragraph 8 as an expression of customary law. The provision institutes a specific procedure which is not accessible to non-member States. Article 76, paragraph 8, is thus *res inter alios acta* for Colombia."[147]

On September 16, 2013, Nicaragua filed an application instituting proceedings against Colombia, which was again based on its claim to a continental shelf beyond 200 nm. Colombia raised five preliminary objections to the Court's jurisdiction. The third and fifth preliminary objections put forward by Colombia are relevant for the present discussion. In the third objection, Colombia argued that Nicaragua's claim was barred by the principle of *res judicata*. In the fifth objection, Colombia argued that Nicaragua's claim was inadmissible because the CLCS has not made recommendations to Nicaragua with respect to its entitlement to the continental shelf beyond 200 nm.[148]

After establishing its jurisdiction over the dispute between Nicaragua and Colombia on the Pact of Bogotá,[149] the Court characterized Colombia's third objection as an objection to admissibility.[150] Considering whether subparagraph 3 of the operative clause of the judgment of the *Nicaragua* v. *Colombia I* case ("the 2012 judgment") constitutes *res judicata*, the Court found that the central question is whether it made a decision on the delimitation of the continental shelf beyond 200 nm from the Nicaraguan coast.[151] Key to this question is the interpretation of paragraph 129 of the 2012 judgment, in which the Court concluded that "Nicaragua, in the present proceedings, has not established that it has a continental margin that extends far enough to overlap with Colombia's 200-nautical-mile entitlement." The Court found that it did not engage with geological or geomorphological evidence of Nicaragua's continental shelf beyond 200 nm, nor did it analyze the substantive legal standards for Nicaragua to establish an entitlement vis-à-vis Colombia. On the contrary, what the Court emphasized in the 2012 judgment was the obligation of Nicaragua to

(eds.), *Oceans Law and Policy: 20 Years under UNCLOS* (Brill Nijhoff Publishers 2016), 374.

147 *Nicaragua* v. *Colombia I* (n 127), 771 [19] (Declaration of Judge ad hoc Cot).

148 See *Question of the Delimitation of the Continental Shelf between Nicaragua and Colombia beyond 200 Nautical Miles from the Nicaraguan Coast (Nicaragua* v. *Colombia) (Preliminary Objections) [2016] ICJ Rep 100, 109–110* [15].

149 See ibid., 123 [46].

150 Ibid., 123 [48].

151 See ibid., 125 [57].

submit information to the CLCS,[152] which was not fulfilled by Nicaragua at that time.

Based on this interpretation, the Court determined that it "did not take a decision on whether or not Nicaragua had an entitlement to a continental shelf beyond 200 nautical miles from its coast."[153] Instead, what the 2012 judgment decided was that "delimitation of the continental shelf beyond 200 nautical miles from the Nicaraguan coast was conditional on the submission by Nicaragua of information on the limits of its continental shelf beyond 200 nautical miles."[154] Since Nicaragua had filed a submission to the CLCS on June 24, 2013, the Court found that the condition imposed by the 2012 judgment had been fulfilled in the present case, and that Nicaragua's claim was not precluded by the *res judicata* principle.

As to Colombia's fifth objection regarding the role of the CLCS, the Court endorsed the conceptual distinction between delineation and delimitation and concluded that:

> [S]ince the delimitation of the continental shelf beyond 200 nautical miles can be undertaken independently of a recommendation from the CLCS, the latter is not a prerequisite that needs to be satisfied by a state party to UNCLOS before it can ask the Court to settle a dispute with another State over such a delimitation.[155]

The Court also rejected the other preliminary objections raised by Colombia and, as a result, found that it had jurisdiction over the delimitation request of Nicaragua and the claim was admissible.[156]

The Court's decision on the third preliminary objection was so controversial that it split the Court in two.[157] The split primarily stems from the two different readings of the ambiguities in the 2012 judgment, as summarized earlier. Whereas the majority of the 2016 judgment of the *Nicaragua* v. *Colombia II* case ("the 2016 judgment") read out of the 2012 judgment a procedural obligation on Nicaragua to file a submission to the CLCS, the dissenting judges found that the 2012 judgment had made a decision on the merits, rejecting Nicaragua's claim for its lack of

152 See ibid., 131 [82].
153 Ibid., 131–132 [83].
154 Ibid., 132 [85].
155 Ibid., 137 [114].
156 See ibid., 139–140 [126].
157 The operative clause on the rejection of Colombia's third preliminary objection was passed by the casting vote of the President. See ibid., 139 [126(1)(b)].

factual basis.[158] It is submitted that the 2016 judgment is correct to the extent that the 2012 judgment did not make a decision either on Nicaragua's entitlement to the continental shelf beyond 200 nm or the delimitation thereof, but it reached the right conclusion with a flawed reasoning.

There is no doubt that, as a matter of treaty law, there is no obligation on a coastal State to make a submission to the CLCS prior to the delimitation of the continental shelf beyond 200 nm. This finding is inconsistent with State practice and it also contradicts the Court's own finding that delineation and delimitation can be undertaken independently from each other. Moreover, Article 76(8) contains a three-step procedure of establishing the outer limits of the continental shelf, which includes the submission by a coastal State, the recommendations of the CLCS, and the eventual establishment of the outer limits of the continental shelf by the coastal State on the basis of such recommendations. As rightly pointed out by the dissenting judges, it is illogical and without textual support from Article 76(8) to consider that only the first step constituted a procedural bar to the delimitation of the continental shelf beyond 200 nm whereas the other two did not.[159] Besides, singling out submission to the CLCS left out the complexities of the delineation as a dialogue between the submitting State and the CLCS, for the CLCS may recommend the revision of the original submission. More importantly, even if a procedural obligation to file a submission prior to a request for delimitation existed, it is doubtful that it would be applicable between Nicaragua and Colombia, the latter being a non-party to UNCLOS.[160]

In addition, the phrasing that "Nicaragua has not established that it has a continental margin which overlaps with Colombia's 200-nm shelf" appears to require more than a procedural obligation to file a submission, because, in any event, filing a submission to the CLCS is not equivalent to *having proved* the existence or extent of the entitlement to the continental shelf beyond 200 nm.[161] As the example of Ascension Island shows,

[158] Ibid., 148 [20] (Joint Dissenting Opinion of Vice-President Yusuf, Judges Cançado Trindade, Xue, Gaja, Bhandari, Robinson and Judge ad hoc Brower); ibid., 189 [8] (Dissenting Opinion of Judge Donoghue).

[159] See *Nicaragua* v. *Colombia II* (Preliminary Objections) (n 148), 156 [50] (Joint Dissenting Opinion).

[160] See ibid., 201 [51] (Dissenting Opinion of Judge Donoghue); ibid., 211–214 [11–18] (Declaration of Judge Robinson).

[161] M. Lando, "Delimiting the Continental Shelf Beyond 200 Nautical Miles at the International Court of Justice: The *Nicaragua* v. *Colombia* Cases" (2017), 16 *Chinese JIL* 137, 153–154.

the CLCS may recommend that a coastal State is not entitled to a continental shelf beyond 200 nm. A submission to the CLCS is only procedural in nature, which is confirmed by the fact that, as generally agreed, if a coastal State does not submit information to the CLCS within the 10-year period, its rights over the continental shelf beyond 200 nm should not be affected.[162] Judge Gaja thus commented that "the basis of a claim concerning the delimitation of an extended continental shelf does not change because of a submission to the CLCS in respect of that shelf."[163] While a submission provides more detailed information than the preliminary obligation and therefore may constitute the basis for reaching a factual determination, it cannot be referred to as the decisive proof of the existence of the entitlement.

For these reasons, the dissenting judges believed that the Court had made a decision on the merit of Nicaragua's entitlement. According to them, the reference to the preliminary information does not necessarily imply that Nicaragua had a procedural obligation; it may instead be an indicator of the inadequacy of evidence supplied by Nicaragua to demonstrate the existence of its entitlement.[164] When Nicaragua's preliminary information was relied on by Nicaragua as evidence, it can be reasonably expected that such evidence was insufficient for the Court to reach a factual conclusion on Nicaragua's entitlement, since the preliminary information itself would not be considered by the CLCS either.[165] Moreover, the structure of the reasoning in the 2012 judgment faithfully reflects the two-step process of maritime delimitation in the jurisprudence: first the determination of overlapping entitlements and

[162] See International Law Association, "Report of Committee on Legal Issues of the Outer Continental Shelf," *Report of the Seventy-First Conference* (Berlin 2004), 814; A. G. Oude Elferink, "Article 76 of the LOSC on the Definition of the Continental Shelf: Questions Concerning Its Interpretation from a Legal Perspective" (2006), 21 *IJMCL* 269, 279; R. Wolfrum, "The Delimitation of the Outer Continental Shelf: Procedural Considerations," *liber amicorum Jean-Pierre Cot: Le procès international.* (Bruylant 2009), 357; F. Armas-Pfirter, "Submissions on the Outer Limit of the Continental Shelf: Practice to Date and Some Issues of Debate," in D. Vidas (ed.), *Law, Technology and Science for Oceans in Globalisation: IUU Fishing, Oil Pollution, Bioprospecting, Outer Continental Shelf* (Martinus Nijhoff Publishers 2010), 492.

[163] *Nicaragua* v. *Colombia II* (Preliminary Objections) (n 148), 202 (Declaration of Judge Gaja).

[164] See ibid., 200 [48] (Dissenting Opinion of Judge Donoghue).

[165] See *Nicaragua* v. *Colombia I* (n 127), 754 [12] (Separate Opinion of Judge Donoghue); ibid., 766 [11] (Declaration of Judge ad hoc Mensah).

second the division of the area of overlap.[166] If there was no entitlement or no overlapping entitlements, the question of delimitation simply would not arise, and consequently should be rejected.

Although carrying particular force, the opinion of the dissenting judges is not necessarily compatible with the legal reasoning of the 2012 judgment. The crucial factor in this respect is that the Court did not decide on the applicable law to determine Nicaragua's entitlement to the continental shelf beyond 200 nm vis-à-vis Colombia. How could the Court have determined the existence or the extent of Nicaragua's entitlement without first ascertaining the legal standards applicable between the parties? In fact, the parties have conflicting views regarding the customary status of the provisions of Article 76 on the establishment of the outer limits of the continental shelf,[167] and the Court explicitly stated that "it does not need to decide whether other provisions of Article 76 of UNCLOS form part of customary international law."[168] The existence and the extent of the continental shelf beyond 200 nm is a *legal* fact, which is to be determined by evaluating the geomorphological or geological evidence in accordance with the legal rules governing the definition of the continental shelf beyond 200 nm, either under Article 76 of UNCLOS or customary international law.

Had the 2012 judgment rejected Nicaragua's claim for the lack of factual certainty regarding the existence or the extent of its entitlement to the continental shelf beyond 200 nm, the *res judicata* force attached to this decision may prevent Nicaragua from claiming a continental shelf beyond 200 nm vis-à-vis Colombia subsequent to the judicial decision. Admittedly a preliminary question in this regard is whether the effect of the *res judicata* principle is substantive or procedural.[169] Nonetheless, the juxtaposition of Judge Greenwood's and Judge Donoghue's views is illustrative of the legal uncertainty that Nicaragua might encounter should the ICJ reject its claim to a continental shelf beyond 200 nm on its merits. As considered by Judge Greenwood,

[166] *Maritime Delimitation in the Black Sea (Romania v. Ukraine) [2009] ICJ Rep 61,89* [77]. See also *Nicaragua* v. *Colombia II* (Preliminary Objections) (n 148), 196–197 [35] (Dissenting Opinion of Judge Donoghue).

[167] See the written replies of Nicaragua and Colombia to Judge Bennuna's question, available at: http://www.icj-cij.org/en/case/124/other-documents.

[168] *Nicaragua* v. *Colombia I* (n 127), 666 [118].

[169] *Nicaragua* v. *Colombia II* (Preliminary Objections) (n 148), 178–179 [5] (Separate Opinion of Judge Greenwood).

> [I]f a court or tribunal, in a case between two States, determines that one of those States has no entitlement to a continental shelf in a particular area, international law does not permit that State thereafter to assert such an entitlement in that area vis-à-vis the other State party.[170]

In contrast, Judge Donoghue argued that, while the doctrine of *res judicata* denies Nicaragua a second chance to meet the burden of proof to demonstrate its entitlement in court, "it does not preclude Nicaragua from pursuing the delineation of the outer limits of its continental shelf within the framework of UNCLOS."[171] Even if one agrees with Judge Donoghue's view on the effect of *res judicata*, it is unlikely that such an option was open to Nicaragua unless Colombia and other relevant States withdrew their objections to the consideration of Nicaragua's submission by the CLCS.[172]

Notwithstanding the twists in the Court's reasoning in the 2016 judgment, the ICJ eventually partook in the approach adopted by the *Bay of Bengal* cases that distinguished delineation from delimitation. However, limited by the line of argumentation of the parties, the ICJ did not have opportunity to appreciate the circumstances of the *Nicaragua* v. *Colombia II* case further. The Court did not consider whether the conceptual distinction between delineation and delimitation was practically sustainable in the geographical context between Nicaragua and Colombia. In contrast with the *Bay of Bengal* cases and the *Ghana/Côte d'Ivoire* case, where the relevant parties share an adjacent coast, Nicaragua and Colombia are opposite to each other. To determine the area of overlapping entitlements, the Court would have to determine, at least approximately, Nicaragua's outer limits of the continental shelf. Similarly, to appreciate the merits of Nicaragua's claim that the boundary line should divide the area between Nicaragua's outer limits of the continental shelf and Colombia's 200 nm limits, the Court would in effect undertake the same work as the CLCS and might risk reaching different factual conclusions from the CLCS.[173] Likewise, the Court did not consider whether in this specific case the distinction between entitlement and delimitation, as purported by ITLOS in the *Bangladesh/*

170 Ibid.

171 Ibid., 199 [45] (Dissenting Opinion of Judge Donoghue).

172 See Note Verbale of Colombia, Costa Rica, Panama dated September 23, 2013 and Note Verbale of Colombia dated September 24, 2013, available at www.un.org/Depts/los/clcs_new/submissions_files/submission_nic_66_2013.htm.

173 See Busch (n 96), 344–345; *Nicaragua* v. *Colombia I* (n 127), 757 [23] (Separate Opinion of Judge Donoghue).

*Myanmar* case, would be tenable. Moreover, the Court had not addressed the factual certainty of the existence or the extent of the entitlement to the continental shelf of Nicaragua, although the 2012 judgment had alluded to the differences in the factual situations between *Nicaragua* v. *Colombia* and the *Bangladesh/Myanmar* case.[174]

Still, there are certain legal issues to be considered by the ICJ before it can actually delimit the continental shelf beyond 200 nm between Nicaragua and Colombia. The first question is, whether the remaining paragraphs of Article 76 form part of customary rules so that the Court could apply them to determine Nicaragua's entitlement to the continental shelf beyond 200 nm vis-à-vis Colombia.[175] More importantly, as between Nicaragua and Colombia, the key issue is whether a continental shelf beyond 200 nm may overlap with the 200-nm continental shelf of another State. Should the Court focus on this issue, the question of whether Nicaragua is entitled to a continental shelf beyond 200 nm may not be in need of an answer, and no question of delimitation will arise.

### 5 *Somalia* v. *Kenya* Case

In 2014, Somalia filed an application instituting proceedings against Kenya before the ICJ and requested the Court to determine "the complete course of the single maritime boundary dividing all the maritime areas appertaining to Somalia and to Kenya in the Indian Ocean, including in the continental shelf beyond 200 [nautical miles]."[176] Somalia sought to found the jurisdiction of the Court on the declarations made by the two parties pursuant to Article 36(2) of the Statute of the ICJ.[177] Kenya raised preliminary objections to the jurisdiction of the Court and to the admissibility of the Application. Kenya contended that the reservation attached to its optional clause declaration would apply, because, first, by signing a Memorandum of Understanding (MOU) that grants each other no-objection in respect of submissions to the CLCS, the two parties had agreed on a method of settlement of their maritime boundary dispute other than having recourse to the ICJ; second, since Kenya and Somalia are parties to UNCLOS, Part XV of UNCLOS, in particular the

[174] *Nicaragua* v. *Colombia I* (n 127), 668 [125].
[175] See Chapter 3, Section III.E.
[176] *Maritime Delimitation in the Indian Ocean (Somalia v. Kenya), Preliminary Objections, 2017 ICJ Rep 3,* 10 [11].
[177] See ibid., 9 [1].

Annex VII arbitration, constitutes "some other method or methods of settlement" within the meaning of its reservation.[178] As to admissibility of Somalia's claim, Kenya argued that Somalia instituted the proceedings in breach of the MOU and the "clean hands" doctrine prevented the claim from being admissible.[179]

Apparently, Kenya did not challenge the ICJ's competence to delimit the continental shelf beyond 200 nm. Instead, the case predominantly relates to the interpretation of whether the parties had agreed to a method of dispute settlement that precluded either party from resorting to the ICJ. Addressing Kenya's argument that negotiations on maritime delimitation can only be finalized after the recommendations of the CLCS have been received, the Court commented on the relationship between delineation and delimitation:

> A lack of certainty regarding the outer limits of the continental shelf, and thus the precise location of the endpoint of a given boundary in the area beyond 200 nautical miles, does not, however, necessarily prevent either the States concerned or the Court from undertaking the delimitation of the boundary *in appropriate circumstances* before the CLCS has made its recommendations.[180]

It is notable that the qualification "in appropriate circumstances" tends to circumscribe the conceptual distinction between delineation and delimitation. Eventually, the ICJ found that neither the MOU nor Part XV of UNCLOS fell within Kenya's reservation to its optional clause declaration,[181] and rejected the "clean hands" doctrine as a valid objection to the admissibility of the claim. The Court decided, therefore, that it had jurisdiction to entertain the Application filed by Somalia and the Application was admissible.[182]

Since Kenya did not challenge the Court's jurisdiction or the admissibility of the Application to delimit the continental shelf beyond 200 nm, it seems that, given the adjacent coastal relationship between Kenya and Somalia, the ICJ could delimit the continental shelf beyond 200 nm without prejudicing the establishment of the outer limits of the continental shelf, following the approach of the *Bay of Bengal* cases.

178 Ibid., 16–17 [32–33].
179 Ibid., 51 [139].
180 Ibid., 38 [94] (emphasis added).
181 Ibid., 51 [134].
182 Ibid., 53 [145(3)].

Nevertheless, one particularity about the *Somalia* v. *Kenya* case is that Kenya proposed to establish its outer limits of the continental shelf by invoking the Statement of Understanding Concerning a Specific Method to be used in Establishing the Outer Edge of the Continental Margin (Statement of Understanding), which was adopted in Annex II to the Final Act of UNCLOS III.[183] The Statement of Understanding responds to the concerns of Sri Lanka that the application of the two formulae under Article 76(4) of UNCLOS would result in inequity for the States in the southern part of the Bay of Bengal, and provides a specific method to establish the outer edge of the continental margin.[184] Article 3 of Annex II to UNCLOS provides that the CLCS shall make recommendations in accordance with Article 76 and the Statement of Understanding. As a result, the Statement of Understanding is considered to be on equal footing with other provisions of Article 76.[185]

However, since the Statement of Understanding requests the CLCS to apply the terms of the Statement of Understanding to "these States in the southern part of Bay of Bengal,"[186] it is not clear at first sight whether Kenya could apply the Statement of Understanding to establish its outer edge of the continental margin. Kenya argued that the Statement of Understanding should be applied as long as the special characteristics of the continental margin as envisaged by the text of the Statement of Understanding and the inequity resulted from the application of Article 76(4) were present, irrespective of the regions where such continental margins are located.[187] Sri Lanka, on the other hand, believed that only the States in the southern part of Bay of Bengal could invoke the Statement of Understanding.[188] To be sure, under Article 3 of Annex II to UNCLOS the CLCS is competent to determine if a State correctly applies the specific method contained in the Statement of Understanding. However, the *applicability* of the Statement of Understanding is a preliminary issue which precedes the application of the

[183] UN Doc. A/CONF.62/121 (October 27, 1982).

[184] See the Statement of Understanding; S. N. Nandan and S. Rosenne (eds.), *United Nations Convention on the Law of the Sea 1982: A Commentary, Volume II* (Martinus Nijhoff Publishers 1993), 859.

[185] See Busch (n 8), 194–195.

[186] Last paragraph of the Statement of Understanding.

[187] See Note Verbale of Kenya dated 30 April 2009 in reaction to Myanmar's submission (December 16, 2008), available at www.un.org/Depts/los/clcs_new/submissions_files/submission_mmr.htm.

[188] Note Verbale of Sri Lanka dated July 22, 2009, available at www.un.org/Depts/los/clcs_new/submissions_files/submission_ken_35_2009.htm.

Statement of Understanding and is thus beyond the competence of the CLCS.[189] Nevertheless, taking note of the differences of the views expressed by Sri Lanka and Kenya, the Commission acknowledged that "States, not the Commission, interpreted the Convention" and it instructed the subcommission to consider the submission made by Kenya on a scientific and technical basis under the provisions of article 76 of the Convention and the Statement of Understanding.[190]

Whether Kenya is entitled to invoke the Statement of Understanding is a legal interpretation issue that should be addressed by the ICJ in the *Somalia* v. *Kenya* case before it delimits the continental shelf beyond the 200 nm, as it underlies Kenya's entitlement to the continental shelf beyond 200 nm. What matters is not whether the physical continental margin of Kenya extends beyond 200 nm. Rather, Kenya should, in the first place, apply Article 76(4) to establish that its outer edge of the continental margin extends beyond 200 nm, and if the "test of appurtenance" under Article 76(4) fails, it is arguable that Kenya would not be entitled to a continental shelf beyond 200 nm. It is not obvious from the text of the Statement of Understanding that a State outside the southern part of Bay of Bengal can invoke the specific method contained therein. Nevertheless, one may also argue that it was because of the limit of knowledge that only the special characteristics of the Bay of Bengal were brought to the attention of UNCLOS III. As the concerns of Sri Lanka received considerable support,[191] and the Statement of Understanding is fairly specific about the conditions of its application, the objective and purpose of the Statement of Understanding might be interpreted to support a broader scope of its applicability. In a word, it is essential for the ICJ to determine the legal criteria that apply to determine the parties' entitlement to the continental shelf beyond 200 nm in the *Somalia v. Kenya* case if it decides to delimit the continental shelf beyond 200 nm.

### C *Towards a Contextualized Approach to the Competence of International Courts and Tribunals*

The review of the cases above has illustrated that various factors have featured in courts and tribunals' evaluation of their competence to

[189] Busch (n 8), 197–198.

[190] "Progress of work in the Commission on the Limits of the Continental Shelf (Thirty-eighth session, New York, 20 July–4 September 2015) (CLCS/90)," [19–21].

[191] Nandan and Rosenne (n 184), 859.

delimit the continental shelf beyond 200 nm prior to receiving recommendations of the CLCS. Notwithstanding the consistency reached in the jurisprudence that distinguishes delineation from delimitation, it is submitted that a more contextualized and case-specific approach to the competence of international courts and tribunals to delimit the continental shelf is preferable. Three considerations support this proposition. First, any case concerning a continental shelf beyond 200 nm arises in its own procedural and substantive framework, subject to the legal and factual relations between the relevant parties. To determine the jurisdiction and admissibility of such a claim, a court or tribunal must appreciate all the relevant factors particular to this specific context. Second, the conceptual distinction between delimitation and delineation based on the separateness between Article 76 and Article 83 has to be assessed against concrete factual and legal circumstances, because only in light of the specific circumstances can the relationship between delineation and delimitation *in that context* be spelled out. Finally, on many occasions the line of argumentation of the relevant parties to a large extent determines the scope of the issues analyzed by a court or a tribunal. One should therefore not lose sight of other potentially relevant factors that may impact on the competence of a court or tribunal. The following discussion will thus present the relevant factors that have been or should have been addressed in connection with the competence to delimit the continental shelf beyond 200 nm.

### 1 "Single Maritime Delimitation" and "Single Continental Shelf"

Empirically, the concepts of single maritime delimitation and single continental shelf were relied upon by the relevant tribunals to determine if the delimitation of the continental shelf beyond 200 nm fell within the scope of the Special Agreement signed by the parties or within the scope of the dispute, with a view to ascertaining the scope of jurisdiction.[192] In contrast, where the parties agree that the jurisdiction of a court or tribunal includes the delimitation of the continental shelf beyond 200 nm, neither the interpretation of a single maritime delimitation or reference to the single continental shelf is legally required. It is irrelevant to consider the legal connotation of single maritime delimitation in a case

[192] See L. D. M. Nelson, "Claims to the Continental Shelf Beyond the 200-Mile Limit," in C. Philipp (ed.), *Liber amicorum Günther Jaenicke – Zum 85. Geburtstag* (Springer 1998), 574–575.

such as the *Somalia* v. *Kenya* case, in which the applicant requests the ICJ to delimit a single maritime boundary dividing the territorial sea, the EEZ, and the continental shelf, including the continental shelf beyond 200 nm.[193] In fact, to interpret single maritime delimitation to mean a delimitation that simultaneously divides the continental shelf and the EEZ, as the *St. Pierre and Miquelon Arbitration* did, is simply incompatible with the desire of the parties to have a single line that delimits their territorial sea and the continental shelf beyond 200 nm in addition to the delimitation of the EEZ and the continental shelf up to 200 nm. In a similar vein, in the *Bay of Bengal* cases and the *Ghana/Côte d'Ivoire* case, it is practically unnecessary for the tribunals to refer to the concept of the single continental shelf because the parties agree that the jurisdiction of a court or tribunal includes the delimitation of the continental shelf beyond 200 nm.

As a result, the normative value of the concept of the single continental shelf and the single maritime delimitation is very limited in determining the competence of international courts or tribunals to delimit the continental shelf beyond 200 nm. Essentially, it is the ascertainment of the scope of the dispute submitted to the third-party dispute settlement that is crucial. The concept of the single continental shelf only serves a descriptive function to capture the continental shelf definition under Article 76,[194] and it is neutral to issues such as the existence or extent of the entitlement to the continental shelf.

### 2 Factual Certainty of the Entitlement to the Continental Shelf beyond 200 NM

It is submitted that international courts and tribunals should refrain from exercising jurisdiction over the delimitation of the continental shelf beyond 200 nm if the existence of the entitlement or overlapping entitlements is subject to "significant uncertainty."[195] As the review of the *Bay of Bengal* cases and the *Ghana/Côte d'Ivoire* case shows, the factual certainty of the existence of entitlement to the continental shelf beyond 200 nm of the parties underlies the tribunals' decisions to delimit the continental shelf beyond 200 nm.[196] In these three cases the factual

193 See Section III.B.5 above.

194 See B. Kunoy, "The Delimitation of an Indicative Area of Overlapping Entitlement to the Outer Continental Shelf" (2013), 83 *BYIL* 61, 66.

195 *Bangladesh/Myanmar* (n 90), 115 [443].

196 Similarly, the Newfoundland and Labrador and Nova Scotia Arbitration also acknowledged the certainty of the existence of the continental shelf beyond 200 nm. *Newfoundland and Labrador and Nova Scotia Arbitration* (n 53), [2.30].

certainty of the existence of the entitlement is established by two methods, one based on reference to uncontested scientific evidence, and the other on the parties' mutual agreement of each other's entitlement. Neither of the two methods have valid legal basis.

The *Bay of Bengal* cases relied on uncontested scientific evidence. Since the unique nature of the Bay of Bengal had been recognized during UNCLOS III, ITLOS in fact proceeded to the delimitation of the continental shelf beyond 200 nm on "a very narrow factual and legal ground."[197] It is unlikely the certainty of entitlement to the continental shelf beyond 200 nm will be present in other disputes.[198] Accordingly, as "delimitation presupposes an area of overlapping entitlements,"[199] it should be a general rule that a court or tribunal makes an independent assessment of the existence of entitlement to the continental shelf beyond 200 nm in accordance with Article 76 of UNCLOS. However, as the interpretation and application of Article 76 require the consideration of scientific and technical data, it is also sensible to consider that international judges may not be comfortable ruling on questions of fact by reference to geomorphological or geological evidence, which is beyond their professional experience.[200] As Judge Al-Khasawneh and Judge Simma in the *Pulp Mills* case pointed out: "The adjudication of disputes in which the assessment of scientific questions by experts is indispensable [...] requires an interweaving of legal process with knowledge and expertise that can only be drawn from experts properly trained to evaluate the increasingly complex nature of the facts put before the Court."[201] A court or tribunal may thus lack the expertise that is otherwise necessary in deciding a fact-intensive dispute. This is especially the case where the parties invoke conflicting scientific or technical evidence to justify their legal claims. The adversarial nature of the contentious proceeding poses further challenges of discharging the judicial function, and it is doubtful that a court or a tribunal is well-equipped to carry out

197 See T. Treves, "Law and Science in the Jurisprudence of the International Tribunal for the Law of the Sea," in H. N. Scheiber et al. (eds.), *Science, Technology, and New Challenges to Ocean Law* (Brill Nijhoff 2015), 26.

198 Busch (n 96), 335.

199 *Bangladesh/Myanmar* (n 90), 105 [397].

200 See D. Anderson, *Modern Law of the Sea: Selected Essays* (Martinus Nijhoff Publishers 2008), 573; M. M. Mbengue, "Scientific Fact-Finding by International Courts and Tribunals" (2012), 3 *JIDS* 509, 511.

201 *Pulp Mills on the River Uruguay (Argentina v. Uruguay) [2010] ICJ Rep 14, 110* [3] (Joint Dissenting Opinion of Judges Al-Khasawneh and Simma).

such exercises in the first place. These difficulties are effectively summarized by Judge Bhandari in the *Nicaragua* v. *Colombia II* case:

> [I]t is to be recalled that the CLCS is a specialized agency with a specific mandate to investigate and pronounce upon continental shelf claims. The Commission consists of 21 members who are world-renowned experts in such relevant fields as geology, geophysics and hydrology. By contrast, the judges of this Court can lay claim to no such expertise, and consequently the Court would necessarily have to rely on the testimony of expert witnesses in order to resolve Nicaragua's continental shelf claim at the merits phase of these proceedings. Not only would this constitute a regrettably inefficient use of valuable Court resources, but the nature of the adversarial process dictates that the Parties would bring witnesses most likely to advance their respective and competing claims, whose opinions could be very well at odds with those of the expert members of the CLCS. This, in turn, could potentially lead to the uneasy situation wherein the CLCS and the Court reach incompatible conclusions regarding Nicaragua's continental shelf claim.[202]

Therefore, to exercise jurisdiction over a case where the parties dispute heavily over the facts concerning the existence or the extent of the continental shelf beyond 200 nm, a court or a tribunal may fall into factual errors and make a decision that turns out to be at odds with the recommendations of the CLCS,[203] which as a result is also a failure to discharge its judicial function properly.[204]

It should also be stressed that the delimitation of the continental shelf beyond 200 nm is qualitatively different from contentious cases where scientific uncertainty can be overcome by adopting a precautionary approach,[205] because the former requires a positive decision on the existence (or not) of the entitlement and overlapping entitlements to

[202] See *Nicaragua* v. *Colombia II* (Preliminary Objections) (n 148), 205–206 [8] (Declaration of Judge Bhandari).

[203] See Churchill (n 86), 149–150.

[204] See M. Benzing, "Evidentiary Issues," in A. Zimmermann et al. (eds.), *The Statute of the International Court of Justice: A Commentary* (2nd ed., Oxford University Press 2012), 1236; A. Riddell, "Evidence, Fact-Finding, and Experts," in C. P. R. Romano et al. (eds.), *The Oxford Handbook of International Adjudication* (Oxford University Press 2013), 848–849.

[205] For instance, in the *Southern Bluefin Tuna* cases, ITLOS found that "although the Tribunal cannot conclusively assess the scientific evidence presented by the parties, it finds that measures should be taken as a matter of urgency to preserve the rights of the parties and to avert further deterioration of the southern bluefin tuna stock." *Southern Bluefin Tuna (New Zealand v. Japan; Australia v. Japan), Request for provisional orders, Order 27 August 1999, ITLOS Reports 1999 280, 296* [80]. See also Treves (n 197), 20.

the continental shelf beyond 200 nm as a precondition to delimitation, which must be drawn from the concrete evaluation of scientific and technical evidence.[206] This task may require courts or tribunals to deal with the determination of the FOS, the distinction between submarine ridges and submarine elevations, and the thickness of the sedimentary rocks, etc. which in themselves can be sometimes challenging for the CLCS as well.[207]

One may consider whether international courts or tribunals could resort to experts in the determination of the entitlement to the continental shelf beyond 200 nm in order to improve the accuracy and transparency of scientific evidence.[208] Despite the practical desirability and procedural feasibility of resort to experts, the underlying legal issue is whether a court or tribunal could make a decision on the entitlement or extent of the entitlement to the continental shelf beyond 200 nm in the light of the function of the CLCS. For instance, even if a court or tribunal has obtained expert opinion on the location of the outer limits of the continental shelf, it might still have to explain why it could substitute for the CLCS to determine the outer limits of the continental shelf, if the determination of the outer limits of the continental shelf are necessary for the task of maritime delimitation. Therefore, it is for a court or tribunal to decide, on a case-by-case approach, the appropriateness of involving experts in the delimitation process.

It has also been suggested that significant uncertainty around the existence or extent of the entitlement could be overcome through assistance from the CLCS. This essentially raises the question of whether and to what extent the CLCS can be involved in the delimitation of the continental shelf beyond 200 nm in a third-party dispute settlement forum. Kim argues that the role assigned to the CLCS by UNCLOS includes assisting international courts and tribunals to analyze contested

206 Nelson (n 192), 588.

207 Chapter 2, Section III.C.

208 For instance, according to the Statute of the International Court of Justice, the ICJ could resort to two types of experts, i.e., assessors (Article 30 (2)) and court-appointed experts (Article 50). See H. Thirlway, "Article 30," in A. Zimmermann et al. (eds.), *The Statute of the International Court of Justice: A Commentary* (2nd ed., Oxford University Press 2012), 528–529; C. J. Tams, "Article 50," in A. Zimmermann et al. (eds.), *The Statute of the International Court of Justice: A Commentary* (2nd ed., Oxford University Press 2012), 1288–1299; Lando (n 161), 157–159; X. Liao, "Evaluation of Scientific Evidence by International Courts and Tribunals in the Continental Shelf Delimitation Cases," (2017), 48 *ODIL* 136, 148–152.

scientific and technical data in the determination of the entitlement to the continental shelf beyond 200 nm.[209] Judge Ndiaye in the *Bangladesh/Myanmar* case proposed for a "preliminary ruling" procedure from the CLCS before a court or tribunal delimited the continental shelf beyond 200 nm.[210] Busch proposed that the CLCS could include in its Rules of Procedure provisions that address the relationship between judicial decisions and the work of the CLCS, such as a speedier procedure that endorses the decision of a court or tribunal on the entitlement to the continental shelf beyond 200 nm, provided that the considerations and findings by the court or tribunal are in accordance with Article 76(8) of UNCLOS.[211] Other authors examined the possibility for a court or tribunal to include individual members of the CLCS as court-appointed experts.[212]

It might be difficult, however, to implement these proposals given the current legal framework of UNCLOS and the Rules of Procedure of the CLCS. That the mandate of the CLCS consists of assisting an international court or tribunal may go beyond a proper interpretation of Article 3 of Annex II to UNCLOS, which limits the mandate of the CLCS to giving recommendations and providing scientific and technical assistance to *coastal States*. Whereas Article 3(2) of Annex II provides that the CLCS may cooperate with the International Hydrographic Organization and other competent international organizations, the objective of such cooperation is to assist in "discharging the Commission's responsibilities," therefore its interpretation is subject to the limited mandate provided for under Article 3(1) of Annex II. The "preliminary ruling" procedure finds no legal basis under UNCLOS, and in fact there has been no recourse to such procedure in international law. As Judge Ndiaye admitted, the "preliminary ruling" procedure is a concept in European Union law, and it allows national courts to seek views from the Court of Justice of the European Union with the aim of "ensuring legal certainty through the uniform application of Community

209 H.-J. Kim, "La délimitation de la frontière maritime dans le golfe du Bengale: courir deux lièvres à la fois avec succès dans le règlement de la délimitation maritime" (2012), 58 *AFDI* 443, 459–460.

210 See *Bangladesh/Myanmar* (n 90), 179–183 [98–120] (Separate Opinion of Judge Ndiaye).

211 See Busch (n 8), 388–389.

212 See Liao (n 208), 152; G. Vega-Barbosa, "The Admissibility of Outer Continental Shelf Delimitation Claims Before the ICJ Absent a Recommendation by the CLCS" (2018) 49 *ODIL* 103, 112.

law."[213] It should be pointed out that there is no comparable vertical relationship between the CLCS and the tribunals established by UNCLOS, therefore a "preliminary ruling" from the CLCS is essentially *lex ferenda*.

As to requesting expert opinion from the CLCS, either by appointing individual members of the CLCS as court-appointed experts or by entrusting the CLCS the task of carrying out an enquiry, this might encounter a number of legal and legitimacy problems. The Rules of Procedure of the CLCS require the consideration of submissions on a first-come, first-served basis in that the submissions will be queued in the order they are received.[214] If a court or tribunal was seized by the parties to delimit their continental shelf beyond 200 nm when none of their submissions were ready to be considered by the CLCS, it would be unfair for other States whose submissions are queuing in the line if the court or tribunal requests the CLCS to spend their time on informing the dispute settlement procedure. This consideration carries particular weight because, currently, the waiting time between the making of a submission and the establishment of a subcommission is approximately 10 years.[215] The workload of the CLCS, which has already exceeded what was expected of it during UNCLOS III,[216] would require a compelling justification for the CLCS to be involved in missions that have no direct legal basis under UNCLOS. Furthermore, in cases where the CLCS had already been barred from considering the submission(s) of the parties to the dispute due to the objection raised under Rule 46 of the Rules of Procedure, would not seeking advice from the CLCS about the parties' entitlement place the Commission in a position to overstep its own Rules of Procedure?[217] In addition, expenses and confidentiality issues should not be overlooked when analyzing the feasibility of seeking expert opinion from the CLCS.[218] Finally, one may ask if a court or tribunal may

213 *Bangladesh/Myanmar* (n 90), 179 [100] (Separate Opinion of Judge Ndiaye).

214 Rule 51 of the Rules of Procedure.

215 Letter dated April 5, 2019 from the Chair of the CLCS addressed to the President of the ninth SPLOS (UN Doc. SPLOS/29/April 6, 8, 2019) [11].

216 See L. Parson, "Observations on the Article 76 Process: Coastal States' Submissions and the Work Outstanding for the Commission on the Limits of the Continental Shelf," in J. Barrett and R. Barnes (eds.), *Law of the Sea: UNCLOS as a Living Treaty* (BIILC 2016), 125.

217 Vega-Barbosa (n 212), 112.

218 Article 2(5) of Annex II to UNCLOS and Annex II to the Rules of Procedure of the CLCS.

order the parties to the dispute to withdraw their objection to each other's submission in order to allow the CLCS to examine their entitlement to the continental shelf beyond 200 nm. This proposition has to be considered in the light of the preceding discussion. In particular, even if it was desirable, it would not interrupt the "first-come-first-served" rule of the CLCS to review the submissions. Besides, the practical value of such a proposition might be limited where the submissions of the parties were objected to by third parties to the dispute.[219]

To proceed to the delimitation of the continental shelf beyond 200 nm by relying on the mutual agreement of the parties of each other's entitlement is even more legally precarious. First, by taking note of the parties' agreement, the tribunals in fact avoided making an independent assessment of the facts in accordance with the applicable legal standards. The agreement between the parties can hardly be a substitute for a court or tribunal's own examination of evidence,[220] inasmuch as the parties' agreement on the customary status of some treaty rules does not prevent the court or tribunal from having to ascertain the status of these rules and their applicability to the States itself.[221] Second, in a case such as *Somalia* v. *Kenya*, to proceed on the basis of the parties' agreement on the existence of overlapping entitlements – should there be any – would bypass the most critical question, namely, the applicability of the Statement of Understanding as the legal standard governing the establishment of one party's entitlement to the continental shelf beyond 200 nm.

Where one of the parties has received the recommendations from the CLCS, the factual certainty of the existence of overlapping entitlements would be significantly enhanced if the parties share an adjacent coastal relationship and the relevant party can prove that the continental margin has similar geomorphological or geological characteristics, such as in the *Ghana/Côte d'Ivoire* case. The recommendations of the CLCS are the most authoritative evidence that one party can use to demonstrate its entitlement to the continental shelf beyond 200 nm and it is exactly for this reason that a court or tribunal should be cautious about the propriety

219 For example, Nicaragua's submission to the CLCS (June 24, 2013) was objected to by Costa Rica and Panama, in addition to Colombia. See Note Verbale of Colombia, Costa Rica, Panama dated September 23, 2013, available at www.un.org/Depts/los/clcs_new/submissions_files/submission_nic_66_2013.htm.

220 Lando (n 161), 162–163.

221 *Military and Paramilitary Activities in and against Nicaragua (Nicaragua v. United States of America) (Merits) [1986] ICJ Rep 14, 97-98* [184].

of exercising jurisdiction of the continental shelf beyond 200 nm in the absence of the recommendations from the CLCS. It is recalled that in the *St. Pierre and Miquelon Arbitration*, the Court of Arbitration declined jurisdiction partly because of deficiency in the factual basis of the French claim.[222] This factor, though not present in the *Bay of Bengal* cases and the *Ghana/Côte d'Ivoire* case, should not be ignored in future delimitation cases concerning the continental shelf beyond 200 nm. Admittedly, ITLOS's formulation of "significant uncertainty" may not be wholly satisfactory due to its inherent ambiguities as to what degree of uncertainty there should be for a court or tribunal to decline the exercise of jurisdiction. However, the certainty of the entitlement is essentially a question of fact, to be ascertained under applicable legal rules. Therefore, it is a matter to be addressed in the concrete circumstances of a given case.

### 3 The Relationship between Delineation and Delimitation

It should not be forgotten that there are several unique circumstances in the *Bay of Bengal* cases that sustain the practical distinction between delineation and delimitation. To start with, Bangladesh and India, as well as Bangladesh and Myanmar, have an adjacent coastal relationship, thus the lateral delimitation of maritime boundaries does not require the identification of the seaward extent of the overlapping entitlements between parties. As a result, the delimitation would not preclude the CLCS's examination of the outer limits of the respective party. More importantly, the existence of the parties' entitlements to the continental shelf beyond 200 nm is not subject to uncertainty or dispute, with which the CLCS is highly likely to agree. To make things easier for the tribunals, the area subject to delimitation in the *Bay of Bengal* cases is also situated far from the Area, and the risk of prejudicing the rights of the international community did not arise.[223] Clearly, the more one relates to the specific circumstances of the *Bay of Bengal* cases, the more one realizes their exceptional character.

In particular, the distinction between delineation and delimitation is tenable only to the extent that the determination of overlapping entitlements would not require the establishment of the outer limits of the continental shelf, which is a matter to be assessed each and every time in

[222] See *St. Pierre and Miquelon Arbitration* (n 58), 1172 [80-81].
[223] See *Bangladesh/Myanmar* (n 90), 97 [368].

a given geographical context. As a result, to understand the interaction between delineation and delimitation one cannot ignore the role played by the determination of the entitlement to the continental shelf beyond 200 nm. In this respect as well, the distinction between entitlement and delineation made by ITLOS should also be taken as a case-specific observation.

In fact, the coastal relationship between coastal States is an important factor that substantiates the distinction between delineation and delimitation. Where coastal States share an adjacent coastal relationship, a court or tribunal can determine the entitlement of each party by determining that the outer edge of the continental margin extends beyond 200 nm in accordance with Article 76(4), without clarifying the seaward limits of the continental shelf. Admittedly this exercise overlaps with the function of the CLCS in the delineation of the outer limits for it is essentially the "test of appurtenance" provided for in the Scientific and Technical Guidelines of the CLCS.[224] Nevertheless, it would not prejudice the function of the CLCS to the extent that the factual certainty of the outer edge of the continental margin extending beyond 200 nm can be established, otherwise it would be a case where courts or tribunals should refrain from exercising jurisdiction for lack of certainty of the existence of the entitlement. Once the existence of the overlapping entitlements is established, the boundary line can be drawn without a precise endpoint, and can be described as extending "until it reaches the area where the rights of third States may be affected,"[225] or "until it reaches the outer limits of the continental shelf" as established in accordance with international law.[226] The former formulation could also accommodate the situation where the Area might be affected.

In contrast, between opposite coasts, the relationships between entitlement and delineation and between delineation and delimitation are subject to greater complexities. Geomorphological or geological circumstances of the seabed play a more significant role in ascertaining the existence or scope of overlapping entitlements. In State practice, the continental shelf beyond 200 nm of two opposite States may be part of a continuous continental margin that is shared by the relevant parties, as

[224] *Scientific and Technical Guidelines of the Commission on the Limits of the Continental Shelf (13 May 1999, Doc. CLCS/11)* [2.2].

[225] *Bangladesh/Myanmar* (n 90), 132 [506(6)].

[226] *Ghana/Côte d'Ivoire* (n 92), [660(3)].

in the Loop Hole between Norway and Russia.[227] Under such circumstances the two States may proceed to delimitation without knowing the exact extent of each other's entitlement. This would be essentially similar with the situation between two adjacent States, as application of Article 76(4) alone could determine the existence of overlapping entitlements. In other situations, the area of overlapping entitlements is determined on the basis of the parties' proposed outer limits of the continental shelf. This is the case for Denmark (Greenland) and Iceland.[228] In a case such as *Nicaragua* v. *Colombia*, it is reasonable to expect that the outer limits of the continental shelf of Nicaragua have to be ascertained in order to determine the area of overlap. However, should the ICJ proceed to delimit the area of overlap between Nicaragua and Colombia on the basis of a decision on the location of Nicaragua's outer limits of the continental shelf, the maritime boundary decided by the Court may not be adjusted if the CLCS recommended differently from the ICJ, given the principle of *res judicata*. This is in sharp contrast with the 2013 Denmark (Greenland)–Iceland Agreed Minutes, which allow for adjustment of the provisional delimitation line.[229] Therefore, a maritime boundary decided by a court or tribunal between two opposite States is subject to a higher risk of being at odds with the recommendations of the CLCS.[230] What follows is that a continental shelf delimitation beyond 200 nm effected by an international court or tribunal is more likely to prejudice the parties' rights to delineate their outer limits or assert their entitlement before the CLCS, as it might preclude the examination of the proposed outer limits of the continental shelf by the CLCS.

Moreover, delimiting the continental shelf beyond 200 nm between two opposite States without first ascertaining the accurate area of overlapping entitlements may also fail the objective of maritime delimitation to achieve an equitable solution. In the *Nicaragua* v. *Colombia I* case, Nicaragua proposed that the Court could define the boundary as "the median line between the outer edge of Nicaragua's continental shelf fixed in accordance with UNCLOS Article 76 and the outer limit of Colombia's

[227] See "Summary of Recommendations to Norway in respect of Areas in the Arctic Ocean, the Barents Sea and the Norwegian Sea adopted on 27 March 2009," [20], available at www.un.org/Depts/los/clcs_new/submissions_files/nor06/nor_rec_summ.pdf.

[228] See paragraph 5 of the 2013 Denmark (Greenland)–Iceland Agreed Minutes, Magnússon (n 18), 5270.

[229] Section II.A above.

[230] See *Nicaragua* v. *Colombia I* (n 127), 757 [23] (Separate opinion of Judge Donoghue).

200-mile zone."[231] Although this formula attempts to allow the CLCS to function after the delimitation, it is doubtful that this formula could lead to an equitable delimitation. As pointed out by Judge Donoghue, this formula proposed to use a median line "without an appreciation of the size of the area to be delimited and without a factual basis to consider any circumstances calling for adjustment of the median line or disproportionality."[232] The assessment of the equity of a delimitation result is an exercise by reference to the overall geography,[233] which includes the area of overlapping entitlements. As a result, without an accurate determination of the area of overlapping entitlements it will be difficult to assess the relevance of other circumstances and the weight accorded to each circumstance in the pursuit of an equitable solution.[234]

Accordingly, the conceptual distinction between delineation and delimitation may not always correspond to the actual interplay of these two processes. Sometimes, especially between opposite coasts, the relationship between entitlement, delineation, and delimitation is inextricable, because determination of the entitlement is integral to both the delineation procedure and the delimitation process. As a result, the "delineation–delimitation" dichotomy should be more accurately presented as the "entitlement–delineation–delimitation" trilogy. The competence of international courts and tribunals to delimit the continental shelf beyond 200 nm cannot be rightly established without fully appreciating the conceptual and factual role that the determination of entitlement plays in the interaction between delineation and delimitation.

### 4 The Impasse in the Delineation Procedure

A final factor that has played a role in the tribunals' decision to proceed with the delimitation of the continental shelf beyond 200 nm in the *Bay of Bengal* cases is the impasse in the delineation procedure before the CLCS. As ITLOS observed, it has an obligation to adjudicate the dispute of the continental shelf beyond 200 nm, otherwise "it would be contrary

231 Ibid., 669 [128].

232 Ibid., 755 [15] (Separate Opinion of Judge Donoghue).

233 See *Black Sea* (n 166), 129 [213].

234 *Nicaragua* v. *Colombia II* (Preliminary Objections) (n 148), 202–203 (Declaration of Judge Gaja). See also A. G. Oude Elferink, "ITLOS's Approach to the Delimitation of the Continental Shelf Beyond 200 Nautical Miles in the Bangladesh/Myanmar Case: Theoretical and Practical Difficulties," in R. Wolfrum et al. (eds.), *Contemporary Developments in International Law: Essays in Honour of Budislav Vukas* (Brill 2015), 236.

to the object and purpose of the Convention not to resolve the existing impasse,"[235] and the parties "may be unable to benefit fully from their rights over the continental shelf."[236] This view was also invoked by Nicaragua in the *Nicaragua* v. *Colombia II* case,[237] though the ICJ did not comment on this point.

The validity of these observations has been questioned. As pointedly observed by Oude Elferink, UNCLOS allows States parties to exclude maritime delimitation disputes from the compulsory dispute settlement mechanisms, which may in practice result in prolonged absence of a boundary and the continuing existence of a dispute.[238] The practical result would be the same with the deadlock in the delineation procedure, as the parties cannot benefit from the certainty of their continental shelf rights. Furthermore, if a dispute of delimiting the continental shelf beyond 200 nm is submitted to a court or a tribunal while the parties' submissions are on the waiting list of the CLCS without an objection being raised, would the "practical impasse" argument lose relevance at all?[239] Indeed, it is not likely that the "impractical impasse" argument is tenable in such a case because the delineation procedure is in perfect operation.

In fact, as will be further elaborated in the next section, an impasse is reached mainly because of the invocation of the Rules of Procedure of the CLCS by one State to object to the consideration of another State's submission. In contrast with the view that by delimiting the continental shelf beyond 200 nm a court or a tribunal can remove the obstacle to the work of the CLCS, it is found that as long as coastal States are empowered to block the delineation process under the Rules of Procedure, there is a persistent risk of impasse, even if the delimitation disputes have been settled. As a matter of fact, with the judgment of the *Bangladesh/ Myanmar* case at hand, Bangladesh still requested the Commission not to establish a subcommission to consider Myanmar's submission because

235 *Bangladesh/Myanmar* (n 90), 102 [392].

236 Ibid.

237 *Nicaragua* v. *Colombia II* (Preliminary Objections) (n 148), 126 [104].

238 A. G. Oude Elferink, "Paragraph 5(a) of Annex I to the Rules of Procedure of the Commission on the Limits of the Continental Shelf: Solution to a Problem or Problem without a Solution?," in M. H. Nordquist et al. (eds.), *Legal Order in the World's Oceans: UN Convention on the Law of the Sea* (Brill Nijhoff 2017), 311.

239 See Ø. Jensen, "Maritime Boundary Delimitation Beyond 200 Nautical Miles: The International Judiciary and the Commission on the Limits of the Continental Shelf" (2015), 84 *Nordic JIL* 580, 590.

in its view "the circumstances which led to the postponement of the consideration of Myanmar's submission continue to exist."[240] One should be reminded that it was Bangladesh, not Myanmar, that availed itself of the opportunity to block the consideration of Myanmar's submission in the first place.[241]

To conclude, a range of factors have influenced the courts or tribunals' decision to proceed (or not) to the delimitation of the continental shelf beyond 200 nm before the parties receive recommendations from the CLCS. Which factor(s) has a more direct or decisive role is, however, a question subject to the specific circumstances of a particular case. It is hoped that the preceding discussion has demonstrated the inadequacy of the conceptual distinction between delineation and delimitation to capture the dynamics of the interaction between the two processes. In this connection, it is necessary to recall the observation of ITLOS that "the determination of whether an international court or tribunal should exercise its jurisdiction depends on the procedural and substantive circumstances of each case."[242] This statement cautions against developing general ideas arising out of case-specific contexts.

## IV Resolving the Impasse in Delineation and Delimitation

States have availed themselves of the opportunities offered by the Rules of Procedure of the CLCS to object to other States' submissions, thus blocking, in whole or in part, the establishment of the outer limits of the continental shelf of other States. As a comprehensive study shows, States have indicated a range of diverse reasons when they objected to the consideration of other States' submissions.[243] Among them, maritime delimitation disputes and territorial disputes account for the major reasons for objection.[244] States also objected to other States' submissions on the basis of interpretation and application of UNCLOS provisions, such as Article 7, Article 76, and Article 121(3) (see Appendix 3).

240 See Note Verbale of Bangladesh's dated on October 22, 2015, in which Bangladesh objected to the Commission's consideration of Myanmar's amended submission (July 30, 2015), available at www.un.org/Depts/los/clcs_new/submissions_files/mmr08/2012_09_30_BGD_NV_UN.pdf.

241 *Bangladesh/Myanmar* (n 90), 101–102 [387–388].

242 Ibid., 101 [384].

243 See Busch (n 8), 121–127.

244 Ibid., 130.

Different views have been expressed with regard to the legitimacy of the de facto veto allowed under the Rules of Procedure of the CLCS. For some authors, the positive effect of this procedure is that it enables States to intervene so that they will not be deemed to have acquiesced to a position revealed in the submission of another State.[245] It also reflects the Commission's awareness of its own limitations as a scientific and technical body, which is however situated and operates in a "political world." As a result, the procedure created by the Rules of Procedure helps the Commission to attune itself to the politics involved in the establishment of the outer limits of the continental shelf.[246] Other authors, however, disapprove of veto power.[247] Oude Elferink argues that two interpretations may apply to paragraph 5(a) of Annex I to the Rules of Procedure. One is that prejudice might result from the consideration by the Commission of a submission, while the other is that no actions taken by the CLCS in its consideration of a submission can result in such prejudice.[248] He further argues that the latter interpretation is more advantageous and the CLCS should amend its Rules of Procedure and delete paragraph 5(a) of Annex I to the Rules of Procedure.[249]

It is submitted that the applicability of the procedure under paragraph 5(a) of Annex I to the Rules of the Procedure should be determined by distinguishing different legal bases invoked by the interested States to block the consideration of other States' submissions. As a point of departure, the CLCS is not competent to interpret or apply the provisions of UNCLOS other than Article 76 or the Statement of Understanding, and the CLCS has no role in settling disputes between States.[250] However,

[245] S.-T. Gau, "Third Party Intervention in the Commission on the Limits of the Continental Shelf Regarding a Submission Involving a Dispute" (2009), 40 *ODIL* 61, 74.

[246] See McDorman (n 3), 301.

[247] Serdy (n 31), 362.

[248] See Oude Elferink (n 238), 312.

[249] Ibid., 317–318.

[250] A. G. Oude Elferink, "The Continental Shelf beyond 200 NM: The Relationship between the CLCS and Third Party Dispute Settlement," in A. G. Oude Elferink and D. R. Rothwell (eds.), *Oceans Management in the 21st Century: Institutional Frameworks and Responses* (Martinus Nijhoff Publishers 2004), 123. For a different view, see E. D. Brown, *Sea-Bed Energy and Minerals: The International Legal Regime* (Martinus Nijhoff Publishers 1992), 31; S. Karagiannis, "Observations sur la Commission des Limites du Plateau Continental" (1994), 8 Espaces et ressources maritimes 163, 167–168; E. Beigzadeh, "La Commission des Limites du Plateau Continental" (2000), 5 *Annuaire du Droit de la Mer* 71, 76; L. D. M. Nelson, "The Continental Shelf: Interplay of Law and Science, " in N. Ando, E. McWhinney and R. Wolfrum (eds.), *Liber Amicorum Judge Shigeru Oda, Volume II* (Kluwer Law International 2002), 1238;

it does not follow that whatever the Commission does is not capable of prejudicing other States' rights or positions in the interpretation and application of UNCLOS provisions. If an interested party challenges the very existence of the entitlement of the continental shelf beyond 200 nm for reasons other than interpretation of Article 76 of UNCLOS, the Commission should act with caution lest its action prejudices the interests or rights of other States.

Take the territorial disputes and the disputes concerning Article 121 (3) as examples. According to the principle that the land dominates the sea, it is territorial sovereignty that determines a coastal State's entitlement to establish the outer limits of the continental shelf beyond 200 nm.[251] If the CLCS considers a submission based on contested territory, it would prejudice the rights of the other claimant State(s) because its work should have been grounded in the fact that the submitting State was *the* coastal State that was entitled to make such submissions. Therefore, territorial disputes cast doubt on the question of "which is the coastal State" that is entitled to initiate the delineation procedure in accordance with Article 76(8).[252] The consideration and qualification by the CLCS of a submission in such a situation may be understood as endorsing the position of the submitting State, and therefore can be perceived as prejudicial to the other claimants. Similarly, Article 121(3) also relates to the legal basis of the entitlement to the continental shelf beyond 200 nm, as it provides that "rocks which cannot sustain human habitation or economic life of their own shall have no exclusive economic zone or continental shelf." Article 121(3) thus concerns the legal capacity for a maritime feature to generate an entitlement to the continental shelf.

Surya P. Subedi, "Problems and Prospects for the Commission on the Limits of the Continental Shelf in Dealing with Submissions by Coastal States in Relation to the Ocean Territory beyond 200 Nautical Miles" (2011), 26 *IJMCL* 413, 429–430.

251 See *Aegean Sea Continental Shelf (Greece v. Turkey) [1978] ICJ Rep 3, 36* [86].

252 In the *Chagos Marine Protected Area Arbitration*, Mauritius requested the Annex VII Arbitral Tribunal to adjudge and declare that, *inter alia*, "the United Kingdom is not entitled to declare an 'MPA' or other maritime zones because it is not the 'coastal State' within the meaning of *inter alia* Articles 2, 55, 56 and 76 of the Convention." The Arbitral Tribunal found that this submission of Mauritius is "properly characterized as relating to land sovereignty over the Chagos Archipelago. The Parties' differing views on the 'coastal State' for the purposes of the Convention are simply one aspect of this larger dispute." As a result, the Arbitral Tribunal found itself without jurisdiction to address this submission because it does not concern the interpretation and application of UNCLOS. See *Chagos Marine Protected Area Arbitration (Mauritius v. United Kingdom), (2015) XXXI RIAA 359* [212] and [221].

When Japan proposed to establish its outer limits of the continental shelf on the basis of Oki-no-Tori Shima, its legal status was questioned by China and the Republic of Korea.[253] Should Oki-no-Tori Shima be a rock under Article 121(3), Japan would not be entitled to establish the outer limits of the continental shelf on this basis. In this respect, the interpretation and application of Article 121(3) precede the application of Article 76, hence are indispensable for the CLCS to make relevant recommendations.[254] Had the Commission issued recommendations in respect of Oki-no-Tori Shima on the assumption that it was a fully entitled island,[255] its recommendations may have been based on a precarious legal basis.

On the contrary, if States raised objections to other States' submissions out of concerns relating to the implications of the application of Article 76 of UNCLOS for maritime delimitation, the use of paragraph 5(a) of Annex I to the Rules of Procedure may run the risk of impeding the effective operation of the CLCS. It should be emphasized that Article 76 (10) provides the legal basis for the relationship between the delineation and delimitation of the continental shelf beyond 200 nm, and the Rules of Procedure adopted by the CLCS should not be implemented in a manner inconsistent with the text or the object and purpose of Article 76(10).

The de facto veto power created by the Rules of Procedure where a maritime delimitation dispute exists may frustrate the object and purpose of Article 76(8) and Article 76(10).[256] The objective and purpose of Article 76(10) is to guarantee that the delineation process does not prejudice coastal States' positions or legal rights in relation to other States on matters of delimitation. This is irrespective of whether a dispute

[253] See Note Verbale of China dated on February 6, 2009 and Note Verbale of Republic of Korea dated on February 27, 2009, available at www.un.org/Depts/los/clcs_new/submissions_files/submission_jpn.htm.

[254] S.-T. Gau, "Recent Decisions by the Commission on the Limits of the Continental Shelf on Japan's Submission for Outer Continental Shelf" (2012), 11 *Chinese JIL* 487, 492.

[255] The CLCS instructed the subcommission to consider the full submission of Japan, but eventually decided not to take action to make recommendations on the part relating to the Oki-no-Tori Shima. See the Statement by the Chairman of the Commission on the Limits of the Continental shelf on the Progress of Work in the Commission, Twenty-fourth session (UN Doc. CLCS/64, October 1, 2009) [26]; "Summary of Recommendations to Japan adopted on 19 April 2012" [20], available at www.un.org/Depts/los/clcs_new/submissions_files/jpn08/com_sumrec_jpn_fin.pdf.

[256] See Ø. Jensen, *The Commission on the Limits of the Continental Shelf: Law and Legitimacy* (Martinus Nijhoff Publishers 2014), 65; Serdy (n 31), 366.

exists between the coastal States. It follows that, as long as the CLCS is applying Article 76 for purposes of ascertaining the existence and the outer limits of the continental shelf beyond 200 nm, by definition nothing it does is capable of bringing about such prejudice.[257] As a result, the invocation of paragraph 5(a) of Annex I to the Rules of Procedure in cases concerning maritime delimitation disputes is not legally necessary, but rather unwarrantedly impedes the function of the CLCS. As argued by Jensen, under Article 76(8) the Commission *shall* issue recommendations to coastal States, and the "prior consent" rule is thus incompatible with the obligation of the CLCS in accordance with Article 76.[258] The practical effect of paragraph 5(a) of Annex I to the Rules of Procedure is the creation of an exception to the CLCS's obligation to issue recommendations, and it is legally questionable whether the CLCS is competent to do so.[259]

More importantly, "questions of delimitation" under Article 76(10) and "disputes" under Annex I to the Rules of Procedure are not identical.[260] Under international law, a dispute is "a disagreement on a point of law or fact, a conflict of legal views or of interests" between parties.[261] In order for a dispute to exist, "[i]t must be shown that the claim of one party is positively opposed by the other."[262] Yet, coastal States may disagree over whether a dispute exists. It is not uncommon that States in their submissions deny the existence of any dispute, whereas diplomatic notes sent by other interested parties indicate otherwise.[263] The

257 Serdy (n 31), 364.

258 See Jensen (n 256), 66–68. See also K. B. Lee, "Should the Invocation of Paragraph 5(a) of Annex I to the CLCS Rules of Procedure Result in an Automatic Deferral of the Consideration of a Submission?" (2014), 13 *Chinese JIL* 605, 618–619.

259 See Busch (n 8), 98–99.

260 See Serdy (n 31), 362.

261 *Mavrommatis Palestine Concessions (Greece v. United Kingdom), Judgment on Jurisdiction [1924] PCIJ Rep, Series A*, 11; *Obligations concerning Negotiations relating to Cessation of the Nuclear Arms Race and to Nuclear Disarmament (Marshall Islands v. United Kingdom), Preliminary Objections [2016] ICJ Rep, 833,849* [37].

262 *South West Africa (Ethiopia v. South Africa; Liberia v. South Africa), Preliminary Objections [1962] ICJ Rep 319*, 328.

263 For instance, Myanmar in its submission states that "the subject of this submission is not subject to any dispute between Myanmar and other States," but Bangladesh believed that "[t]he unresolved delimitation in the Bay of Bengal is [. . .] to be considered as a dispute for the purposes of Rule 46 of the Rules, and of Annex I thereto." See "Executive summary of Myanmar's submission (16 December 2008)" and Note Verbale of Bangladesh dated on July 23, 2009, available at www.un.org/Depts/los/clcs_new/submissions_files/submission_mmr.htm.

legal criterion in this regard is that "[w]hether there exists an international dispute is a matter for objective determination. The mere denial of the existence of a dispute does not prove its non-existence."[264] It is beyond doubt that the CLCS, as a scientific and technical body, lacks competence to decide whether a dispute exists, which is in essence a legal question.[265] As recognized by the CLCS, "the competence with respect to matters regarding disputes which may arise in connection with the establishment of the outer limits of the continental shelf rests with States."[266]

Although "in cases of a dispute" seems to connote a narrower scope than "questions of delimitation," in practice paragraph 5(a) of Annex I to the Rules of Procedure may be invoked inasmuch as there are merely different views of the relevant parties. The CLCS also acknowledged that Annex I to the Rules of Procedure "dealt with the complex issue of how the Commission should treat possible submissions containing areas under actual or *potential* delimitation dispute."[267] As a result, the threshold of paragraph 5(a) of the Annex I to the Rules of Procedure can be much lower than a judicial determination of the existence of a dispute.[268] The practice of the CLCS confirms that, in general, the CLCS refrains from considering the submission if another State requests it, even without the explicit invocation of paragraph 5(a) of the Rules of Procedure.[269] In fact, in a few cases even though the interested party did not object to the consideration of the submission by the CLCS, the CLCS still deferred the consideration of the submission "in order to take into account any further developments that might occur in the intervening period," as the CLCS decided in respect of Bangladesh's submission.[270]

The "counterproductive oversensitivity to disputes" reflected in the practice of the CLCS may have a negative impact on the delimitation of

[264] *Interpretation of Peace Treaties with Bulgaria, Hungary and Romania (Advisory Opinion) (First Phase) [1950] ICJ Rep 65*, 74.

[265] McDorman (n 3), 293; Oude Elferink (n 4), 266.

[266] Paragraph 1 of Annex I to the Rules of Procedure of the CLCS.

[267] Statement by the Chairman of the Commission on the Limits of the Continental Shelf on the Progress of Work in the Commission, Third session (May 15, 1998) [5] (emphasis added).

[268] See Busch (n 8), 105–106.

[269] The only exception is that the CLCS proceeded to consider Guyana's submission even though Venezuela objected to its consideration, ibid., 111–112.

[270] Statement by the Chairman of the Commission on the progress of work in the Commission (CLCS/72, September 16, 2011) [22].

the continental shelf beyond 200 nm[271] because it prevents States from having authoritative evidence of the existence and scope of their continental shelf beyond 200 nm, the lack of which may also handicap a court or tribunal that is seized to delimit the continental shelf beyond 200 nm. Therefore, it is no wonder that Judge Gaja suggested that "[i]t would therefore be appropriate for the CLCS to modify its Rules of Procedure and consider submissions also when the delimitation is under dispute."[272]

Based on the above analysis, a modification of the Rules of Procedure to allow consideration of a submission where the interested States are solely concerned with the application of Article 76 in connection with maritime delimitation issues should be welcome.[273] Alternatively, restricting the use of paragraph 5(a) of Annex I to the Rules of Procedure in the practice of the CLCS may well serve the same purpose. It is noted that Rule 46 and Annex I to the Rules of Procedure specify three categories of disputes, namely, "dispute in the delimitation of the continental shelf between States with opposite or adjacent coasts," "unresolved land disputes," and "unresolved maritime disputes."[274] Paragraph 2 of Annex I to the Rules of Procedure provides in general that submissions involving any of the three types of disputes should inform the CLCS about the existence of the dispute and assure the latter that the submission would not prejudice matters relating to the delimitation of boundaries between States. Although in practice the CLCS does not classify the disputes in accordance with these three categories, nor is it clear how "land or maritime disputes" are defined,[275] it is notable that paragraph 5(a) of Annex I to the Rules of Procedure only applies "in cases where a land or maritime dispute exists," whereas paragraph 2 of Annex I to the Rules of Procedure applies to the three categories of disputes. It is thus arguable that the text of Rule 46 and Annex I to the Rules of Procedure only allow the States to invoke paragraph 5(a) of Annex I to the Rules of Procedure when the dispute or disagreement relates to unresolved land or maritime disputes that are qualitatively distinct from "dispute in the delimitation of the continental shelf between

271 Serdy (n 31), 362.
272 *Nicaragua* v. *Colombia II* (Preliminary Objections) (n 148), 202 (Declaration of Judge Gaja).
273 See Oude Elferink (n 238), 317–318.
274 Rule 46, paragraph 1 and Paragraph 2 of Annex I to the Rules of Procedure.
275 See Busch (n 8), 121.

States with opposite or adjacent coasts." In consequence, territorial disputes, disputes concerning the interpretation and application of Article 7, Article 121(3), and the Statement of Understanding may be considered as "land or maritime disputes," whereas disagreements or disputes over the application of Article 76, such as those regarding the existence or scope of another State's entitlement to the continental shelf beyond 200 nm should be considered "disputes in the delimitation of the continental shelf between States with opposite or adjacent coasts." The latter cannot trigger paragraph 5(a) of Annex I to the Rules of Procedure, because their implications for maritime delimitation have been fully addressed by Article 76(10), Article 9 of Annex II to UNCLOS, and paragraph 2 of Annex I to the Rules of Procedure. This interpretation could enable the CLCS to proceed with consideration of submissions concerning maritime delimitation disputes without going through a formal procedure of amendment to the Rules of Procedure. Nevertheless, it may meet opposition from States that have invoked paragraph 5(a) to withhold their consent in cases of maritime delimitation. It is therefore desirable that the CLCS reconsiders the use of paragraph 5(a) of Annex I to the Rules of Procedure or amends the Rules of Procedure in consultation with the Meetings of States Parties to UNCLOS.[276]

[276] See Oude Elferink (n 238), 317–318.

# PART II

# Delimitation Methodology for the Continental Shelf beyond 200 Nautical Miles

# 5

# Conceptual Framework of Delimitation Methodology

Maritime delimitation is a process which starts from a given geographical framework and arrives at an equitable solution expressed by boundary line(s). This process can be understood from two perspectives. First, maritime delimitation is a legal–political operation,[1] in which different considerations and factors of a legal, political, and technical nature come into play. Second, it is a constructive and practical exercise which separates the jurisdictions between coastal States by drawing lines on maps.[2] Questions naturally arise as to what the law governing maritime delimitation is, how the disputed area is determined, what methods should be employed to draw the boundary line(s), and how different considerations are addressed and balanced in this process, etc. When it comes to the delimitation of the continental shelf beyond 200 nautical miles (nm), as the concerned maritime area extends further seaward and the entitlement is solely based on natural prolongation to the outer edge of the continental margin, the above-mentioned questions need to be reflected on. Delimitation methodology responds to these questions in the process of translating the law and facts into a precise line, which is the theme of the following chapters.

This chapter provides the conceptual framework which will guide the subsequent analysis of the delimitation methodology for the continental shelf beyond 200 nm. It is not intended as a recount of the law of maritime delimitation in general.[3] Instead, it is aimed at developing an

1 See *Delimitation of the Maritime Boundary in the Gulf of Maine Area (Canada/United States of America) [1984] ICJ Rep 246, 277* [56].

2 See M. D. Evans, *Relevant Circumstances and Maritime Delimitation* (Oxford University Press 1989), 63.

3 For guidance on this, see, for instance, P. Weil, *The Law of Maritime Delimitation: Reflections* (Grotius 1989); S. Fietta and R. Cleverly, *A Practitioner's Guide to Maritime Boundary Delimitation* (Oxford University Press 2016); A. G. Oude Elferink et al., *Maritime Boundary Delimitation: The Case Law: Is It Consistent and Predictable?* (Cambridge University Press 2018); M. Lando, *Maritime Delimitation as a Judicial*

approach to the delimitation beyond 200 nm on the basis of the current law of maritime delimitation. To this end, Section I will explain the sources of the law of maritime delimitation relating to the delimitation of the continental shelf beyond 200 nm. Section II introduces the elements of delimitation methodology and the formulations of delimitation methodology that evolve over time. On that basis, Section III raises the methodological questions arising out of the context of the continental shelf delimitation beyond 200 nm, which paves the way for a coherent and logical approach to examining the delimitation methodology for the continental shelf beyond 200 nm in subsequent chapters.

## I Sources of the Law of Maritime Delimitation

Between coastal States which are parties to UNCLOS, the applicable law of delimiting the continental shelf is Article 83. Article 83(1) reads:

> The delimitation of the continental shelf between States with opposite or adjacent coasts shall be effected by agreement on the basis of international law, as referred to in Article 38 of the Statute of the International Court of Justice, in order to achieve an equitable solution.

This article is impressive for its emptiness, which is an inevitable result of the protracted negotiations and irreconcilable positions between the "equidistance school" and the "equitable principles school" during the Third United Nations Conference on the Law of the Sea (UNCLOS III).[4] Without referring to any method, this provision is devoid of substance in guiding maritime delimitation.[5] Nonetheless, as a formal source of the law of maritime delimitation, Article 83 equally applies to the delimitation of the continental shelf beyond 200 nm. This is the position of international tribunals that have dealt with the delimitation of the continental shelf beyond 200 nm.[6] Article 83(1) has also been declared to be

*Process* (Cambridge University Press 2018); Y. Tanaka, *Predictability and Flexibility in the Law of Maritime Delimitation* (2nd ed., Hart 2019).

4 See G. J. Tanja, *The Legal Determination of International Maritime Boundaries: The Progressive Development of Continental Shelf, EFZ and EEZ Law* (Kluwer 1990), 94–116; S. N. Nandan and S Rosenne (eds.), *United Nations Convention on the Law of the Sea 1982: A Commentary, Volume II* (Martinus Nijhoff Publishers 1993), 954–980.

5 See R. R. Churchill and A. V. Lowe, *The Law of the Sea* (3rd ed., Manchester University Press 1999), 191.

6 See *Delimitation of the Maritime Boundary in the Bay of Bengal (Bangladesh/Myanmar) (Judgment) [2012] ITLOS Rep 4*, 117 [454]; *Bay of Bengal Maritime Boundary Arbitration (Bangladesh v. India) (2014) 167 ILR 1,146* [438].

part of customary international law, thus applicable to non-State parties to UNCLOS.[7]

In contrast, Article 6 of the 1958 Convention on the Continental Shelf (CCS) contains a combined rule of "equidistance-special circumstances" applicable in situations of opposite or adjacent coasts between the parties.[8] According to Article 311(1) of UNCLOS, UNCLOS prevails over the CCS as between the parties to UNCLOS.[9]

However, regardless of whether it is the UNCLOS, CCS, or customary international law that applies to maritime delimitation between specific States, the contents of the applicable law, including how they should be applied to effect the delimitation, have been mainly developed through international jurisprudence.[10]

Indeed, international jurisprudence is the main source of the law of maritime delimitation, and it influenced and continues to influence the articulation of rules governing maritime delimitation to the extent that the law of maritime delimitation is frequently referred to as "judge-made law."[11] The lack of substance of Articles 74(1) and 83(1) of UNCLOS, to some extent, facilitates this development. On the one hand, it leaves to international courts and tribunals the task of finding applicable principles, rules, and methods in concrete delimitation cases, which "open[s] the door to continuation of the development effected in this field by international case law."[12] On the other, the text of Articles 74(1) and 83(1) itself refers to the sources of international law as provided by Article 38 of the Statute of the International Court of Justice, which includes judicial decisions.[13] As maritime delimitation is the most

[7] See *Maritime Delimitation and Territorial Questions (Qatar v. Bahrain) (Merits) [2001] ICJ Rep 40, 91* [167].

[8] See *Delimitation of the Continental Shelf between the United Kingdom of Great Britain and Northern Ireland, and the French Republic (United Kingdom/France) (1978) 18 RIAA 3* [68]; Convention on the Continental Shelf (April 29, 1958), 499 UNTS 311.

[9] Article 311 (1) of UNCLOS provides: "This Convention shall prevail, as between States Parties, over the Geneva Conventions on the Law of the Sea of 29 April 1958."

[10] See P. Weil, "A propos du droit coutumier en matière de délimitation maritime, " *Écrits de droit international* (Presses Universitaires de France 2000) 151; Fietta and Cleverly (n 3), 26–27.

[11] A. G. Oude Elferink et al., "The Judiciary and the Law of Maritime Delimitation: Setting the Stage," in A. G. Oude Elferink et al. (eds.), *Maritime Boundary Delimitation: The Case Law: Is It Consistent and Predictable?* (Cambridge University Press 2018), 3.

[12] *The Gulf of Maine* (n 1), 294 [95].

[13] See T. A. Mensah, "Delimitation of the Continental Shelf: The Methodology," in J. C. Sainz-Borgo et al. (eds.), *Liber Amicorum: In Honour of a Modern Renaissance Man His Excellency Guomundur* (Universal Law Publishing 2017), 33–34.

litigated field in international adjudication, a body of judicial decisions concerning the law of maritime delimitation has become consolidated throughout the years. The Arbitral Tribunal of the *Bangladesh* v. *India* case goes even as far as to declare that "[t]he ensuing—and still developing—international case law constitutes [. . .] an *acquis judiciaire*, a source of international law under article 38(1)(d) of the Statute of the International Court of Justice, and should be read into articles 74 and 83 of the Convention."[14] Although it is doubtful whether "international case law" concerning the delimitation methodology should be read into the delimitation rules of UNCLOS,[15] it is correct that judicial decisions provide the substantive source of the law of maritime delimitation.

State practice, for its part, has a very limited role in the normative development of the law of maritime delimitation. For one thing, it is hardly the case that State practice would give rise to customary international law in respect of maritime delimitation, since States have a high degree of freedom to delimit their maritime boundaries as long as they can reach agreement.[16] For another, it is more often than not the case that the details of negotiations remain secret and, as a result, it is difficult to establish how States have reached agreement and what factors have influenced the negotiations.[17] Perhaps more importantly, the objective of concluding maritime delimitation agreements is to specify a fixed boundary rather than formulate rules applicable for future conduct.[18] Nonetheless, a survey of relevant delimitation agreements concerning the continental shelf beyond 200 nm between States is still necessary for

[14] *Bangladesh* v. *India* (n 6) 112 [339].

[15] Since the lack of substance of Articles 74(1) and 83(1) is the result of irreconcilable positions of the delegates during UNCLOS III, it is reasonable to infer that the intention of the parties to UNCLOS was to maintain the ambiguity of the delimitation rules, and leave the actual delimitation to be decided on a case-by-case basis, either through negotiations or third-party dispute settlement. Consequently, to read international jurisprudence, in particular a delimitation methodology which subscribes to a particular method into the provisions would go against the intention of the parties. Furthermore, as will become apparent in subsequent sections, it is doubtful whether the approach taken by international courts and tribunals is sufficiently consistent and concrete so as to be read into the provisions.

[16] See P. Weil, "Geographical Considerations in Maritime Delimitation," in J. I. Charney and L. M. Alexander (eds.), *International Maritime Boundaries, Volume I* (Martinus Nijhoff Publishers 1993), 123.

[17] See Tanaka (n 3), 454.

[18] See A. G. Oude Elferink et al., "Conclusions," in A. G. Oude Elferink et al. (eds.), *Maritime Boundary Delimitation: The Case Law: Is It Consistent and Predictable?* (Cambridge University Press 2018), 380.

understanding the delimitation methodology, as it reflects coastal States' perception of the delimitation of the continental shelf beyond 200 nm, especially its relation with maritime delimitation within that distance. Similarly, it has been suggested that a gradual accreted State practice could reveal what States regard as equitable, which is a sort of *opinio aequitatis*.[19]

As a result, while Article 83 of UNCLOS represents the starting point of identifying the sources of law in the delimitation of the continental shelf beyond 200 nm, the content of the rules has to be found in international jurisprudence, which comprises the practices of the ICJ, ITLOS, arbitral tribunals constituted under Annex VII of UNCLOS, and other ad hoc tribunals. In recent jurisprudence, focus has shifted from spelling out the content of applicable law to formulating the delimitation methodology.[20] In consequence, it is through the formulation of delimitation methodology that the law governing maritime delimitation is articulated.

## II Delimitation Methodology: An Overview

### *A Determination of Geographical Frameworks*

The reason why determination of a geographical framework is indispensable from consideration of delimitation methodology is three-fold. To start with, it provides the factual background for the operation of delimitation methodology. As observed by the ICJ in the *Cameroon* v. *Nigeria* case: "The geographical configuration of the maritime areas that the Court is called upon to delimit is a given. It is not an element open to modification by the Court but a fact on the basis of which the Court must effect the delimitation."[21] Second, the geographical framework provides the basis for the consideration and evaluation of relevant circumstances

19 See M. Mendelson, "On the Quasi-Normative Effect of Maritime Boundary Agreements," in N. Ando et al. (eds.), *Liber Amicorum Judge Shigeru Oda, Volume II* (Kluwer Law International 2002), 1079–1083; D. Anderson, "Developments in Maritime Boundary Law and Practice," in D. A. Colson and R. W. Smith (eds.), *International Maritime Boundaries, Volume V* (Brill Nijhoff Publishers 2005), 3204.

20 See D. McRae, "The Applicable Law: The Geneva Convention on the Continental Shelf, the LOSC, and Customary International Law," in A. G. Oude Elferink et al. (eds.), *Maritime Boundary Delimitation: The Case Law: Is It Consistent and Predictable?* (Cambridge University Press 2018), 105.

21 *Land and Maritime Boundary between Cameroon and Nigeria (Cameroon v. Nigeria: Equatorial Guinea intervening) [2002] ICJ Rep 303, 443-445* [295].

and delimitation methods, which are key to the practical exercise of delimitation. It has been expressed on many occasions that "the appropriateness of the equidistance or any other method for the purpose of effecting an equitable delimitation is a function or reflection of the geographical and other relevant circumstances of each particular case."[22] In addition, defining a geographical framework relevant for a particular case may also contribute to restricting the range of circumstances that may be relevant for that delimitation.[23]

Last but not least, the geographical framework provides parameters to assess the equity of delimitation outcomes. The ultimate goal of any delimitation methodology is to achieve an equitable solution, but "[t]here can never be any question of completely refashioning nature."[24] Whether an equitable solution has been achieved is thus a question to be assessed against the geographical framework. The disproportionality test, which compares the ratios between coastal lengths and the ratios between attributed maritime areas, is such a tool developed for this end as it intends to "check, *ex post facto*, on the equitableness of the delimitation line."[25] As the ICJ emphasized, how the disproportionality test is implemented "remains in each case a matter for the Court's appreciation, which it will exercise by reference to the overall geography of the area."[26]

In general, a geographical framework might include the following factors.

*Relevant coasts and relevant areas*: International courts and tribunals determine relevant coasts and relevant areas as a step to determine the area in dispute and the area relevant to the delimitation.[27] The importance of relevant coasts derives from the principle that "[t]he title of a State to the continental shelf and to the exclusive economic zone is based on the principle that the land dominates the sea through the projection of

[22] *Anglo-French Arbitration* (n 8) [97]. In the *Libya/Malta* case, the ICJ stated that "the method chosen and its results must be faithful to the actual geographical situation," *Continental Shelf (Libyan Arab Jamahiriya/Malta) [1985] ICJ Rep 13, 44-45* [57].

[23] See M. D. Evans, "Maritime Delimitation and Expanding Categories of Relevant Circumstances" (1991) 40 *ICLQ* 1, 24.

[24] *North Sea Continental Shelf Cases (Federal Republic of Germany/Denmark; Federal Republic of Germany/Netherlands) [1969] ICJ Rep 3, 49-50* [91]; *Anglo-French Arbitration* (n 8) [249].

[25] See *Maritime Delimitation in the Black Sea (Romania v. Ukraine) [2009] ICJ Rep 61, 129* [211].

[26] Ibid., 129 [213].

[27] *Continental Shelf (Tunisia/Libyan Arab Jamahiriya) [1982] ICJ Rep 18, 60-61* [72]; *Libya/ Malta* (n 22) 20 [14].

the coasts or the coastal fronts."[28] The relevant area is where maritime delimitation takes place, and it is regarded as a legal concept embedded in the methodology of maritime delimitation.[29] Whereas the two concepts contribute to identifying delimitation methods, assessing relevant circumstances, and conducting the disproportionality test, their definition or determination is far from consistent in the jurisprudence.[30] Nevertheless, it is frequently the case that international courts and tribunals dedicate separate sections in their judgments or awards to the identification of relevant coasts and relevant areas, implying that the two assume methodological importance in the delimitation process.[31]

*Coastal lengths:* The identification of relevant coasts may serve a separate function in the delimitation process, namely, as one of the relevant circumstances that influences the application of the delimitation method. As consistently held in the jurisprudence, "a substantial difference in the lengths of the parties' respective coastlines may be a factor to be taken into consideration in order to adjust or shift the provisional delimitation line."[32]

*Coastal configuration:* Configuration of the coast was acknowledged as a relevant circumstance as early as in the *North Sea* cases, which may present "special" or "unusual" features that should be addressed in the delimitation process.[33]

*Coastal relationship:* States are adjacent to each other where their land boundary reaches the coast, and States are opposite where their coastlines face each other and are nearly parallel.[34] Under the CCS, the characterization of "opposite" or "adjacent" coastal relationship may determine whether it is paragraph 1 or paragraph 2 of Article 6 that applies,[35]

[28] See *Black Sea* (n 25) 89 [77].

[29] Ibid., 99 [110].

[30] See A. G. Oude Elferink, "Relevant Coasts and Relevant Area – The Difficulty of Developing General Concepts in a Case-Specific Context," in A. G. Oude Elferink et al. (eds.), *Maritime Boundary Delimitation: The Case Law: Is It Consistent and Predictable?* (Cambridge University Press 2018), 239–247; Lando (n 3) 34–101.

[31] Lando (n 3) 35–36.

[32] *Cameroon* v. *Nigeria* (n 21) 446 [301]; *Maritime Delimitation in the Area between Greenland and Jan Mayen (Denmark v. Norway) [1993] ICJ Rep 38, 68-69* [68]; *Territorial and Maritime Dispute (Nicaragua v. Colombia) [2012] ICJ Rep 624, 702* [209–211].

[33] *North Sea* (n 24), 54 [101(D)(1)].

[34] See R. W. Smith, "Geographic Considerations in Maritime Boundary Delimitations," in D. G. Dallmeyer and L. DeVorsey, Jr. (eds.), *Rights to Oceanic Resources* (Martinus Nijhoff 1989), 5.

[35] See *Anglo-French Arbitration* (n 8) [237].

though the rules concerned are essentially the same.[36] Articles 74 and 83 of UNCLOS do not make a distinction between opposite or adjacent coasts, and it seems that "there is no justification to approach the process of delimitation from the perspective of a distinction between opposite and adjacent coasts and apply different criteria."[37] The classification per se may not be important, and sometimes not feasible. Nevertheless, the importance of determining the actual geographical relationship between the parties remains.[38]

*Coastal direction, including a major change of direction*: Determination of the coastal direction is crucial when a bisector line is employed to delimit maritime boundaries, because how the coastal fronts are measured depends on how the general direction of the coasts is determined.[39] In other situations, a major change of the direction of coasts may amount to a relevant circumstance that indicates the choice of, or change of, delimitation methods.[40]

*Presence of islands, rocks, islets, etc.*: The status of maritime features as well as their effect in the delimitation process is a quintessential topic in the law of maritime delimitation, and a proper assessment of their relevance to the delimitation process is often what defines an equitable solution.[41]

[36] See *Anglo-French Arbitration* (n 8) [238]. See also S. Yanai, "International Law Concerning Maritime Boundary Delimitation," in D. Attard et al. (eds.), *The IMLI Manual on International Maritime Law, Volume I: The Law of the Sea* (Oxford University Press 2014), 306–307; M. D. Evans, "Maritime Boundary Delimitation: Whatever Next?," in J. Barrett and R. Barnes (eds.), *Law of the Sea: UNCLOS as a Living Treaty* (BIILC 2016), 45.

[37] *Maritime Boundary Arbitration (Barbados v. Trinidad and Tobago) (2006) XXVII RIAA 147* [315].

[38] See M. D. Evans, "Relevant Circumstances," in A. G. Oude Elferink et al. (eds.), *Maritime Boundary Delimitation: The Case Law: Is It Consistent and Predictable?* (Cambridge University Press 2018), 249.

[39] See *Territorial and Maritime Dispute between Nicaragua and Honduras in the Caribbean Sea (Nicaragua v. Honduras) [2007] ICJ Rep 659, 748-749* [295–298].

[40] In the *Tunisia/Libya* case, the major change in direction from an adjacent to an opposite coastal relationship made the "equidistance line become a factor to be given more weight in the balancing of equitable considerations than would otherwise be the case," *Tunisia/Libya* (n 27) 88 [126]. In the *Black Sea* case, as the coastal relationship between Romania and Ukraine goes from an adjacent one to an opposite one, the ICJ considered that the choice of basepoints has to result in "a turning-point on the equidistance line where the effects of adjacency give way to those of the coasts on the opposite side," *Black Sea* (n 25) 105 [128].

[41] See *Qatar* v. *Bahrain* (n 7) 98–104 [190–216]; D. Bowett, "Islands, Rocks, Reefs, and Low-Tide Elevations in Maritime Boundary Delimitations," in J. I. Charney and L. M.

*Macrogeography*: It is debatable whether a macrogeographical perspective of the geographical framework would be legally relevant for the delimitation process. In the *Guinea/Guinea-Bissau* case, the Tribunal considered that "a valid method consists of looking at the whole of West Africa and of seeking a solution which would take overall account of the shape of its coastline," and it sought "a delimitation which is integrated into the present or future delimitation of the region as a whole."[42] In contrast, the Special Chamber of ITLOS in the recent *Ghana/Côte d'Ivoire* case, addressing Côte d'Ivoire's argument that a bisector line would make it possible to take into account "the macrogeography" of the area concerned, responded that "such consideration is alien to the application of articles 74 and 83 of the Convention," and that "interests of neighbouring States or of the region would have to be voiced by the other States," which are not parties to the proceedings.[43]

The above illustration of potential elements of a geographical framework shows the interaction between the geographical framework and the delimitation methodology: the geographical framework of a given case provides at the same time the context for the operation of delimitation methodology and the parameters that assess the equitableness of the outcome of such a methodology. It is because of this interaction that the determination of a geographical framework is constructive for delimitation methodology, not descriptive.[44] Determination of the geographical framework underlies the process of maritime delimitation, perhaps apart from the exception where pre-existing delimitation agreements are found. In the jurisprudence the terminology "geographical framework" is not consistently used,[45] and other terminologies such as "geographical context,"[46] "geographical circumstances,"[47] "geographical

Alexander (eds.), *International Maritime Boundaries, Volume I* (Martinus Nijhoff Publishers 1993).

42 *Delimitation of the Maritime Boundary between Guinea and Guinea-Bissau (Guinea/Guinea-Bissau) (1985) XIX RIAA 149* [108].

43 *Delimitation of the Maritime Boundary in the Atlantic Ocean (Ghana/Côte d'Ivoire), [2017] ITLOS Rep 4, 87* [283].

44 The Court of Arbitration in the *Anglo-French Arbitration* considered that it "will begin by identifying the geographical and other features which *establish* the legal framework for its decision regarding the course of the continental shelf boundary," *Anglo-French Arbitration* (n 8) [232] (emphasis added).

45 See ibid., [181].

46 See *Nicaragua* v. *Colombia I* (n 32), 707–708 [229].

47 See *Anglo-French Arbitration* (n 8), [96] and [183].

considerations,"[48] and "geographic realities"[49] are frequently adopted. But the message is clear. It is in this sense that Weil suggests that "geographic considerations inspire, if they do not dictate, most delimitation."[50]

The delimitation of the continental shelf beyond 200 nm cannot be considered in a legal vacuum without referring to geographical frameworks. To state the obvious, the claims to a continental shelf beyond 200 nm, in addition to being in accordance with Article 76 (4)–(7), are part of the geographical realities that characterize the overall delimitation process. For instance, short coastlines of States and proximity with neighboring States may place an immediate restriction on the extent of the continental margin that may be attributed to one of the States in the delimitation process.[51] Likewise, the determination of relevant coasts and relevant areas is also necessary for a delimitation of the continental shelf beyond 200 nm, though this step may take into account the specific characteristics of the entitlement to the continental shelf beyond 200 nm.[52] The same can be said about other geographical circumstances, because how they interact with the entitlement to the continental shelf beyond 200 nm can be the key to the pursuit of an equitable solution in the delimitation of the continental shelf beyond this distance.

## B *Elements of Delimitation Methodology*

When one delves into international jurisprudence for the substance of delimitation methodology, the first problem one encounters is the kaleidoscope of terminologies. The jurisprudence is littered with terminologies such as "equitable principles," "equitable criteria," "equitable considerations," "special circumstances," "relevant circumstances," "features and considerations," "factors," "methods," and "approach," etc. Notwithstanding the diverse usages, these terminologies can be categorized into three basic elements that underlie any delimitation process, namely, equitable principles, relevant circumstances, and practical

48 For instance, *North Sea* (n 24), 47–48 [87].

49 See *Bangladesh/Myanmar* (n 6), 67 [235].

50 Weil (n 16), 119.

51 See V. Prescott, "Resources of the Continental Margin and International Law," in P. J. Cook and C. M. Carleton (eds.), *Continental Shelf Limits: The Scientific and Legal Interface* (Oxford University Press 2000), 67.

52 See Chapter 6, Section II.

methods. These elements constitute the substance of delimitation methodology.

Equitable principles featured in the early judicial decisions of the ICJ prior to 2000. The concept of equitable principles was first used in the Truman Proclamation, which was regarded by the ICJ as "the starting point of the positive law" on the subject of the continental shelf.[53] In the *North Sea* cases, the Court was requested to decide what principles and rules of international law are applicable to the delimitation between the parties. Rejecting the use of equidistance either as a treaty rule or customary international rule,[54] the Court placed "equitable principles" at the center of the customary international law for maritime delimitation.[55] Nonetheless, whereas the parties to the disputes frequently resorted to equitable principles in their pleadings, the Court rarely elucidated the precise content of equitable principles.[56] It was in the *Libya/Malta* case that the ICJ, by way of giving examples, mentioned certain "well-known" equitable principles:

> [T]he principle that there is to be no question of refashioning geography, or compensating for the inequalities of nature; the related principle of non-encroachment by one party on the natural prolongation of the other, which is no more than the negative expression of the positive rule that the coastal State enjoys sovereign rights over the continental shelf off its coasts to the full extent authorized by international law in the relevant circumstances; the principle of respect due to all such relevant circumstances; the principle that although all States are equal before the law and are entitled to equal treatment, "equity does not necessarily imply equality" [. . .] nor does it seek to make equal what nature has made unequal; and the principle that there can be no question of distributive justice.[57]

Since the 2000s, reference to equitable principles has largely decreased; instead, the emphasis of international courts and tribunals shifted to "equitable solution,"which is the legal requirement under Articles 74(1) and 83(1) of UNCLOS. Although international courts and tribunals ceased to articulate the content or role of equitable principles, it has been

53 *North Sea* (n 24), 32–33 [47].

54 See ibid., 24–45 [25–81].

55 See ibid., 35–36 [55].

56 See L. Delabie, "The Role of Equity, Equitable Principles, and the Equitable Solution in Maritime Delimitation, " in A. G. Oude Elferink et al. (eds.), *Maritime Boundary Delimitation: The Case Law: Is It Consistent and Predictable?* (Cambridge University Press 2018), 150–152.

57 *Libya/Malta* (n 22) 39–40 [46].

observed that the judiciary still engages with evaluative assessments that find origins from equitable principles.[58] Indeed, almost all the equitable principles listed in the above-quoted passage continue to exert an influence in courts or tribunals' reasoning in maritime delimitation cases. Equitable or not, these principles of general application form part of the normative framework of the law of maritime delimitation.[59]

Instead of the content of equitable principles, it is the application of equitable principles that really matters, which is through the function of relevant circumstances.[60] As stated in the *Tunisia/Libya* case, the task of the Court was "to apply equitable principles as part of international law, and to balance up the various considerations which it regards as relevant in order to produce an equitable result."[61] Similarly, the *Libya/Malta* case explicitly observed that the application of equitable principles "leaves the Court with the task of appreciation of the weight to be accorded to the relevant circumstances in any particular case of delimitation."[62]

Consideration of relevant circumstances has been included in the law of maritime delimitation from the very beginning. As early as the International Law Commission (ILC) drafted the articles on the delimitation of the continental shelf, it was acknowledged that the elasticity of special circumstances prevents the formulation of a single, all-embracing method, which is capable of general application.[63] Under Article 6 of the CCS, the delimitation rule states that "in the absence of agreement, and unless another boundary line is justified by special circumstances, the boundary shall be determined by application of the principle of equidistance."[64] "Special circumstances" is therefore a concept under the treaty rule, while "relevant circumstances" is a concept of customary international law.[65] Although different in origin and in name, the ICJ in the *Jan Mayen* case has already noted that "there is inevitably a tendency towards assimilation between the special circumstances of Article 6 of the 1958 Convention and the relevant circumstances under customary law."[66] According to Evans, in the context of delimitation of the

[58] See Oude Elferink et al. (n 18), 381.
[59] *Libya/Malta* (n 22), 39–40 [45–46].
[60] See Evans (n 2), 76–78.
[61] *Tunisia/Libya* (n 27), 60 [71].
[62] *Libya/Malta* (n 22), 40 [48].
[63] See Evans (n 2), 10.
[64] Article 6(2) of the CCS.
[65] See *North Sea* (n 24), 46–47 [85].
[66] *Jan Mayen* (n 32), 62–63 [56].

continental shelf and the EEZ, even if "special circumstances" and "relevant circumstances" may have been different at one time, today they are not.[67] Since "special circumstances" is part of the territorial delimitation rule under UNCLOS,[68] "relevant circumstances" will be used in the context of delimitation concerning the EEZ and the continental shelf, including the continental shelf beyond 200 nm.

Relevant circumstances considered in the continental shelf and the EEZ delimitation are generally divided into two subcategories, i.e., geographical circumstances and non-geographical circumstances.[69] While the former includes those mentioned earlier in connection with the geographical framework, the latter includes circumstances relating to the interests and activities of parties in disputed maritime areas, such as the conduct of parties, access to resources, and security considerations, etc.[70] Although in State practice evidently all sorts of circumstances may be considered relevant, international jurisprudence shows that the relevant circumstances have "increasingly been attached to geographical considerations."[71] Nevertheless, non-geographical circumstances, such as security considerations, may form part of the assessment of the overall equitability of the delimitation result.[72]

For the present study, methods are used in the strict sense, referring to the techniques employed to draw or create the boundary line(s). This note of terminology is necessary because, sometimes, courts or tribunals refer to the overall delimitation methodology as a "method."[73] Delimitation methods can be geometrical, such as equidistance, angle-bisector, enclaving, perpendicular, etc., or non-geometrical, such as the so-called "natural" boundaries.[74] Although jurisprudence is cautious not

67 Evans (n 38), 228.

68 Article 15 of UNCLOS.

69 This classification is made by Tanaka, though he refers to "geographical factors" and "non-geographical factors." See Y. Tanaka, *The International Law of the Sea* (1st ed., Cambridge University Press 2012), 198–212.

70 See Evans (n 38), 252–260; Tanaka (n 3), 370–438.

71 *Barbados* v. *Trinidad and Tobago* (n 37), [233].

72 See Evans (n 38), 256–258.

73 For example, the ICJ in the *Cameroon* v. *Nigeria* case referred to the "equitable principles/relevant circumstances method," *Cameroon* v. *Nigeria* (n 21), 441 [288]. The *Bay of Bengal* cases labelled the delimitation methodology as an "equidistance/relevant circumstances method," *Bangladesh/Myanmar* (n 6) 67 [238]; *Bangladesh* v. *India* (n 6), 114 [346].

74 See V. Prescott and C. H. Schofield, *The Maritime Political Boundaries of the World* (2nd ed., Martinus Nijhoff Publishers 2005), 224–235.

to give any method a normatively prestigious or compulsory status,[75] it widely acknowledges the intrinsic value of equidistance being scientific, convenient, and improving the certainty of maritime delimitation.[76] In recent years, due to the proliferation of the two-stage or three-stage approach to maritime delimitation, under which equidistance is applied as a first step, international courts and tribunals "have come to embrace a clear role for equidistance."[77]

What stands out from this brief overview of equitable principles, relevant circumstances, and methods in maritime delimitation is that none of these can operate without reference to the others. Equitable principles, such as "the land dominates the sea," "delimitation cannot completely refashion nature," "equity does not necessarily imply equality," or indeed, "the principle of respect due to all such relevant circumstances," are given effect through the identification and evaluation of relevant circumstances. Relevant circumstances, for its part, cannot be selected or assessed in the delimitation process without normative values expressed in equitable principles.[78] Methods provide the technical tools to translate the principles and circumstances into concrete lines, and the choice and application of methods "has therefore to be determined in the light of those circumstances and of the fundamental norm that the delimitation must be in accordance with equitable principles."[79]

### *C Formulations of Delimitation Methodology*

Given the different weights or roles accorded to equitable principles, relevant circumstances, and methods, delimitation methodology may assume different formulations. Above all, the structural force that shapes the formulation of delimitation methodology is the changing perceptions of the nature and function of equity in the delimitation methodology, which can be summarized as "autonomous equity" and "corrective equity."[80] The changing perceptions of equity can be identified in the formulation of delimitation methodology through two indicia: first,

[75] See *Libya/Malta* (n 22), 55–56 [77]; *Barbados* v. *Trinidad and Tobago* (n 37) [306]; *Nicaragua* v. *Honduras* (n 39), 741 [272].

[76] *North Sea* (n 24) 23 [23]; *Nicaragua* v. *Honduras* (n 39), 741 [272]; *Barbados* v. *Trinidad and Tobago* (n 37) [306].

[77] *Maritime Boundary Arbitration (Guyana v. Suriname) (2007) XXX RIAA 1* [335].

[78] See Weil (n 3), 211–212.

[79] *Anglo-French Arbitration* (n 8), [97].

[80] See Weil (n 3), 165–167; Delabie (n 56), 150–154; Tanaka (n 3), 164–165.

whether a specific method is required in a particular delimitation methodology, and, second, the role of relevant circumstances in relation to the choice of and application of delimitation methods. To give an example, Article 6 of the CCS incorporates a specific method, namely equidistance. It also opens up considerations of equity through "special circumstances."[81] Nevertheless, the text of Article 6 of the CCS is not clear-cut as to whether equidistance or special circumstances comes first,[82] nor is it certain whether the consideration of special circumstances justifies the choice of a different method or corrects the equidistance line when the application of equidistance leads to inequitable results. Thus the text is open to different perceptions of the role of equity.

It is generally agreed that the *North Sea* cases inaugurated the trend towards a "result-oriented" approach to maritime delimitation, under which equity has an autonomous role. An equitable result is predominant, while equitable principles are subordinate to this ultimate goal.[83] This delimitation methodology emphasizes that each maritime delimitation is a *unicum*,[84] and involves extensive examinations of relevant circumstances. Equidistance method is neither a rule nor principle, but merely one of many delimitation methods, whose applicability depends on the circumstances of each particular case. Relevant circumstances have an indicative role in the sense that the identification and examination of relevant circumstances would directly indicate the primary methods to be applied.[85] The *Tunisia/Libya* case and the *Gulf of Maine* case represent the high watermark of this result-oriented approach. Whereas a result-oriented approach maximizes the flexibility of the delimitation process, it falls short of ensuring the predictability and certainty of the jurisprudence, and therefore risks undermining the normativity of the law of maritime delimitation.[86]

The *Anglo-French Arbitration* developed the corrective concept of equity on the basis of Article 6 of the CCS. Addressing the effect of the Scilly Isles in the delimitation process, the Court of Arbitration found that the problem arises from the "distorting effect of a geographical feature in circumstances in which the line equidistant from the coasts

[81] *North Sea* (n 24), 35–36 [55]; *Anglo-French Arbitration* (n 8), 45–46 [70].
[82] See McRae (n 20), 93.
[83] *Tunisia/Libya* (n 27), 59 [70].
[84] *Guinea/Guinea-Bissau* (n 42), [89].
[85] For the "indicative" role of relevant circumstances, see Evans (n 2), 80–83.
[86] Weil (n 3), 160–161; Tanaka (n 3), 164; Lando (n 3), 19.

of the two States would otherwise constitute the appropriate boundary," and the solution is "a method modifying or varying the equidistance method rather than to have recourse to a wholly different criterion of delimitation."[87] In effect, the Court of Arbitration applied Article 6 in the manner that equidistance was adopted provisionally whereas the consideration of special circumstances served to correct the inequities produced by the equidistance line.[88] Despite the employment of a corrective-equity approach, the Court of Arbitration assimilated the result-oriented approach with Article 6 of the CCS by stating that "even under Article 6 it is the geographical and other circumstances of any given case which indicate and justify the use of the equidistance method as the means of achieving an equitable solution rather than the inherent quality of the method as a legal norm of delimitation."[89]

Between 1969 and the early 1990s, the delimitation methodology applied by international courts and tribunals embraced an autonomous function of equity, under which relevant circumstances and delimitation methods were selected and applied in order to produce an equitable result. However, the emphasis on an equitable solution or an equitable result, if not bound by parameters of legal principles and rules, "leads straight into pure judicial discretion and a decision based upon nothing more than the court's subjective appreciation of what appears to be a 'fair' compromise of the claims of either side."[90] Furthermore, if the focus is exclusively on relevant circumstances, and if the evaluative exercises demonstrate no consistency between judicial decisions, there will be no discernible line between equity and a decision *ex aequo et bono*. As noted by Higgins:

> The invocation of the concept of equity provides no guidance in selecting among those various factors, and at the end of the day the "appreciation individualisée d'un cas concret" remains subjective if the invocation of equity is the only guide to the task.[91]

Aware of the excessive subjectivity of this result-oriented approach, international courts and tribunals gradually detached themselves from

[87] *Anglo-French Arbitration* (n 8), 116 [249].
[88] Ibid.
[89] Ibid., 45–46 [70].
[90] R. Jennings, "The Principles Governing Maritime Boundaries," in K. Hailbronner (ed.), *Staat und Völkerrechtsordnung, Festschrift für Karl Doehring* (Springer 1989), 31.
[91] R. Higgins, *Problems and Process: International Law and How We Use It* (Reprinted, Oxford University Press 2010), 222.

it by emphasizing the consistency of the jurisprudence and the predictability of the delimitation process.[92] What followed was a definite turn to a two-stage approach: a provisional equidistance line is drawn as a starting point, and the relevant circumstances are examined in the second stage in order to adjust the provisional line, should the provisional line lead to inequitable results. This trend was demonstrated by the series of cases decided during the two decades after the *Libya/Malta* case, which include the *Jan Mayen* case, the *Qatar* v. *Bahrain* case, and the *Cameroon* v. *Nigeria* case decided by the ICJ, and the *Barbados* v. *Trinidad and Tobago* and *Suriname* v. *Guyana* cases by tribunals constituted under Annex VII of UNCLOS. The name of this approach varies across the jurisprudence; it is sometimes referred to as the "equitable principles/relevant circumstances method,"[93] and, at other times, as the "equidistance/relevant circumstances principle,"[94] but the formulation of the delimitation methodology is the same. Under the two-stage approach, the role of relevant circumstances is transformed into an ameliorative one, in that it does not indicate a primary method but corrects or adjusts the provisional equidistance line.[95] This is also the reason why the two-stage approach is also called a corrective-equity approach. Another step in enhancing the normativity of the delimitation methodology during this period is the narrowing down of the scope of relevant circumstances.[96]

The *Black Sea* case took an even more rigorous approach to maritime delimitation and entrenched the corrective-equity approach when it reformulated the delimitation methodology as a three-stage approach. The three-stage approach supplements the two-stage approach by introducing the disproportionality test as the last step of the delimitation process, whose function is "[a] final check for an equitable outcome [that] entails a confirmation that no great disproportionality of maritime areas is evident by comparison to the ration of coastal lengths."[97]

The three-stage approach strengthened the role of equidistance even further, because "[s]o far as delimitation between adjacent coasts is concerned, an equidistance line will be drawn unless there are compelling

[92] See *Libya/Malta* (n 22), 39 [45]; Barbados *v.* Trinidad and Tobago (n 37), [242].

[93] *Cameroon* v. *Nigeria* (n 21), 441 [288]; *Nicaragua* v. *Honduras* (n 39), 741 [271].

[94] *Barbados* v. *Trinidad and Tobago* (n 37), [242].

[95] See Evans (n 38), 229. The "ameliorative" role of relevant circumstances is explained in Evans (n 2) 279–280.

[96] *Barbados* v. *Trinidad and Tobago* (n 37), [233–241].

[97] *Black Sea* (n 25), 103 [122].

reasons that make this unfeasible in the particular case" and in cases of opposite coasts, no exception is provided for departure from the provisional equidistance line.[98] This formulation treats equidistance not merely as "a hypothesis and a practical starting point,"[99] but amounts to a quasi-rule, because the sole exception to equidistance is the "unfeasibility" test. Given that the second stage is meant to verify or adjust a provisional equidistance line, the role of equidistance under the three-stage approach appears to be dominant.[100]

Ever since the *Black Sea* case, all judicial decisions or awards adopted the three-stage approach to delimit the single delimitation of the EEZ and the continental shelf, including the continental shelf beyond 200 nm, and sometimes the territorial sea.[101] The three-stage approach is applied regardless of whether the applicable law is UNCLOS or customary international law. According to Tanaka, this demonstrates the trend towards the unification of the law of maritime delimitation under the corrective-equity approach or the three-stage approach.[102]

At first sight, the three-stage approach, or the equidistance/relevant circumstances approach, achieves a certain degree of balance between certainty and flexibility, as it enhances the objectivity and scientific facet of the delimitation process by employing the equidistance method and the disproportionality test,[103] and it constrains the subjectivity involved in the judicial discretion by assigning a more modest role to relevant circumstances.[104] However, several years after the *Black Sea* case, international courts and tribunals seemed to have retreated from the rigorous application of the three-stage approach. In the *Nicaragua* v. *Colombia I* case, the ICJ cautioned that "[t]he three-stage process is not, of course, to be applied in a mechanical fashion and the Court has recognized that it will not be appropriate in every case to begin with a provisional equidistance/median line," citing the departure from equidistance in the *Nicaragua* v. *Honduras* case.[105] The retreat from the three-stage

[98] Ibid., 101[116].

[99] *Barbados* v. *Trinidad and Tobago* (n 37), [242].

[100] Evans (n 36), 50.

[101] *Ghana/Côte d'Ivoire* (n 43), [260].

[102] Tanaka (n 3), 164–167.

[103] See M. Kamto, "Considérations actuelles sur la méthode de délimitation maritime devant la Cour Internationale de Justice. de Charybde en Scylla?," in J. Crawford et al. (eds.), *The International Legal Order: Current Needs and Possible Responses* (Brill Nijhoff 2017), 393.

[104] Evans (n 36), 49–50.

[105] *Nicaragua* v. *Colombia I* (n 32), 696 [194].

approach was further confirmed by the *Peru* v. *Chile* case, in which the ICJ stated that "[t]he methodology which the Court *usually* employs in seeking an equitable solution involves three stages" and that "it constructs a provisional equidistance line unless there are compelling reasons preventing that."[106] The applicability of the three-stage approach and the provisional equidistance seems to be circumscribed in these two cases in comparison to the formulations in the *Black Sea* case.[107]

The *Ghana/Côte d'Ivoire* judgment also expanded the exception to the first stage, as it stated that "in the absence of any compelling reasons that make it impossible or inappropriate to draw a provisional equidistance line, the equidistance/relevant circumstances methodology should be chosen for maritime delimitation."[108] From an "unfeasibility" test to an "inappropriateness" test, the scope of exception to equidistance is naturally expanded, though international courts and tribunals have not actually departed from applying equidistance in the first stage so far. In the *Bangladesh/Myanmar* case, however, ITLOS cast into doubt the applicability of the three-stage approach in a more general fashion by observing that "the issue of which method should be followed in drawing the maritime delimitation line should be considered in light of the circumstances of each case. The goal of achieving an equitable result must be the paramount consideration guiding the action of the Tribunal in this connection."[109] It compared the bisector method proposed by Bangladesh and the "equidistance/relevant circumstances method" and decided that "in the present case the appropriate method [...] is the equidistance/relevant circumstances method."[110] The Tribunal's rhetoric thus appears to be closer to the result-oriented approach prevailing in the earlier judicial decisions than to that of the ICJ in the *Black Sea* case.[111]

Nevertheless, the three-stage approach has become the "established methodology" in the law of maritime delimitation.[112] Several points are in order to conclude the overview of the delimitation methodology

106 *Maritime Dispute (Peru v. Chile) [2014] ICJ Rep 3, 65* [180] (emphasis added).

107 See M. D. Evans, " Maritime Boundary Delimitation," in D. R. Rothwell et al. (eds.), *The Oxford Handbook of the Law of the Sea* (Oxford University Press 2015), 260.

108 *Ghana/Côte d'Ivoire* (n 43), [289].

109 *Bangladesh/Myanmar* (n 6), 67 [235].

110 Ibid., 67 [236–239].

111 Evans (n 36), 50–54.

112 *Maritime Delimitation in the Caribbean Sea and the Pacific Ocean (Costa Rica v. Nicaragua) and Land Boundary in the Northern Part of Isla Portillos (Costa Rica v. Nicaragua) [2018] ICJ Rep 139, 190* [135].

developed throughout the jurisprudence. First, the significance of equidistance has been gradually recognized, as it constitutes a starting point and a basis for working towards the final line. This is in sharp contrast with the equity-based approach adopted by the *North Sea* cases and other early judicial decisions. Second, the role of relevant circumstances has been considerably reduced under the current formulation of the delimitation methodology. Instead of playing an indicative role for determining the primary methods, the concept of relevant circumstances tends to work as a corrective in the application of equidistance. Third, the corrective equity approach has largely replaced the result-oriented approach. Nevertheless, the latter has its own *raison d'être* in the primitive stage of the development of the law of maritime delimitation,[113] because resort to equity allowed international courts and tribunals to fill in the lacunae of the law of maritime delimitation.[114] In this regard, equity may be characterized as belonging to the dynamic side of the law, where the law is evolving and is not always fully endorsed by the *opinio juris* of States.[115] The corrective-equity approach is advantageous because it attempts to combine objectivity with flexibility in order to achieve an equitable solution. Nonetheless, many judges and arbitrators have noticed that the application of the three-stage approach is not always robust or consistent in the jurisprudence subsequent to the *Black Sea* case.[116] It

[113] See J. I. Charney, "Ocean Boundaries between Nations: A Theory for Progress" (1984), 78 *AJIL* 582, 589–590; T. Scovazzi, "Where the Judge Approaches the Legislator: Some Cases Relating to Law of the Sea," in N. Boschiero et al. (eds.), *International Courts and the Development of International Law: Essays in Honour of Tullio Treves* (TMC Asser Press 2013), 300.

[114] See E. Lauterpacht, "Equity, Evasion, Equivocation and Evolution in International Law," *Proceedings and Committee Reports of the American Branch of the International Law Association* (New York 1977), 33.

[115] See *Jan Mayen* (n 32), 256–257 [161–162] (Separate Opinion of Judge Weeramantry). See also S. Rosenne, "The Position of the International Court of Justice on the Foundations of the Principle of Equity in International Law," in A. Bloed and P. van Dijk (eds.), *Forty Years International Court of Justice: Jurisdiction, Equity and Equality* (Europa Instituut 1988), 108.

[116] See critiques of the application of the three-stage approach in the *Bangladesh/Myanmar* case. *Bangladesh/Myanmar* (n 6), 189–195 (Separate Opinion of Judge Cot); ibid., 205–216 [27–58] (Separate Opinion of Judge Gao). Critiques of the application of the three-stage approach in the *Nicaragua* v. *Colombia I* case, *Nicaragua* v. *Colombia* I (n 32), 743–745 [9–13] (Declaration of Judge Keith); ibid., 747–749 [3–10] (Separate Opinion of Judge Xue); ibid., 735–739 [21–35] (Separate Opinion of Judge Abraham). For academic critiques of the three-stage approach as applied in the jurisprudence, see Fietta and Cleverly (n 3), 575–583 (On "The Creeping Subjectivity of Base-Point Selection: A Lurch toward a 'Four-State Approach' (or a Return to Equitable

therefore remains the task of international courts and tribunals to further refine delimitation methodology as well as the manner of its application.[117]

## III Delimitation Methodology for the Continental Shelf beyond 200 NM

### *A The Limits of the Three-Stage Approach*

The trend towards the unification of delimitation methodology under the three-stage approach in the jurisprudence provokes the question of whether the three-stage approach provides the frame of reference to discuss the delimitation methodology for the continental shelf beyond 200 nm.[118] Such an approach may be understandable and reasonable, as the *Bay of Bengal* cases and the *Ghana/Côte d'Ivoire* case adopted the three-stage approach to delimit the continental shelf beyond 200 nm. However, upon closer examination, the choice and application of the three-stage approach in these cases rather demonstrate the limits of the three-stage approach to address the methodological questions concerning the delimitation of the continental shelf beyond 200 nm.

As a starting point, the three cases differ slightly on the legal basis for the applicability of the three-stage approach. In the *Bangladesh/Myanmar* case, ITLOS based its choice on the applicable law. For the Tribunal, "article 83 of the Convention addresses the delimitation of the continental shelf between States with opposite or adjacent coasts without any limitation as to area. [...] Article 83 applies equally to the

Principles?)"); McRae (n 20), 105–114; N. Marques Antunes and V. Becker-Weinberg, "Entitlement to Maritime Zones and Their Delimitation: In the Doldrums of Uncertainty and Unpredictability," in A. G. Oude Elferink et al. (eds.), *Maritime Boundary Delimitation: The Case Law: Is It Consistent and Predictable?* (Cambridge University Press 2018), 81; C. G. Lathrop, "The Provisional Equidistance Line: Charting a Course Between Objectivity and Subjectivity?," in A. G. Oude Elferink et al. (eds.), *Maritime Boundary Delimitation: The Case Law: Is It Consistent and Predictable?* (Cambridge University Press 2018); Evans, "Relevant Circumstances" (n 38), 232–243; Y. Tanaka, "The Disproportionality Test in the Law of Maritime Delimitation," in A. G. Oude Elferink et al. (eds.), *Maritime Boundary Delimitation: The Case Law: Is It Consistent and Predictable?* (Cambridge University Press 2018), 304–316; Evans, "Maritime Boundary Delimitation: Whatever Next?" (n 36), 50–70.

[117] See Tanaka (n 3), 443–468.

[118] For academic works so framed, see B. M. Magnússon, *The Continental Shelf beyond 200 Nautical Miles: Delineation, Delimitation and Dispute Settlement* (Brill Nijhoff Publishers 2015), 142–180; Lando (n 3), 41–42, 95–97, 128–142, 221–226, 259.

delimitation of the continental shelf both within and beyond 200 nm."[119] Without any reasoning, the Tribunal decided that "the delimitation method to be employed in the present case for the continental shelf beyond 200 nautical miles should not differ from that within 200 nm. Accordingly, the equidistance/relevant circumstances method continues to apply for the delimitation of the continental shelf beyond 200 nm."[120]

The *Bangladesh* v. *India* case and the *Ghana/Côte d'Ivoire* case, for their part, based their reasoning on the concept of the single continental shelf. The Arbitral Tribunal in the *Bangladesh* v. *India* case simply noted that "[t]he Parties and the Tribunal agree that there is a single continental shelf. The Tribunal considers that the appropriate method for delimiting the continental shelf remains the same, irrespective of whether the area to be delimited lies within or beyond 200 nm."[121] The Special Chamber of ITLOS more explicitly linked the concept of the single continental shelf to the same delimitation methodology within and beyond 200 nm:

> As far as the methodology for delimiting the continental shelf beyond 200 nm is concerned, the Special Chamber recalls its position that there is only one single continental shelf. Therefore it is considered inappropriate to make a distinction between the continental shelf within and beyond 200 nm as far as the delimitation methodology is concerned.[122]

It is submitted that neither Article 83 as the applicable law nor the concept of single continental shelf should be interpreted to require application of the same delimitation methodology within and beyond 200 nm, much less the three-stage approach. There is no logical reason to base the choice of the same delimitation methodology on Article 83 because, as recognized by the *Bay of Bengal* cases and the *Ghana/Côte d'Ivoire* case, Article 83(1) is silent as to the delimitation methodology or method.[123] Since different methods can be adopted to address different relevant circumstances in various cases, even if Article 83 continues to be the applicable law,[124] is it not arguable that there might exist distinct

119 *Bangladesh/Myanmar* (n 6), 117 [454].

120 Ibid., 117 [455].

121 *Bangladesh* v. *India* (n 6), 158 [465].

122 *Ghana/Côte d'Ivoire* (n 43), [526].

123 *Bangladesh/Myanmar* (n 6), 64 [225]; *Bangladesh* v. *India* (n 6), 112 [338]; *Ghana/Côte d'Ivoire* (n 43), [281].

124 For example, bisector method was applied in the *Nicaragua* v. *Honduras* case and equidistance method was applied in the *Black Sea* case, though in both cases the

relevant circumstances in the delimitation of the continental shelf beyond 200 nm that call for a different methodology? Consequently, Article 83 in itself does not indicate that the same delimitation methodology should be applied within and beyond 200 nm.[125]

The concept of the single continental shelf is also not a helpful tool to justify the same delimitation methodology within and beyond 200 nm. For one thing, it does not take into account whether there are circumstances exclusively relevant to the continental shelf beyond 200 nm. For another, the tribunals of the *Bangladesh* v. *India* case and the *Ghana/Côte d'Ivoire* case left out the fact that the maritime delimitation within 200 nm was not a continental shelf delimitation, but a single delimitation that delimited both the continental shelf and the EEZ.[126] The leap of reasoning in this respect is particularly striking given the common belief that a single maritime delimitation of the EEZ and the continental shelf shall take into account "neutral" criteria common to both regimes,[127] as well as the fact that the three-stage approach was developed through the judicial practices concerning single maritime delimitation.[128] In fact, when the Arbitral Tribunal in the *Ghana/Côte d'Ivoire* case denied the relevance of the parties' oil practice with the delimitation process, it noted that "a *de facto* line or *modus vivendi* related to oil practice cannot *per se* be a relevant circumstance in the delimitation of an all-purpose maritime boundary with respect to superjacent water as well as the seabed and subsoil."[129] Apparently, the concept of the single continental shelf in itself cannot respond to the question of whether there are circumstances relevant only to the delimitation of the continental shelf beyond 200 nm.

applicable law was Article 83. See *Nicaragua* v. *Honduras* (n 39), 738 [261]; *Black Sea* (n 25), 74–75 [31].

125 A. G. Oude Elferink, "ITLOS's Approach to the Delimitation of the Continental Shelf Beyond 200 Nautical Miles in the Bangladesh/Myanmar Case: Theoretical and Practical Difficulties," in R. Wolfrum et al. (eds.), *Contemporary Developments in International Law: Essays in Honour of Budislav Vukas* (Brill 2015), 240; Ø. Jensen, "The Delimitation of the Continental Shelf beyond 200 NM: Substantive Issues," in A. G. Oude Elferink et al. (eds.), *Maritime Boundary Delimitation: The Case Law: Is It Consistent and Predictable?* (Cambridge University Press 2018), 367.

126 In the two cases the tribunals were requested to delimit the territorial sea, the EEZ, and the continental shelf between the parties. See *Bangladesh* v. *India* (n 6), 33 [83]; *Ghana/Côte d'Ivoire* (n 43), [74]. See Jensen (n 125), 367.

127 See *The Gulf of Maine* (n 1), 327 [194]. For more discussion on this point, see Chapter 9, Section II.

128 *Black Sea* (n 25), 101 [115].

129 *Ghana/Côte d'Ivoire* (n 43), [477].

The above discussion by no means questions the validity of using the three-stage approach to pursue an equitable solution in the *Bay of Bengal* cases and the *Ghana/Côte d'Ivoire* case. Rather, the point is that Article 83 and the concept of the single continental shelf, by themselves, cannot justify the employment of the same delimitation methodology within and beyond 200 nm.

Moreover, given the limited number of judicial decisions applying the three-stage approach in the delimitation of the continental shelf beyond 200 nm, it might be too early to use this approach as a generally valid conceptual framework to analyze the methodological questions in the continental shelf delimitation beyond 200 nm. The limits of the three-stage approach are accentuated by the fact that the three cases dealt with essentially one geographical situation, namely, between two States with adjacent coasts where the parties have overlapping entitlements within and beyond 200 nm. The precedential value of these three decisions might be limited for cases concerning two opposite States where the parties have overlapping entitlements (or simply claims) to the continental shelf beyond 200 nm only, much less for a peculiar case such as the *Nicaragua* v. *Colombia II* case. In addition, the parties to each of the three decisions agreed that the same delimitation methodology should apply to the delimitation of the continental shelf beyond 200 nm, though they differed on the specific methodology or method to be applied.[130] This fact may have made it easier for the tribunals' choice of the same delimitation methodology.[131] Clearly, if one party argues for a different methodology to delimit the continental shelf beyond 200 nm, there has to be concrete legal reasoning behind the judiciary's choice of the delimitation methodology, which is so far absent. From an academic point of view, to confine the discussion to the framework of the three-stage approach may also overlook the practices of the delimitation of the continental shelf beyond 200 nm in State practice.

A second reason why the three-stage approach may not be the point of departure for considering the delimitation methodology for the continental shelf beyond 200 nm lies in the lack of clearly defined criteria for the applicability (or, indeed, inapplicability) of equidistance as a first step of the delimitation methodology. Uncertainties in this respect may be acute in the delimitation of the continental shelf beyond 200 nm. For

[130] See *Bangladesh/Myanmar* (n 6), 116 [452–453]; *Bangladesh* v. *India* (n 6), 146 [438] and 151 [449]; *Ghana/Côte d'Ivoire* (n 43), [259].

[131] Marques Antunes and Becker-Weinberg (n 116), 82.

instance, in the *Bangladesh/Myanmar* case, Bangladesh argued that an equidistance line would cut-off its access to the continental shelf beyond 200 nm completely and therefore should not be applied.[132] ITLOS did not address the relevance of this circumstance because it decided to adjust the provisional equidistance line even before it reached the 200 nm limits.[133] Therefore, it remains unclear whether cutting off a coastal State's access to the continental shelf beyond 200 nm should be one of the "factors which make it inappropriate to use the methodology of [the three-stage approach]."[134] Furthermore, in some circumstances a provisional equidistance line constructed from respective coasts might be located outside the area of overlapping entitlements to the continental shelf beyond 200 nm, as in the 2013 Denmark (Greenland)–Iceland Agreed Minutes.[135] Is it a circumstance that renders a provisional equidistance line infeasible or inappropriate? Should a court in the face of such a circumstance adopt an entirely different method or draw a provisional equidistance line anyway but adjust it by moving it to the area of the overlap? These problems illustrate that in the delimitation of the continental shelf beyond 200 nm, the interaction between equidistance (or other methods) and relevant circumstances may be subject to more complications and therefore cannot be easily sorted out using the framework of the three-stage approach.

A third consideration that advises against using the three-stage approach as the conceptual framework stems from the tension between the formulation of this approach and its application. Since the three-stage approach reflects the corrective-equity approach, an objectively constructed equidistance line is vital for the subsequent examination of the relevant circumstances.[136] Some authors thus disapprove of the widening up of the exception to equidistance and argue for a strict equidistance line without manipulating the choice of appropriate basepoints in the first stage.[137] Notwithstanding the merits of these suggestions, a circumstance-free equidistance line objectively drawn on the basis of coastal geography may result in a line that is so inequitable that the

132 See Bangladesh/Myanmar, Memorial of Bangladesh, Volume I (July 1, 2010) 83 [6.45].

133 See *Bangladesh/Myanmar* (n 6), 81–82 [291–297].

134 *Nicaragua* v. *Honduras* (n 39), 741 [272].

135 See B. Kunoy, "Agreed Minutes on the Delimitation of the Continental Shelf beyond 200 Nautical Miles between Greenland and Iceland in the Irminger Sea" (2013), 12 *Chinese JIL* 125, 135–136.

136 McRae (n 20), 110.

137 See Lathrop (n 116), 221; Fietta and Cleverly (n 3), 579–590.

second stage must in effect overturn its use. The *Bay of Bengal* cases are cases in point. To address the pronounced cut-off effect created by the application of equidistance to the concave coasts of Bangladesh, the eventual maritime boundaries took the shape of two geodetic lines that almost look identical to the bisector lines proposed by Bangladesh.[138] Likewise, the maritime boundaries drawn in the *Nicaragua* v. *Colombia I* case combine the use of a weighted equidistance line, enclaves, and parallel lines of latitudes.[139] Even if nothing in the formulation of the three-stage approach suggests that adjustment in the second stage should be minor,[140] one cannot explain how it is compatible with the corrective perception of equity, in particular with the modest role assigned to relevant circumstances under this approach. This was, nevertheless, what the ICJ explicitly approved in the *Nicaragua* v. *Colombia I* case, as the Court stated that: "Where the relevant circumstances so require, the Court may also employ other techniques, such as the construction of an enclave around isolated islands, in order to achieve an equitable result."[141] However, should this be allowed under the three-stage approach, it would be very difficult to see how the second stage of the three-stage approach could be distinguished from the result-oriented approach.

All in all, the formulation of the three-stage approach and the uncertainties found in its application do not support its use as a proper frame of reference to discuss the delimitation methodology for the continental shelf beyond 200 nm. These observations should not be read as

[138] *Bangladesh/Myanmar* (n 6), 90 [340]; *Bangladesh* v. *India* (n 6), [478]. For the critiques of the resemblance of the boundary lines with the bisector lines, see *Bangladesh/Myanmar* (n 6), 283 (Dissenting Opinion of Judge Lucky); ibid., 213 [53] (Separate Opinion of Judge Gao); D. H. Anderson, "Delimitation of the Maritime Boundary in the Bay of Bengal (Bangladesh/Myanmar) – Case No. 16" (2012), 106 *AJIL* 817, 823; *Bangladesh* v. *India* (n 6), 191 [9] (Concurring and Dissenting Opinion of Dr P. S. Rao).

[139] *Nicaragua* v. *Colombia I* (n 32), 709–715 [232–238].

[140] This point is debated and debatable. The *Nicaragua* v. *Colombia I* case explicitly acknowledged that "the second stage of the three-stage approach does not preclude very substantial adjustment to, or shifting of, the provisional line in an appropriate case," ibid., 697 [197]. See critiques of the substantial adjustment under the three-stage approach, ibid., 744 [9] (Declaration of Judge Keith); ibid., 748 [8] (Separate Opinion of Judge Xue); ibid., 738 [32–33] (Separate Opinion of Judge Abraham); *Bangladesh/Myanmar* (n 6) 191–192 (Separate Opinion of Judge Cot); ibid., 208–209 [38–40] (Separate Opinion of Judge Gao); Evans, 'Maritime Boundary Delimitation: Whatever Next?' (n 36), 60. For an opposite view, see Lando (n 3), 241–244.

[141] *Nicaragua* v. *Colombia I* (n 32), 696 [192].

challenging the applicability of this approach in the jurisprudence in general, or play down its applicability in future judicial cases concerning the continental shelf beyond 200 nm. Rather, the point is, from a methodological point of view, much confusion still obfuscates the delimitation of the continental shelf beyond 200 nm, in particular with regard to the identification of relevant circumstances, and these questions cannot be coherently or comprehensively analyzed under the corrective-equity approach. As will be discussed below, methodological questions concerning the continental shelf beyond 200 nm relate more to the *scope* of relevant circumstances and their normative implications for the delimitation process.

### *B Methodological Questions in the Continental Shelf Delimitation beyond 200 NM*

As mentioned at the beginning of this chapter, many methodological issues have to be re-examined in the light of the specific context of the continental shelf beyond 200 nm, because a feeling widely shared is that the delimitation of the continental shelf beyond 200 nm should somehow differ from that within 200 nm. This common feeling or belief may stem from what the ICJ stipulated in the *Libya/Malta* case when it rejected natural prolongation as one of the relevant circumstances for continental shelf delimitation:

> [T]o rely on this jurisprudence would be to overlook the fact that where such jurisprudence appears to ascribe a role to geophysical or geological factors in delimitation, it finds warrant for doing so in a régime of the title itself which used to allot those factors a place which now belongs to the past, in so far as sea-bed areas less than 200 miles from the coast are concerned.[142]

This observation gives rise to various hypotheses of the implications of the special characteristics of the entitlement to the continental shelf beyond 200 nm for the delimitation process, which can be summarized in the following four categories.

The first derives from a "fundamentalist aspect" of the law of maritime delimitation;[143] that is, the delimitation methodology has to be connected with the legal basis of title. Some authors argue, since equidistance has a

[142] *Libya/Malta* (n 22), 35–36 [40].

[143] To use the word of the ICJ. See *North Sea* (n 24), 28–29 [37].

normative link with the basis of title (distance),[144] that the entitlement to the continental shelf beyond 200 nm should also require a delimitation method that is consistent with it.[145]

The second category of methodological questions concerns the determination of the area of overlap. It has been suggested that since the extent of the entitlement to the continental shelf beyond 200 nm depends on the location of the outer limits of the continental shelf, the relevant area cannot be determined by simply referring to the coasts of States.[146] In addition, under some circumstances, it is the FOS located in accordance with Article 76(4) that provides precise baselines for determining the area of overlap.[147]

If the area of overlap in the delimitation of the continental shelf beyond 200 nm is established differently, it would seem that a method applied to a coast-to-coast delimitation scenario cannot achieve an equitable solution in the delimitation of the continental shelf beyond 200 nm.[148] This is the main thrust of the third category of hypotheses, which focuses on the choice and application of delimitation methods. Some argue that the FOS of each State should serve as the respective line for constructing an equidistance line,[149] or a boundary line.[150] Others, however, find solutions from the entitlement to the continental shelf beyond 200 nm. For example, the delimitation method should aim at discovering the "most natural prolongation" of the States through the examination of scientific and technical evidence.[151]

[144] See Weil (n 3), 79–83; Tanaka (n 3), 194–203; Lando (n 3), 30–32.

[145] B. Kunoy, "A Geometric Variable Scope of Delimitations: The Impact of a Geological and Geomorphologic Title to the Outer Continental Shelf"(2006), 11 *Austrian RIEL* 49, 67–69. Lando argues that there is an element of distance in the entitlement to the continental shelf beyond 200 nm, therefore applying equidistance to the continental shelf beyond 200 nm is also consistent with the entitlement. See Lando (n 3), 131–135. Similarly, see Marques Antunes and Becker-Weinberg (n 116), 75.

[146] B. Kunoy, "The Delimitation of an Indicative Area of Overlapping Entitlement to the Outer Continental Shelf" (2013), 83 *BYIL* 61, 74–78.

[147] D. Colson, "The Delimitation of the Outer Continental Shelf between Neighboring States" (2003), 97 *AJIL* 91, 103.

[148] See Fietta and Cleverly (n 3), 617–618.

[149] Colson (n 147), 103.

[150] See Hedberg's proposal concerning the maritime delimitation in the Gulf of Mexico between Mexico and the United States. H. D. Hedberg, "Ocean Floor Boundaries" (1979), 204 *Science* 135, 135.

[151] See C. Schofield et al., "A Tribunal Navigating Complex Waters: Implications of the Bay of Bengal Case" (2013), 44 *ODIL* 363, 375.

Above all, the most widely held hypothesis relates to the identification of relevant circumstances in the continental shelf delimitation beyond 200 nm. This fourth category directly flows from the first, because propositions in this regard find justifications from the special characteristics of entitlement to the continental shelf beyond 200 nm. There are several variations under this category. One relates to the relevance of geophysical factors with the delimitation process in the continental shelf delimitation beyond 200 nm.[152] Related to this proposition is that geographical circumstances, which predominantly shape the delimitation lines within 200 nm, will not necessarily be relevant, for instance in a "pure" continental shelf beyond 200 nm delimitation between two opposite coasts. Alternatively, the influence of coastal geography should be minimized between two adjacent States, where there is a need to extend the boundary line beyond 200 nm.[153] Other propositions attribute different weights to the methods to establish the establishment of the continental shelf beyond 200 nm under Article 76. For example, Kunoy argued that an entitlement established on the basis of submarine elevations is by nature "stronger" than an entitlement based on submarine ridges, in accordance with the distinction made by Article 76(5) and Article 76(6),[154] therefore the delimitation process should give effect to the differences in the establishment of the entitlement.

The preceding hypotheses find the intellectual sources from early judicial decisions decided before the *Libya/Malta* case, sometimes by throwing new light on principles of natural prolongation and non-encroachment with reference to Article 76 of UNCLOS.[155] In addition to these specific propositions touching upon different aspects of delimitation methodology, another more broadly construed argumentation is that delimitation of the continental shelf beyond 200 nm should have a different methodology because an equitable solution for a continental shelf delimitation may differ from that of the EEZ. As summarized by Churchill and Lowe:

> [A] boundary that might be equitable for EEZ purposes may not be equitable for continental shelf purposes because of the different

[152] K. Highet, "The Use of Geophysical Factors in the Delimitation of Maritime Boundaries," in J. I. Charney and L. M. Alexander (eds.), *International Maritime Boundaries, Volume I* (Martinus Nijhoff Publishers 1993), 196.

[153] See Colson (n 147), 105–106.

[154] Kunoy (n 145), 75.

[155] *North Sea* (n 24), 46–47 [85]; *Libya/Malta* (n 22), 39–40 [46].

> considerations that are relevant to achieving an equitable solution in each case – for example, the location of fish stocks in the case of the EEZ, the geological characteristics of the sea bed and the location of sea bed mineral deposits in the case of continental shelf.[156]

This view is in fact widely shared[157] and reinforced by the Chamber of the ICJ in the *Gulf of Maine* case.[158] Following this line of thinking, from the moment the delimitation of the continental shelf is not concerned with superjacent waters, the considerations that are solely relevant to the regime of the continental shelf may take over the delimitation process.

To sum up, key to understanding the delimitation methodology for the continental shelf beyond 200 nm is whether and how the entitlement to the continental shelf beyond 200 nm bears on the determination of the area of overlap and the identification of relevant circumstances, in particular the implications of the relevant circumstances for the drawing of the boundary lines. The following chapters will therefore examine these issues in turn, before which several clarifications are in order.

First, the focus of the following chapters is placed on the identification of the relevant circumstances for the continental shelf delimitation beyond 200 nm, which includes four sets of circumstances: (1) those relating to the basis of entitlement; (2) geomorphological or geological circumstances; (3) geographical circumstances; and (4) regime-specific circumstances.

Second, some circumstances whose potential relevance is recognized in the delimitation process within 200 nm are excluded from the present study, either due to their remote relevance with the delimitation of the continental shelf beyond 200 nm, or due to their lack of contribution to the choice of delimitation methods. The first category includes security and defense considerations,[159] and the second category includes conduct of States that amounts to evidence of a tacit agreement.[160]

156 Churchill and Lowe (n 5), 160.

157 See Charney (n 113), 601; D. J. Attard, *The Exclusive Economic Zone in International Law* (Oxford University Press 1987), 214–216; F. Orrego Vicuña, *The Exclusive Economic Zone: Regime and Legal Nature under International Law* (Cambridge University Press 1989), 198–199; Weil (n 3), 132–134; Magnússon (n 118), 160.

158 "The Chamber observed that all that it is necessary [. . .] to rule out the application of any criterion found to be typically and exclusively bound up with the particular characteristics of one alone of the two natural realities that have to be delimited in conjunction," *The Gulf of Maine* (n 1), 326–327 [192–193].

159 *Black Sea* (n 25), 128 [204]; *Anglo-French Arbitration* (n 8), [188]; *Libya/Malta* (n 22), 46 [51].

160 *Cameroon* v. *Nigeria* (n 21), 447–448 [304].

Third, delimitation methods, whether equidistance or others, will not be discussed separately; instead, they will be addressed in connection with the discussion of the identification of relevant circumstances. The subsequent chapters are not based on a corrective-equity approach to delimitation methodology, and the discussion rather focuses on articulating the relevant circumstances for choice and application of delimitation methods in the delimitation beyond 200 nm.

Last but not least, the following analysis will not address the disproportionality test as a separate stage in the delimitation methodology either, because, first, the disproportionality test has its own conceptual and operative problems as applied in the jurisprudence and, second, its applicability in the delimitation of the continental shelf beyond 200 nm is largely dependent on the identification of relevant coasts and relevant areas. Therefore, the disproportionality test and its application in the delimitation of the continental shelf beyond 200 nm will be examined in connection with the relevant coasts and relevant areas.[161]

[161] See Chapter 6, Section II.B.1.

# 6

# Determination of the Area of Overlapping Entitlements

## I Relevant Coasts, Relevant Area, and Area of Overlapping Entitlements

The concepts of relevant coasts and relevant area find their origin in the practice of international courts and tribunals. The significance of relevant coasts derives, first, from the principle that the land dominates the sea[1] and, second, from the task of maritime delimitation, which aims at dividing the area of overlapping entitlements generated from the coasts of the respective party.[2] The most frequently applied formula to identify the relevant coasts was developed by the ICJ in the *Tunisia/Libya* case, as summarized by the *Black Sea* case:

> [T]hat the coast, in order to be considered as relevant for the purpose of the delimitation, must generate projections which overlap with projections from the coast of the other Party. Consequently "the submarine extension of any part of the coast of one Party which, because of its geographic situation, cannot overlap with the extension of the coast of the other, is to be excluded from further consideration by the Court."[3]

Although the coast is the starting line to "ascertain how far the submarine areas appertaining to each of them extend in a seaward direction,"[4] it is by reference back to the possibility of overlap that the relevance of the coasts is assessed.[5] Therefore, relevant coasts, relevant area, and the area of overlapping entitlements are inextricable from each other. The terminology of "area of overlapping entitlements" is, however, not consistently employed in the jurisprudence, because international courts and

1 *Maritime Delimitation in the Black Sea (Romania v. Ukraine) [2009] ICJ Rep 61, 89* [77].
2 Ibid.
3 Ibid., 96–97 [99].
4 *Continental Shelf (Tunisia/Libyan Arab Jamahiriya) [1982] ICJ Rep 18, 61* [74].
5 M. D. Evans, *Relevant Circumstances and Maritime Delimitation* (Oxford University Press 1989) 127.

tribunals not infrequently refer to "area of overlapping claims,"[6] "area of overlapping potential entitlements,"[7] and "area of overlapping projections,"[8] etc. It seems that the area of overlapping claims is not necessarily identical with the area of overlapping entitlements, as the former may be defined by reference to the parties' proposed maritime boundaries, while the latter may be defined by reference to the parties' maximum maritime entitlements in accordance with international law.[9] Despite the variations of the terminology, it is clear that only on the basis of an area of overlapping entitlements can a delimitation proceed to divide the jurisdictions of the respective parties.[10] In this sense, the term "area of overlapping entitlements" is preferred, and it must be stressed that the maritime entitlements to be delimited must possess an *actual*, rather than potential, existence under international law, though it is understood that "potential entitlement" is used to convey the non-absolute character of maritime entitlement in contrast to territorial title.[11] This last point is particularly relevant when it comes to the determination of the area of overlapping entitlements to the continental shelf beyond 200 nautical miles (nm).

The relevant area is determined, to a large extent, by identifying the area of overlapping entitlements, but the two are not always identical because in some circumstances the relevant area can be limited by agreements concluded between one of the parties and a third State,[12] or by the claims of third parties.[13] Nevertheless, the basic idea is that the relevant coasts and the relevant area reciprocally define each other

[6] *Maritime Boundary Arbitration (Barbados v. Trinidad and Tobago) (2006) XXVII RIAA 147* [239].

[7] *Territorial and Maritime Dispute (Nicaragua v. Colombia) [2012] ICJ Rep 624, 678* [145]. *Maritime Delimitation in the Caribbean Sea and the Pacific Ocean (Costa Rica v Nicaragua) and Land Boundary in the Northern Part of Isla Portillos (Costa Rica v. Nicaragua) [2018] ICJ Rep 139, 210* [180–181].

[8] *Bay of Bengal Maritime Boundary Arbitration (Bangladesh v. India) (2014) 167 ILR 1, 97* [295].

[9] See *Maritime Delimitation in the Area between Greenland and Jan Mayen (Denmark v. Norway) [1993] ICJ Rep 38, 47* [18–19].

[10] *Delimitation of the Maritime Boundary in the Bay of Bengal (Bangladesh/Myanmar) (Judgment) [2012] ITLOS Rep 4, 105* [397].

[11] N. Marques Antunes, *Towards the Conceptualisation of Maritime Delimitation: Legal and Technical Aspects of a Political Process* (Martinus Nijhoff 2003), 133–134.

[12] See *Nicaragua* v. *Colombia I* (n 7) 686 [164–165]; S. Fietta and R. Cleverly, *A Practitioner's Guide to Maritime Boundary Delimitation* (Oxford University Press 2016), 601–602.

[13] See *Continental Shelf (Libyan Arab Jamahiriya/Malta) [1985] ICJ Rep 13, 25-28* [21–22].

through the determination of the area of overlapping entitlements.[14] In maritime delimitation within 200 nm, since the maritime entitlements are distance-based, the determination of the area of overlapping entitlements is a geometrical exercise through the identification of coastal projections. In this regard, the relevant area "has become secondary to, and largely a function of, the identification of the 'relevant coasts'."[15] On the contrary, the entitlement to the continental shelf beyond 200 nm is based on natural prolongation to the outer edge of the continental margin. The extent of the entitlement cannot be determined by referring to the coasts, but to its seaward limits, whose location varies from case to case in accordance with Article 76(4)–(6) of UNCLOS.[16] The "relevant coasts – area of overlapping entitlements – relevant area" equation has to be revisited in the context of the delimitation of the continental shelf beyond 200 nm.

Section II examines how the judiciary dealt with these concepts in the delimitation concerning the continental shelf beyond 200 nm thus far and discusses the problems detected in these exercises. Section III turns to consider the factors that may contribute to a precise determination of the area of overlapping entitlements to the continental shelf beyond 200 nm, and Section IV concludes.

## II Practices and Problems

### A *Decisions Concerning the Continental Shelf beyond 200 NM*

As a preliminary remark, notwithstanding the normative status of relevant coasts and relevant area in the delimitation process, the jurisprudence has not determined relevant coasts or relevant area in a consistent manner in maritime delimitation even within 200 nm. In addition to the *Tunisia/Libya* formula, it has been observed that several other approaches were adopted to determine relevant coasts and relevant area from time to time.[17] Nor are the exercises free from criticism of being

[14] See A. G. Oude Elferink, "Relevant Coasts and Relevant Area – The Difficulty of Developing General Concepts in a Case-Specific Context," in A. G. Oude Elferink et al. (eds.), *Maritime Boundary Delimitation: The Case Law: Is It Consistent and Predictable?* (Cambridge University Press 2018), 178.

[15] M. D. Evans, "Maritime Boundary Delimitation," in D. R. Rothwell et al. (eds.), *The Oxford Handbook of the Law of the Sea* (Oxford University Press 2015), 267.

[16] Fietta and Cleverly (n 12), 48–49.

[17] Oude Elferink (n 14), 242–247.

subjective or arbitrary. For one thing, there is no objective method to measure the coastal lengths or the size of the relevant area.[18] For another, the methods to construe coastal projections seem to vary from case to case. Whereas some cases employ frontal projections, under which coastal projections generate maritime entitlements along lines perpendicular to the general direction of the coast, some other cases adopt radial projections, which entail that a point on a coast generates entitlements along a radius equal in length with the maritime entitlement.[19] Other than these uncertainties, determination of relevant coasts and relevant area can be "particularly impressionistic" in certain geographical contexts, such as between adjacent coasts facing the open seas.[20]

These problems are equally visible in decisions concerning the delimitation of the continental shelf beyond 200 nm. As will be elaborated below, all the three decisions concerning the continental shelf delimitation beyond 200 nm applied the *Tunisia/Libya* formula without distinguishing the entitlement within and beyond 200 nm, though they differed in the treatment of the following issues: first, how coastal projections are constructed, and second, the role of the outer limits of the continental shelf in determining the relevant area.

### 1 *Bangladesh/Myanmar* Case

The judgment of the *Bangladesh/Myanmar* case did not specifically deal with the relationship between the relevant coasts and the parties' entitlements to the continental shelf beyond 200 nm. In fact, relevant coasts were considered in section VIII of the decision, which is entitled "exclusive economic zone and continental shelf *within* 200 nautical miles."[21] Nonetheless, the disagreement between the parties over the relevance of one segment of Myanmar's coast illustrates the uncertainties in determining the relevant coasts when it comes to the continental shelf beyond 200 nm. According to Myanmar, its relevant coast extended from the land boundary terminus between Myanmar and Bangladesh up to Cape Negrais.[22] Bangladesh, however, contended that the coast between Bhiff Cape and Cape Negrais was not relevant, "since the entire length of

18 See Fietta and Cleverly (n 12), 597–599.

19 See M. Lando, *Maritime Delimitation as a Judicial Process* (Cambridge University Press 2018), 73–81.

20 See Evans (n 15), 272.

21 *Bangladesh/Myanmar* (n 10), 56–60 [185–205] (emphasis added).

22 See ibid., 58 [194].

Myanmar's coast below Bhiff Cape is more than 200 M from Bangladesh (i.e., beyond any possible projection the Bangladesh coast might generate), the projection of Myanmar's coast between Bhiff Cape and Cape Negrais could not possibly overlap with that of Bangladesh."[23] The ITLOS did not accept Bangladesh's argument, and the Tribunal simply stated that "the coast of Myanmar from the terminus of its land boundary with Bangladesh to Cape Negrais does [...] indeed generate projections that overlap projections from Bangladesh's coast" and decided that this segment must be relevant (see Figure 6.1).[24] It is not entirely clear from the judgment whether the segment of Myanmar's coast between Bhiff Cape and Cape Negrais was included because it generated a projection that overlaps with Bangladesh's entitlement to the continental shelf beyond 200 nm, but Bangladesh considered this to be the case.[25] In any event, the Tribunal did not consider the question of relevant coasts in the delimitation of the continental shelf beyond 200 nm again.

As to the relevant area, the Tribunal did not determine the relevant area in connection with the relevant coasts, but rather at the final stage for the purpose of the disproportionality test.[26] This seems to suggest that for the delimitation to proceed, a precise identification of the relevant area is not indispensable. The relevant area determined by the Tribunal includes parts of overlapping entitlements to the continental shelf beyond 200 nm of the parties, but it does not correspond to the entire area of overlapping entitlements.[27] It is clear that the Tribunal determined the relevant area using frontal projections of the coasts, as "[t]he southern limit of the relevant area will be marked by the parallel westward from Cape Negrais,"[28] and "the western limit of the relevant area is marked by a straight line drawn from point ß2 due south."[29] Thus, the Tribunal applied the geometrical exercise without referring to the extent of the parties' entitlement to the continental shelf beyond 200 nm, and did not find it necessary to refer to the outer

23 *Bangladesh/Myanmar*, Reply of Bangladesh, Volume I (March 15, 2011), 100 [3.151].

24 *Bangladesh/Myanmar* (n 10), 59 [203].

25 In the proceedings of the *Bangladesh* v. *India* case, Bangladesh argued that this segment of Myanmar's coast generated "a projection [that] would overlap only with Bangladesh's claim to the continental shelf beyond 200 nm." *Bangladesh* v. *India* (n 8), 94–95 [290].

26 See *Bangladesh/Myanmar* (n 10), 123 [477].

27 See R. Churchill, "Bangladesh/Myanmar Case: Continuity and Novelty in the Law of Maritime Boundary Delimitation" (2012) 1 *CJICL* 137, 145.

28 *Bangladesh/Myanmar* (n 10), 125 [491].

29 Ibid., 126 [495].

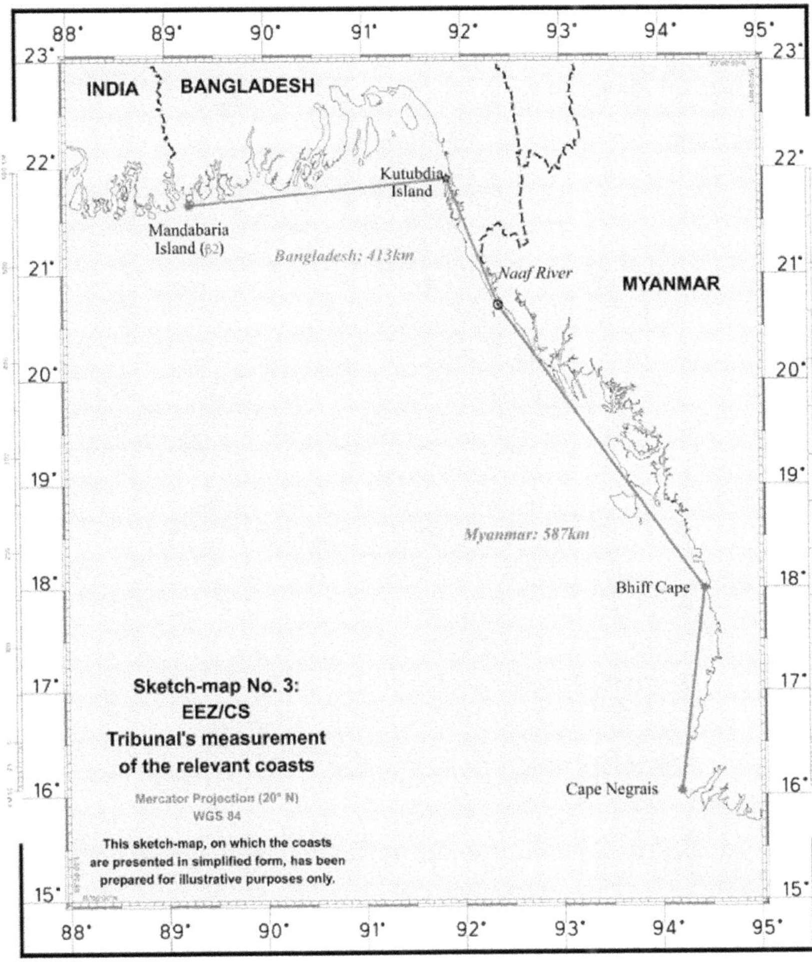


**Figure 6.1** Relevant coasts in the *Bangladesh/Myanmar* case.
Source: [2012] ITLOS Rep 60

limits of the continental shelf (see Figure 6.2). The relevant area thus defined is smaller in size than the actual area of overlapping entitlements of the parties due to the exclusion of certain parts of the continental shelf beyond 200 nm. It is therefore doubtful whether the disproportionality test based on an inaccurate determination of the relevant area enhanced the objectivity of the assessment of the equity of the delimitation result.

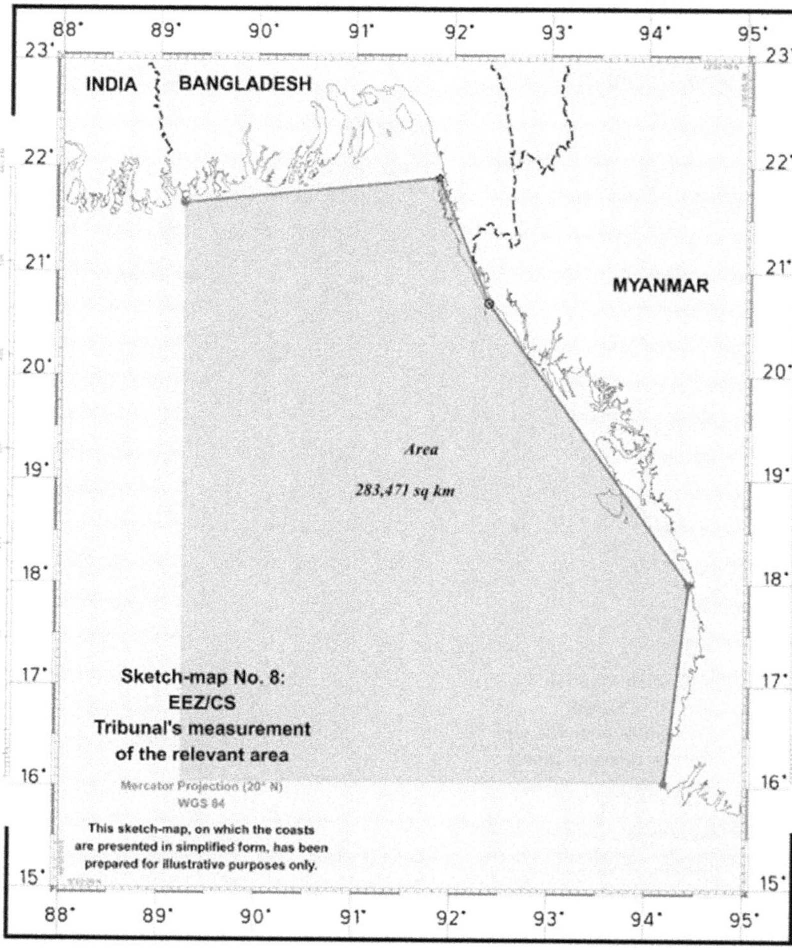


**Figure 6.2** Relevant area in the *Bangladesh/Myanmar* case.
Source: [2012] ITLOS Rep 127

## 2 *Bangladesh* v. *India* Case

The Arbitral Tribunal in the *Bangladesh* v. *India* case more explicitly explained its approach to determining relevant coasts and relevant area in connection with the continental shelf beyond 200 nm. Bangladesh and India disputed whether India's coast from Devi Point to Sandy Point should be included as part of India's relevant coast. Bangladesh contended that this segment should be included because "the projection from India's coast overlaps with the projection extending beyond 200 nm from Bangladesh's coast."[30] India, on the other hand, rejected this argument because it considered that this segment of coast faced in a south-easterly direction and did not face back into the head of the Bay of Bengal.[31]

The Arbitral Tribunal accepted Bangladesh's argument and recognized the relevance of the coast between Devi Point and Sandy Point.[32] It reached this conclusion because the Arbitral Tribunal did not distinguish between coastal projections within and beyond 200 nm:

> In keeping with its view that there is a single continental shelf [...], this Tribunal sees no basis for distinguishing between projections within 200 nm and those beyond that point. Accordingly, the Tribunal considers the Indian coast to be relevant to the extent that its projection generates any overlap with the projection generated by the coast of Bangladesh. That being so, the coast is relevant, *irrespective of whether that overlap occurs within 200 nm of both coasts, beyond 200 nm of both coasts, or within 200 nm of one and beyond 200 nm of the other.*[33]

The Arbitral Tribunal, however, did not explain how the entitlement to the continental shelf beyond 200 nm, which was established on the basis of geomorphological or geological factors, was compatible with coastal projections determined in a geometrical exercise. In fact, the exercise of determining the relevant coasts involved a considerable degree of flexibility. While the Arbitral Tribunal recognized that "a radial line drawn to the north-east from a point south of Sandy Point would also overlap with the projection of the coast of Bangladesh beyond 200 nm,"[34] it did not find it necessary to determine if a line drawn south of that point would represent the projection of that coast, since "neither Party has suggested that the Indian coastline remains relevant."[35] Nonetheless, the main reason not to include the coast south of Sandy Point was that it lay "too far to the south to be fairly considered to generate projections that overlap with those of the coast of Bangladesh."[36] This explanation seems to confirm that the

30 *Bangladesh* v. *India* (n 8), 94 [289].
31 Ibid., 97 [296].
32 Ibid., 99 [300].
33 Ibid., [299] (emphasis added).
34 Ibid., 100 [302].
35 Ibid.
36 This reasoning was given in the context where the Arbitral Tribunal decided that the southern coast of the island chain of the Andaman Islands should be excluded from the relevant coast. The complete quotation is as follows: "*As with the coast of mainland India*

Arbitral Tribunal adhered to the frontal projection method even though it explicitly endorsed the radial projection method.[37] Similarly, in reaction to India's argument that the Indian coast north of Devi Point could also generate projections that overlap with the areas beyond 200 nm claimed by Bangladesh, the Tribunal simply noted that this had no bearing on the relevance of the Indian coast between Devi Point and Sandy Point, as "[t]he projection of the coast of one Party can easily be overlapped by the projections of multiple segments of the coast of the other."[38]

By treating the entitlement to the continental shelf beyond 200 nm as part of coastal projections and by not distinguishing the coasts that generate entitlement to the continental shelf within 200 nm from those beyond 200 nm, the Arbitral Tribunal's approach may significantly expand the scope of the coasts and the area that are deemed relevant. By including the segment of the coast between Devi Point and Sandy Point, which only generates projections that overlap with Bangladesh's entitlement to the continental shelf beyond 200 nm, the Arbitral Tribunal also included in the relevant area the maritime area within the 200 nm limits of India, even though this area does not overlap with Bangladesh's entitlement at all, either within or beyond 200 nm – unless one understood Bangladesh's coasts to generate radial projections that overlap with the 200 nm continental shelf of India, but this would be inconsistent with Bangladesh's claim to the continental shelf beyond 200 nm in its submission to the CLCS.[39] The expansion of relevant coasts is further illustrated by the Arbitral Tribunal's inclusion of the northern part of the coasts of the Andaman Islands as relevant coasts, even though neither party argued for their inclusion.[40] As acknowledged by the Arbitral Tribunal, the projections generated by the Andaman Islands only overlap with Bangladesh's entitlement to the continental shelf beyond 200 nm.[41] It later became apparent that the coast of the Andaman Islands and the

*to the south of Sandy Point*, the Tribunal excludes the coast of the island chain to the south of Interview Island (as well as the Nicobar Islands further to the south)," ibid., 101–102 [304] (emphasis added).

37 See ibid., 99–100 [300–302]. See Oude Elferink (n 14), 189–190; Lando (n 19), 79–81.

38 See *Bangladesh* v. *India* (n 8), 99–100 [301].

39 The proposed outer limits of the continental shelf in the executive summary of Bangladesh's submission does not seem to overlap with India's 200 nm limits. See "Executive summary of Bangladesh's submission (25 February 2011)," 9–10, available at www.un.org/Depts/los/clcs_new/submissions_files/bgd55_11/Executive%20summary%20final.pdf.

40 See *Bangladesh* v. *India* (n 8),100 [303].

41 Ibid.

coast between Devi Point and Sandy Point did not contribute to the drawing of the boundary line.[42] As a result, these two segments of coast were only relevant for the purpose of the disproportionality test in the entire delimitation process.[43]

One last point concerns the calculation of relevant coasts. It is noted that the projections generated by the Andaman Islands overlap partially with the same area generated by the mainland of India. In other words, for the same relevant area, the lengths of the Indian coasts have been calculated twice.[44] This seems to be at odds with the approach of the ICJ when it dealt with the relevant coast of Nicaragua in the *Nicaragua* v. *Colombia I* case, in which the Court decided that "the east-facing coasts of the Nicaraguan islands are parallel to the mainland and do not, therefore, add to the length of the relevant coast, although they contribute to the baselines from which Nicaragua's entitlement is measured."[45] There is no doubt that the east-facing coasts of the Nicaraguan islands also generate projections into the area of the overlapping entitlements, yet their coastal lengths were not calculated. One may argue that the inclusion of the coast of the Andaman Islands in the *Bangladesh* v. *India* case is similar to that of the *Black Sea* case, in which two segments of Ukrainian coasts were included as relevant, whereas they projected into the same area of overlapping entitlements.[46] Yet, a difference between the *Bangladesh* v. *India* case and the *Black Sea* case is that both segments of the Ukrainian coasts contributed to the construction of the equidistance line, whereas the coast of the Andaman Islands did not.[47]

The Arbitral Tribunal referred to the proposed outer limits of the parties in their submissions to the CLCS to determine the relevant area. It is recalled that the Arbitral Tribunal "sees no ground why it should refrain from exercising its jurisdiction to decide on the lateral delimitation of the continental shelf beyond 200 nm before its outer limits have been established."[48] Therefore, the reference to the proposed outer limits of the continental shelf was solely for the purpose of calculating the size

[42] No basepoints south of Devi Point were selected for constructing the provisional equidistance line, nor were the coasts of the Andaman Islands considered in this respect. Ibid., 158 [463].

[43] Ibid., 168–169 [495–497].

[44] See ibid., 102 [305].

[45] See *Nicaragua* v. *Colombia I* (n 7), 678 [145].

[46] See *Black Sea* (n 1), 97–98 [98–103].

[47] See ibid., 111–112 [153–154].

[48] *Bangladesh* v. *India* (n 8), 31 [76].

of the relevant area in order to conduct the disproportionality test. However, the validity of such an exercise is questionable because the proposed outer limits of a coastal State in its submission may not be accepted by the CLCS.[49] Therefore, to determine the relevant area with the proposed outer limits of the continental shelf may be inaccurate, which further undermines the credibility of the disproportionality test. It may also encounter legitimate issues in light of the functions of the CLCS.[50] Given the uncertainties of determining the relevant area without precise outer limits of the continental shelf, Lando argues that international courts and tribunals should refrain from delimiting the continental shelf beyond 200 nm before the delineation of the outer limits of the continental shelf in accordance with Article 76.[51] It is submitted that whether this argument is valid depends on which stage of the delimitation process requires the outer limits of the continental shelf beyond 200 nm. If the outer limits of the continental shelf are necessary for determining the area of overlapping entitlements, it would be advisable for international courts and tribunals not to exercise jurisdiction.[52] However, if, as in the *Bangladesh* v. *India* case, the outer limits of the continental shelf are resorted to for the sole purpose of the disproportionality test, they would not be indispensable for the delimitation to proceed, as long as the existence of overlapping entitlements could be ascertained.

### 3 *Ghana/Côte d'Ivoire* Case

In the *Ghana/Côte d'Ivoire* case, the Special Tribunal of the ITLOS endorsed the approach of the *Bangladesh* v. *India* case. The Special Tribunal invoked the concept of the single continental shelf to justify that there is no basis for distinguishing between projections within 200 nm and those beyond, and observed that "the coasts of the two Parties are relevant, irrespective of whether an overlap occurs within 200 nm of both coasts, beyond 200 nm of both coasts, or within 200 nm of one and beyond 200 nm of another coast."[53] In terms of the relevant coasts of Ghana, the Special Tribunal did not take into account its coasts

[49] Chapter 2, Section III.C.

[50] See B. Kunoy, "The Delimitation of an Indicative Area of Overlapping Entitlement to the Outer Continental Shelf" (2013) 83 *BYIL* 61, 77–78.

[51] See Lando (n 19), 96.

[52] See Chapter 4, Section III.C.3.

[53] *Delimitation of the Maritime Boundary in the Atlantic Ocean (Ghana/Côte d'Ivoire), [2017] ITLOS Rep 4, 105* [373].

eastward of Cape Three Points because beyond that feature the coast "faces away from the area to be delimited and is not, therefore, relevant."[54] As to Côte d'Ivoire's relevant coasts, the Special Tribunal considered that the coast between Sassandra and the land boundary with Liberia is not relevant, because "this part of the coast of Côte d'Ivoire does not have a projection to the sea in a way that overlaps with the disputed area."[55] This statement is confusing because coastal projections are relevant not because they "overlap with the disputed area," but because they overlap with the projections of the coast of another party. Furthermore, unlike Ghana's coasts eastward of Cape Three Points, the segments of Ivorian coasts between Sassandra and the boundary with Liberia do face onto the disputed area.

The relevant area as identified by the Special Tribunal was bounded by limits to the east, to the south, and to the west. In the east and west, the relevant area was bounded by two meridian lines running due south from the points Cape Three Points and Sassandra respectively, until they reached the outer limits of the continental shelf claimed by Ghana and Côte d'Ivoire in their submissions to the Commission (see Figure 6.3).[56] Considering that Côte d'Ivoire had not received the recommendations, the Special Chamber emphasized that "it is only possible to give an approximation of the size of the relevant area since [. . .] the outer limits of the continental shelf beyond 200 nm have not yet been established."[57] Therefore, the *Ghana/Côte d'Ivoire* case also referred to the outer limits of the parties for the only purpose of the disproportionality test, whereas the lateral delimitation process did not require a prior determination of the location of the outer limits of the continental shelf.

### *B Assessment*

#### 1 The Crux of the Problems

The three decisions discussed above did not distinguish the entitlement to the continental shelf beyond 200 nm from coastal projections, and continued to identify the relevant coasts and the relevant area by employing the *Tunisia/Libya* formula. To some extent, such an approach can be justified by the principle that "the land dominates the sea through

54 Ibid., [376].
55 Ibid., [378].
56 See ibid., [383–384].
57 Ibid., [386].

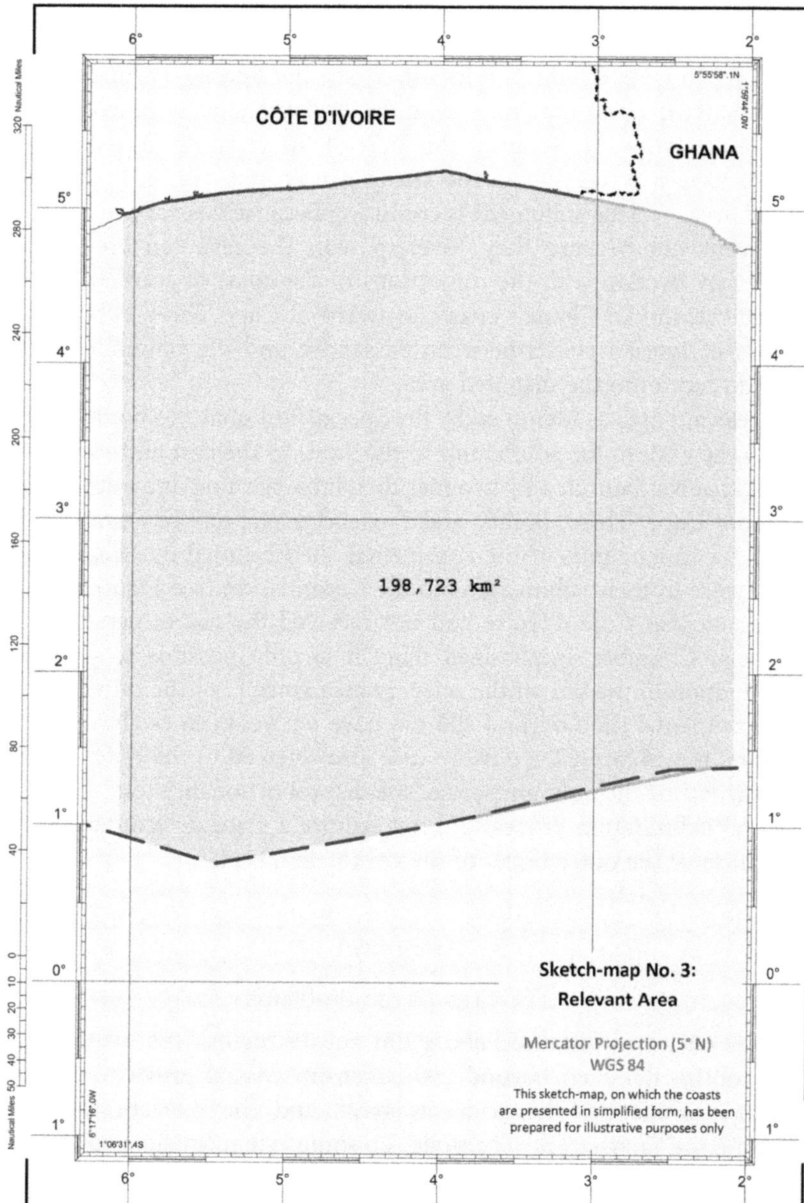


**Figure 6.3** Relevant area in the *Ghana/Côte d'Ivoire* case.
Source: [2017] ITLOS Rep 109

the projection of the coasts or the coastal fronts."[58] Despite the technicalities to establish the outer limits of the continental shelf, the basis of the entitlement rests on the sovereignty over the land territory,[59] and the entitlement to the continental shelf beyond 200 nm is also measured from the coasts, regardless of where the outer limits of the continental shelf are located. In this sense, the coast remains the intermediary for all maritime entitlements, including the entitlement to the continental shelf beyond 200 nm. In addition, the area beyond 200 nm abuts the coasts and its continuity with the maritime areas within 200 nm is not interrupted. However, one should not overlook the fact that the entitlement to the continental shelf beyond 200 nm and coastal projections are not identical, and the tribunals glossed over their differences.

A major problem of the three judicial decisions in their determination of the relevant coasts and relevant area is the employment of the *Tunisia/Libya* formula in a geographical framework in which that formula was not viable. The *Bay of Bengal* cases and the *Ghana/Côte d'Ivoire* case share the common geographical circumstance, i.e. adjacent coasts facing the open sea. The validity of using the *Tunisia/Libya* formula to such a geographical context had already been questioned.[60] In the *Libya/Malta* case, Judge Mosler criticized the method of defining the relevant area by drawing notional lines and suggested that "[i]n geographical conditions where the coasts of two laterally neighbouring States are not in a concave situation no definition of relevant maritime areas is possible."[61] When the *Tunisia/Libya* formula was strictly implemented, the *Bangladesh/Myanmar* case excluded part of the area of overlapping entitlements to the continental shelf beyond 200 nm, while the *Bangladesh* v. *India* case expanded the scope of relevant coasts and relevant areas. These uncertainties are further exacerbated because there is no consistent approach to the construction of coastal projections in the jurisprudence. It is recalled that the *Bangladesh* v. *India* case stated that: "[T]here is a margin of appreciation in determining the projections generated by a segment of coastline and a point at which a line drawn at an acute angle to the general direction of the coast can no longer be fairly said to represent the

[58] *Black Sea* (n 1), 89 [77].

[59] See *Aegean Sea Continental Shelf (Greece v. Turkey) [1978] ICJ Rep 3, 36* [86].

[60] L. L. Herman, "The Court Giveth and the Court Taketh Away: An Analysis of the Tunisia–Libya Continental Shelf Case" (1984) 33 *ICLQ* 825, 851–852.

[61] See *Libya/Malta* (n 13), 115 (Dissenting Opinion of Judge Mosler).

seaward projection of that coast."[62] The vagueness inherent in this statement does not seem helpful in clarifying the conceptual problems in the determination of relevant coasts and relevant area.[63]

It is submitted that the above-mentioned problems could have been avoided had not the tribunals engaged with the disproportionality tests. The ICJ perceived a twin role of relevant coasts and relevant area, namely, one relating to determining the area of overlapping claims and the other to the disproportionality test.[64] The practices of the *Bay of Bengal* cases and the *Ghana/Côte d'Ivoire* case demonstrate that the exercises of identifying relevant coasts and relevant areas have been increasingly attached to the latter. However, due to the conceptual and operational problems of the disproportionality test,[65] it is doubtful that the latter would yield meaningful input in a coherent approach to delimitation of the continental shelf beyond 200 nm.

Since the disproportionality test has to rely on the calculation of coastal lengths and the size of maritime areas, the lack of objectivity in the latter also undermines the credibility of the former. As pointed out by Fietta and Cleverly, in most cases the parties engaged with a self-serving determination of relevant coasts and relevant areas that suited their specific situation and case objectives.[66] But it would be unrealistic to expect that international courts and tribunals can calculate coastal lengths or the size of maritime areas in a more scientifically convincing manner than the parties.[67] More importantly, as formulated by the ICJ,

[62] *Bangladesh* v. *India* (n 8), 100 [302].

[63] Lando (n 19), 79–81.

[64] As summarized by the ICJ, the roles of relevant coasts to determine the area of overlapping claims and to test the disproportionality of the boundary lines are "two different though closely related legal aspects in relation to the delimitation of the continental shelf and the exclusive economic zone," *Black Sea* (n 1) 89 [78].

[65] See R. Ida, "The Role of Proportionality in Maritime Delimitation Revisited: The Origin and Meaning of the Principle from the Early Decisions of the Court," in N. Ando et al. (eds.), *Liber Amicorum Judge Shigeru Oda, Volume II* (Kluwer Law International 2002), 1052; J.-H. Paik, "The Role of Proportionality in Maritime Delimitation: State of Jurisprudence," in H. P. Hestermeyer et al. (eds.), *Coexistence, Cooperation and Solidarity: Liber Amicorum Rüdiger Wolfrum, Volume I* (Martinus Nijhoff 2012), 209–213; Fietta and Cleverly (n 12), 602–609; Y. Tanaka, "The Disproportionality Test in the Law of Maritime Delimitation," in A. G. Oude Elferink et al. (eds.), *Maritime Boundary Delimitation: The Case Law: Is It Consistent and Predictable?* (Cambridge University Press 2018), 314–316.

[66] Fietta and Cleverly (n 12), 594.

[67] See *Decision in Case concerning Delimitation of Maritime Areas (St Pierre and Miquelon), (1992) 31 ILM 1145*, 1206 [24] (Dissenting Opinion of Mr Weil).

the disproportionality test is to check if there is "significant"[68] or "marked"[69] or "gross"[70] disproportion in the ratios between maritime areas and coastal lengths. However, there are no objective criteria to measure the degree of disproportion.[71] As the ICJ found, various tribunals and the Court itself drew different conclusions as to what "significant disproportionality" is. Inevitably, "[t]his remains in each case a matter for the Court's appreciation, which it will exercise by reference to the overall geography of the area,"[72] and the disproportionality test can only be approximate.[73]

To incorporate the disproportionality test into the three-stage approach also provokes the question of whether the final stage of the delimitation process could overthrow the delimitation outcomes reached in the preceding delimitation process, should significant disproportionality be found. However, this is not how international courts or tribunals view the function of the disproportionality test. According to the ICJ, "What constitutes such a disproportionality will vary according to the precise situation in each case, for the third stage of the process cannot require the Court to disregard all of the considerations which were important in the earlier stages."[74] This cannot be clearer than when the Court conducted the disproportionality test in the *Nicaragua* v. *Colombia I* case by "taking account of all the circumstances of the present case."[75] These statements almost disregard the disproportionality test as such, because a contextualized analysis of disproportionality seems to blur the distinction between the second and the third stage of the three-stage approach. Eventually, it is the second stage of the delimitation methodology that really matters in determining the equity of the delimitation result.

Furthermore, the function of the disproportionality is inherently limited. Tanaka points out that since the number of lines capable of producing the same proportion is limitless in a given area, the disproportionality test cannot verify the validity of the *location* of the maritime

68 *Black Sea* (n 1), 129 [210].
69 *Maritime Dispute (Peru v. Chile) [2014] ICJ Rep 3, 65* [180].
70 *Nicaragua* v. *Colombia I* (n 7), 716 [242].
71 See Tanaka (n 65), 305–306.
72 *Black Sea* (n 1), 129 [213].
73 Ibid., [212]; *Ghana/Côte d'Ivoire* (n 53), 144 [534].
74 *Nicaragua* v. *Colombia I* (n 7), 715 [240].
75 See ibid., 716–717 [244–247].

boundary established by a court or tribunal.[76] Likewise, as the disproportionality test is a geographical concept in itself, it can hardly test the equitableness of the result if the boundary line was established on the basis of relevant circumstances other than geographical ones.[77] This latter observation has been confirmed by the *Peru* v. *Chile* case. Due to the existence of a 80 nm boundary line established on the basis of tacit agreement between the parties, the Court found that "it would make difficult, if not impossible, the calculation of the length of the relevant coasts and of the extent of the relevant area," thus "in this final phase of the delimitation process, the calculation does not purport to be precise and is approximate," and the Court only engaged "in a broad assessment of disproportionality" without presenting any specific figures about the relevant coasts or relevant area.[78]

It seems that the disproportionality test in a delimitation of the continental shelf beyond 200 nm may be subject to further theoretical and practical difficulties. As mentioned earlier, the approaches in the *Bay of Bengal* cases cast into doubt the correctness of applying the disproportionality test in a delimitation of the continental shelf beyond 200 nm before the parties receive the recommendations of the CLCS.[79] It has also been argued that if geomorphological or geological factors have been taken into account in the delimitation of the continental shelf beyond 200 nm, the equity of the delimitation could hardly be justified by resorting to the disproportionality test.[80]

In the *Bay of Bengal* cases and the *Ghana/Côte d'Ivoire* case, no significant disproportion was found, which also occurred in all previous cases where a disproportionality test was conducted. This fact alone seems to suggest that the disproportionality test is more of a rhetorical tool to declare the equity of the delimitation result.[81] That said, it is likely that future judicial decisions concerning the continental shelf beyond

[76] Tanaka (n 65), 317.

[77] Paik (n 65), 200.

[78] *Peru* v. *Chile* (n 69), 69 [193]. Evans criticized the statement as being "less of a 'broad assessment' and more of a bare assertion," M. D. Evans, "Maritime Boundary Delimitation: Whatever Next?," in J. Barrett and R. Barnes (eds.), *Law of the Sea: UNCLOS as a Living Treaty* (BIILC 2016), 65.

[79] See Lando (n 19), 278–280.

[80] See Paik (n 65), 210.

[81] See M. D. Evans, "Maritime Boundary Delimitation: Where Do We Go From Here?," in D. Freestone et al (eds.), *The Law of the Sea: Progress and Prospects* (Oxford University Press 2006), 155.

200 nm will continue to engage with the disproportionality test if the three-stage approach is found to be applicable. Yet, one should not underestimate the force of the arguments that the use of the disproportionality test should be restricted,[82] if not abandoned,[83] for its exercise is full of subjectivity and its value as an independent stage of the delimitation process is essentially and empirically limited.

### 2 Refining the Relevance of Coasts with the Delimitation Process

The preceding discussion has demonstrated that the problems involved in the determination of relevant coasts and relevant area in the *Bay of Bengal* cases and the *Ghana/Côte d'Ivoire* case derived from the overriding need to apply the disproportionality test. Part of the confusion also stems from the unclarified role of coasts in relation to the delimitation of the continental shelf beyond 200 nm, in particular the undefined relationship between the coast and the entitlement to the continental shelf beyond 200 nm. This question could only be elucidated by refining the relevance of coasts with the delimitation process.

In the jurisprudence, coasts are relevant to maritime delimitation first because they contribute to determining the area of overlapping entitlements of the parties.[84] As maritime delimitation can only take place in areas of overlapping entitlements, determination of the latter has a direct influence over the location of the boundary.[85] This aspect of the coasts is closely related to the nature of maritime delimitation, which is an exercise that spells out the spatial relationship between maritime areas

[82] See Tanaka (n 65), 318; Fietta and Cleverly (n 12), 608–609. These authors argue that the use of the disproportionality test should be restricted to its original use in the *North Sea* cases, namely that disproportionality should be considered only where an equidistance line would create the cut-off effect by a markedly concave or convex coastline, even though relevant coasts are comparative in length. This proposition in effect argues that the role of disproportionality should be confined to the evaluation of relevant circumstances.

[83] Evans, "Maritime Boundary Delimitation: Where Do We Go From Here?," (n 81), 156. Weil more profoundly challenged the concept of proportionality as such. According to him: "There is nothing riskier than models of proportionality, which experience shows to be of such flexibility that they make it possible to prove, in an allegedly scientific way, almost anything one wants to. Theoretically unjustifiable, impossible to put into practice, the test of proportionality is, moreover, useless." See also P. Weil, *The Law of Maritime Delimitation: Reflections* (Grotius 1989), 244.

[84] *Black Sea* (n 1), 89 [78].

[85] Ibid., [77].

and coasts.[86] It should be stressed that the *Tunisia/Libya* formula should not be rigorously applied to determine the area of overlapping entitlements in every geographical context, as its value can be very limited in certain circumstances. In the *Nicaragua* v. *Honduras* case, it would be difficult to maintain that the coasts of Nicaragua and Honduras generate overlapping entitlements in a seaward facing direction, for the coasts of Nicaragua face the direction of the northeast, whereas the coasts of Honduras face the direction of the southeast.[87] Indeed, in this case the ICJ refrained from engaging with the precise measurement of relevant coasts or relevant areas or the disproportionality test. It is therefore advisable not to overconceptualize the correlation between the coasts and the area of overlapping entitlements. In the *Bay of Bengal* cases and the *Ghana/Côte d'Ivoire* case, the overlapping entitlements to the continental shelf beyond 200 nm lie off the coasts of the parties and can be safely considered to be the natural prolongation of the relevant parties. Also given the adjacent coastal relationship between the parties in the three cases, the area under dispute is practically limited. Therefore, it does not seem necessary to determine the area of overlapping entitlements by reference to the coasts.[88]

Coasts are also relevant to the delimitation process because of their implications for the choice and application of delimitation methods. As stressed by the ICJ, "If it is 'to be faithful to the actual geographical situation' [. . .], the method of delimitation should seek a solution by reference first to the States' 'relevant coasts'."[89] In fact, a number of judicial decisions determined relevant coasts by referring to the delimitation method. For instance, in the *Jan Mayen* case, between the opposite coasts of Denmark and Norway, the ICJ observed that "[i]t is appropriate to treat as relevant the coasts [. . .], in view of their role in generating the complete course of the [equidistance] line."[90] This is also the case in the *Cameroon* v. *Nigeria* case,[91] as well as the

[86] See M. D. Evans, "Relevant Circumstances," in A. G. Oude Elferink et al. (eds.), *Maritime Boundary Delimitation: The Case Law: Is It Consistent and Predictable?* (Cambridge University Press 2018), 260; Oude Elferink (n 14), 173.

[87] See *Territorial and Maritime Dispute between Nicaragua and Honduras in the Caribbean Sea (Nicaragua v. Honduras) [2007] ICJ Rep 659, 749* [296-298]. See also Oude Elferink (n 14), 180.

[88] See Section III.A. below.

[89] *Nicaragua* v. *Honduras* (n 87), 747 [289].

[90] *Jan Mayen* (n 9), 68 [67].

[91] As the ICJ stated, "the Court must, however, define the relevant coastlines of the Parties by reference to which the location of the base points to be used in the construction of the equidistance line will be determined," *Land and Maritime Boundary between Cameroon*

*Guyana* v. *Suriname* case.[92] It would seem that the *Bay of Bengal* cases and the *Ghana/Côte d'Ivoire* case could have adopted the same approach. In the *Bangladesh* v. *India* case, the basepoints selected did not include any points on the coast of mainland India to the south of Devi Point, nor on the coast of the Andaman Islands. In the *Ghana/Côte d'Ivoire* case, the basepoints on the coasts of each State are concentrated in the immediate proximity of the land boundary terminus, whereas the relevant coasts identified by the Special Chamber extend much further away from the land boundary terminus (see Figure 6.4).[93] Therefore, the coasts relevant for the delimitation methods and the coasts relevant for the disproportionality test were not identical. Some scholars suggest that the relevant coasts can be determined more objectively by reference to the delimitation methods, which may serve as an alternative to the *Tunisia/Libya* formula.[94] It is also desirable that international courts and tribunals endeavor to distinguish the role of coasts in relation to delimitation methods and to the disproportionality test so that the relevance of the coasts can be coherently and clearly presented.

Moreover, coasts are relevant to the delimitation process because they may constitute the relevant circumstances that shape the boundary lines. For instance, significant disproportion in coastal lengths "may be a factor to be taken into consideration in order to adjust or shift the provisional delimitation line"[95] and for addressing this relevant circumstance, the lengths of the parties' coasts are measured. This usage of disproportionality should be distinguished from the disproportionality test as an *ex post facto* test.[96] In a similar vein, where the coasts are deemed not relevant, they would not form part of the relevant circumstances to be

*and Nigeria (Cameroon v Nigeria: Equatorial Guinea intervening) [2002] ICJ Rep 303, 442* [290].

92 The Arbitral Tribunal observed that "it seems logical and appropriate to treat as relevant the coasts of the Parties which generate 'the complete course' of the provisional equidistance line," *Maritime Boundary Arbitration (Guyana v. Suriname) (2007) XXX RIAA 1* [352].

93 See *Ghana/Côte d'Ivoire* (n 53), 106 [378] and 112–113 [399].

94 See Y. Tanaka, "Reflections on the Concept of Proportionality in the Law of Maritime Delimitation" (2001) 16 *IJMCL* 433, 461; L. Lucchini, "La Délimitation des Frontières Maritimes dans la Jurisprudence International: Vue d'ensemble," in R. Lagoni and D. Vignes (eds.), *Maritime Delimitation* (Martinus Nijhoff Publishers 2006), 12; Evans, "Maritime Boundary Delimitation: Where Do We Go From Here?" (n 81), 154; Oude Elferink (n 14), 192.

95 *Cameroon* v. *Nigeria* (n 91), 446–447 [301]; *Nicaragua* v. *Colombia I* (n 7), 702 [209–211].

96 See Chapter 8, Section III.A.

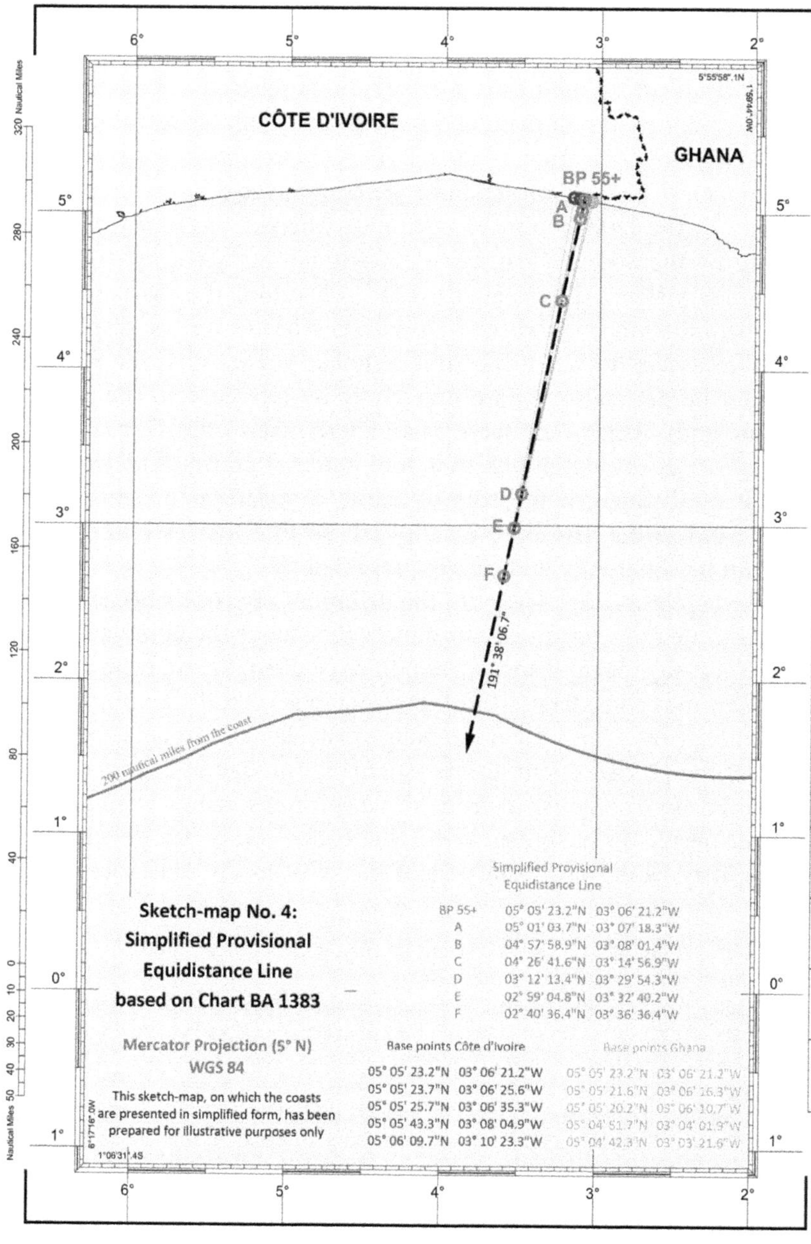


**Figure 6.4** Construction of the equidistance line in the *Ghana/Côte d'Ivoire* case.
Source: [2017] ITLOS Rep 114

considered in the delimitation process. In the *Cameroon* v. *Nigeria* case, the ICJ excluded the relevance of the coasts forming part of the Gulf of Guinea but belonging to third parties to the dispute, as well as the coast of the Bioko Island – an island whose sovereignty rests on the third party, Equatorial Guinea.[97] Subsequently, the Court did not consider these coasts relevant in relation to the assessment of the concavity of the coasts or the disproportion in coastal lengths.[98]

By refining the relevance of coasts with the delimitation process, it becomes clear that coasts are relevant not only to the disproportionality test, but also to the determination of the area of overlapping entitlements, the choice and application of delimitation methods, and the consideration of relevant circumstances. The decisions concerning the delimitation of the continental shelf beyond 200 nm up to date determined the relevant coasts primarily for the purposes of the disproportionality test, but fell short of explaining how the coasts thus identified were relevant with other aspects of the delimitation process in a more explicit manner. As a result, the coherence of identifying relevant coasts and relevant area could be improved if international courts and tribunals spell out the multiple dimensions of the relevance of the coasts with the delimitation process, which is also the case in the delimitation of the continental shelf beyond 200 nm.

## III Factors Contributing to the Determination of the Area of Overlapping Entitlements

With the relevance of coasts put in perspective, this section addresses the relevance of coasts with the determination of the area of overlapping entitlements to the continental shelf beyond 200 nm.

### *A Coastal Relationship as a Starting Point*

In recent jurisprudence, the wide acceptance of the three-stage approach lessens the discussions of the coastal relationship in that the delimitation methodology applies regardless of whether the coasts are opposite or adjacent in relation to each other.[99] Nevertheless, the coastal relationship

[97] See *Cameroon* v. *Nigeria* (n 91), 442–443 [291].
[98] See ibid., 446–447 [297–301].
[99] See Evans, "Relevant Circumstances" (n 86), 249.

does provide a useful starting point to consider the area of overlapping entitlements to the continental shelf beyond 200 nm.

Notwithstanding a risk of over-simplifying, where the coastal relationship is opposite, the area of overlapping entitlements is situated "between" the coasts of the parties, while where the parties share a common land boundary terminus and therefore the coastal relationship is adjacent, the areas of overlapping entitlements lie "off" the coasts of both parties.[100] These two situations are different in several aspects. First, between adjacent coastal States, regardless of how the area of the overlapping entitlements to the continental shelf beyond 200 nm is determined, the boundary line normally commences from the land boundary terminus that intersects with the coasts, which is an important factor that restricts the area relevant to the delimitation as well as the possible location of the boundary line.[101] As pointed out in the *North Sea* cases, "Evidently any dispute about boundaries must involve that there is a disputed marginal or fringe area, to which both parties are laying claim."[102] In terms of opposite coastal States, the boundary line has to be situated within the area of overlapping entitlements to the continental shelf beyond 200 nm. If the distance between the two States is greater than 400 nm apart, the area of overlapping entitlements is found between the 200 nm limits of the coasts. Therefore, the formulae or the constraints of Article 76 of UNCLOS in relation to the extent of the continental shelf beyond 200 nm may come into play in order to accurately determine the area of overlap.

Second, between adjacent coastal States, the boundary line continues throughout the maritime areas of the territorial sea, the EEZ, and the continental shelf until it reaches the outer limits of the continental shelf, therefore the seaward limits of the maritime zones are not necessary for the delimitation to proceed.[103] On the contrary, for opposite coastal States, the outer limits of the continental shelf beyond 200 nm may be

[100] The distinction between "opposite" and "adjacent" coasts may become blurred when the maritime area extends further into the open sea. See *Delimitation of the Continental Shelf between the United Kingdom of Great Britain and Northern Ireland, and the French Republic (United Kingdom/France) (1978) 18 RIAA 3* [88–93]; *Barbados* v. *Trinidad and Tobago* (n 6), [121–124].

[101] The ICJ in the *Tunisia/Libya* case considered that "the position of the land frontier, or more precisely, the position of its intersection with the coastline" was a relevant circumstance. See *Tunisia/Libya* (n 4), 64–65 [81].

[102] *North Sea Continental Shelf Cases (Federal Republic of Germany/Denmark; Federal Republic of Germany/Netherlands) [1969] ICJ Rep 3, 22-23* [20].

[103] Chapter 4, Section III.B.3.

indispensable for determining the area of overlap for purposes of maritime delimitation. This point is not trivial, as it underlies the admissibility of a claim to the continental shelf beyond 200 nm if the dispute is submitted to an international court or tribunal.

A third difference between opposite and adjacent coastal relationships concerning the continental shelf beyond 200 nm is that an adjacent coastal relationship may be a strong indicator of the existence of a common continental margin "shared" by the adjacent coastal States.[104] The determination of the overlapping entitlements in the *Ghana/Côte d'Ivoire* case is a clear example.[105] In contrast, there is less certainty as to the existence of a common continental margin between opposite coasts.[106]

With these observations in mind, looking back at the *Bay of Bengal* cases and the *Ghana/Côte d'Ivoire* case, it becomes clear that due to the adjacent coastal relationship, the area to be delimited is considerably limited. As to the area of the continental shelf beyond 200 nm, in all three cases there is a common continental margin shared by the coastal States to the disputes. Therefore, there is little practical purpose in determining the area of overlapping entitlements by reference to the coasts. The continuity between the maritime areas within and beyond 200 nm also necessitates the continuity of the maritime boundary. Therefore, between adjacent coasts, the exercise of determining the existence of overlapping entitlements to the continental shelf beyond 200 nm can and should be separated from determining relevant coasts. This, however, does not seem to be the case for States with opposite coasts. As will be elaborated upon further below, other factors may be important to specify the area of overlapping entitlements to the continental shelf beyond 200 nm.

### *B 200-NM-Limit Opening*

Lilje-Jensen and Thamsborg found an analogy between the 200 nm opening and the coast. According to them, the area of the continental

[104] See M. Zahraa, "Natural Prolongation and Delimitation of Maritime Boundaries" (1996) 7 *Finnish YIL* 378, 396–397; T. L. McDorman, "The Continental Shelf beyond 200 NM: A First Look at the Bay of Bengal (Bangladesh/Myanmar) Case," in M. H. Nordquist et al. (eds.), *The Regulation of Continental Shelf Development: Rethinking International Standards* (Martinus Nijhoff 2013), 100.

[105] *Ghana/Côte d'Ivoire* (n 53), 136 [491].

[106] See C. M. Carleton, "Delimitation Issues," in P. J. Cook and C. M. Carleton (eds.), *Continental Shelf Limits: The Scientific and Legal Interface* (Oxford University Press 2000), 314–316.

shelf beyond 200 nm can only be legally belonging to coastal States when they are situated in front of the coastal States, in the sense that "the outer and inner part of the shelf meet along the 200 nm line off the individual State (200 nm opening) over a certain distance, long or short."[107] They also argued that in the delimitation process, "the length of the opening should be given status of basic parameter (equitable principle) as to the allocation of share of outer shelf to the individual claiming State."[108]

This analogy is not, however, convincing or appropriate. Coasts are the starting line from which the entitlements to maritime zones are measured, in accordance with the principle that "the land dominates the sea," while the 200-nm-limit opening is not. To make such an analogy suggests that the continental shelf beyond 200 nm is, in the opinion of the authors, something surplus or extra.[109] This argument is not consistent with Article 76, which does not provide an "inner" or "outer" continental shelf distinction. The authors' thesis is based on the presumption that the existence of the area of the continental shelf beyond 200 nm precedes the identification of the 200-nm-limit opening, where the continental shelf within and beyond 200 nm converges.[110] In other words, the 200-nm-limit opening is the line that determines the continuity of the continental shelf beyond 200 nm. However, the continuity of the continental shelf under UNCLOS is established by reference to Article 76(4). This baseline hypothesis thus deviates from the entitlement to the continental shelf beyond 200 nm and from the foundation of the law of maritime delimitation.[111]

In fact, the role of the 200 nm limits in determining the area of overlapping entitlements to the continental shelf beyond 200 nm is secondary to the application of Article 76. It is possible that an area of the continental shelf beyond 200 nm surrounded by the 200 nm limits of the coastal States is subject to the overlapping claims of all these States. For instance, the Loop Hole in the Barents Sea is surrounded by the 200 nm limits of Norway and Russia, and is part of the common continental margin of both States.[112] In this case, the 200 nm limits have

[107] See J. Lilje-Jensen and M. Thamsborg, "The Role of Natural Prolongation in Relation to Shelf Delimitation beyond 200 Nautical Miles" (1995) 64 *Nordic JIL* 619, 639.

[108] Ibid., 643.

[109] Ibid., 626.

[110] Ibid., 635.

[111] See B. M. Magnússon, *The Continental Shelf beyond 200 Nautical Miles: Delineation, Delimitation and Dispute Settlement* (Brill Nijhoff Publishers 2015), 156–157.

[112] See "Summary of Recommendations to Norway in respect of Areas in the Arctic Ocean, the Barents Sea and the Norwegian Sea adopted on 27 March 2009," 23, available at www.un.org/Depts/los/clcs_new/submissions_files/nor06/nor_rec_summ.pdf.

a descriptive role to define the area of overlapping entitlements once the application of Article 76 confirms that it is a "shared" continental shelf. Nevertheless, in some other circumstances, not every one of the coastal States could claim the entire area bounded by the 200 nm limits of all the relevant parties. This is the case of the Banana Hole, which is bounded by the 200 nm limits of Norway, Iceland, and Denmark (Faroe Islands). While Norway has an entitlement to almost the entire Banana Hole, Denmark and Iceland only claim part of it.[113] Accordingly, the precise area of overlapping entitlements between any two of the coastal States can only be correctly defined on the basis of the application of Article 76 for each State, not by reference to the 200 nm limits of the States.

The relevance of the 200-nm-limit opening to define the area of overlapping entitlements between adjacent coastal States may be even less obvious because the coasts remain the reference line for measuring the maritime entitlement.

### C *The Foot of the Continental Slope*

Due to the central role of the foot of the continental slope (FOS) to establish the entitlement to the continental shelf beyond 200 nm, it has been suggested that the FOS may provide an alternative baseline for determining the area of overlapping entitlements other than the coasts.[114] Colson suggested one specific scenario (Scenario A): suppose that State A and State B were opposite and 500 nm apart, which would create a 100 nm strip lying between the 200 nm limits of both States. Suppose that the FOS of State A was located 180 nm from its coasts and the FOS of State B 220 nm from its coasts. Applying the Hedberg formula, the area of overlapping entitlements would be situated between 220 nm and 240 nm from the coasts of State A.[115] In this scenario, it is

[113] Iceland has claimed the western part of the Banana Hole, while Denmark (Faroe Islands) claims the western and southern part of the Banana Hole. All the three States have received recommendations from the CLCS with respect to their continental shelf beyond 200 nm in the Banana Hole. See the summary of the recommendations of the CLCS to Norway (March 27, 2009), to Denmark (March 12, 2014), and to Iceland (March 10, 2016), available at www.un.org/Depts/los/clcs_new/commission_submissions.htm.

[114] See Fietta and Cleverly (n 12), 616–618. For an opposite view, see International Law Association, "Preliminary Report of the Committee on Legal Issues of the Outer Continental Shelf," Report of the Seventieth Conference (2002, New Dheli) 752; B. M. Magnússon, "The Rejection of a Theoretical Beauty: The Foot of the Continental Slope in Maritime Boundary Delimitations beyond 200 Nautical Miles" (2014) 45 *ODIL* 41, 48–49.

[115] See D. Colson, "The Delimitation of the Outer Continental Shelf between Neighboring States" (2003) 97 *AJIL* 91, 103.

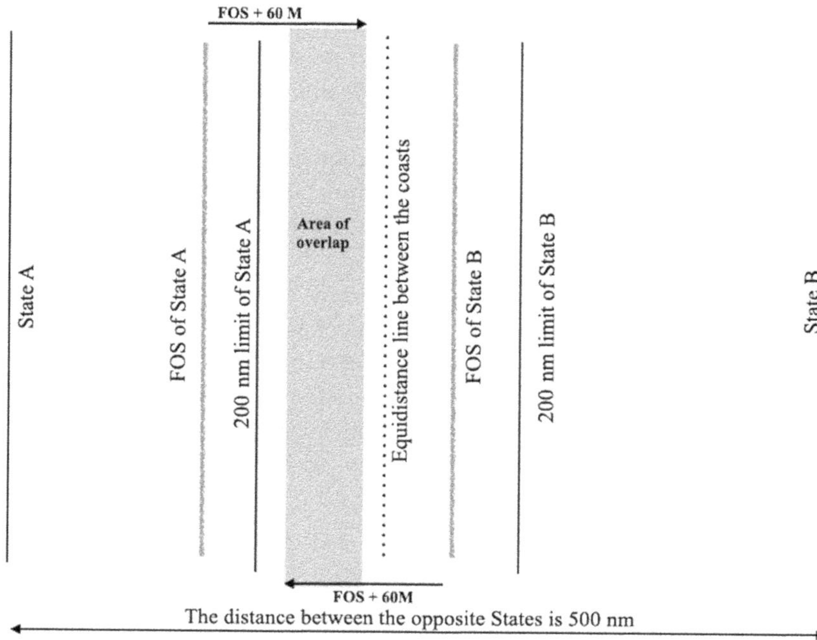


**Figure 6.5** Determination of the area of overlap (Scenario A): application of the Hedberg formula

the FOS, rather than the coasts of the respective States, that provides a reliable criterion for determining the area of overlapping entitlements. What follows is that the boundary line should divide the area between the respective FOS instead of the respective coasts (Figure 6.5).

Notwithstanding this illustrative scenario, whether the FOS contributes to determining the area of overlapping entitlements to the continental shelf beyond 200 nm depends on the locations of the FOS in specific situations, as well as the applicable formula under Article 76(4) of UNCLOS. In the Scenario A proposed by Colson, if the Gardiner formula were to be applied, it could also be possible that the entire area in the 100 nm strip between the 200 nm limits of State A and State B were covered by the sedimentary rocks that could be equally claimed by both States. As a result, the 100 nm strip area would be the area of overlapping entitlements of the two States regardless of the locations of the respective FOS (see Figure 6.6). What follows is the delimitation in this scenario continues to be governed by reference to the respective coasts.

Similarly, considering a Scenario B where State A and State B were opposite and 500 nm apart, and assuming that the FOS of State A was

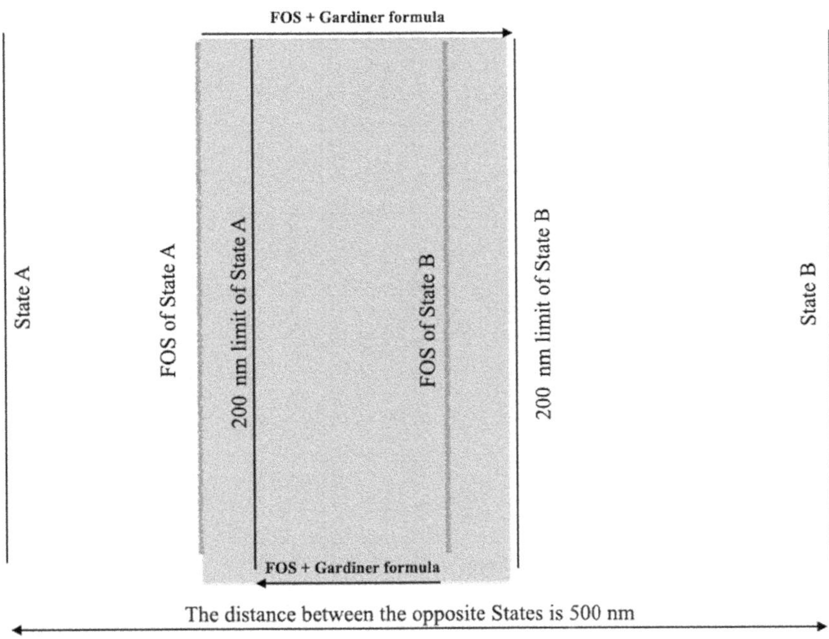


**Figure 6.6** Determination of the area of overlap (A variation of Scenario A): application of the Gardiner formula

located 40 nm seaward from its 200 nm limit, and the FOS of State B was located 50 nm seaward from its 200 nm limit, should the Hedberg formula apply, the 100 nm strip between the 200 nm limits of the two States would also be the area of overlapping entitlements. In this scenario, the respective FOS points also contribute to the accurate definition of the area of overlapping entitlements, yet they lose relevance in the delimitation process, as the 100 nm strip can be divided by reference to the coasts of the States (see Figure 6.7).

Whereas using the FOS to determine the area of overlapping entitlements to the continental shelf beyond 200 nm is theoretically possible between two opposite coasts under certain circumstances, it seems that the same does not hold true for States with adjacent coasts. This is so in cases where the respective FOS points of the two adjacent States are approximately parallel to the coasts.[116] As a consequence, the potential

[116] For instance, see the executive summaries of submissions of Brazil (September 8, 2017) and France (May 22, 2007), available at www.un.org/Depts/los/clcs_new/commission_submissions.htm.

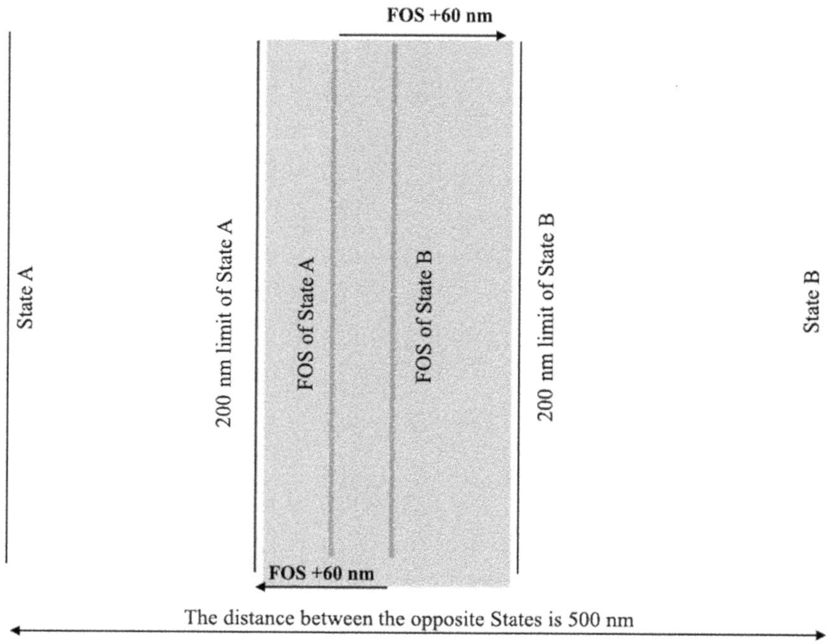


**Figure 6.7** Determination of the area of overlap (Scenario B): application of the Hedberg formula

role of the FOS in the delimitation between adjacent States is also limited. It has also been argued that if the FOS of the parties were located seaward from the 200 nm limits of the States, the question of connecting the terminus of the maritime boundary at the 200 nm limit with the boundary beyond 200 nm (starting from the FOS) would arise,[117] which is another factor that argues against the use of the FOS for delimitation of the continental shelf beyond 200 nm between two adjacent States.

To sum up, the role of FOS in determining the area of overlapping entitlements has to be examined in concrete scenarios, taking into account factors such as the coastal relationship, locations of the FOS, and the applicable formulae of Article 76(4). Note also that in reality the actual display of the FOS in geomorphological or geological terms could be much more complicated, which renders the exercise even less viable.[118]

[117] See Magnússon (n 114), 48.

[118] Chapter 8, Section II.C.1.

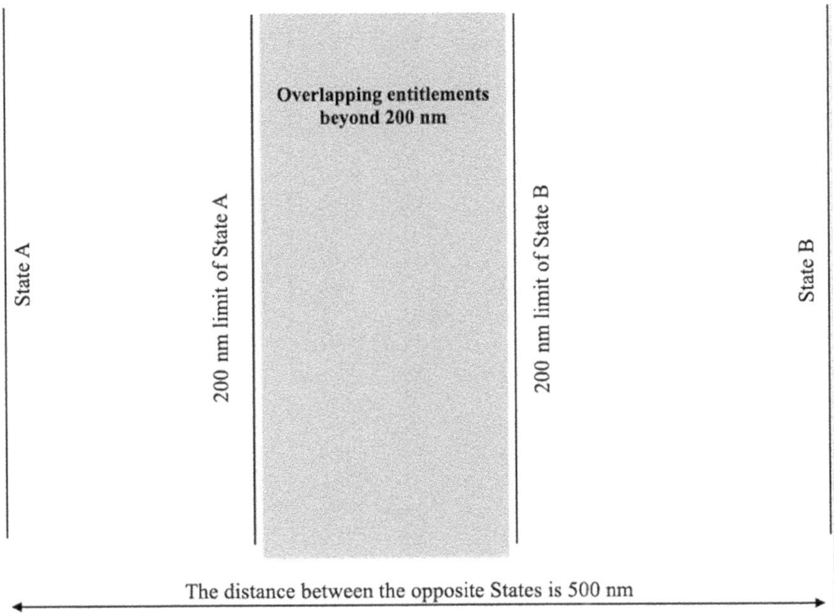


**Figure 6.8** A common continental margin "shared" by two coastal States

### *D The Outer Limits of the Continental Shelf*

As illustrated by the survey of State practice in Chapter 3, whether outer limits of the continental shelf are necessary in determining the relevant area is not a question that can be answered *in abstracto*.[119] As between adjacent States, coastal States can proceed to delimit the continental shelf beyond 200 nm without necessarily knowing the exact extent of overlapping entitlements. Even for situations other than those between adjacent coasts, the outer limits of the continental shelf may not be necessary in cases where the continental shelf beyond 200 nm can safely be said to fall within a common continental margin shared by the coastal States (see Figure 6.8). The delimitation of the continental shelf beyond 200 nm between Mexico and the United States in the western polygon in the Gulf of Mexico,[120] as well as between Norway and Russia in the

[119] Chapter 3, Section II.A.

[120] See R. W. Smith, "Mexico – United States, Report Number 1-5(2)," in J. I. Charney and R. W. Smith (eds.), *International Maritime Boundaries, Vol.IV* (Martinus Nijhoff 2002), 2623. It should be pointed out that, whereas Mexico and the United States are adjacent States given that they share the land boundary, when their maritime boundary extends

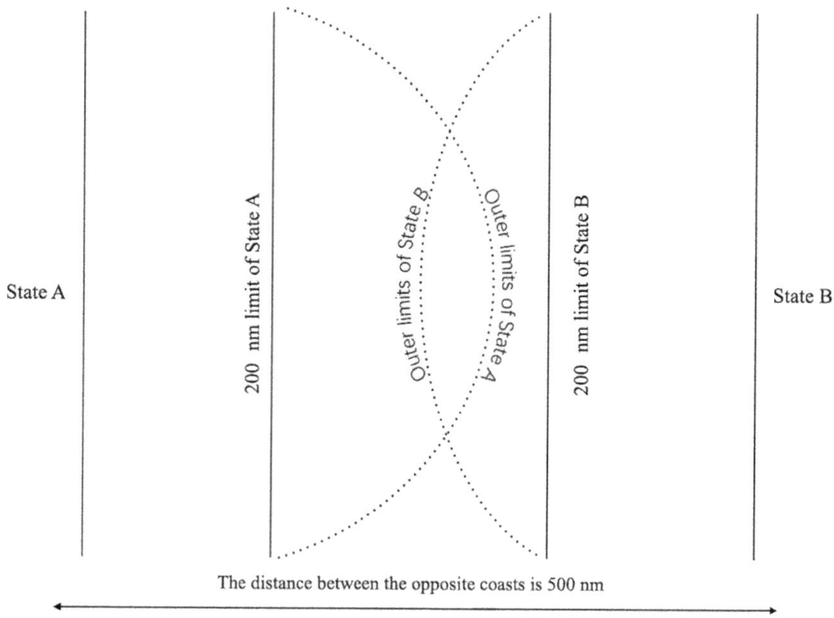


**Figure 6.9** The area of overlapping entitlements defined by the respective outer limits of the continental shelf

Loop Hole,[121] illustrates that the area of overlapping entitlements can be identified without determining the outer limits of the continental shelf.

In other circumstances, at least approximate outer limits of the continental shelf have to be identified in order to accurately determine the area of overlapping entitlements. This is likely to occur between opposite States where the application of Article 76 results in the situation that either party may claim part of the continental shelf beyond 200 nm between them, but not in its entirety (see Figure 6.9). This situation can be found in the 2013 Denmark (Greenland)–Iceland Agreed Minutes,[122] which also suggests that once it is the outer limits of the

further into the Gulf of Mexico and where the delimitation of the continental shelf beyond 200 nm is concerned, their coastal relationship demonstrates characteristics of opposite coasts as well.

121 See R. E. Fife, "Norway–Russia Federation, Report Number 9-6(3)," in C. G. Lathrop (ed.), *International Maritime Boundaries, Vol. VII* (Brill Nijhoff Publishers 2016), 5183–5184.

122 See Paragraph 2 of 2013 Agreed Minutes, reproduced in B. M. Magnússon, "Denmark (Greenland)–Iceland, Report Number 9-22 (2)," in C. G. Lathrop (ed.), *International Maritime Boundaries, Vol. VII* (Brill Nijhoff Publishers 2016), 5269.

continental shelf that determine the area of overlapping entitlements, there tends to be no role for the coasts in this respect.

In this latter situation, one may consider that a boundary line can be construed from the respective outer limits of the continental shelf rather than from the coasts of the parties. Such a method was proposed by Nicaragua in the *Nicaragua* v. *Colombia I* case, but the ICJ has not addressed the feasibility of this proposal.[123] It is recalled that the 2013 Denmark (Greenland)–Iceland Agreed Minutes provisionally delimit the area of overlapping entitlements by a defined ratio that shares out the area of interest.[124] Such a method, though perfectly viable in negotiations between States, may not fit easily with the distinction between delimitation and apportionment under the law of maritime delimitation,[125] as the jurisprudence is consistent in holding that "judicial treatment of maritime delimitation does not involve the sharing-out of something held in undivided shares."[126]

## IV Determination of the Area of Overlapping Entitlements in Prospect

This chapter has demonstrated that the practices in the jurisprudence fall short of providing a consistent and objective approach to determining the area of overlapping entitlements to the continental shelf beyond 200 nm, primarily because the tribunals did not clarify the relationship between the coasts and the entitlement to the continental shelf beyond 200 nm, and they determined relevant coasts and relevant area almost exclusively for the purpose of the disproportionality test. It is found that coastal relationships, the 200 nm limit opening, the FOS, and the outer limits of the continental shelf might be useful for an accurate identification of the area of overlapping entitlements.

This chapter has also appreciated the merits of the hypotheses that the FOS or the outer limits of the continental shelf could serve as the baseline for constructing the delimitation line in cases concerning the continental shelf beyond 200 nm between two opposite coasts. These hypotheses may

[123] *Nicaragua* v. *Colombia I* (n 7), 669 [128]. See also discussion on this point in Chapter 4 III.C.3.

[124] Paragraph 3 of 2013 Agreed Minutes, Magnússon (n 122), 5270.

[125] *North Sea* (n 102), 21–22 [18].

[126] *Anglo-French Arbitration* (n 100), [101]; *Delimitation of the Maritime Boundary between Guinea and Guinea-Bissau (Guinea/Guinea-Bissau) (1985) XIX RIAA 149* [120]; *Jan Mayen* (n 9), 66–67 [64]; *Black Sea* (n 1), 99–100 [110–111].

not easily be put into practice because of the diversity and complexity of geographical, geomorphological, and geological realities. In addition, these hypotheses mainly address opposite coasts, thus fail to address the relevance of the FOS or the outer limits of the continental shelf in cases concerning adjacent coasts, where the continuity of the continental shelf beyond 200 nm with the maritime area within 200 nm rather suggests the continuous relevance of coasts. Furthermore, to date, neither State practice nor judicial practice has employed the FOS or the outer limits of the continental shelf as baselines for drawing maritime boundaries in the delimitation of the continental shelf beyond 200 nm, though the 2013 Denmark (Greenland)–Iceland Agreed Minutes refer to the parties' outer limits of the continental shelf to determine the area of overlap. Although these practices by no means exhaust all possible geographical situations, they attest to the fact that coasts remain valid reference lines in the delimitation of the continental shelf beyond 200 nm in a considerable number of geographical frameworks. In any event, delimiting a continental shelf beyond 200 nm based on the FOS or outer limits of the continental shelf could be plausible if the relevant parties agree that such a delimitation would lead to an equitable solution. Such a prospect is unlikely to materialize in the third-party dispute settlement, at least before the parties receive recommendations from the CLCS. As will be further explored in Chapter 7, there is in general little prospect for the judiciary to resort to geomorphological or geological factors in the delimitation of the continental shelf beyond 200 nm.

# 7

# Geomorphological and Geological Circumstances

## I Re-Emergence of Geophysical Circumstances into the Continental Shelf Delimitation beyond 200 NM

That the delimitation has to somehow reflect the basis of maritime entitlement has always been part of the vocabulary of the law of maritime delimitation. Undoubtedly, it has some traces in the jurisprudence. In the *Libya/Malta* case, the International Court of Justice (ICJ or "the Court") alluded to the connection between maritime delimitation and the basis of the title in several parts of the judgment. It pronounced on the connection between the entitlement to maritime zones and the law of maritime delimitation in a general fashion:

> That the questions of entitlement and of definition of continental shelf, on the one hand, and of delimitation of continental shelf on the other, are not only distinct but are also complementary is self-evident. The legal basis of that which is to be delimited, and of entitlement to it, cannot be other than pertinent to that delimitation.[1]

Later on, the Court linked the nature of the maritime zone with the scope of relevant circumstances in order to narrow down the considerations that a court could take into account in effecting maritime delimitation:

> [I]t is evident that only those that are pertinent to the institution of the continental shelf as it has developed within the law, and to the application of equitable principles to its delimitation, will qualify for inclusion. Otherwise, the legal concept of continental shelf could itself be fundamentally changed by the introduction of considerations strange to its nature.[2]

Perhaps more unequivocally, in connection with the delimitation methodology, the Court observed that the criterion to employ at the outset to

[1] *Continental Shelf (Libyan Arab Jamahiriya/Malta) [1985] ICJ Rep 13, 29-30* [27].
[2] Ibid., 40 [48].

achieve an equitable solution "is linked with the law relating to a State's legal title to the continental shelf," which in that case was found to be the distance criterion.[3] Consequently, "It therefore seems logical to the Court that the choice of the criterion and the method which it is to employ in the first place to arrive at a provisional result should be made in a manner consistent with the concepts underlying the attribution of legal title."[4]

Although international courts and tribunals did not explain or elaborate upon why the entitlement to maritime zones should bear on the law of maritime delimitation, it has been widely accepted among intellectuals that the use of equidistance in the delimitation process as a provisional step flows directly from the distance-based entitlement to the continental shelf and the EEZ.[5] As Weil saw it, since distance is a fundamental part of the concept of the continental shelf, it is logically necessary to apply equidistance in maritime delimitation, which "has a character of so to speak juristic inevitability."[6] Equidistance is thus inherent in the distance criterion.

In the same line of argumentation, since the entitlement to the continental shelf beyond 200 nm is established not on the basis of distance, but on geomorphological or geological factors in accordance with Article 76 of UNCLOS, the delimitation of the continental shelf beyond 200 nm would naturally require a method that is more consistent with the entitlement.[7] This question has a preliminary character in addressing

3 Ibid., 46–47 [61].

4 Ibid.

5 See P. Weil, *The Law of Maritime Delimitation: Reflections* (Grotius 1989), 79–83; L. Lucchini and M. Voelckel, *Droit de la Mer, Tome II, Délimitation* (Pedone 1996), 213; N. Marques Antunes, *Towards the Conceptualisation of Maritime Delimitation: Legal and Technical Aspects of a Political Process* (Martinus Nijhoff 2003), 241; S. Fietta and R. Cleverly, *A Practitioner's Guide to Maritime Boundary Delimitation* (Oxford University Press 2016), 576; N. Marques Antunes and V. Becker-Weinberg, "Entitlement to Maritime Zones and Their Delimitation: In the Doldrums of Uncertainty and Unpredictability," in A. G. Oude Elferink et al. (eds.), *Maritime Boundary Delimitation: The Case Law: Is It Consistent and Predictable?* (Cambridge University Press 2018), 74–75; M. Lando, *Maritime Delimitation as a Judicial Process* (Cambridge University Press 2018), 30–32, 104–109; Y. Tanaka, *Predictability and Flexibility in the Law of Maritime Delimitation* (2nd ed., Hart 2019), 196–203.

6 Weil (n 5), 80–81.

7 See V. Prescott and C. H. Schofield, *The Maritime Political Boundaries of the World* (2nd ed., Martinus Nijhoff 2005), 221, 234; D. Anderson, "Developments in Maritime Boundary Law and Practice," in D. A. Colson and R. W. Smith (eds.), *International Maritime Boundaries, Volume V* (Brill Nijhoff Publishers 2005), 3214; B. Kunoy, "A Geometric Variable Scope of Delimitations: The Impact of a Geological and Geomorphologic Title to

the delimitation methodology for the continental shelf beyond 200 nm, because, should the different bases of entitlement to the continental shelf indicate different applicable delimitation methods, the scope of potentially available methods could be significantly reduced, which contributes to a predictable starting point of the delimitation process. Three more specific propositions are made in this respect. First, equidistance, as a method implied by the distance criterion of entitlement, loses its a priori applicability in the continental shelf delimitation beyond 200 nm and its use is subject to geophysical circumstances of a given context.[8] Second, the delimitation of the continental shelf beyond 200 nm should aim at discovering the most natural prolongation of the respective party.[9] Third, geophysical factors should be a relevant circumstance in the delimitation of the continental shelf beyond 200 nm.[10] If the three-stage approach is applied, geophysical factors should be weighted and balanced with other relevant circumstances in the second stage of the delimitation process for purposes of adjusting the provisional equidistance line.

Arguably, the normative link argument has certain theoretical attractions. At first, it provides a logical and legal support for the employment of a particular method.[11] The choice of a method is thus not opportune, but based on a legal ground, namely, "the rules governing the existence, '*ipso jure* and *ab initio*,' and the exercise of sovereign rights of the coastal State over areas of continental shelf situate off its coasts."[12] In addition, practically speaking, if a method is inherent, implied, or a logical necessity of the maritime entitlement, it could significantly enhance the certainty and predictability of maritime delimitation, as well as reduce the discretion of international courts and tribunals in selecting and applying delimitation methods.[13]

The following sections will investigate these widely held presumptions about the normative link between entitlement and delimitation as well as

the Outer Continental Shelf" (2006) 11 *Austrian RIEL* 49, 64–69; Fietta and Cleverly (n 5), 109.

8 See Fietta and Cleverly (n 5), 617–618.

9 C. Schofield, A. Telesetsky and S. Lee, "A Tribunal Navigating Complex Waters: Implications of the Bay of Bengal Case" (2013) 44 *ODIL* 363, 375.

10 D. Colson, "The Delimitation of the Outer Continental Shelf between Neighboring States" (2003) 97 *AJIL* 91, 107.

11 See J.-M. Arbour, "Les fondements du titre de l'État sur les espaces maritimes et ses rapports avec l'opération de délimitation," in D. Pharand and U. Leanza (eds.), *The Continental Shelf and the Exclusive Economic Zone* (Martinus Nijhoff 1993), 17.

12 *Libya/Malta* (n 1), 29–30 [27].

13 See Weil (n 5), 161–162.

its implications for the delimitation of the continental shelf beyond 200 nm. Section II examines whether the geomorphology or geology-based entitlement to the continental shelf beyond 200 nm might influence the choice and application of delimitation methods. Section III discusses the use of geophysical factors in the delimitation process as a relevant circumstance. Section IV concludes.

## II Entitlement to the Continental Shelf beyond 200 NM and the Delimitation Process

### *A The Basis of Entitlement and Equidistance*

The first attempt to establish a normative link between entitlement and delimitation in the jurisprudence was made by Denmark and the Netherlands in the *North Sea* cases, and was intended to justify the use of the equidistance method. Denmark and the Netherlands built their arguments on the understanding of the concept of continental shelf as codified in Article 1 of the 1958 Convention on the Continental Shelf (CCS), which, according to them, supports that adjacency of the areas in question to the coast is the legal nexus creating the coastal State's rights to the continental shelf.[14] The idea of proximity was thus rooted in continental shelf rights,[15]and the application of the equidistance method was "logically necessary,"[16] because only equidistance could "leave to each one of the States concerned all those areas that are nearest to its own coast."[17] This argument in fact embraces an idea of absolute proximity, namely that coastal States should retain the maritime areas that are closer to their territory than to their neighbors'.[18]

The ICJ flatly rejected this argument. It first rejected the idea that the notion of proximity can be identified with that of adjacency. According to the Court, the latter "only implies proximity in a general sense, and

14 Article 1 of the CCS provides: "For the purpose of these articles, the term 'continental shelf' is used as referring (a) to the seabed and subsoil of the submarine areas *adjacent to* the coast but outside the area of the territorial sea, to a depth of 200 metres or, beyond that limit, to where the depth of the superjacent waters admits of the exploitation of the natural resources of the said areas" (emphasis added). Convention on the Continental Shelf (April 29, 1958), 499 UNTS 311.

15 *North Sea cases, Pleadings, Oral arguments, Documents, Volume II (1968)* 93.

16 See *North Sea Continental Shelf Cases (Federal Republic of Germany/Denmark; Federal Republic of Germany/Netherlands) [1969] ICJ Rep 3, 29* [38].

17 See ibid., 29 [39].

18 Ibid.

does not imply any fundamental or inherent rule the ultimate effect of which would be to prohibit any State (otherwise than by agreement) from exercising continental shelf rights in respect of areas closer to the coast of another State."[19] In the Court's view, it was the principle of natural prolongation, rather than the notion of proximity that was fundamental in determining the continental shelf rights,[20] and equidistance could not be identified with the notion of natural prolongation, because

> the use of the equidistance method would frequently cause areas which are the natural prolongation or extension of the territory of one State to be attributed to another, when the configuration of the latter's coast makes the equidistance line swing out laterally across the former's coastal front, cutting it off from areas situated directly before that front.[21]

The Court thus rejected equidistance being a logically necessary method flowing from the concept of the continental shelf by rejecting proximity as the basis of the entitlement.[22]

However, the Court was silent as to whether the equidistance method can be identified with the idea of proximity.[23] Nonetheless, the Court more generally rejected the idea that there existed a normative link between the entitlement and the delimitation method. According to the Court, it is not possible "to maintain that there is a rule of law ascribing certain areas to a State as a matter of inherent and original right, without also admitting the existence of some rule by which those areas can be obligatorily delimited."[24] The Court separated the law of entitlement from the law of maritime delimitation by stating that "[t]he appurtenance of a given area, considered as an entity, in no way governs the precise delimitation of its boundaries, any more than uncertainty as to boundaries can affect territorial rights."[25]

[19] Ibid., 30–31 [42].
[20] Ibid., 31 [43].
[21] Ibid., 31–32 [44].
[22] Ibid., 32 [46].
[23] Judge Tanaka and Judge Morelli believed that the concept of the continental shelf was geographically defined, and should be understood on the basis of proximity. Therefore, equidistance is a method prescribed in law as a necessary consequence of the concept of continental shelf. See ibid., 180 (Dissenting Opinion of Judge Tanaka) and 202 (Dissenting Opinion of Judge Morelli).
[24] Ibid., 32 [46].
[25] Ibid.

Although not recognized by the ICJ, the incorporation of the distance criterion into Article 76 of UNCLOS provides another basis for the revival of the normative link between equidistance and adjacency. In the *Gulf of Maine* case, Canada relied on geographic adjacency to deduce rules of maritime delimitation, arguing that adjacency was the fundamental legal foundation for a 200 nm zone, and that equidistance was a method that reflected both the coastal configuration and the distance parameters.[26] The Chamber did not accept this argument. It first refuted the idea that the mere natural fact of adjacency could produce legal consequences in determining the entitlement or in the delimitation process, because " 'legal title' to certain maritime or submarine areas is always and exclusively the effect of a legal operation," and the "boundary results from a rule of law, and not from any intrinsic merit in the purely physical fact."[27] Next, it more explicitly rejected Canada's arguments that customary rules governing maritime delimitation could be deduced from the idea of adjacency, because, in its view,

> [I]t amounts to just one more, still unconvincing, endeavour to instil the idea that "equidistance" [. . .] is a concept endorsed by customary law, since the objective is to assert that whatever lies less far from the coasts of one State than from those of another should automatically appertain to the former State.[28]

The Chamber rather regarded equidistance as "a practical method that can be applied for the purposes of delimitation."[29] The Chamber observed that equidistance "has not thereby become a rule of general international law, a norm logically flowing from a legally binding principle of customary international law."[30] If the Chamber's reasoning was followed, could it be argued that had the distance criterion become part of customary international law, a norm logically flowing from it would also acquire the status of a customary rule?[31] It does not seem that such a line of argument is tenable, because customary international law is determined through ascertaining a general State practice that is accepted

[26] See Tanaka (n 5), 200.
[27] See *Delimitation of the Maritime Boundary in the Gulf of Maine Area (Canada/United States of America) [1984] ICJ Rep 246, 296* [103].
[28] Ibid., 297 [106].
[29] Ibid.
[30] Ibid., [107].
[31] Tanaka takes this stance. According to him, "where the legal title based on the distance criterion is based on customary law, the method derived from the legal title would be customary law as well." Tanaka (n 5), 202.

as law (*opinio juris*), not from deduction.[32] In addition, the Chamber did not approve the normative link between equidistance and proximity/ adjacency, for it agreed with the *North Sea* cases that Article 6 of the CCS did not "adopt a rule of equidistance because this gave expression to, and translated into linear terms, a principle of proximity inherent in the basic concept of the continental shelf."[33]

In the *Libya/Malta* case, Malta argued that continental shelf rights were controlled by the concept of distance from the coasts.[34] Accordingly, equidistance, "at least between opposite coasts, is virtually a required method if only as the first stage in a delimitation."[35] Malta did not argue that the equidistance method is fundamental or inherent, or that equidistance has a legally obligatory character, but it contended that the distance criterion, as the legal basis of continental shelf rights, "requires that as a starting point of the delimitation process consideration must be given to a line based on equidistance."[36] The Court explicitly rejected this argument, stating that "[t]he Court is unable to accept that, even as a preliminary and provisional step towards the drawing of a delimitation line, the equidistance method is one which *must* be used."[37] The Court further pointed out that "[s]uch a rule would come near to an espousal of the idea of 'absolute proximity,' which was rejected by the Court in 1969 [. . .], and which has since, moreover, failed of acceptance at the Third United Nations Conference on the Law of the Sea."[38] Likewise, the Court did not believe that equidistance should always apply, even as a first step, where the entitlement is based on distance:

> That a coastal State may be entitled to continental shelf rights by reason of distance from the coast, and irrespective of the physical characteristics of the intervening sea-bed and subsoil, does not entail that equidistance is

[32] See Conclusion 2 of "Draft conclusions on identification of customary international law, with commentaries," Report of the International Law Commission covering the work of its seventieth session, UN Doc. A/73/10, (April 30–June 1 and July 2–August 10, 2018), 119. For a critical view of the identification of customary international law through deduction, see S. Talmon, "Determining Customary International Law: The ICJ's Methodology between Induction, Deduction and Assertion" (2015) 26 *EJIL* 417.

[33] See *The Gulf of Maine* (n 27), 296–297 [104–105] and [107].

[34] See *Libya/Malta* (n 1), 31–32 [30–31].

[35] Ibid., 34 [35].

[36] See ibid., 37 [42].

[37] Ibid., 37–38 [43] (emphasis added).

[38] Ibid.

> the only appropriate method of delimitation, even between opposite or quasi-opposite coasts, nor even the only permissible point of departure.[39]

It appears that the Court later contradicted itself by in fact employing a median line as a provisional line and then adjusted it in accordance with other circumstances,[40] in particular taking into account the Court's remarks on the general relationship between entitlement and delimitation as quoted at the beginning of this chapter.[41] How should one interpret the seeming inconsistency between the words and deeds of the Court?

Read in the context of the judgment, it is clear that the equidistance method was applied provisionally not because it flowed from the distance criterion, but because the distance criterion as the basis of the entitlement to the continental shelf *between two opposite States* made the choice of equidistance equitable and appropriate. To start with, the delimitation by stages was decided by the Court in accordance with equitable principles and in the light of the relevant circumstances.[42] The Court decided to "first make a provisional delimitation by using a criterion and a method both of which are clearly destined to play an important role in producing the final result"; that is, to fulfil the call of an equitable solution.[43] Accordingly, even the first step of drawing an equidistance was not a circumstance-free exercise. Next, the Court considered that "the choice of the criterion *and* the method" should be consistent with the concepts underlying the attribution of legal title.[44] In the next paragraph, the Court again emphasized the "fundamental norm" of the law of delimitation,[45] and found it necessary "to examine the equities of the distance criterion and of the results to which its application may lead."[46] It soon became apparent what the Court had in mind was the circumstance of the case, i.e., the opposite coastal relationship.[47] Here, it is evident that

39 Ibid.

40 See ibid., 46 [60].

41 Hence Marques Antunes and Becker-Weinberg argued that the *Libya/Malta* case was a turning point in the jurisprudence that conceptualizes the relationship between entitlement and delimitation. See Marques Antunes and Becker-Weinberg (n 5), 72.

42 *Libya/Malta* (n 1), 46 [60].

43 Ibid.

44 Ibid., 46–47 [61] (emphasis added).

45 Ibid., 47 [62].

46 Ibid.

47 Ibid. In this connection, the Court also cited the *North Sea* cases to reinforce the appropriateness of a median line for delimitation between opposite coasts.

the reference to the circumstances is decisive for the applicability of equidistance, for the Court observed that "the equitable nature of the equidistance method is particularly pronounced in cases where delimitation has to be effected between States with opposite coasts," and that "[i]t is clear that, in these circumstances, the tracing of a median line between those coasts, by way of a provisional step in a process to be continued by other operations, is the most judicious manner of proceeding with a view to the eventual achievement of an equitable result."[48] That the choice of equidistance was made in the light of the relevant circumstances is further strengthened by the following observation:

> [T]he equidistance method is not the only method applicable to the present dispute, and it does not even have the benefit of a presumption in its favour. Thus, under existing law, it must be demonstrated that the equidistance method leads to an equitable result in the case in question. To achieve this purpose, the result to which the distance criterion leads must be examined in the context of applying equitable principles to the relevant circumstances.[49]

Therefore, it is the equitableness and appropriateness of the method in the particular case that suggests its applicability rather than some inherent connection between distance and equidistance. The opposite coastal relationship between Libya and Malta in this present case and the "rival claims" of both parties based on the distance criterion made the application of a median line prima facie equitable. Indeed, Vice-President Sette-Camara in the *Libya/Malta* case explicitly stated that "[t]he Court resorts to equidistance because equidistance is a method – among others – which recommends itself in cases like this – not on account of the so-called 'distance principle'."[50]

This aspect is even more clearly spelled out in the *Jan Mayen* case, in which the Court stated that "the provisional drawing of an equidistance line was not a necessary or obligatory step in every case; yet in two of the cases mentioned (*Gulf of Maine* and the *Libya/Malta* case), where the delimitation was between opposite coasts, it was found entirely appropriate to begin with such a provisional line."[51] Attention should be paid to the choice of words, as it was "appropriate" to begin with a median

[48] Ibid.
[49] Ibid., 47 [63].
[50] Ibid., 71 (Separate Opinion of Vice-President Sette-Camara).
[51] *Maritime Delimitation in the Area between Greenland and Jan Mayen (Denmark v. Norway) [1993] ICJ Rep 38, 60-61* [51].

line, not "necessary," nor "required." The equitableness of the equidistance line in cases of opposite coasts is further summarized by the Arbitral Tribunal of the *Eritrea/Yemen Arbitration*:

> It is a generally accepted view, as is evidenced in both the writings of commentators and in the jurisprudence, that between coasts that are opposite to each other the median or equidistance line normally provides an equitable boundary in accordance with [Articles 74 and 83 of UNCLOS].[52]

The reason why equidistance is appropriate between two opposite coasts stems from the consideration that, in such situations, the application of equidistance can result in an equal division of the area of overlapping entitlements. As early as in the *North Sea* cases, the ICJ observed that "[t]he continental shelf area off, and dividing, opposite States, can be claimed by each of them to be a natural prolongation of its territory. These prolongations meet and overlap, and can therefore only be delimited by means of a median line."[53] An equal division of the area of overlapping entitlements finds its rationale in the law of maritime delimitation in that it is conceptually attached to the idea of equity and equality. Although the *North Sea* cases found that "[e]quity does not necessarily imply equality,"[54] the ICJ in the *Burkina Faso/Mali* case qualified that "where there are no special circumstances the latter is generally the best expression of the former."[55] Note that these observations were made before the legal continental shelf was defined on the basis of distance.

The connection between equidistance and equal division of the area of overlap has been established in the jurisprudence. As the *Anglo-French Arbitration* observed, "Between opposite States [. . .] a median line boundary will in normal circumstances leave broadly equal areas of continental shelf to each State and constitute a delimitation in accordance with equitable principles."[56] More explicitly, the Chamber in the *Gulf of Maine* case recognized that the equidistance method enshrined in

52 *Second Stage of the Proceedings between Eritrea and Yemen (Maritime Delimitation) (Eritrea/Yemen) (1999) XXII RIAA 335* [131].

53 *North Sea* (n 16), 36–37 [57].

54 Ibid., 49–50 [91].

55 *Frontier Dispute (Burkina Faso/Mali) [1986] ICJ Rep 554, 633* [150].

56 *Delimitation of the Continental Shelf between the United Kingdom of Great Britain and Northern Ireland, and the French Republic (United Kingdom/France) (1978) 18 RIAA 3* [182].

Article 6 of the CCS "derives from a particular equitable criterion: namely, that the equitable solution, at least prima facie, is an equal division of the areas of overlap of the continental shelves of the two litigant States."[57] Proceeding to the delimitation, the Chamber further commented that:

> [T]he Chamber's basic choice should favour a criterion long held to be as equitable as it is simple, namely that in principle, while having regard to the special circumstances of the case, one should aim at an equal division of areas where the maritime projections of the coasts of the States between which delimitation is to be effected converge and overlap.[58]

Although it has been questioned whether an equidistance method can in fact result in an exact equal division of the area,[59] the point is that the "equal division" does not purport to be precise in numerical terms. In any event, methods are secondary to the primary principle of equal division. When the ICJ in the *Nicaragua* v. *Honduras* case applied the bisector method because of the impossibility of choosing stable base-points for constructing an equidistance line, it observed that "[l]ike equidistance, the bisector method is a geometrical approach that can be used to give legal effect to the [equitable criterion of equal division]."[60] It is hence the idea of equal division, rather than the particular method that gives effect to the idea, that is dominant.

Another proof that equidistance is expressive of equal division of the area of overlap than of the distance-based entitlement is the asymmetry in the use of equidistance in cases concerning opposite coasts and those concerning adjacent coasts. An updated comprehensive survey of bilateral delimitation agreements shows that approximately 84 percent of agreements have recourse to equidistance for all or part of the maritime boundaries between opposite coasts, whereas at best 56 percent of the agreements between adjacent coasts use the equidistance method for all

57 *The Gulf of Maine* (n 27), 300–301 [115].

58 Ibid., 327 [195].

59 See R. Jennings, "The Principles Governing Maritime Boundaries," in K. Hailbronner (ed.), *Staat und Völkerrechtsordnung, Festschrift für Karl Doehring* (Springer 1989) 408; Prescott and Schofield (n 7), 226; D. Anderson, *Modern Law of the Sea: Selected Essays* (Martinus Nijhoff Publishers 2008), 393.

60 *Territorial and Maritime Dispute between Nicaragua and Honduras in the Caribbean Sea (Nicaragua v. Honduras) [2007] ICJ Rep 659, 746* [287]. Subsequently, the *Bangladesh/Myanmar* case also shared this view. See *Delimitation of the Maritime Boundary in the Bay of Bengal (Bangladesh/Myanmar) (Judgment) [2012] ITLOS Rep 4, 66* [234].

or part of their maritime boundaries.[61] A similar trend was dictated in a 1993 survey which covers 134 instances of delimitation agreements concluded between coastal States, and it shows that 55 of 62 boundaries (89 percent) between opposite States employed the equidistance method, while 37 of 43 boundaries (86 percent) involving mixed coastal relationships adopted equidistance for a substantial portion of the boundary. In contrast, only 12 of 30 boundaries (40 percent) between adjacent States used equidistance.[62] This result is not surprising, as between adjacent coasts the equidistance method may unreasonably cut-off the entitlement to the maritime zones of one party, therefore not faithfully reflecting the basis of the entitlement of the relevant parties.[63] As illustrated by the 1993 survey, eight of these boundaries between adjacent coasts (27 percent) follow parallels of latitude or meridians, a method which is capable of avoiding the cut-off effect produced by equidistance on concave or convex coasts.[64]

The preceding discussion demonstrates that a normative link is unlikely to exist between the entitlement and the delimitation method, which has never been explicitly accepted by the jurisprudence. Indeed, even in the *Libya/Malta* case, the ICJ refused to accept that the use of equidistance was legally required by the distance-based entitlement, even though the Court acknowledged the general connection between entitlement and delimitation.[65] The employment of equidistance has always

61 See Tanaka (n 5), 190–191.

62 See L. Legault and B. Hankey, "Method, Oppositeness and Adjacency, and Proportionality in Maritime Boundary Delimitation," in J. I. Charney and L. M. Alexander (eds.), *International Maritime Boundaries, Volume I* (Martinus Nijhoff Publishers 1993), 215–216.

63 *North Sea* (n 16), 37 [58].

64 See Legault and Hankey (n 62), 211 and 216.

65 *Libya/Malta* (n 1), 47 [63]. Some Judges also linked the appropriateness of equidistance in this case with the equal division of the area of overlap or with the opposite coastal relationship. Judges Ruda, Bedjaoui, and Jiménez de Aréchaga stated that "[i]n certain special circumstances, equal division appears to be self-recommending as a means of fully satisfying the requirements of equity," ibid., 91 [38] (Separate Opinion of Judges Ruda, Bedjaoui, and Jiménez de Aréchaga). Judge Valticos considered that, "If adjacency or distance becomes the sole criterion of title to the continental shelf up to a distance of 200 nautical miles, representing the domination of land sovereignty over the sea, the method of the median line acquires increased importance as a delimitation method between opposite coasts [. . .] while the 'distance' criterion does not imply that equidistance is the sole appropriate method of delimitation in the case of opposite coasts, the aptness of this method is all the greater when there are no special circumstances to hinder its use," ibid., 106–107 [9] (Separate Opinion of Judge Valticos). Judge Mosler observed that "the areas in which the conflicting claims of coastal States overlap shall be equally

been a choice based on considerations of relevant circumstances, especially in cases concerning opposite coasts, because in such cases equidistance could achieve equal division of the area of overlap. In recent jurisprudence, the rhetoric in favor of a provisional equidistance line is more grounded in the merits of equidistance to ensure the certainty and predictability of the delimitation process rather than any normative link between the equidistance method and the distance criterion.[66]

Therefore, there is no a priori reason why equidistance should be applied in maritime delimitation within 200 nm. Likewise, there is no a priori reason why equidistance should not be applied in the delimitation of the continental shelf beyond 200 nm due to its lack of a direct link with the basis of entitlement. Equal division of the area of overlap may still be considered an equitable solution in the delimitation of the continental shelf beyond 200 nm, even though the entitlement to the continental shelf beyond 200 nm is not established on the basis of the distance criterion. Here it should be stressed that the application of the criterion of equal division requires two conditions. The first condition is to identify the areas that "converge and overlap,"[67] and the second is that the coastal lengths of the relevant States should be comparable. As stated by the *Anglo-French Arbitration*,

> [W]here the coastlines of two opposite States are themselves approximately equal in their relation to the continental shelf not only should the boundary in normal circumstances be the median line but the areas of shelf left to each Party on either side of the median line should be broadly equal or at least broadly comparable.[68]

The first condition is of particular significance in the delimitation of the continental shelf beyond 200 nm, as there might be situations where the area of overlapping entitlements cannot be determined by reference to coasts,[69] and equidistance is therefore incapable of giving effect to the

divided. Since in the present case the distance from the opposite coasts generates the title, a median line between the coasts of the Parties suggests itself as the principal consideration for arriving at an equitable result," ibid., 119–120 (Dissenting Opinion of Judge Mosler).

66 See *Maritime Boundary Arbitration (Barbados v. Trinidad and Tobago) (2006) XXVII RIAA 147* [306]; *Bay of Bengal Maritime Boundary Arbitration (Bangladesh v. India) (2014) 167 ILR 1, 112* [339].

67 *The Gulf of Maine* (n 27), 327 [195]; *Nicaragua* v. *Honduras* (n 60), 746 [287].

68 *Anglo-French Arbitration* (n 56), [182].

69 See Chapter 6, Section III.B. and C.

criterion of equal division of the area of overlap.[70] The second condition highlights that equal division of the area of overlap is only one facet of the multi-faceted concept of equity of the law of maritime delimitation. As emphasized by the *North Sea* cases, there cannot be any question of "rendering the situation of a State with an extensive coastline similar to that of a State with a restricted coastline."[71] It is recalled that in the *Gulf of Maine* case, where the Chamber decided to apply equidistance in order to give effect to the equitable criterion of equal division, the Chamber added that "[t]he multiplicity and diversity of geographical situations frequently call for this criterion to be adjusted or flexibly applied to make it genuinely equitable, not in the abstract, but in relation to the varying requirements of a reality that takes many shapes and forms."[72] Nothing suggests that these observations would not continue to be relevant in the delimitation of the continental shelf beyond 200 nm.[73]

### B *Identification of Natural Prolongations*

Somewhat driven by the *North Sea* cases, coastal States litigating before international courts and tribunals engaged in identifying physical natural prolongations as a means to delimit the continental shelf.[74] This view was said to be grounded in a declaratory approach to maritime delimitation, which arguably was adopted by the ICJ in the *North Sea* cases when the Court observed that, "Delimitation is a process which involves establishing the boundaries of an area already, in principle, appertaining to the coastal State and not the determination *de novo* of such an area."[75] Since the Court considered that natural prolongation constitutes the basis of coastal States' entitlement to the continental shelf, the delimitation process is in fact one of discovering how far the natural prolongation of each State extends under the sea, because it is an exercise of determining the

70 B. Kunoy, "Agreed Minutes on the Delimitation of the Continental Shelf beyond 200 Nautical Miles between Greenland and Iceland in the Irminger Sea" (2013) 12 *Chinese JIL* 125, 140.

71 *North Sea* (n 16), 49–50 [91].

72 *The Gulf of Maine* (n 27), 327–328 [196].

73 See Chapter 8, Section III.B.

74 See K. Highet, "Whatever Became of Natural Prolongation?," in D. Dorinda and L. De Vorsey (eds.), *Rights to Oceanic Resources: Deciding and Drawing Maritime Boundaries* (Martinus Nijhoff Publishers 1989), 89.

75 *North Sea* (n 16), 21–22 [18].

extent of the areas which "already" belong to the coastal States.[76] Nonetheless, neither the declaratory approach nor the identification of separate natural prolongations survived the development of the law of maritime delimitation.

In fact, it is even doubtful whether a declaratory approach to maritime delimitation ever existed in the first place. When the ICJ observed that delimitation does not involve a *de novo* delimitation of the area, it was addressing the argument of a just and equitable share proposed by the Federal Republic of Germany,[77] and it was making the point that coastal States' rights to the continental shelf were inherent.[78] More importantly, the Court recognized that delimitation involved an area of overlapping claims throughout the judgment,[79] including the operative part in which the Court suggested that "if [. . .] the delimitation leaves to the Parties areas that overlap, these are to be divided between them in agreed proportions."[80] Subsequent cases also explicitly or implicitly proceeded on the basis that an area of overlapping entitlements was a precondition to delimitation. The Court of Arbitration in the *Anglo-French Arbitration* stated that "[t]he problem of delimitation arises precisely because in situations where the territories of two or more States abut on a single continuous area of continental shelf, it may be said geographically to constitute a natural prolongation of the territory of each of the States concerned."[81] The *Tunisia/Libya* case also proceeded with the observation that "[t]he need for delimitation of areas of continental shelf between the Parties can only arise within the submarine region in which claims by them to the exercise of sovereign rights are legally possible according to international law."[82] Given these observations, it is difficult to argue that maritime delimitation was ever considered a matter of discovering the "true" extent of the entitlement based on facts of nature.

It was in the *Tunisia/Libya* case and the *Libya/Malta* case that the identification of physical natural prolongations was extensively contested between the relevant parties. In both cases the ICJ rejected the identification of physical natural prolongations as a means to delimitation, though on different grounds. In the *Tunisia/Libya* case, the Court distinguished

[76] See Weil (n 5), 22–23.
[77] See *North Sea* (n 16), 21–22 [18].
[78] Ibid., [19].
[79] See ibid., [20], [46], [57–58], [89(b)], [99].
[80] Ibid., 53 [101(C)(2)].
[81] *Anglo-French Arbitration* (n 56), [79].
[82] *Continental Shelf (Tunisia/Libyan Arab Jamahiriya) [1982] ICJ Rep 18, 42* [34].

natural prolongation as the basis of entitlement from a rule of delimitation, and stated that the former would not necessarily be sufficient or appropriate to determine the latter.[83] In the view of the Court, the identification of the natural prolongation may, "where the geographical circumstances are appropriate, have an important role to play in defining an equitable delimitation, in view of its significance as the justification of continental shelf rights in some cases."[84] The Court thus reduced the usefulness of natural prolongations to situations "where the geographical circumstances are appropriate," which amounts to rejecting the applicability of identifying physical natural prolongations in a general fashion. In the *Libya/Malta* case, the rejection of the identification of natural prolongations was based on a different, and more definite legal ground. Applying the distance criterion as the basis of entitlement to the continental shelf for both parties, the Court considered that natural prolongation has no role in verifying the entitlement or the delimitation process.[85]

Although in no case did international courts and tribunals delimit maritime boundaries based on discovering physical natural prolongations, they never rejected such a possibility outright either. Instead, rejection of the relevance of geophysical features was always made in a case-specific manner. In the *Anglo-French Arbitration*, the Court of Arbitration did not accept that the Hurd Deep provided a basis for the boundary line because these geological faults did not disrupt the essential unity of the continental shelf concerned.[86] Similarly, the *Tunisia/Libya* case also left considerable room for further exploring the circumstances which may permit the identification of separate natural prolongations in the physical sense.[87] In the *Gulf of Maine* case, the comment of the Chamber that "the most accentuated of these features [. . .] does not have the characteristics of a real trough marking the dividing-line between two geomorphologically distinct units" was also ambiguous as to the feasibility of arguing the relevance of geophysical factors.[88] In the *Guinea/Guinea-Bissau* case, it was even explicitly acknowledged that "the rule of natural prolongation can be effectively invoked for purposes of

[83] Ibid., 46 [43].
[84] Ibid., 46–47 [44].
[85] *Libya/Malta* (n 1), 35 [39].
[86] *Anglo-French Arbitration* (n 56), [107].
[87] See K. Highet, "The Use of Geophysical Factors in the Delimitation of Maritime Boundaries," in J. I. Charney and L. M. Alexander (eds.), *International Maritime Boundaries, Volume I* (Martinus Nijhoff 1993), 173–175.
[88] *The Gulf of Maine* (n 27), 274–275 [46].

delimitation only where there is a separation of continental shelves," and that "[t]he characteristics of a continental shelf may serve to demonstrate the existence of a break in the continuity of the shelf or in the prolongation of territories of the States which are parties to a delimitation."[89] Even in the *Libya/Malta* case, where the rejection of the relevance of identification of natural prolongations was the most decisive, the ICJ still left open the possibility of identifying physical natural prolongations in the delimitation of the continental shelf beyond 200 nm.[90]

It is doubtful that identification of physical natural prolongations may find a renaissance in the delimitation of the continental shelf beyond 200 nm. The idea of discovering the respective extent of the entitlement of each coastal State goes against the precondition to maritime delimitation; that is, the existence of an area of overlapping entitlements.[91] This principle is reinforced in the delimitation of the continental shelf beyond 200 nm as well, since the *Bay of Bengal* cases and the *Ghana/Côte d'Ivoire* case proceeded on the basis of overlapping entitlements to the continental shelf beyond 200 nm.[92] If a separation of continental shelves is plausible, there are in fact two continental shelves rather than a common continental shelf shared by two parties, and it would turn into a question of establishing the outer limits of the continental shelf of the respective party, rather than a question of delimitation.[93]

Moreover, identifying physical natural prolongations as a delimitation method is attached to the idea of natural boundary, which is alien to the constructive nature of the law of maritime delimitation. In the *Anglo-French Arbitration*, responding to the United Kingdom's arguments to take the Hurd Deep-Hurd Deep Fault Zone as an alternative to the median line in the Channel region westward of the Channel Islands and in the Atlantic region, the Court of Arbitration considered the feature simply "a fact of nature," and that "there is no intrinsic reason

89 *Delimitation of the Maritime Boundary between Guinea and Guinea-Bissau (Guinea/Guinea-Bissau) (1985) XIX RIAA 149* [116–117].

90 *Libya/Malta* (n 1), 55–56 [77].

91 See *Maritime Delimitation in the Black Sea (Romania v. Ukraine) [2009] ICJ Rep 61*, 89 [77].

92 See *Bangladesh/Myanmar* (n 60), 105 [397]. *Bangladesh v. India* (n 66), [457]. *Delimitation of the Maritime Boundary in the Atlantic Ocean (Ghana/Côte d'Ivoire), [2017] ITLOS Rep 4* [496].

93 See M. D. Evans, *Relevant Circumstances and Maritime Delimitation* (Oxford University Press 1989), 103; E. D. Brown, "The Anglo-French Continental Shelf Case" (1978), 16 *San Diego LR* 461, 477; Marques Antunes and Becker-Weinberg (n 5), 67–68.

why a boundary along that axis should be the boundary."[94] Maritime delimitation is a legal and political operation, and "it is not the case that where a natural boundary is discernible, the political delimitation necessarily has to follow the same line."[95] As pointed out by Vice-President Sette-Camara in the *Libya/Malta* case:

> [I]t is one thing for any State to be free to conclude with another State a delimitation agreement that would take into account geomorphological features of whatever dimension; for a tribunal to feel obliged to decide on the basis of any accidental feature of the sea-bed is quite another.[96]

Whereas being the basis of the entitlement, there is no intrinsic reason why a boundary line that follows the configuration of the physical natural prolongation would be an equitable solution under the law of maritime delimitation,[97] nor is it a practical method that is capable of general application. As pointed out by Highet, the original reason for the usefulness of a natural boundary on land was to make it easy to identify, which does not seem to apply to submarine features beneath the seas and oceans, especially given the availability of the technology to pinpoint the exact location of a maritime boundary and the development of other navigational aids.[98] Moreover, it is highly probable that even the most dramatic geological rifting in the seabed presents itself as a zone (such as the "rift zone" in the *Libya/Malta* case) rather than a line, and there is no legal standard why a line among a range of possibilities within that zone could be an equitable solution.[99] Arguments in this respect never prevailed in the judicial practice, and it is not likely that they will in the future. Perhaps only where the salient geophysical features of the seabed coincide with a line that allows the maritime entitlements of the parties

[94] *Anglo-French Arbitration* (n 56), [107–108].

[95] *The Gulf of Maine* (n 27), 277 [56].

[96] *Libya/Malta* (n 1), 62 (Separate Opinion of Vice-President Sette-Camara).

[97] Weil (n 5), 28–29.

[98] See Highet (n 74), 94–95. Similarly, in the *Guinea-Bissau/Senegal* case Arbitrator Bedjaoui opined that: "The idea of 'natural boundaries' formed by mountains, waterways or various accidents of nature, has never been able to commend itself to States for purposes of delimitation of their land frontiers, although these limits are visible to the naked eye. Legal science is unlikely to accept for maritime spaces what it rejects for land spaces and to confer legal standing on those 'natural boundaries' constituted by an important and significant geological feature when that boundary is not even visible to the naked eye." *Case concerning the Arbitral Award of 31 July 1989 (Guinea-Bissau/Senegal), (1990) 83 ILR 1, 101* [114] (Dissenting Opinion of Mr Bedjaoui).

[99] See Highet (n 87), 180–181; Evans (n 93), 118.

to produce effect in a reasonable and mutually balanced way,[100] would such features feed into the overall assessment of the equitableness of the delimitation result.[101]

### C The Elusive Search For a "Logically Necessary" Method

Previous sections have demonstrated that the jurisprudence has never upheld the validity of a normative link between the entitlement and the delimitation method, much less of the proposition that equidistance is a logically necessary method flowing from the very basis of the entitlement to maritime zones within 200 nm. With this basic premise clarified, the arguments that the entitlement to the continental shelf beyond 200 nm shall indicate a different method than that of equidistance are hardly convincing, because these propositions have started from the misperceived presumption that equidistance is *the* method of maritime delimitation within 200 nm. In fact, the applicability of equidistance is always a matter of appreciating the relevant circumstances of a particular geographical context, regardless of the delimitation within or beyond 200 nm.

The search for a normative link between the entitlement and delimitation methods also finds no support from the treaty rules governing maritime delimitation. Equidistance was incorporated into Article 6 of the CCS not because it gave expression to the principle of proximity underlying the concept of the continental shelf.[102] Instead, the *travaux préparatoires* made clear that "no one single method of delimitation was likely to prove satisfactory in all circumstances," and the emphasis was placed on delimitation in accordance with agreement.[103] Therefore it is not surprising that the ICJ found the argument of "logical necessity" "an *ex post facto* construct directed to providing a logical juristic basis for a

[100] See *Black Sea* (n 91), 127 [201].

[101] As expressed by Arbitrator Bedjaoui, "At most, the geological or morphological indicators, however discrete, may constitute supporting elements for verifying *a posteriori* the equitable character of the delimitation obtained by a combination of other factors," *Guinea-Bissau/Senegal Arbitration* (n 98), 104 [121] (Dissenting Opinion of Mr Bedjaoui). See also D. N. Hutchinson, "The Concept of Natural Prolongation in the Jurisprudence Concerning Delimitation of Continental Shelf Areas" (1985) 55 *BYIL* 133, 184.

[102] See the ICJ's review of the genesis and development of the equidistance method of delimitation in the context of the CCS. *North Sea* (n 16), 32–35 [47–54].

[103] Ibid., 35–36 [55].

method of delimitation propounded largely for different reasons, cartographical and other."[104]

The same holds true for the delimitation rules governing the continental shelf and the EEZ under UNCLOS. The silence on delimitation methods in Articles 74 and 83 was intended by the drafters, and "[b]oth those parties negotiating an agreement and those deciding a delimitation dispute are free under article 83 (and 74) to choose any method that will lead to an equitable solution."[105] International courts and tribunals are wise to reject this line of argument, because otherwise it would amount to judicial law-making, which goes against the intention of the drafters of both the CCS and UNCLOS.[106] Judge Schwebel made this point when he commented on the Chamber's rejection of the normative link between equidistance and adjacency in the *Gulf of Maine* case:

> The Chamber is right to reject an interpretation of the "distance principle" which in substance maintains that the intention of the Third United Nations Conference on the Law of the Sea was indirectly to prescribe the application of the equidistance method while directly declining, in the governing provisions of the Convention which it drafted, even to make mention of that method.[107]

It is intriguing that the *Bangladesh/Myanmar* case appears to imply that there is a normative link between the three-stage approach and the sovereignty of coastal States: "This method is rooted in the recognition that sovereignty over the land territory is the basis for the sovereign rights and jurisdiction of the coastal State with respect to both the exclusive economic zone and the continental shelf."[108] The implications of this observation are unclear. It is difficult to see that any delimitation methods can be inferred from sovereignty over the land territory.[109] Sovereignty over the land territory, though being the legal source of maritime entitlements, is remotely concerned with the rules or principles governing the choice or application of delimitation methods.

104 Ibid., 36 [56].

105 S. N. Nandan and S. Rosenne (eds.), *United Nations Convention on the Law of the Sea 1982: A Commentary, Volume II* (Martinus Nijhoff Publishers 1993), 983.

106 T. A. Mensah, "Delimitation of the Continental Shelf: The Methodology," in J. Carlos Sainz-Borgo et al. (eds.), *Liber Amicorum: In Honour of a Modern Renaissance Man His Excellency Guomundur* (Universal Law Publishing 2017) 48.

107 *The Gulf of Maine* (n 27), 353 (Separate Opinion of Judge Schwebel).

108 *Bangladesh/Myanmar* (n 60), 117 [455].

109 See A. G. Oude Elferink, "ITLOS's Approach to the Delimitation of the Continental Shelf Beyond 200 Nautical Miles in the Bangladesh/Myanmar Case: Theoretical and Practical Difficulties," in R. Wolfrum et al. (eds.), *Contemporary Developments in International Law: Essays in Honour of Budislav Vukas* (Brill 2015), 242.

In effect, the rules conferring on coastal States rights to maritime zones and the rules governing maritime delimitation are two sets of rules, with different objectives. The rules of entitlement provide coastal States with the legal basis to claim maritime zones, but the fact that coastal States may have equally valid claims over the same maritime areas entails that neither State is able to enjoy the maximum reach of its entitlement as allowed by international law.[110] The latter is the very *raison d'être* of the law of maritime delimitation, which is aimed at dividing the area of overlapping entitlements in order to achieve an equitable solution. To establish a logical link between the two bodies of rules may unnecessarily complicate the exercise of maritime delimitation. For instance, applying equidistance regardless of its appropriateness in the light of the relevant circumstances may undermine the flexibility of maritime delimitation in the pursuit of an equitable solution.[111] Similarly, to achieve an equitable solution a provisional equidistance line may be subject to substantial adjustment that involves the choice of a different method or a combination of various methods, a process that replaces the provisional equidistance line rather than correcting it.[112]

Based on the above considerations, it is futile to search for a method implied by the basis of the entitlement to maritime zones. This by no means suggests that the basis of the entitlement has nothing to do with the delimitation process. The role of the basis of the entitlement primarily lies in characterizing the area of overlapping entitlements, either in maritime delimitation within 200 nm or beyond that distance, and in this regard the entitlement to the continental shelf beyond 200 nm may call for methods not based on a coast-to-coast delimitation.[113] However, this is conceptually distinct from the suggestion that a particular delimitation method carries special force due to its logical link with the basis of the entitlement.

## III Geophysical Factors as a Relevant Circumstance

### A "The Most Natural Prolongation" Argument

Whereas identification of physical natural prolongations may not be a delimitation method for the continental shelf beyond 200 nm since it goes against the precondition to maritime delimitation, there is still a

110 See *Bangladesh* v. *India* (n 66), 160–161 [469].

111 See H. Thirlway, "The Law and Procedure of the International Court of Justice 1960–1989 Part Five" (1994) 64 *BYIL* 1, 34.

112 See Chapter 5, Section III.A.

113 See Chapter 6, Section III.C and Section III.D.

need to consider whether geomorphological or geological factors, which are constitutive of the entitlement to the continental shelf beyond 200 nm, may play a role in the delimitation process as a relevant circumstance.

Whereas during UNCLOS III several States proposed that the delimitation between coastal States should take into account geophysical factors, these proposals never made it to the several Negotiating Texts nor the Draft Convention.[114] Nonetheless, the early judicial decisions decided prior to the entry into force of UNCLOS may be the intellectual sources for arguing the relevance of geomorphological or geological factors in the delimitation of the continental shelf beyond 200 nm, among which "the most natural prolongation" argument merits attention. A word of caution is needed, since the observations and analysis were made in very different contexts at a time when the notion of natural prolongation was not applied as a treaty concept under UNCLOS. Therefore, their relevance with the delimitation of the continental shelf beyond 200 nm should be carefully articulated.

The genesis of "the most natural prolongation" argument is the *North Sea* cases, as the Court observed that:

> [W]henever a given submarine area does not constitute a natural – or the most natural – extension of the land territory of a coastal State, even though that area may be closer to it than it is to the territory of any other State, it cannot be regarded as appertaining to that State; – or at least it cannot be so regarded in the face of a competing claim by a State of whose land territory the submarine area concerned is to be regarded as a natural extension, even if it is less close to it.[115]

What the term "the most natural prolongation" entails is an idea of "comparative naturalness."[116] As analyzed in Chapter 2, this observation does not necessarily imply a geomorphological/geological understanding of natural prolongation. Instead, the *North Sea* judgments may use the notion of natural prolongation in a geographical sense, namely the

[114] Doc. A/CONF.62/C.2/L.18 (July 23, 1974), *Official Records of the Third United Nations Conference on the Law of the Sea, Volume III* (United Nations 1975) 195–196 (Romania); Doc. A/CONF.62/C.2/L.34 (August 1, 1974), ibid., 213 (Turkey); Doc. A/CONF.62/C.2/L.28 (July 30, 1974), ibid., 205 (Kenya and Tunisia). See also proposals of Morocco and Turkey to revise the articles of Informal Single Negotiating Text. See texts reproduced in R. Platzöder, *Third United Nations Conference on the Law of the Sea: Documents, Volume IV* (Oceana 1982), 320 and 389.

[115] *North Sea* (n 16), 31 [43].

[116] See Highet (n 87), 168.

coastal projections of the respective parties.[117] Nonetheless, the *North Sea* cases acknowledged the relevance of geology,[118] and, more importantly, parties to subsequent cases instilled geomorphological or geological meaning into the notion of natural prolongation and attempted to persuade the ICJ to delimit their maritime boundaries on the basis of geophysical features of the seabed. Although such efforts were not successful, the relevance of geophysical factors was not rejected by the ICJ in a definite manner. For instance, whereas the *Tunisia/Libya* case did not uphold the existence of two separate physical natural prolongations, the ICJ acknowledged that:

> [C]ertain geomorphological configurations of the sea-bed, which do not amount to such an interruption of the natural prolongation of one Party with regard to that of the other, may be taken into account for the delimitation, as relevant circumstances characterizing the area.[119]

As any other observation made by international courts and tribunals, this excerpt cannot be read out of its context. It became apparent that when the Court was re-examining the seabed features in order to determine their relevance in the delimitation process, geomorphological configurations of the sea-bed were, after all, irrelevant:

> [U]nless [the seabed feature] were such as to disrupt the essential unity of the continental shelf so as to justify a delimitation on the basis of its identification as the division between areas of natural prolongation, it would be an element inappropriate for inclusion among the factors to be balanced up with a view to equitable delimitation.[120]

At the end of the day, the *Tunisia/Libya* case amounts to the suggestion that unless identification of separate natural prolongations is plausible, salient geophysical features cannot be a relevant circumstance. However, subsequent jurisprudence assumes a homogeneous continental shelf as the precondition to the continental shelf delimitation.[121] Hence no question of identifying separate natural prolongations arises.

In the *Bangladesh/Myanmar* case, Bangladesh attempted to bring "the most natural prolongation" argument back to life in order to justify a

[117] See Chapter 2, Section II.A.2.

[118] *North Sea* (n 16), 54 [101(D)(2)].

[119] *Tunisia/Libya* (n 82), 58 [68].

[120] ibid., 64 [80].

[121] H. Thirlway, *Law and Procedure of the International Court of Justice: Fifty Years of Jurisprudence, Volume II* (Oxford University Press 2013), 1378.

larger share in the delimitation of the continental shelf beyond 200 nm. According to Bangladesh, the reference by the ICJ to "the most natural prolongation" in the *North Sea* cases "suggests that natural prolongation can be a relative concept, and where one State has the more compelling physical connection," it will be very relevant to an equitable delimitation.[122] In its opinion, "Myanmar at best enjoys only geomorphological continuity between its own landmass and the outer continental shelf," whereas Bangladesh enjoys geomorphological as well as geological continuity to the Bay of Bengal.[123] As a result, an equitable delimitation should "take full account of the fact that Bangladesh has 'the most natural' prolongation in the Bay of Bengal and on this basis attribute the whole of the disputed shelf beyond 200 M to Bangladesh."[124] The essence of Bangladesh's argument is to interpret "the most natural prolongation" to imply a superiority of geology over geomorphology.

ITLOS did not accept that "were the Tribunal to decide that Myanmar is entitled to a continental shelf beyond 200 nm, Bangladesh would be entitled to a greater portion of the disputed area because it has 'the most natural prolongation'."[125] The Tribunal found that the notion of natural prolongation did not have a separate meaning other than the continental margin, which is to be determined by the application of Article 76(4).[126] Therefore, as long as Article 76(4) is satisfied, there is no room for the consideration of "fundamental discontinuity" in geological terms. In other words, the role of geomorphological or geological factors is confined to the proof of the existence of entitlement in accordance with Article 76, and they cannot be utilized to establish a stronger entitlement, nor to warrant a larger share of the attributed area in the delimitation process. In this regard, ITLOS denies any possible practical value of the "most natural prolongation" argument in the delimitation process.

Bangladesh also invoked "the most natural prolongation" argument in relation to the Bengal depositional system in order to determine that Bangladesh's natural prolongation is "more natural" in terms of the origins of the sediments covering the Bay of Bengal.[127] However, the Tribunal did not find it a relevant circumstance in the delimitation, either

122 See *Bangladesh/Myanmar*, Verbatim Record on September 16, 2011 (ITLOS/PV.11/6/Rev.1), 25.
123 Bangladesh/Myanmar, Reply of Bangladesh, Volume I (March 15, 2011), 142 [4.76].
124 Ibid.
125 *Bangladesh/Myanmar* (n 60), 118 [460].
126 See ibid., 113–114 [435–437].
127 See *Bangladesh/Myanmar*, Memorial of Bangladesh, Volume I (July 1, 2010), 23 [2.32].

within or beyond 200 nm,[128] which further confirms that the natural and scientific evolution of geomorphological or geological factors is not the concern of a tribunal applying international law. This is resonant with the observation on the irrelevance of geology in the *Tunisia/Libya* case:

> The function of the Court is to make use of geology only so far as required for the application of international law. It is of the view that what must be taken into account in the delimitation of shelf areas are the physical circumstances as they are today [. . .]. It is the outcome, not the evolution in the long-distant past, which is of importance.[129]

Nevertheless, some scholars do not find it necessary to generalize the irrelevance of geomorphological or geological factors in the delimitation of the continental shelf beyond 200 nm.[130] They emphasize the uniqueness of the Bay of Bengal, in which there is no clear geomorphological or geological distinction, thus one is unable to compare the entitlements to the continental shelf beyond 200 nm of the parties. It has been suggested that where such geophysical distinctions are more clear-cut – for instance, where a major geomorphic or geological feature (e.g., a trough or plate boundary) exists – then such a feature could be used as the basis for the alignment of the continental shelf boundary beyond 200 nm.[131] Others, more radically contend that the delimitation process should give more weight to the more natural component in the establishment of the continental shelf beyond 200 nm under Article 76. For example, Magnússon suggests that an international court or tribunal shall compare the thickness of the sedimentary rocks of the parties and decide that a party with thicker sedimentary rocks has a stronger claim to the continental shelf beyond 200 nm.[132] Kunoy also argued that entitlement based on submarine elevations is stronger than that based on submarine ridges with reference to Article 76(5)–(6).[133]

[128] See *Bangladesh/Myanmar* (n 60), 87 [322] and 118 [460].

[129] *Tunisia/Libya* (n 82), 54 [61].

[130] See R. Churchill, "Bangladesh/Myanmar Case: Continuity and Novelty in the Law of Maritime Boundary Delimitation" (2012) 1 *CJICL* 137, 150; Fietta and Cleverly (n 5), 616–618; Schofield, Telesetsky and Lee (n 9), 375; Ø. Jensen, "The Delimitation of the Continental Shelf beyond 200 Nm: Substantive Issues," in A. G. Oude Elferink et al. (eds.), *Maritime Boundary Delimitation: The Case Law: Is It Consistent and Predictable?* (Cambridge University Press 2018) 370–371.

[131] See Schofield, Telesetsky and Lee (n 9), 375.

[132] See B. M. Magnússon, *The Continental Shelf beyond 200 Nautical Miles: Delineation, Delimitation and Dispute Settlement* (Brill Nijhoff Publishers 2015), 172.

[133] Kunoy (n 7), 75.

However, none of the above-mentioned arguments is likely to succeed in the third-party dispute settlement forum seized to delimit the continental shelf beyond 200 nm, because, neither Article 76 nor Article 83 (or customary international law of maritime delimitation) provides legal criteria that measure the comparative naturalness of the entitlement. Equally obscure is how the comparative naturalness, even if their relative hierarchy could be established, should be reflected in the drawing of the boundary lines. The formulae and the constraints in Article 76(4)–(6) are adopted for coastal States to choose the best combination of positive formulae and constraint lines in order to maximize their claim to the continental shelf beyond 200 nm.[134] It is therefore the choice and freedom of coastal States to use one or the other or the combination of them. Article 76 does not prescribe any hierarchy between these formulae or between the constraints in terms of "naturalness." Interpreting Article 76 to accord different degrees of naturalness to the geophysical elements so as to justify different qualities of the entitlements finds no textual support under Article 76 and overlooks the objective and purpose of Article 76. Article 76(4) provides two formulae for coastal States to locate their outer edge of the continental margin because the drafters recognized the diverse geological and geomorphological characteristics of continental margins worldwide. Likewise, Article 76(5) and Article 76(6) distinguish submarine elevations from submarine ridges because of the drafters' concern that certain mid-ocean ridges can be so lengthy and elevated that some coastal States may have undue advantage if the 2,500 metre isobath plus 100 nm constraint is applied to such ridges.[135] None of the considerations derived from an assessment of the "naturalness" of the geomorphological or geological criteria. In effect, geomorphological or geological factors are only relevant to the extent of defining the existence and extent of the continental shelf beyond 200 nm, since they are "agreed categories of geological and geomorphological facts that are legally relevant for the purpose of determining title to the outer

[134] See United Nations, *The Law of the Sea: Definition of the Continental Shelf* (United Nations 1993), 14; R. Macnab, "Initial Assessment," in P. J. Cook and C. M. Carleton (eds.), *Continental Shelf Limits: The Scientific and Legal Interface* (Oxford University Press 2000), 261; S. V. Suarez, *The Outer Limits of the Continental Shelf: Legal Aspects of Their Establishment* (Springer 2008), 154; *Scientific and Technical Guidelines of the Commission on the Limits of the Continental Shelf* (May 13, 1999, Doc. CLCS/11) [2.3.1–2.3.4].

[135] See L. Parson, "Article 76," in A. Proelss (ed.), *The United Nations Convention on the Law of the Sea: A Commentary* (Hart 2017), 595–598.

continental shelf."[136] Troughs, "marked disruption of the seabed,"[137] or "fundamental discontinuity in the sea-bed and subsoil,"[138] are accidents of nature. True, maritime delimitation does not seek to "make equal what nature has made unequal,"[139] but the very pursuit of an equitable solution requires the elimination of the inequitableness created by circumstances that "appear on the face of them to be extraordinary, unnatural or unreasonable."[140] International courts and tribunals acknowledge that "[t]here can never be any question of *completely* refashioning nature," but it is also the task of the judiciary to abate "the effects of an incidental special feature from which an unjustifiable difference of treatment could result."[141] Therefore, to suggest that international courts and tribunals should accept the work of nature where there are salient submarine features in geophysical terms would be wholly incompatible with the jurisprudence that aims to eliminate unwanted effects of peculiar or unusual or incidental geographical natures. It would also come into conflict with the overall objective of maritime delimitation, namely that, "so far as possible, the line of delimitation should allow the coasts of the Parties to produce their effects in terms of maritime entitlements in a reasonable and mutually balanced way."[142]

Coastal States may put geomorphological or geological considerations at the centre of their negotiations,[143] but international courts and tribunals are not obliged to.[144] Despite the lack of legal criteria for this end, international courts and tribunals also lack the incentive to address arguments based on superiority of geomorphological or geological factors, given the potential magnitude of disagreement between the parties. Shedding light on the rejection of "the most natural prolongation" argument by ITLOS, Judges ad hoc Mensah and Oxman commented that:

> Bangladesh invited the Tribunal to undertake an evaluation of the relative strengths of the natural prolongations of the Parties, based on geological

[136] Colson (n 10), 102.
[137] *Tunisia/Libya* (n 82), 57 [66].
[138] *Libya/Malta* (n 1), 45–46 [58].
[139] Ibid., 39–40 [46].
[140] *North Sea* (n 16), 23–24 [24].
[141] Ibid., 49–50 [91] (emphasis added).
[142] *Territorial and Maritime Dispute (Nicaragua v. Colombia) [2012] ICJ Rep 624, 703-704* [215].
[143] See discussion in Tanaka (n 5), 297–304.
[144] *Tunisia/Libya* (n 82), 117–118 [62] (Separate Opinion of Judge Jiménez de Aréchaga).

> and related factors. Acceptance of this idea would, in our view, introduce a new element of difficulty and uncertainty into the process of maritime delimitation in this case. We are concerned that it could have an unsettling effect on the efforts of States to agree on delimitation of the continental shelf beyond 200 miles.[145]

To delimit the continental shelf beyond 200 nm by dictating geomorphological or geological features would in effect open the door for confrontations over scientific matters, as the *Tunisia/Libya* case and the *Libya/Malta* case remind us.[146] One should not underestimate the unwillingness of international courts and tribunals to engage with divergent interpretations of scientific or technical data. As explained by the ICJ when it rejected the rift-zone argument of Libya in the *Libya/Malta* case:

> The Court is unable to accept the position that in order to decide this case, it must first make a determination upon a disagreement between scientists of distinction as to the more plausibly correct interpretation of apparently incomplete scientific data; for a criterion that depends upon such a judgment or estimate having to be made by a court, or perhaps also by negotiating governments, is clearly inapt to a general legal rule of delimitation.[147]

The frustration of the judges when they were caught between heavily disputed scientific and technical propositions was also vividly summarized by Judge Jiménez de Aréchaga in the *Tunisia/Libya* case: "The impression gained from the lengthy and instructive discussion was that the criticism by each Party of the scientific arguments presented by the other was far stronger and more convincing than their affirmative contentions."[148] Indeed, it has been suggested that the "interplay of geology and law is probably one of the most important of the factors contributing to uncertainty in the rules relating to boundary delimitation on the continental shelf" at an early stage of the development of the law of maritime delimitation.[149] International courts and tribunals would not be an ideal arena for such confrontations to prevail, as the unwillingness of international judges to make a decision over disputed scientific and

145 *Bangladesh/Myanmar* (n 60), 150 [11] (Joint Declaration of Judges ad hoc Mensah and Oxman).

146 See Hutchinson (n 101), 144–145.

147 *Libya/Malta* (n 1), 36–37 [41].

148 *Tunisia/Libya* (n 82), 110 [38] (Separate Opinion of Judge Jiménez de Aréchaga).

149 D. M. McRae, "Delimitation of the Continental Shelf between the United Kingdom and France: The Channel Arbitration" (1977), 15 *Canadian YIL* 173, 197.

technical evidence has been clearly registered,[150] which is not a singular phenomenon in maritime delimitation disputes.[151]

One may consider if international courts and tribunals may be capable of finding "the most natural prolongation" of the respective party if the recommendations of the CLCS are available.[152] It is submitted that the recommendations of the CLCS may significantly contribute to determining the factual certainty of the existence and extent of the entitlement to the continental shelf beyond 200 nm, and, if things so require, to determining the area of overlap with the information on the FOS, the outer edge of the continental margin or the outer limits of the continental shelf. Nevertheless, the recommendations of the CLCS provide no justification for comparing the naturalness or superiority of one natural component of the seabed over others. What force should be attached to them is a matter of judgment based on law, the lack of which is fundamental to the unfeasibility of arguing a larger share of the continental shelf beyond 200 nm on the basis of relative naturalness. Importantly, if the recommendations of the CLCS confirm that both parties are equally entitled to the continental shelf beyond 200 nm concerned, it is unlikely that the court or tribunal would linger over the question of the superiority of entitlement to the continental shelf beyond 200 nm,[153] as already being demonstrated by the *Tunisia/Libya* case.[154] Furthermore, it is even less likely that geomorphological or geological

150 See D. Anderson, "Scientific Evidence in Cases under Part XV of the LOSC," in M. H. Nordquist et al. (eds.), *Law, Science & Ocean Management* (Martinus Nijhoff Publishers 2007), 508; T. Treves, "Law and Science in the Interpretation of the Law of the Sea Convention: Article 76 Between the Law of the Sea Tribunal and the Commission on the Limits of the Continental Shelf" (2012) 3 *JIDS* 483, 485.

151 Criticizing the ICJ's approach to scientific evidence in the *Pulp Mills* case, Judges Al-Khasawneh and Simma commented that "the Court has an unfortunate history of persisting, when faced with sophisticated scientific and technical evidence in support of the legal claims made by States before it, in resolving these issues purely through the application of its traditional legal techniques; and it has come under considerable criticism in this regard, particularly in very recent scholarly commentary on its working methods," *Pulp Mills on the River Uruguay (Argentina v. Uruguay) [2010] ICJ Rep 14, 113* [12] (Joint Dissenting Opinion of Judges Al-Khasawneh and Simma). See also Bruno Simma, "The International Court of Justice and Scientific Expertise" (2012), 106 Proceedings of the Annual Meeting (American Society of International Law), 230.

152 See Colson (n 10), 102.

153 See Fietta and Cleverly (n 5), 617.

154 In the *Tunisia/Libya* case, the Court found that a common continental shelf (natural prolongation) was shared by the two parties, and that "the ascertainment of the extent of the areas of shelf appertaining to each State must be governed by criteria of international law other than those taken from physical features," *Tunisia/Libya* (n 82), 58 [67].

factors will be relevant in cases concerning adjacent coasts, as courts could determine the maritime boundary without a terminus, but indicate that the boundary extends until it reaches the outer limits of the continental shelf.[155]

Therefore, "the most natural prolongation" argument is unlikely to succeed in the delimitation of the continental shelf beyond 200 nm where international courts and tribunals are seized. In contrast to the opinion that the *Bangladesh/Myanmar* case did not set a precedent by rejecting "the most natural prolongation" argument,[156] it is submitted that the Tribunal significantly contributed to the clarity of the law of maritime delimitation by confining the relevance of geomorphological or geological factors to the establishment of entitlement to the continental shelf beyond 200 nm in accordance with Article 76 of UNCLOS. It also wisely distanced the notion of natural prolongation from its ambiguous, and sometimes contradictory connotations manifested in early jurisprudence. By taming the notion of natural prolongation under the legal framework of Article 76, the Tribunal cautioned against the past fever to "search for natural boundaries in the dark blue depths of depressions and troughs or in the pale shallownesses of ridges and plateaus."[157] This aspect of the *Bangladesh/Myanmar* case may turn out to be a leading precedent for arguments with similar objectives.

### B The Use of Geophysical Factors in State Practice

Analysis of State practice concerning maritime delimitation can be in danger of being superficial. Perhaps it is inevitable because of the paucity of first-hand information relating to the conclusion of agreements available to researchers outside the official circles. The texts of agreements are more often than not silent on what principles, circumstances, or factors were taken into account and how much weight has been accorded to a particular factor. Accordingly, to some extent speculation is inevitable.[158] In addition, offsetting gains and losses of each side in a single agreement delimiting maritime zones can be widely identified. Coastal States may be guided principally by legal principles or legally relevant factors, but other

[155] See *Ghana/Côte d'Ivoire* (n 92), [660(3)].
[156] See Churchill (n 130), 150; Schofield, Telesetsky and Lee (n 9), 375.
[157] *Libya/Malta* (n 1), 62 (Separate Opinion of Vice-President Sette-Camara).
[158] P. Beazley, "Technical Aspects of Maritime Boundary Delimitation" (1994) 1 *Maritime Briefing* 1, 7.

factors which would normally be disregarded by international courts or tribunals may well come into play.[159] After all, Articles 74 and 83 of UNCLOS are deprived of substantive rules. This section will thus aim at describing whether coastal States use geophysical factors in the delimitation of the continental shelf beyond 200 nm, and, if so, under what circumstances.

A comprehensive study of 134 maritime delimitation agreements conducted in 1993 concludes that "geophysical factors have been ignored far more frequently than they have been used,"[160] but it predicts that a principal exception to this conclusion will be the delimitation of the continental shelf beyond 200 nm.[161] So far, there have been 15 agreements concerning the delimitation of the continental shelf beyond 200 nm concluded between coastal States (see Appendix 4).[162] Most of these maritime boundary agreements were concluded before the relevant parties submitted information to the CLCS in respect of their continental shelf beyond 200 nm, and some of them were concluded before the entry into force of UNCLOS. It is therefore clear that the parties proceeded to delimit the continental shelf beyond 200 nm on the assumption that all of them were entitled to a continental shelf beyond 200 nm. Among these 15 agreements, only in two agreements do geophysical factors play a role in shaping the course of the maritime boundaries, whereas in the remaining agreements, the knowledge of geomorphological and geophysical features of the seabed contributes to determining the existence of the area of overlapping continental shelves and the terminus of the maritime boundaries.

159 See B. H. Oxman, "Political, Strategic, and Historical Considerations," in J. I. Charney and L. M. Alexander (eds.), *International Maritime Boundaries, Volume I* (Martinus Nijhoff Publishers 1993), 11; A. G. Oude Elferink, "International Law and Negotiated and Adjudicated Maritime Boundaries: A Complex Relationship" (2015) 58 *GYIL* 231, 247–250.

160 Highet (n 87), 195.

161 Ibid., 196.

162 The Agreement between the Republic of Ireland and the United Kingdom of Great Britain and Northern Ireland Concerning the Delimitation of the Continental Shelf between the Two Countries (November 7, 1988, 1765 UNTS 421) was amended in 2013, yet for the present study only the 1988 agreement is examined because the amendment treaty in 2013 did not change the main course of the continental shelf boundaries extending beyond 200 nm. The Agreement on Maritime Delimitation between the Government of Australia and the Government of the French Republic (January 4, 1982, 1329 UNTS 107) involves two maritime boundaries, one between Australia (Heard/McDonald Islands) and France (Kerguelen Islands) and the other between Australia and France (New Caledonia).

The two agreements in which geophysical factors play a positive role are the 1997 Australia–Indonesia agreement[163] and the 2004 Australia–New Zealand agreement.[164] The 1997 Australia–Indonesia agreement completed the delimitation of maritime boundaries between Australia and Indonesia.[165] It is obvious that geophysical considerations played a central role in shaping the seabed boundary line in the western Timor Sea, which extended the seabed boundary in the 1972 Australia–Indonesia agreement concerning the Timor Sea and the Arafura Sea.[166] The distance between Australia and Indonesia in the Timor Sea, where the delimitation took place, is less than 400 nm. Nonetheless, Australia managed to secure part of the continental shelves which lie beyond 200 nm from its territorial baselines.[167] The delimitation method to effect the boundary is derived from Article 76(4) of UNCLOS, for the western boundary between Points A79 and A82 coincides with a line 60 nm seaward of the foot of the Australian continental slope.[168] In this sense, Australia's entitlement to the continental shelf beyond 200 nm seems to prevail over the 200 nm continental shelf of Indonesia. However, one should not overlook the fact that the delimitation of the continental shelf in the 1997 Australia–Indonesia agreement was negotiated as part of a "package-deal," in which three maritime boundaries were negotiated.[169] The negotiations were premised on the basis that nothing was agreed until everything was agreed,[170] and the gain of Australia in the seabed delimitation is offset by its loss to Indonesia in the delimitation between Christmas Island and Java and in the delimitation of the EEZ boundary. Indonesia gained two-thirds of the seas and seabed in the disputed area

[163] Treaty between Australia and Indonesia Establishing an Exclusive Economic Zone Boundary and Certain Seabed Boundaries (March 14, 1997), (1997) 36 ILM 1053.

[164] Treaty between Australia and New Zealand Establishing certain Exclusive Economic Zone and Continental Shelf Boundaries (July 25, 2004), 2441 UNTS 235 117.

[165] J. R. V. Prescott, "Australia–Indonesia, Report Number 6-2(6)," in J. I. Charney and R. W. Smith (eds.), *International Maritime Boundaries, Vol. IV* (Martinus Nijhoff Publishers 2002), 2697.

[166] Agreement between the Government of the Commonwealth of Australia and the Government of the Republic of Indonesia Establishing Certain Seabed Boundaries in the Area of the Timor and Arafura Seas Supplementary to the Agreement of 18 May 1971 (October 9, 1972), 974 UNTS 319.

[167] See Prescott, "Australia–Indonesia, Report Number 6-2(6)" (n 165), 2708.

[168] Ibid.

[169] See B. M. Magnússon, "Outer Continental Shelf Boundary Agreements" (2013) 62 *ICLQ* 345, 357.

[170] See Prescott, "Australia–Indonesia, Report Number 6-2(6)" (n 165), 2698.

north of Christmas Island, and it secured more than half of the disputed area in the EEZ delimitation.[171]

The consideration of the characteristics of the seabed and subsoil in the 1997 Australia–Indonesia agreement reflects the position of Australia, that in the Timor Sea there were two continental shelves separated by the deep Timor Trough, which was also a paramount consideration in fixing the 1972 seabed agreement between Australia and Indonesia.[172] So far Indonesia has not ratified the 1997 Australia–Indonesia agreement.[173] Whereas Australia continued to take this view in its negotiations with Timor-Leste in delimiting the maritime boundaries in the central Timor Sea,[174] the Treaty between Australia and the Democratic Republic of Timor-Leste Establishing their Maritime Boundaries in the Timor Sea (2018 Treaty) represents an amicable solution in which the relevance of geophysical factors cannot be judged by reference to the terms of the 2018 Treaty.[175] As stated by the Preamble of the 2018 Treaty, "the settlement contained in this Treaty is based on a mutual accommodation between the Parties without prejudice to their respective legal positions." Australia and Timor-Leste reached the 2018 Treaty with the assistance of the Conciliation Commission constituted under Article 298(i)(a)(i) and Annex V of UNCLOS, which was the first time that States Parties to UNCLOS utilized the compulsory conciliation procedure.[176] The southern boundary takes the form of a single maritime boundary; it partially follows a median line and partially runs to the north of the median line along an agreed course.[177] The western and eastern boundaries are two continental shelf boundaries, and they are provisional in the sense that they are subject to adjustments once the

171 See ibid., 2705.

172 See J. R. V. Prescott, "Australia–Indonesia (Timor and Arafura Seas), Report Number 6-2(2)," in J. I. Charney and Lewis M. Alexander (eds.), *International Maritime Boundaries, Vol. I* (Martinus Nijhoff 1993), 1211.

173 Though it was reported that the parties acted as if the 1997 treaty were in force. See A. Serdy, "Is There a 400-Mile Rule in UNCLOS Article 76(8)?" (2008) 57 *ICLQ* 941, 951.

174 See Timor Sea Conciliation (*Timor-Leste* v. *Australia*), *Report and Recommendations of the Compulsory Conciliation Commission between Timor-Leste and Australia on the Timor Sea, 9 May 2018* [231–234], available at: pca-cpa.org/en/cases/132/.

175 Treaty between Australia and the Democratic Republic of Timor-Leste Establishing Their Maritime Boundaries in the Timor Sea (March 6, 2018), ATS [2019] 16.

176 X. Liao, "The Timor Sea Conciliation under Article 298 and Annex V of UNCLOS: A Critique" (2019) 18 *Chinese JIL* 281, 281–282.

177 Report of the Conciliation Commission (n 174), [261].

oil fields at stake are depleted and Timor-Leste and Indonesia conclude their maritime boundaries.[178]

The 2004 Australia–New Zealand agreement involves two areas, namely, the northern area between Lord Howe Island and the North Island of New Zealand and between Norfolk Island and the Three Kings Islands, and the southern area between Macquarie Island and Auckland and Campbell Islands.[179] The delimitation of overlapping EEZs was determined by equidistance, whereas the delimitation of the continental shelf beyond 200 nm of the two parties reflects the parties' agreement on the entitlement of each to the continental shelf beyond 200 nm.[180] The delimitation of the continental shelf beyond 200 nm starts from the termini (northern and southern) which are located at points that are "either agreed by the two countries as being the outer limit of the continental shelf beyond 200 nm or, where there was no such agreement, at points slightly beyond the furthest possible extent of such continental shelf."[181] The boundary lines delimiting the continental shelf beyond 200 nm are more favorable for New Zealand because they follow the 200 nm limit of the Australian island, but are well beyond the 200 nm limit from the New Zealand coast. This is suggested to reflect the more pronounced entitlement of New Zealand along the Three Kings Ridge when compared with Australia's eastward natural prolongation from Norfolk Island.[182] It seems that the reason why New Zealand's entitlement to the continental shelf beyond 200 nm was the central consideration in the delimitation of the continental shelf beyond 200 nm boils down to the question of evidence of the existence of the entitlement.

Other than the 1997 Australia–Indonesia agreement and the 2004 Australia–New Zealand agreement, in no other agreements concerning the continental shelf beyond 200 nm did coastal States refer to geomorphological or geological factors to shape the course of maritime boundaries. Instead, the majority of the agreements rely on the knowledge of geomorphology or geology for determining the terminus of the maritime boundary, or for specifying the geographical scope of the area to be delimited.

178 Ibid., [263–264].

179 Articles 2 and 3 of the 2004 Australia–New Zealand agreement.

180 See N. Fyfe and G. French, "Australia–New Zealand, Report Number 5-26," in D. A. Colson and R. W. Smith (eds.), *International Maritime Boundaries, Vol. V* (Martinus Nijhoff 2005), 3763–3764.

181 Ibid., 3763.

182 See ibid., 3764.

In four agreements geophysical factors are taken into account in connection with the termini of the boundary lines. Some agreements apply the formulae and constraints under Article 76(4)–(5) of UNCLOS so that the terminus of the maritime boundary is located on the outer edge of the continental margin or on the potential outer limits of the continental shelf. The 1988 Ireland–United Kingdom agreement determines termini Point 94 and Point 132 based on the FOS plus 60 nm formula under Article 76(4) and the 2,500-meter-isobath plus 100 nm constraint under Article 76(5) respectively.[183] The 1990 Trinidad and Tobago–Venezuela agreement locates the terminus of the maritime boundary on the outer edge of the continental margin, determined by calculating the thickness of the sedimentary rocks.[184] Likewise, the 1982 Australia–France (New Caledonia) agreement locates the terminus close to the foot of the slope of the eastern side of the Norfolk Ridge.[185] It is also the case that coastal States may extend the maritime boundary as far as the outer edge of the continental margin was known to them, as in the 1982 Australia (Heard/McDonald Islands)–France (Kerguelen Islands) agreement.[186]

Other agreements simply decide to defer the determination of the terminus of the maritime boundary until the time the parties' outer limits of the continental shelf beyond 200 nm are established in accordance with the procedure under Article 76 of UNCLOS. Article 3 of the 2009 Kenya–Tanzania agreement provides that the boundary extends eastward along the parallel to "a point that [. . .] intersects the outermost limits of the continental shelf."[187] The 2010 Norway–Russia agreement adopts a formula to determine the northern termini of the delimitation line in the

[183] See D. H. Anderson, "Ireland-United Kingdom, Report Number 9-5," in J. I. Charney and L. M. Alexander (eds.), *International Maritime Boundaries, Vol. II* (Martinus Nijhoff 1993), 1770.

[184] See K. G. Nweihed, "Trinidad and Tobago–Venezuela, Report Number 2-13(3)," in J. I. Charney and L. M. Alexander (eds.), *International Maritime Boundaries, Vol. I* (Martinus Nijhoff Publishers 1993), 681.

[185] See C. H. Park, "Australia–France (New Caledonia), Report Number 5-1," in J. I. Charney and L. M. Alexander (eds.), *International Maritime Boundaries, Vol. I* (Martinus Nijhoff Publishers 1993), 912–913.

[186] See J. R. V. Prescott, "Australia (Heard/McDonald Islands)–France (Kerguelen Islands), Report Number 6-1," in J. I. Charney and L. M. Alexander (eds.), *International Maritime Boundaries, Vol. II* (Martinus Nijhoff Publishers 1993), 1188.

[187] Article 2 of Agreement between the United Republic of Tanzania and the Republic of Kenya on the Delimitation of the Maritime Boundary of the Exclusive Economic Zone and the Continental Shelf (June 23, 2009), 2603 UNTS 37.

Arctic Ocean, which is to be specified upon the establishment of the outer limits of the continental shelf on the basis of the recommendations of the CLCS.[188] The 1990 United States–Soviet Union agreement, for its part, more generally provides that the boundary line between the parties extends into the Arctic Ocean "as far as permitted under international law."[189] The 2017 France (French Guiana)–Suriname agreement consists of a single and open-ended maritime boundary, as the agreement simply provides that the maritime delimitation "is the delimitation of the maritime areas in which the States respectively exercise or will exercise their sovereignty, their sovereign rights or their jurisdiction," and the agreement allows the boundary line to be extended without specifying the endpoint.[190] It should be noted that when France and Suriname reached this agreement, both of them had received recommendations from the CLCS that confirmed the location of their respective outer limits of the continental shelf.[191] Therefore, it will be comparatively straightforward as to where the boundary line specified in the 2017 agreement will intersect with the respective outer limits of the continental shelf of the parties.

The 1982 Australia–Papua New Guinea agreement[192] and the 1988 Australia–Solomon Islands agreement,[193] on the other hand, includes short segments of boundary lines that extend beyond 200 nm from the respective party, though it is unclear if the parties resorted to Article 76 of

[188] See Article 1.1 of Treaty between the Kingdom of Norway and the Russian Federation concerning Maritime Delimitation and Cooperation in the Barents Sea and the Arctic Ocean (September 15, 2010), 2791 UNTS 3.

[189] E. G. Verville, "United States–Soviet Union, Report Number 1-6," in I. L. Charney and L. M. Alexander (eds.), *International Maritime Boundaries, Vol. I* (Martinus Nijhoff Publishers 1993), 457.

[190] See Article 1.2 and Article 1.4 of Agreement on Maritime Delimitation between the Government of the French Republic and the Government of the Republic of Suriname (November 8, 2017), published at Official Gazette of the French Republic (December 16, 2018), NOR: EAEJ1831584D.

[191] Suriname received the recommendations from the CLCS on March 30, 2011 while France received the recommendations in respect of French Guiana on September 2, 2009.

[192] Treaty between Australia and the Independent State of Papua New Guinea Concerning Sovereignty and Maritime Boundaries in the Area between the Two Countries, including the Area known as Torres Strait, and Related Matters (December 18, 1978), 1429 UNTS 207.

[193] Agreement between the Government of Solomon Islands and the Government of Australia establishing certain sea and seabed boundaries (September 13, 1988), (1988) 12 LoSB 19.

UNCLOS during their negotiations. It is noted that the eastern endpoint of the 1982 Australia–Papua New Guinea agreement and the western endpoint of the 1988 Australia–Solomon Islands agreement, plus the southernmost terminus of the 1989 Solomon Islands–Papua New Guinea agreement,[194] form a tiny triangular "grey area," in which the seabed might be the continental shelf beyond 200 nm of the three States whereas the water column is part of the high seas.[195] Nevertheless, up to date only the Solomon Islands claimed this triangular area beyond 200 nm in its preliminary information to the CLCS,[196] whereas neither Australia or Papua New Guinea included this area in their submissions to the CLCS.

Sometimes, the knowledge of geomorphology or geology could be a crucial factor that qualifies the geographical scope of the area beyond 200 nm to be delimited. The western terminus of the 1982 Australia (Heard/McDonald Islands) and France (Kerguelen Islands) agreement was settled because the parties found it inappropriate to extend the boundary line further to the west in 1982 "because of uncertainty as to the configuration of the continental shelf southwest of the agreed line."[197] In fact, subsequent submissions of Australia and France to the CLCS confirm that the area westward of their 1982 boundary between the Heard/McDonald Islands and Kerguelen Islands is not subject to overlapping continental shelves beyond 200 nm.[198] Similarly, the delimitation

[194] The 1989 Solomon Islands–Papua New Guinea agreement does not concern the continental shelf beyond 200 nm. See C. H. Park, "Papua New Guinea -Solomon Islands, Report Number 5-16," in J. I. Charney and L. M. Alexander (eds.), *International Maritime Boundaries, Vol. I* (Martinus Nijhoff Publishers 1993), 1155.

[195] See C. H. Park, "Australia–Papua New Guinea, Report Number 5-3," in J. I. Charney and L. M. Alexander (eds.), *International Maritime Boundaries, Vol. I* (Martinus Nijhoff Publishers 1993), 933.

[196] See "Preliminary Information of the Solomon Islands," available at: www.un.org/Depts/los/clcs_new/submissions_files/preliminary/slb_preliminaryinfo.pdf.

[197] See Prescott (n 186), 1188–1189.

[198] Whereas the 2004 Australian submission to the CLCS informed the CLCS that "[t]here is a potential outstanding delimitation with France involving an extension of the Australia–France Delimitation Treaty boundary at its western end," the 2009 French submission in respect of the Kerguelen Islands shows that France's proposed outer limits of the continental shelf do not involve the area in the western end of the 1982 Treaty, and France informed the CLCS that "the continental shelf in the area of Kerguelen is not the subject of any dispute between France and any other State." See also, "Executive summary of Australia's submission (November 15, 2004)," 17–18, available at www.un.org/Depts/los/clcs_new/submissions_files/aus04/Documents/aus_doc_es_web_delivery.pdf; "Executive summary of France's partial submission (5 February 2009)," 3–4,

of the continental shelf beyond 200 nm in the 2009 Barbados–France (Guadeloupe and Martinique) agreement is conditional, for the agreement provides that "if the continental shelf of Barbados and that of France overlap beyond two hundred nautical miles" the delimitation line will be extended in the manner as defined by the agreement.[199] Coastal States may also take into account the possibility that their claim to the continental shelf beyond 200 nm would not be confirmed by the CLCS, and provide for methods of adjustment of the maritime delimitation in their provisional delimitation agreements, as in the 2006 Agreed Minutes between Denmark (Faroe Islands), Iceland, and Norway and in the 2013 Denmark (Greenland)–Iceland Agreed Minutes.[200] In the 2006 Agreed Minutes, it is reported that "salient geological and geomorphological features in the area were incidentally largely respected when drawing the provisional delimitation lines,"[201] and that key features which are related to the continental margin of the coastal State remain part of that State's continental shelf following the provisional lines.[202] This suggests that coastal States integrate the delineation and delimitation processes intentionally. It has also been suggested that several provisional delimitation lines of the 2006 Agreed Minutes bear considerable resemblance to equidistance lines with adjustments.[203]

To conclude, several points regarding the survey of State practice are in order. First, the knowledge of geomorphology or geology is important for coastal States' decision to delimit the continental shelf beyond 200 nm and the geographical scope of such delimitation. The latter is expressed through the termini of the maritime boundaries. In fact, the majority of the agreements illustrate that geomorphological or geological elements under Article 76 of UNCLOS were only taken into account to the extent

available at www.un.org/Depts/los/clcs_new/submissions_files/fra09/fra_executivesummary_2009.pdf.

199 See Article 3.1 of the Agreement between the Government of Barbados and the Government of the French Republic on the Delimitation of the Maritime Space between Barbados and France (October 15, 2009), 2663 UNTS 163.

200 See R. E. Fife, "Denmark/The Faroes–Iceland–Norway, Report Number 9-26," in D. A. Colson and R. W. Smith (eds.), *International Maritime Boundaries, Vol. VI* (Martinus Nijhoff Publishers 2011), 4543; B. M. Magnússon, "Denmark (Greenland)–Iceland, Report Number 9-22 (2)," in C. G. Lathrop (ed.), *International Maritime Boundaries, Vol. VII* (Brill Nijhoff Publishers 2016), 5263.

201 Fife (n 200), 4540.

202 Ibid.

203 Ibid., 4543.

of determining the endpoint of the boundary line without affecting the course of the boundaries. This use of geophysical factors is found between adjacent States,[204] between States with a lateral coastal relationship where the States are located in or face towards the open ocean,[205] and sometimes between opposite coasts.[206] This is also irrespective of whether the relevant parties concluded the maritime boundaries before or after they received the recommendations of the CLCS.

Second, the majority of the agreements seem to suggest that once the existence of overlapping entitlements to the continental shelf beyond 200 nm is recognized by the relevant parties, geophysical factors cease to be relevant in the drawing of maritime boundaries. Knowledge of geomorphology and geology contributes to determining the existence of a continuous continental margin that is "shared" by the relevant parties, without having implications for the methods of delimitation. Examples include the 1990 United States–Soviet Union agreement,[207] the 2000 Mexico–United States agreement,[208] the 2010 Norway–Russia agreement,[209] and the 2013 Denmark (Greenland)–Iceland Agreed Minutes.[210] It is important to note that even if the parties have recommendations from the CLCS and thus the geomorphology or geology of the continental shelves to be delimited is underwritten by the CLCS, the parties nonetheless disregarded geophysical factors in their delimitation of the continental shelf beyond 200 nm. This is the case in the 2010 Norway–Russia agreement and the 2017 France (French Guiana)–Suriname agreement.

204 For instance, the 2009 Kenya–Tanzania agreement and 2017 France (French Guiana)–Suriname agreement.

205 Examples are the 2009 Barbados–France (Guadeloupe and Martinique) agreement, the 1990 Trinidad and Tobago–Venezuela agreement, and the 1988 Ireland–United Kingdom agreement.

206 Examples are the 1982 Australia–France (New Caledonia) agreement and the 1988 Australia–Solomon Islands agreement.

207 Agreement between the United States of America and the Union of Soviet Socialist Republics on the maritime boundary (June 1, 1990), (1991) 17 LoSB 15. See Verville (n 189), 455.

208 Treaty between Mexico and the United States on the Delimitation of the Continental Shelf in the Western Gulf of Mexico beyond 200 Nautical Miles (June 9, 2000), (2001) 44 LoSB 71. See R. W. Smith, "Mexico–United States, Report Number 1-5(2)," in J. I. Charney and R. W. Smith (eds.), *International Maritime Boundaries, Vol. IV* (Martinus Nijhoff Publishers 2002), 2623.

209 R. E. Fife, "Norway–Russia Federation, Report Number 9-6(3)," in C. G. Lathrop (ed.), *International Maritime Boundaries, Vol. VII* (Brill Nijhoff Publishers 2016), 5183–5184.

210 Magnússon (n 200), 5263.

Last but not least, the survey demonstrates that, so far, State practice shows no preference for geophysical factors in the delimitation of the continental shelf beyond 200 nm. The 1997 Australia–Indonesia agreement and the 2004 Australia–New Zealand agreement are, after all, outcomes of political decisions. It is the agreement between the parties that attaches force to the natural components of the seabed, not *vice versa*.[211] In consequence, it is unlikely that international courts and tribunals will engage with determining the significance of geophysical factors and on that basis delimit the boundary of the continental shelf beyond 200 nm. It is recalled that the *Anglo-French Arbitration* found that attaching significance to the Hurd Deep-Hurd Deep Fault Zone "would run counter to the whole tendency of State practice on the continental shelf in recent years."[212] Admittedly the current body of State practice concerning the continental shelf beyond 200 nm may be too small a sampling to establish the tendency in State practice, yet the fact that in one agreement geophysical factors are central while in others they are immaterial militates against any legal value that might be inferred from geomorphology or geology.

Eventually, the use of geophysical factors in the delimitation of the continental shelf beyond 200 nm may share the same fate as in maritime delimitation within 200 nm: "[M]ore attention than effect has been given to geophysical features."[213] The State practice concerning the continental shelf beyond 200 nm to date tends to confirm this view.

## IV The Proper Role of Geophysical Circumstances in the Delimitation of the Continental Shelf beyond 200 NM

The preceding discussion leads to the conclusion that it is unpromising to infer delimitation methods or relevant circumstances from the entitlement to the continental shelf beyond 200 nm, in particular when a court or tribunal is requested to delimit the continental shelf beyond 200 nm. The jurisprudence in general, whether prior or subsequent to the *Libya/Malta* case, showed little support for sustaining the normative link between the entitlement and the delimitation methods in the sense that the use of a method is a logically and legally necessary choice flowing

[211] See Weil (n 5), 30–31; *Tunisia/Libya* (n 82), 117–118 [62] (Separate Opinion of Judge Jiménez de Aréchaga).

[212] *Anglo-French Arbitration* (n 56), [107].

[213] Highet (n 87), 164.

from the basis of entitlement. Nor is it likely that geophysical factors will re-enter the judiciary's mind so that the delimitation process shall accord particular weight to certain submarine geomorphological or geological features in the continental shelf delimitation beyond 200 nm. The declaratory approach once prevailing in the early judicial decisions provides no justification for identifying physical natural prolongations, as it amounts to finding the outer limits of the continental shelf of the respective party and the latter is subject to the delineation procedure under Article 76 of UNCLOS. "The most natural prolongation" argument is, for its part, unlikely to guide the delimitation process because there are no rules or criteria to measure the degrees of naturalness, which would allow for a decision on the superiority of one entitlement to the continental shelf beyond 200 nm over the other. Further, the use of geophysical factors in State practice concerning the continental shelf beyond 200 nm is very limited, and geophysical factors were taken into account primarily for determining the existence of overlapping continental shelves and the termini of boundaries.

Accordingly, it is more convincing that the role of geophysical factors in the delimitation process is confined to the establishment of the entitlement to the continental shelf beyond 200 nm and, consequential upon that, the determination of the area of overlapping entitlements. Under certain circumstances, this exercise may call for determining the locations of the respective FOS or the outer limits of the continental shelf, which deviates from a coast-to-coast relationship in determining the area of overlap.[214] It is in this sense that the basis of entitlement to the continental shelf beyond 200 nm bears on the choice and application of delimitation methods. Once the knowledge of geomorphology and geology plays its role in determining the existence and extent of the overlapping entitlements to the continental shelf beyond 200 nm, there is no legally compelling reason to attach special force to them in the delimitation process.[215] On the conceptual and practical level, once established, the area of overlapping entitlements to the continental shelf beyond 200 nm should be treated legally as a featureless continuum, allowing no internal distinction.[216]

[214] See Chapter 6, Section III.C. and D.

[215] See Marques Antunes and Becker-Weinberg (n 5), 67.

[216] See J. Lilje-Jensen and M. Thamsborg, "The Role of Natural Prolongation in Relation to Shelf Delimitation beyond 200 Nautical Miles" (1995) 64 *Nordic JIL* 619, 626–627.

# 8

# Geographical Circumstances

## I The Relevance of Geographical Circumstances

Circumstances related to coastal geography are central to maritime delimitation. Geographical circumstances may contribute to indicating the delimitation method as well as its implementation, for "the appropriateness–the equitable character–of the method is always a function of the particular geographical situation,"[1] and "the method chosen and its results must be faithful to the actual geographical situation."[2] Under the three-stage approach established in the *Black Sea* case, geographical circumstances are considered as part of the "factors calling for the adjustment or shifting of the provisional equidistance line in order to achieve an equitable result" in the second stage.[3] Although formulated as a corrective, relevant circumstances, in particular geographical ones, may require a substantial adjustment of the provisional equidistance line, a process that may involve the use of a different method or combination of methods.[4] The disproportionality test under the three-stage approach, in addition, is also an exercise "by reference to the overall geography of the area."[5]

Notwithstanding the hypotheses that coastal geography would lose relevance in the delimitation of the continental shelf beyond 200 nautical miles (nm), the judicial practice to date indicates the opposite. The *Bangladesh/Myanmar* case found that the concavity of the coast of Bangladesh continued to produce a cut-off effect in the delimitation of

[1] *Delimitation of the Continental Shelf between the United Kingdom of Great Britain and Northern Ireland, and the French Republic (United Kingdom/France) (1978) 18 RIAA 3, 51* [84].

[2] *Continental Shelf (Libyan Arab Jamahiriya/Malta) [1985] ICJ Rep 13, 44-45* [57].

[3] *Maritime Delimitation in the Black Sea (Romania v. Ukraine) [2009] ICJ Rep 61, 101-103* [120].

[4] *Territorial and Maritime Dispute (Nicaragua v. Colombia) [2012] ICJ Rep 624, 696* [192] and 697 [197].

[5] *Black Sea* (n 3), 129 [213].

the continental shelf beyond 200 nm and considered it a relevant circumstance.[6] The *Bangladesh* v. *India* case reached the same conclusion.[7] The *Ghana/Côte d'Ivoire* case, for its part, applied the equidistance method throughout the delimitation within and beyond 200 nm.[8] These decisions attest to the fact that coastal geography continues to be relevant, if not controlling, in the delimitation of the continental shelf beyond 200 nm between adjacent States.

However, coastal geography is by no means a small category, as it may include coastal configuration, coastal lengths, general direction of the coasts, coastal relationship between the parties, and the presence of islands, rocks, islets, etc. Each of these items has received treatment in the jurisprudence, but it is unrealistic and unnecessary to delve into every one of them, for two reasons. First, even if a geographical factor is capable of being a relevant circumstance on the theoretical level, it does not necessarily mean that such a factor would always be present in a particular case. Second, even if the geographical factor is present in a particular case, it does not follow that it will be given weight in shaping the maritime boundary.[9] In a word, the relevance of geographical circumstances has both a general/theoretical dimension as well as a specific/actual dimension.[10] To determine the relevance of geographical circumstances in a specific case, it is crucial to establish the "verifiable link" between the geographical circumstances and the boundary lines.[11] In other words, circumstances are relevant in a specific context because they produce effects that have consequences on the making of boundary lines.[12] It is through these effects that the rules governing relevant circumstances are spelled out. These effects are expressive of the

6 *Delimitation of the Maritime Boundary in the Bay of Bengal (Bangladesh/Myanmar) (Judgment) [2012] ITLOS Rep 4, 118* [461].

7 *Bay of Bengal Maritime Boundary Arbitration (Bangladesh v. India) (2014) 167 ILR 1, 161* [473].

8 *Delimitation of the Maritime Boundary in the Atlantic Ocean (Ghana/Côte d'Ivoire), [2017] ITLOS Rep 4, 142* [527].

9 For example, in the *Ghana/Côte d'Ivoire* case, the Special Chamber "accepts that the coast of Côte d'Ivoire is concave, although such concavity is not as pronounced as in, for example, the case of the Bay of Bengal," but did not consider it a relevant circumstance that warrants the adjustment of the provisional equidistance line, ibid., 120 [424–425].

10 See M. D. Evans, "Maritime Delimitation and Expanding Categories of Relevant Circumstances" (1991) 40 *ICLQ* 1, 5.

11 To use the phrase of Judge Schwebel in the *Libya/Malta* case. *Libya/Malta* (n 2), 183 (Dissenting Opinion of Judge Schwebel).

12 See Evans (n 10), 3.

equitable principles that underlie the value judgments of the geographical circumstances,[13] and thus provide vantage points for analyzing the relevant circumstances without falling into each category of the coastal geography family. Two effects stand out in the jurisprudence, namely, cut-off effect and disproportionality. Section II and Section III explore, respectively, the relevance of these geographical circumstances in the delimitation of the continental shelf beyond 200 nm. By discussing in depth the various aspects of these geographical circumstances and their potential implications for continental shelf delimitation beyond 200 nm, this chapter intends to articulate the role of coastal geography in the delimitation of the continental shelf beyond 200 nm and to explain why coastal geography remains central in the exercise thereof.

## II Cut-Off Effect

Guided by the principle that "[t]here can never be any question of completely refashioning nature,"[14] international courts and tribunals are, while accepting geographical circumstances as given, frequently engaged in eliminating or correcting "extraordinary, unnatural or unreasonable" effects produced by geographical circumstances.[15] The cut-off effect is one such effect that is well documented in the jurisprudence, and it results from the application of geometrical methods to irregular geographical factors. Coastal configurations such as concave or convex coastlines may lead to the swinging of an equidistance line between adjacent coasts, thus cutting off one State's coastal projections.[16] Incidental maritime features of one State, which are located very close to another State, may also produce a cut-off effect that blocks the seaward projections of the other State if that feature is given full effect.[17]

[13] See P. Weil, *The Law of Maritime Delimitation: Reflections* (Grotius 1989), 211.

[14] *North Sea Continental Shelf Cases (Federal Republic of Germany/Denmark; Federal Republic of Germany/Netherlands) [1969] ICJ Rep 3, 49-50* [91].

[15] Ibid., 23–24 [24].

[16] This is the key issue of the *North Sea* cases. As the ICJ stated,

"[W]here two such lines are drawn at different points on a concave coast, they will, if the curvature is pronounced, inevitably meet at a relatively short distance from the coast, thus causing the continental shelf area they enclose, to take the form approximately of a triangle with its apex to seaward and, as it was put on behalf of the Federal Republic, 'cutting off' the coastal State from the further areas of the continental shelf outside of and beyond this triangle," ibid., 17–18 [8].

[17] See *Bangladesh/Myanmar* (n 6), 73 [265].

International jurisprudence is consistent in holding that circumstances producing a cut-off effect which unduly restricts coastal States' projections to maritime areas should be addressed and their effect corrected.[18] A cut-off effect has been accepted as a valid ground for adjusting provisional equidistance lines,[19] a circumstance to be considered during the construction of a provisional equidistance line,[20] or a circumstance in the implementation of the applicable method.[21] The objective of addressing the cut-off effect is to allow the coasts of the respective parties "to produce their effects, in terms of maritime entitlements, in a reasonable and mutually balanced way."[22]

A cut-off effect may be a relevant circumstance in the delimitation of the continental shelf beyond 200 nm based on three different considerations. First, the cut-off effect produced by an irregular coastal configuration may be magnified where the maritime boundary extends further seaward.[23]Accordingly, where the area of the continental shelf beyond 200 nm is part of the maritime area to be delimited in a maritime delimitation within and beyond 200 nm, there may be continuing cut-off effect throughout the areas within and beyond 200 nm.

18 See *Continental Shelf (Tunisia/Libyan Arab Jamahiriya) [1982] ICJ Rep 18, 62-63* [76]; *Delimitation of the Maritime Boundary in the Gulf of Maine Area (Canada/United States of America) [1984] ICJ Rep 246, 312–313* [157]; *Nicaragua* v. *Colombia I* (n 4), 703–704 [215].

19 For instance, ITLOS observed that "when an equidistance line drawn between two States produces a cut-off effect on the maritime entitlement of one of those States, as a result of the concavity of the coast, then an adjustment of that line may be necessary in order to reach an equitable result," *Bangladesh/Myanmar* (n 6), 81 [292].

20 In the *Bangladesh/Myanmar* case, ITLOS constructed the provisional equidistance line without placing basepoints on the St. Martin's Island, because that "would result in a line the blocks the seaward projection from Myanmar's coast," ibid., 73 [265].

21 In the *Nicaragua* v. *Honduras* case, the ICJ compared different coastal fronts for the construction of the bisector line and observed that "[t]he front that extends from Punta Patuca to Wouhnta, would avoid the problem of cutting off Honduran territory and at the same time provide a coastal façade of sufficient length to account properly for the coastal configuration in the disputed area," *Territorial and Maritime Dispute between Nicaragua and Honduras in the Caribbean Sea (Nicaragua v. Honduras) [2007] ICJ Rep 659, 749* [298].

22 *Black Sea* (n 3), 127 [201].

23 As observed in the *Anglo-French Arbitration*, "in the case of lateral boundaries the effect of any irregularity in the coastline on the areas of continental shelf allocated to each State by the equidistance method is automatically magnified, the greater the distance the boundary extends from the shore,"*Anglo-French Arbitration* (n 1), 52 [86].

Second, in a variation of the first situation, the coastal configuration may be so irregular that the use of a particular method may completely cut-off one State's access to the continental shelf beyond 200 nm.

Third, international tribunals have treated the cut-off effect in the continental shelf delimitation beyond 200 nm primarily as a geographical circumstance, and they have not fully clarified whether cutting off the entitlement to the continental shelf should also be part of the assessment of the cut-off effect. The *North Sea* cases pronounced that the delimitations should "leave as much as possible to each Party all those parts of the continental shelf that constitute a natural prolongation of its land territory into and under the sea, without encroachment of the natural prolongation of the land territory of the other."[24] This is the so-called principle of non-encroachment.[25] Since the notion of natural prolongation acquires new contents under Article 76 of UNCLOS, it is of interest to discuss to what extent cutting off the entitlement to the continental shelf beyond 200 nm can fit in a geographically oriented concept of cut-off.

The following sections will examine the three considerations relating to cut-off effects in turn.

### A *The Continuing Cut-Off Effect of Coastal Geography*

The cut-off effect produced by coastal geography has a continuing influence in the delimitation of the continental shelf beyond 200 nm because "the distorting effects of lateral equidistance lines under certain conditions of coastal configuration are nevertheless comparatively small within the limits of territorial waters, but produce their maximum effect in the localities where the main continental shelf areas lie further out."[26] This problem is derived from the use of equidistance to irregular coastal configuration, in particular between adjacent coasts, because between adjacent coasts "any distorting effect of a salient feature might well extend and increase through the entire course of the boundary," while between opposite coasts "the influence of one feature is normally quickly succeeded and corrected by the influence of another, as the course of the

[24] *North Sea* (n 14), 53 [101(C)(1)].

[25] See *Libya/Malta* (n 2), 39–40 [46]; *Maritime Boundary Arbitration (Barbados v. Trinidad and Tobago) (2006) XXVII RIAA 147* [232].

[26] *North Sea* (n 14), 37 [59].

line proceeds between more or less parallel coasts."[27] As a result, since the continental shelf beyond 200 nm is part of the overall relevant area to be delimited between two adjacent coasts, the effect of the coastal configuration is continuous throughout the entire area the two adjacent States are entitled to, and the cut-off effect may prevent one State from enjoying a considerable portion of the continental shelf beyond 200 nm, which it would otherwise be entitled to under Article 76.

The *Bay of Bengal* cases confirmed the continuing relevance of the cut-off effect of coastal geography in the continental shelf delimitation beyond 200 nm. Bangladesh shares a similar geographical position as that of the Federal Republic of Germany in the *North Sea* cases because its coast is concave and it is being sandwiched by Myanmar to the east and India to the west. In the *Bangladesh/Myanmar* case, ITLOS acknowledged that "Bangladesh's coast has been portrayed as a classic example of a concave coast."[28] The Tribunal, citing the *North Sea* cases, observed that "the greater the irregularity and the further from the coastline the area to be delimited, the more unreasonable are the results produced."[29] Observing that "[t]he projection southward from the coast of Bangladesh continues throughout the delimitation area," the Tribunal found that "[t]here is thus a continuing need to avoid cut-off effects on this projection."[30] The Tribunal extended the adjusted delimitation line within 200 nm to the area beyond that limit without a change of direction.[31] The concavity of the coastal configuration was thus a controlling circumstance in both the delimitation within and beyond 200 nm.

The Arbitral Tribunal in the *Bangladesh* v. *India* case shared the view of ITLOS in respect of the continuing cut-off effect of the coastal configuration. As the Arbitral Tribunal found, "[t]he effect is even more pronounced in respect of the southward projection of the south facing coast of Bangladesh [. . .] as far as the area beyond 200 nm is concerned."[32] The adjustment of the provisional equidistance line was thus meant to address the cut-off effect throughout the entire relevant area.[33]

It is clear that the continuing cut-off effect as examined in the *Bay of Bengal* cases is primarily a circumstance of geographical nature. What

27 *Libya/Malta* (n 2), 50–51 [70].
28 *Bangladesh/Myanmar* (n 6), 81 [291].
29 Ibid., [294].
30 Ibid., 89 [333].
31 See ibid., 118 [461–462].
32 *Bangladesh* v. *India* (n 7), 134 [407].
33 See ibid., 161 [473–475].

were being cut off were the coastal projections understood geometrically.[34] The geomorphological or geological elements constituting the continental shelf beyond 200 nm did not seem to be considered in the determination of the cut-off effect. Rather, the relevance of the entitlement to the continental shelf beyond 200 nm seems to be confined to the fact that it added to the distance that the boundary line has to travel. It follows that if the irregularities of the coastal configuration have been severe enough to produce inequitable results within 200 nm, such adverse effects would intensify as the area to be delimited extends further seaward. It is in this sense that the cut-off effect may be considered a relevant circumstance in the continental shelf beyond 200 nm.

Despite these common grounds in the *Bay of Bengal* cases, the assessment of the cut-off effect was more sophisticated in the *Bangladesh* v. *India* case in that the Arbitral Tribunal referred to the area of overlapping entitlements to the continental shelf beyond 200 nm when it examined the cut-off effect. Proceeding from the position that there is only a single continental shelf, the Arbitral Tribunal observed that "the configuration and *extent* of the Parties' entitlements to areas of the continental shelf beyond 200 nm may equally be of relevance."[35] Next the Arbitral Tribunal noted that "the area attributed to Bangladesh in the area beyond 200 nm is limited in scope in comparison to the area in which the entitlements of the Parties overlap."[36] It is recalled that the Arbitral Tribunal determined the area of overlapping entitlements to the continental shelf beyond 200 nm by reference to the submissions made by Bangladesh and India.[37] Therefore, the comparison between the area attributed to Bangladesh beyond 200 nm and the area of overlapping entitlements goes beyond a geometrical exercise by reference to the coasts. However, the Arbitral Tribunal immediately followed with the observation that "a coastal State has an entitlement if its coast projects into the area claimed. [...] In particular, the south facing coast of Bangladesh is given insufficient weight by the provisional equidistance line from Point Prov-3 to the South."[38] This latter observation thus characterized the problem of cut-off as one of geographical nature.

[34] *Bangladesh/Myanmar* (n 6), 89 [333].
[35] *Bangladesh* v. *India* (n 7), 133 [404] (emphasis added).
[36] Ibid., 161 [473].
[37] See ibid., 102–103 [306–311].
[38] Ibid., 161 [474].

Other than coastal configuration, the cut-off effect may also result from incidental maritime features lying close to the coasts, which, if given full effect, would block the seaward projection of one State.[39] International jurisprudence is consistent in eliminating the cut-off effect produced by incidental maritime features, as can be seen in the practices concerning the Channel Islands,[40] the Kerkennah Islands,[41] Serpents' Island,[42] and St. Martin's Island.[43] Similar to that of coastal configuration, the distorting effect of maritime features on the delimitation line may intensify as the boundary line travels seaward. Accordingly, it may also be qualified as a relevant circumstance in the continental shelf beyond 200 nm, and its adverse effects could be pre-empted before the boundary line takes shape and extends to the area beyond 200 nm. State practice supports this approach. In the delimitation between Kenya and Tanzania, the existence of Tanzania's Pemba Island could have given rise to a cut-off effect on Kenya if the parties continued to use the equidistance method. Instead, the 1976 Kenya–Tanzania agreement decided that the delimitation line beyond Point C follows a parallel of latitude, which avoided the cut-off effect to either coast of the parties.[44] In 2009 the two countries concluded a new agreement to extend the

39 See R. W. Smith, "Geographic Considerations in Maritime Boundary Delimitations," in D. G. Dallmeyer and L. De Vorsey, Jr. (eds.), *Rights to Oceanic Resources* (Martinus Nijhoff Publishers 1989), 6.

40 The Court of Arbitration described the inequity if giving the Channel Islands full effect as follows:

> "The presence of these British islands close to the French coast, if they are given full effect in delimiting the continental shelf, will manifestly result in a substantial diminution of the area of continental shelf which would otherwise accrue to the French Republic. This fact by itself appears to the Court to be, prima facie, a circumstance creative of inequity and calling for a method of delimitation that in some measure redresses the inequity."

Eventually, the Court of Arbitration created a 12 nm enclave to the north and west of the Channel Islands while in the region the Court drew a median line. *Anglo-French Arbitration* (n 1), [196] and [201–202].

41 The ICJ gave the Kerkennah Islands half effect instead of full effect because the latter would cut-off Libya's coastal projections. See *Tunisia/Libya* (n 18), 88–89 [128–129].

42 The ICJ did not take Serpents' Island as a basepoint to construct the provisional equidistance line because doing so "would amount to grafting an extraneous element onto Ukraine's coastline; the consequence would be a judicial refashioning of geography, which neither the law nor practice of maritime delimitation authorizes," *Black Sea* (n 3), 110 [149].

43 *Bangladesh/Myanmar* (n 6), 73 [265].

44 See A. O. Adede, "Kenya–Tanzania, Report Number 4-5," in J. I. Charney and L. M. Alexander (eds.), *International Maritime Boundaries, Vol. I* (Martinus Nijhoff 1993), 877.

existing maritime boundary to their outer limits of the continental shelf.[45] Although the geographical feature is located in the vicinity of the coasts, it could have detrimental effects on Kenya in the area beyond that distance had it not been addressed in the first place.

To sum up, the *Bay of Bengal* cases confirmed the relevance of the cut-off effect with the delimitation of the continental shelf beyond 200 nm. The two cases treated the cut-off effect primarily as a geographical circumstance without elaborating on the relevance of the entitlement to the continental shelf beyond 200 nm, though the *Bangladesh* v. *India* case shows certain sympathy with the limited area attributed to Bangladesh beyond 200 nm in comparison with the overlapping entitlements beyond 200 nm. The entitlement to the continental shelf beyond 200 nm contributes to the determination of the cut-off effect to the extent that it adds to the distance that the boundary line has to extend. Accordingly, where coastal projections of one State have been suffering a severe cut-off effect within a distance of 200 nm, such an adverse effect would magnify in the area of the continental shelf beyond 200 nm and should be addressed. The continuing relevance of the cut-off effect is in accord with the observation that "[t]o the extent that a coast is abutting on the area of overlapping claims, it is bound to have a strong influence on the delimitation, an influence which results not only from the general direction of the coast but also from its radial projection in the area in question."[46]

### B Cutting Off the Access to the Continental Shelf beyond 200 NM

The circumstance of "cutting off the access to the continental shelf beyond 200 nm" needs qualification. One situation is where a proposed delimitation line prevents a coastal State from accessing any maritime area beyond the 200 nm limits, whereas there is convincing evidence that the coastal State is entitled to a continental shelf beyond 200 nm. A second situation is where a coastal State is cut off from accessing its outer limits of the continental shelf beyond 200 nm, though the delimitation line attributes part of the continental shelf beyond 200 nm to the State.

[45] See Article 2 of the Agreement between the United Republic of Tanzania and the Republic of Kenya on the Delimitation of the Maritime Boundary of the Exclusive Economic Zone and the Continental Shelf (June 23, 2009), 2603 UNTS 37.

[46] *Barbados* v. *Trinidad and Tobago* (n 25), [239].

In the *Bangladesh/Myanmar* case, Bangladesh argued that if the strict equidistance line was adopted, it would cut off Bangladesh entirely from its entitlement to the continental shelf beyond 200 nm, which was "a separate reason" that warrants the application of a different method than equidistance.[47] ITLOS did not address this aspect of the cut-off effect specifically, because it had decided to adjust a provisional equidistance line already within the 200 nm.[48] As a result, Bangladesh's access to the continental shelf beyond 200 nm was ensured and the question of the relevance of completely cutting off one State's access to its entitlement to the continental shelf beyond 200 nm remains open.

The *Barbados* v. *Trinidad and Tobago* case, on the other hand, seems to disregard the relevance of access to the continental shelf beyond 200 nm. Trinidad and Tobago argued against the use of the equidistance method in delimiting the eastern sector of the disputed area, and proposed a line running along an azimuth of 88 degrees to the outer edge of the continental margin as defined in Article 76.[49] To support this adjustment, Trinidad and Tobago argued that, *inter alia*,

> Moreover the effect of the Barbados claim line is to shelf-lock Trinidad and Tobago despite its coastal frontage of approximately 75 n.m. directly out to the Atlantic. Barbados thereby claims 100% of the outer continental shelf in the area of overlapping potential entitlements. This is evidently inequitable.[50]

As discussed in Chapter 4, the Arbitral Tribunal seems to have rejected Trinidad and Tobago's claim to the continental shelf beyond 200 nm by locating the terminus of the boundary line at a point of the junction of Trinidad and Tobago's 200 nm limit with its southern maritime boundary with Venezuela.[51] Does this mean that completely cutting off Trinidad and Tobago's entitlement to the continental shelf beyond 200 nm was not considered a relevant circumstance in the delimitation process? This question has to be considered in the context of that case, and three factors might account for the reason why Trinidad and Tobago's argument did not prevail.

[47] See *Bangladesh/Myanmar*, Memorial of Bangladesh, Volume I (July 1, 2010), 83 [6.43].
[48] See *Bangladesh/Myanmar* (n 6), 81–82 [291–297].
[49] See *Barbados* v. *Trinidad and Tobago*, Counter-Memorial of Trinidad and Tobago, Volume 1(1) (March 30, 2005), 102 [288].
[50] Ibid. [230].
[51] See *Barbados* v. *Trinidad and Tobago* (n 25), [382].

First of all, the agreement between Venezuela and Trinidad and Tobago is *res inter alios acta* for Barbados.[52] This agreement departed from an equidistance line and shifted northward to allow Venezuela access to part of the maritime zone in the Atlantic (the so-called '*salida al Atlántico*'),[53] which was adverse to Trinidad and Tobago.[54] The Arbitral Tribunal considered that "certainly Barbados cannot be required to 'compensate' Trinidad and Tobago for the agreements it has made by shifting Barbados's maritime boundary in favour of Trinidad and Tobago."[55] Had the boundary line between Venezuela and Trinidad and Tobago been an equidistance line, the maritime boundary as decided by the Tribunal would have left Trinidad and Tobago a window to access the area beyond its 200 nm limit.

Second, the Tribunal did adjust a segment of the provisional equidistance line in the eastern sector to give "a meaningful influence" to a lengthy coastal frontage of Trinidad and Tobago.[56] This adjustment, in the opinion of the Tribunal, "reflects a reasonable influence of the coastal frontages on the overall area of delimitation, with a view to avoiding reciprocal encroachments which would otherwise result in some form of inequity."[57] One may consider that this adjustment is overly modest in comparison with delimitation between States with similar disparities in coastal lengths. The Tribunal did not explicitly dispute Trinidad and Tobago's calculation of the ratio of the coastal lengths (8.2:1 in Trinidad and Tobago's favor),[58] but the deflection of the provisional equidistance line was made only to a small segment of the provisional line. On the contrary, in the *Jan Mayen* case, the ratio between the relevant coasts was more or less 9.1:1, and the adjustment made to the provisional median line was substantial, because the Court shifted the provisional line throughout its length, and the shift resulted in an area of roughly 30,000 km$^2$ between the provisional equidistance line and the final

[52] Ibid., [346].

[53] See *Barbados* v. *Trinidad and Tobago*, Counter-Memorial of Trinidad and Tobago, Volume 1(1) (March 30, 2005), 88 [253].

[54] See *Barbados* v. *Trinidad and Tobago* (n 25), [345].

[55] Ibid., [346].

[56] See ibid., [372].

[57] Ibid. [379].

[58] R. Churchill, "Dispute Settlement under the UN Convention on the Law of the Sea: Survey for 2006" (2007) 22 *IJMCL* 463, 478.

boundary.[59] Nonetheless, each case is unique in its circumstances and therefore can only be equitable in its own right.

A last factor that prevents the adjustment from going further north is, perhaps, that the Tribunal was reluctant to create a "grey area," in which Trinidad and Tobago would enjoy rights to the seabed and subsoil of the continental shelf while Barbados retains the rights to the water column. A delimitation that grants Trinidad and Tobago access to the continental shelf beyond 200 nm, no matter how small that area is, would give rise to a "grey area." Although such a result proves to be acceptable to international tribunals in the *Bay of Bengal* cases,[60] it does not seem to be a reasonable solution for the Tribunal, which emphasized that it "must exercise its judgment in order to decide upon a line that is, in its view, both equitable and as *practically satisfactory* as possible, while at the same time in keeping with the requirement of achieving a stable legal outcome."[61] Undoubtedly the parties would encounter considerable practical difficulties if a grey area was created.[62] However, it is doubtful if policy considerations could be so overriding as to avoid a legal assessment on the scope of the adjustment.

While the approach of the Tribunal in the *Barbados* v. *Trinidad and Tobago* case may be justified by reference to these circumstances, and the outcome that Trinidad and Tobago is "zone-locked" in relation to Barbados may be an equitable solution between the two States, it seems that the Tribunal did not fully appreciate the relevance of Trinidad and Tobago's entitlement to the continental shelf beyond 200 nm. To say the least, it did not assess whether the entitlement exists nor did it determine to what extent the entitlement exists, though the Tribunal found itself with jurisdiction to delimit the continental shelf beyond 200 nm.[63] The Tribunal did not offer legal reasoning why Trinidad and Tobago's entitlement to the continental shelf beyond 200 nm should be ignored, or why the ignorance was a reasonable result after balancing up all the relevant

[59] See A. G. Oude Elferink, "International Law and Negotiated and Adjudicated Maritime Boundaries: A Complex Relationship" (2015) 58 *GYIL* 231, 256–257.

[60] See the discussion in Chapter 3, Section III.D. For an opposite view, see M. Lando, *Maritime Delimitation as a Judicial Process* (Cambridge University Press 2018), 140–143.

[61] *Barbados* v. *Trinidad and Tobago* (n 25), [244] (emphasis added).

[62] B. Kwiatkowska, "The 2006 Barbados/Trinidad and Tobago Award: A Landmark in Compulsory Jurisdiction and Equitable Maritime Boundary Delimitation" (2007) 22 *IJMCL* 7, 55–56.

[63] See *Barbados* v. *Trinidad and Tobago* (n 25), [213].

circumstances.[64] It seems that the Tribunal's approach may be criticized for not acting prudently with regard to Trinidad and Tobago's entitlement to the continental shelf beyond 200 nm, which is in contrast with the approach taken by other courts where one State claims a continental shelf beyond 200 nm. In the *St. Pierre and Miquelon Arbitration*, the Court of Arbitration extended the boundary line to the 200 nm limits of France and explicitly provided that the delimitation does not prejudice either Party's claim to the continental shelf beyond 200 nm.[65] The *Nicaragua* v. *Colombia I* case, being ambiguous about Nicaragua's claim to the continental shelf beyond 200 nm, also extended the maritime boundaries to the 200 nm limit of Nicaragua, which left open the possibility for Nicaragua to maintain its claim to the continental shelf beyond 200 nm.[66] No such option for Trinidad and Tobago was given by the Tribunal.[67] Subsequently in the *Bangladesh* v. *India* case, when the Arbitral Tribunal decided to shift the provisional equidistance line, it decided that "any adjustment of the provisional equidistance line within 200 nm should result in a delimitation line extending into the area beyond 200 nm."[68] This last example of the judicial practice tends to confirm that the delimitation of the continental shelf beyond 200 nm should avoid completely cutting off one State's access to the continental shelf beyond 200 nm.

Turning to the situation where one State is prevented from reaching its proposed outer limits of the continental shelf beyond 200 nm, it essentially raises the question of what qualifies the "cut-off effect" that warrants the choice of a different delimitation method or the adjustment of a provisional equidistance line. In the *Bangladesh/Myanmar* case, ITLOS observed that:

> [C]oncavity *per se* is not necessarily a relevant circumstance. However, when an equidistance line drawn between two States produces a cut-off effect on the maritime entitlement of one of those States, as a result of the

[64] See Oude Elferink (n 59), 258–259.

[65] See *Decision in Case concerning Delimitation of Maritime Areas (St. Pierre and Miquelon), (1992) 31 ILM 1145, 1172* [80].

[66] See *Nicaragua* v. *Colombia I* (n 4), 719–720 [251(4)]. For comments, see M. D. Evans, "Maritime Boundary Delimitation: Whatever Next?," in J. Barrett and R. Barnes (eds.), *Law of the Sea: UNCLOS as a Living Treaty* (BIILC 2016), 77.

[67] See Chapter 4, Section III.B.2.

[68] *Bangladesh* v. *India* (n 7), 144 [437].

> concavity of the coast, then an adjustment of that line may be necessary in order to reach an equitable result.[69]

This observation does not qualify the cut-off effect, though ITLOS invoked the observations in the *North Sea* cases that "the greater the irregularity and the further from the coastline the area to be delimited, the more unreasonable are the results produced. So great an exaggeration of the consequences of a natural geographical feature must be remedied or compensated for as far as possible, being of itself creative of inequity."[70] ITLOS thus appears to suggest that it is where the cut-off effect is severe enough to produce unreasonable and inequitable effects on the entitlement of the coastal State that it calls for remedy. However, ITLOS also cited the view of the Arbitral Tribunal of the *Guinea/Guinea-Bissau* case, which stated that:

> When in fact [. . .] there are three adjacent States along a concave coastline, the equidistance method has the other drawback of resulting in the middle country being enclaved by the other two and thus prevented from extending its maritime territory *as far seaward as international law permits*'.[71]

The *Guinea/Guinea-Bissau* case introduced one criterion to establish what amounts to a cut-off effect, namely, whether the proposed delimitation method would prevent the coastal State from extending its entitlement to the seaward limits permitted under international law. If a coastal State is unable to access its outer limits of the continental shelf, *mutatis mutandis*, such a situation would qualify as a cut-off effect that should be remedied. In the *Bangladesh* v. *India* case, Bangladesh built its arguments on the cut-off effect with the "maximum reach" theory developed by Charney, who contended that the delimitation should avoid "the effect of fully cutting off a disputant's access to the seaward limit of any zone."[72] Bangladesh further argued that the delimitation should allow all disputants to be allocated some access to the areas approaching the maximum distance from the coast permitted for each zone, citing the *North Sea* cases, the *St. Pierre and Miquelon* case and the *Nicaragua* v. *Colombia I*

69 *Bangladesh/Myanmar* (n 6), 81 [292].

70 *North Sea* (n 14), 49 [89].

71 *Delimitation of the Maritime Boundary between Guinea and Guinea-Bissau (Guinea/Guinea-Bissau) (1985) XIX RIAA 149* [104] (emphasis added).

72 J. I. Charney, "Progress in International Maritime Boundary Delimitation Law" (1994) 88 *AJIL* 227, 247.

case.[73] Bangladesh submitted that the boundary line should bend and run along an azimuth of 215 degrees parallel to the Bangladesh–Myanmar delimitation line up to the outer limit of Bangladesh's continental shelf when it reaches the 200 nm limit.[74]

The Arbitral Tribunal rejected this argument, and stated that "international jurisprudence on the delimitation of the continental shelf does not recognize a general right of coastal States to the maximum reach of their entitlements, irrespective of the geographical situation and the rights of other coastal States."[75] As to the cut-off effect, the Arbitral Tribunal considered that "the existence of a cut-off effect should be established on an objective basis and in a transparent manner,"[76] and provided two criteria for evaluating to what extent the cut-off effect calls for adjustment of a provisional equidistance line:

> First, the line must prevent a coastal State from extending its maritime boundary as far seaward as international law permits. Second, the line must be such that—if not adjusted—it would fail to achieve the equitable solution required by articles 74 and 83 of the Convention. This requires an assessment of where the disadvantage of the cut-off materializes and of its seriousness.[77]

According to the two criteria, failure to reach the maximum limits permitted by international law does count for determining a cut-off effect. In the case of the continental shelf beyond 200 nm, it seems that the first criterion should be satisfied if a coastal State would not be able to reach its outer limits of the continental shelf. Note, however, that this criterion may not fully meet the requirement of objectivity if the delimitation of the continental shelf beyond 200 nm takes place before the parties establish their outer limits on the basis of the recommendations of the CLCS, for the parties' proposed outer limits of the continental shelf may not be confirmed by the CLCS, and there is the possibility for the parties to revise their submissions.

Nevertheless, since under the second criterion the cut-off effect has to be severe enough to fail the objective of an equitable solution, it turns out that cut-off effect can hardly be determined on an objective basis, as the evaluation of the "seriousness" of the cut-off effect entails a margin of

[73] See *Bangladesh* v. *India* (n 7), 151 [447].
[74] Ibid., 148 [444].
[75] Ibid., 160–161 [469].
[76] Ibid., 133 [404].
[77] Ibid., 137 [417].

appreciation.[78] The eventual boundary decided by the Arbitral Tribunal in the *Bangladesh* v. *India* case did not permit Bangladesh from accessing its proposed outer limits of the continental shelf, but the Arbitral Tribunal did not consider that Bangladesh suffered from cut-off effect in the continental shelf beyond 200 nm. As the Arbitral Tribunal saw it, "the entitlement of a State to reach the continental shelf beyond 200 nm is not the only relevant consideration. The Tribunal must examine the geographic situation as a whole."[79] Accordingly, whereas not reaching the outer limits of the continental shelf may be an indicator of the cut-off effect, it is ultimately whether such effect can be justified in light of all the circumstances that is decisive. As the Arbitral Tribunal explained, Bangladesh's argument for bending the boundary when it extends beyond 200 nm "would lead to a significant cut-off to the detriment of India's entitlement to the area beyond 200 nm."[80] Eventually, the difference between the "maximum reach" theory and the determination of the cut-off effect by reference to the outer limits of maritime zones lies in the fact that the former requires a positive pursuit of reaching the maximum distance while the latter does not. Reaching the outer limits of the continental shelf permitted by international law may be a solution resulting from correcting the cut-off effect, but it should not always be the objective of a maritime boundary delimitation.

Although a degree of discretion is inevitable in the examination of the seriousness of a cut-off effect, one relevant factor might be the location where the cut-off effect materializes. If the cut-off effect only comes into play at a considerable distance from the coasts, it may not be considered relevant because it goes beyond the original intention of avoiding a cut-off effect, which is to prevent coastal States from losing maritime areas that are in the vicinity of their coasts.[81] As stated by the *Guinea/Guinea-Bissau* case, "In order for any delimitation to be made on an equitable and objective basis, it is necessary to ensure that, as far as possible, each State controls the maritime territories opposite its coasts and in their

78 See M. D. Evans, "Relevant Circumstances," in A. G. Oude Elferink et al. (eds.), *Maritime Boundary Delimitation: The Case Law: Is It Consistent and Predictable?* (Cambridge University Press 2018), 251.

79 *Bangladesh* v. *India* (n 7), 134 [410].

80 Ibid., 160 [469].

81 O. Schachter, "Linking Equity and Law in Maritime Delimitation," in N. Ando et al. (eds.), *Liber Amicorum Judge Shigeru Oda, Volume II* (Kluwer Law International 2002), 1166.

vicinity."[82] In consequence, it is the "nonencroachment perspective that comes into play in deciding that an equidistant line will cut off the extension of the coastal front of the neighboring country."[83] This point was highlighted in the *Ghana/Côte d'Ivoire* case. Côte d'Ivoire argued that its coasts were concave and cut-off effects were produced. The Special Chamber acknowledged that some cut-off effect exists to the detriment of Côte d'Ivoire, but "[s]uch cut-off effect only comes into being 163 nm from BP 55+. The seaward projection of the relevant coast of Côte d'Ivoire from Abidjan to Sassandra, however, extends beyond 200 nm."[84] This observation might imply that if the seaward projection did not extend beyond 200 nm, the Tribunal would have considered the matter differently. Indeed, in this case both parties are able to reach their proposed outer limits of the continental shelf. It is thus arguable that if the cut-off effect takes place at a considerable distance away from the coasts, it is unlikely to be taken as a relevant circumstance, unless one State suffers from the total loss of its access to the continental shelf beyond 200 nm.

To summarize, cutting off a coastal State's reach to the outer limits of the continental shelf beyond 200 nm may be an indicator of the existence of a cut-off effect, but it has to be severe enough to cause inequitable and unreasonable results for one of the coastal States to be corrected. On the other hand, completely cutting off one State's access to the continental shelf beyond 200 nm should be a relevant circumstance in a maritime delimitation within and beyond 200 nm, though the relative weight given to this factor has to be determined in light of all the relevant circumstances of the case.

### C *Cutting Off the Entitlement to the Continental Shelf beyond 200 NM*

International tribunals so far only addressed the cut-off effect in the delimitation of the continental shelf beyond 200 nm between adjacent States, and have not yet considered whether cutting off the entitlement to the continental shelf beyond 200 nm is a relevant circumstance in the delimitation between opposite States, or how such a cut-off effect should be identified. In addition, even in situations between adjacent States,

[82] *Guinea/Guinea-Bissau* (n 71), [92] and [103].

[83] D. Colson, "The Delimitation of the Outer Continental Shelf between Neighboring States" (2003) 97 *AJIL* 91, 102.

[84] *Ghana/Côte d'Ivoire* (n 8), 120 [424].

international tribunals primarily addressed the issue of cut-off as a geographical circumstance without clarifying whether cutting off the entitlement to the continental shelf beyond 200 nm should also be part of the assessment of the cut-off effect.

### 1 Assessment of Cut-Off Effect between Opposite Coasts

Traditionally, a cut-off effect was examined mainly in cases concerning adjacent coasts.[85] Yet, in the *Nicaragua* v. *Colombia I* case, the ICJ acknowledged that a cut-off effect was one of the relevant circumstances between the opposite coasts of Nicaragua and the Colombian Islands:

> The effect of the provisional median line is to cut Nicaragua off from some three quarters of the area into which its coast projects. Moreover, that cut-off effect is produced by a few small islands which are many nautical miles apart. [...] The Court therefore concludes that the cut-off effect is a relevant consideration which requires adjustment or shifting of the provisional median line in order to produce an equitable result.[86]

It is thus submitted that, whether cutting off the entitlement to the continental shelf beyond 200 nm between opposite coasts is a relevant circumstance depends on how the area of overlapping entitlements is determined, which also provides the parameters to assess the seriousness of the cut-off effect. One argument suggests that the FOS may provide an indicator of the encroachment effect between two opposite States, which is essentially based on the idea that the area of overlap is accurately determined by reference to the respective FOS rather than the coasts.[87] Under this scenario, an equidistance line may cut off a significant part of one State's entitlement to the continental shelf beyond 200 nm while awarding the other State its entire continental shelf beyond 200 nm, including even some area that is beyond the latter State's outer limits. Such a result is apparently inequitable as it fails to give sufficient effect to the entitlement to the continental shelf beyond 200 nm of the former State, and the delimitation is not reflective of an accurate determination of the area of overlap (see Figure 6.5). However, as also explained with illustrations in Chapter 6, where the area of overlap encompasses the entire area between the 200 nm limits of the two opposite States (see Figures 6.6, 6.7, and 6.8), there would be no room for determining the

[85] See Lando (n 60), 170–171.
[86] *Nicaragua* v. *Colombia I* (n 4), 703–704 [215].
[87] See Colson (n 83), 103.

cut-off effect by referring to factors other than the coasts.[88] As pointed out by Fietta and Cleverly, in a scenario "where the coasts are separated by one continuous physical shelf [...] jurisprudence and State practice reject any notion that one State should be able to gain advantage in the delimitation through arguments of 'stronger' or 'most' natural prolongation."[89] In fact, such a situation is more likely to occur in practice, because according to research on the continental margins of the world, excluding wide margins around Antarctica, 29 wide margins were found and almost all cases consist of a continuous continental margin.[90] In the delimitation of these continuous continental margins, any boundary line between two opposite coasts will involve a certain degree of encroachment on the entitlement to the continental shelf beyond 200 nm of each State.[91]

Furthermore, in reality geophysical factors such as the FOS may not be reliable factors for determining the cut-off effect, because the actual display of the FOS in specific geomorphological or geological contexts can be more complex than the hypotheses suggest. The potential delimitation of the continental shelf beyond 200 nm between Denmark (Greenland) and Russia in the Arctic Ocean is a case in point. Both countries relied on the Lomonosov Ridge to establish part of their outer limits of the continental shelf in their submissions to the CLCS.[92] Therefore, there is an area of overlap beyond 200 nm because the same ridge is claimed by the two countries. The FOS points chosen by Russia and Denmark (Greenland) along the Lomonosov Ridge, if connected with straight lines, are not parallel with the coasts of Russia or Norway, but rather vertical to them. Accordingly, once the area of overlap between Russia and Denmark (Greenland) in respect of the area concerning the

88 See the relevant discussion in Chapter 6, Section III.C. and D.

89 S. Fietta and R. Cleverly, *A Practitioner's Guide to Maritime Boundary Delimitation* (Oxford University Press 2016), 617.

90 See V. Prescott and C. H. Schofield, *The Maritime Political Boundaries of the World* (2nd ed., Martinus Nijhoff Publishers 2005), 187.

91 See Weil (n 13), 47–48; N. Marques Antunes and V. Becker-Weinberg, "Entitlement to Maritime Zones and Their Delimitation: In the Doldrums of Uncertainty and Unpredictability," in A. G. Oude Elferink et al. (eds.), *Maritime Boundary Delimitation: The Case Law: Is It Consistent and Predictable?* (Cambridge University Press 2018), 72–73.

92 See "Executive summary of Denmark's submission in respect of the Northern Continental Shelf of Greenland on 15 December 2014," 8; "Executive summary of Russia's revised submission in respect of the Arctic Ocean on 3 August 2015," 26, available at: www.un.org/Depts/los/clcs_new/commission_submissions.htm.

Lomonosov Ridge is ascertained, the FOS can hardly provide a useful baseline for drawing the boundary line or determining if any cut-off effect occurs.

In State practice, where the continental shelf beyond 200 nm is delimited as part of the delimitation within and beyond 200 nm of two opposite coasts, it seems that whether the cut-off effect on the entitlement to the continental shelf beyond 200 nm is justifiable has to be examined in the light of the overall objective or delimitation methodology. The 2010 Norway–Russia agreement gives Russia the major part of the continental shelf beyond 200 nm in the Loop Hole, which seems to significantly cut off Norway's entitlement to the continental shelf beyond 200 nm in this area. Nonetheless, the delimitation within and beyond 200 nm in its entirety results in an equal share of the total disputed area for Russia and Norway.[93] Similarly, the 1990 Soviet Union–United States agreement placed almost all the area beyond 200 nm of the Bering Sea (and about 70 percent of the Bering Sea) under the jurisdiction of the United States,[94] but it would be inappropriate to judge the agreement by referring to the fact that the Soviet Union's continental shelf beyond 200 nm in the Bering Sea was significantly cut off, which is only one aspect of the agreement.

### 2 Assessment of Cut-Off Effect between Adjacent Coasts

As to adjacent States with overlapping entitlements within and beyond 200 nm, a pertinent question is whether the direction of the boundary line should be adjusted when it extends beyond 200 nm in order not to encroach unreasonably on one State's entitlement to the continental shelf beyond 200 nm. This issue in effect turns on how a cut-off effect should be identified – by reference to geometrically determined coastal projections or geomorphologically determined entitlement?

One may argue that the principle of non-encroachment formulated in the *North Sea* cases should come into play. The principle of non-encroachment and the notion of natural prolongation were considered as two sides of the same coin in the *North Sea* cases,[95] and non-

93 See R. E. Fife, "Norway–Russia Federation, Report Number 9-6(3)," in C. G. Lathrop (ed.), *International Maritime Boundaries, Vol. VII* (Brill Nijhoff Publishers 2016), 5185.

94 See E. G. Verville, "United States–Soviet Union, Report Number 1-6," in I. L. Charney and L. M. Alexander (eds.), *International Maritime Boundaries, Vol. I* (Martinus Nijhoff Publishers 1993), 451.

95 *North Sea* (n 14), 46–47 [85(c)].

encroachment was understood as "the negative expression of the positive rule that the coastal State enjoys sovereign rights over the continental shelf off its coasts to the full extent authorized by international law in the relevant circumstances."[96] Therefore, a correct understanding of the notion of natural prolongation is critical for a correct understanding of the principle of non-encroachment. If natural prolongation is understood as a geographical concept, as Judge Jiménez de Aréchaga argued in the *Tunisia/Libya* case, "then the 'non-encroachment' in front of and close to the coasts of a State is the correct interpretation of the principle."[97] This understanding of non-encroachment is synonymous with that of non-cut off. In fact, in maritime delimitation within 200 nm, sometimes "non-cut off" and "non-encroachment" are used interchangeably when they refer to coastal projections. For instance, in the *Barbados* v. *Trinidad and Tobago* case, the Tribunal adjusted the provisional equidistance line in a way that "as far as possible, there should be no cut-off effects arising from the delimitation and that the line as drawn by the Tribunal avoids the encroachment that would result from an unadjusted equidistance line."[98] In the view of the Tribunal, the difference between non-encroachment and non-cut-off is simply the framework they relate to, as the former relates to the continental shelf and the latter to the EEZ.[99] However, under Article 76 of UNCLOS, a coastal State's natural prolongation is determined through the application of Article 76(4),[100] thus the principle of non-encroachment has to be understood by referring to geomorphological or geological factors constitutive of the entitlement to the continental shelf beyond 200 nm.[101]

Again, this issue has to be considered by first determining whether there are overlapping entitlements to the continental shelf beyond 200 nm between the two adjacent States, and how the area of overlap is established. If it is a common continental margin shared by two adjacent States, as it was in the *Bay of Bengal* cases and the *Ghana/Côte d'Ivoire* case, it is difficult to discern the encroachment effect by referring to the

96 *Libya/Malta* (n 2), 39–40 [46].

97 *Tunisia/Libya* (n 18), 119 [69] (Separate Opinion of Judge Jiménez de Aréchaga). *St. Pierre and Miquelon Arbitration* (n 65), [58]. See also H. Thirlway, "The Law and Procedure of the International Court of Justice 1960–1989 Part Five" (1994) 64 *BYIL* 1, 27.

98 *Barbados* v. *Trinidad and Tobago* (n 25), [375].

99 Ibid., [232].

100 See *Bangladesh/Myanmar* (n 6), 114 [437].

101 See Fietta and Cleverly (n 89), 619.

geomorphological or geological elements of the entitlement beyond 200 nm. This scenario is more likely to be the case because States with adjacent coasts tend to have similar geophysical characteristics of the seabed.[102] Second, the delimitation of the continental shelf beyond 200 nm between two adjacent States, more often than not, involves the extension of the delimitation line within 200 nm of the two countries. As a result, the existing or potential delimitation within 200 nm is highly relevant, because whether and how the boundary should be adjusted in the area beyond 200 nm cannot be assessed in isolation from maritime delimitation within 200 nm.[103]

In fact, the influence of coasts is commanding in the delimitation between two adjacent States, as the boundary line travels throughout the whole area of overlapping entitlements from territorial seas to the outer limits of the continental shelf of the States. As observed by the Arbitral Tribunal of the *Barbados* v. *Trinidad and Tobago* case:

> [W]hat governs the delimitation essentially are the geographical elements which are at its origin, close to land, and not at its end, except where, as in the Gulf of Maine, the delimitation line might be affected by a major geographical feature further towards the open sea. Otherwise there would be no delimitation that could withstand the effect of distance and, as the *Gulf of Maine* Chamber noted in connection with a comparable argument made in that case, the continuity of the line is the inevitable expression of the principle that the "land dominates the sea."[104]

Fietta and Cleverly put forward a scenario under which State A may enjoy a continental shelf beyond 200 nm through uninterrupted natural prolongation, whereas the adjacent State B does not because of the existence of a deep trough off its coast. According to them, in such a situation "geological and geomorphological evidence should have a role to play so as to safeguard State A's outer shelf rights (and may mandate the boundary running in part along the 200 M limit of State B)."[105] However, such a scenario should be more appropriately characterized as one in which State A and State B do not have overlapping entitlements to the continental shelf beyond 200 nm because State B is not eligible to

[102] See B. J. Van Pay, "Disputed Areas Beyond 200 Nautical Miles: How Many and Will Geophysical Characteristics Matter in Their Resolution?," in M. H. Nordquist and J. N. Moore (eds.), *Maritime Border Diplomacy* (Martinus Nijhoff Publishers 2012), 56.

[103] *Bangladesh* v. *India* (n 7), [410].

[104] *Barbados* v. *Trinidad and Tobago* (n 25), [316].

[105] Fietta and Cleverly (n 89), 618.

assert an entitlement on the basis of Article 76. Accordingly, non-encroachment, which is a principle for maritime delimitation, should not come into play because, simply, no delimitation issues arise between the two States when it comes to the continental shelf beyond 200 nm.

To conclude, whether cutting off the entitlement to the continental shelf beyond 200 nm is a relevant circumstance has to take into account various factors. Between two opposite coasts, cut-off effect has to be assessed first by accurately determining the area of overlap. In this exercise, account should be taken of the FOS or other factors that contribute to the determination of the area of overlap. However, in reality, the usefulness of the FOS may be less obvious if the same submarine feature is claimed by the relevant parties to establish their entitlement to the continental shelf beyond 200 nm. Between adjacent States, since in most situations it is a common continental margin that is "shared" by the relevant States, geographical circumstances deriving from the coasts tend to exert a controlling influence over the delimitation within and beyond 200 nm. In any event, irrespective of the coastal relationship, it seems that the cut-off effect on the entitlement to the continental shelf beyond 200 nm is only one of the factors that should be weighed and balanced with other relevant circumstances in the light of the overall geography.

## III Disproportionality

### A *Meanings and Functions of Disproportionality in Maritime Delimitation*

As observed by Tanaka, the concept of (dis)proportionality has been elaborated through the jurisprudence and it has been taken into account in almost every judgment concerning maritime delimitation.[106] Yet international courts and tribunals have not always been consistent as to the terminology. Whereas the *North Sea* cases stated that "the element of a reasonable degree of proportionality" should be a final factor taken into account in negotiations, which aimed to "bring about between the extent of the continental shelf appertaining to the States concerned and the lengths of their respective coastlines,"[107] the *Anglo-French Arbitration*

[106] Y. Tanaka, *Predictability and Flexibility in the Law of Maritime Delimitation* (2nd ed., Hart 2019), 216.

[107] *North Sea* (n 14), 52 [98].

emphasized that "it is disproportion rather than any general principle of proportionality which is the relevant criterion or factor," whose function was "remedying the disproportionality and inequitable effects produced by particular geographical configurations or features in situations where otherwise the appurtenance of roughly comparable attributions of continental shelf to each State would be indicated by the geographical facts."[108] The divergencies of the terminologies reflect the various meanings and functions of the concept of (dis)proportionality in the law of maritime delimitation. Given the evolution of the meanings and functions of the concept,[109] the terminology "disproportionality" is preferred, although the present study will adopt the term as it appears in the materials.

As summarized by Weil, the term proportionality or disproportionality has been used in the jurisprudence to refer to three distinct, though connected, problems. The first is a comparison of coastal lengths; the second, the considerations based on the equality of surface areas; and the third, considerations drawn from a correlation between the ratio of coastal lengths and the ratio of surface areas.[110] The meanings of disproportionality thus differ, depending upon how disproportionality is identified. However, in the jurisprudence, it is hardly the case that international courts or tribunals will identify the existence of disproportionality by solely referring to the comparison of coastal lengths or to the comparison of surface areas. It is more often than not the case that both coastal lengths and surface areas are assessed for the purpose of determining disproportionality, though Weil was right that the focus of the disproportionality may vary from case to case.

How disproportionality is identified also relates to its functions. On the basis of the jurisprudence, it is submitted that disproportionality may assume two functions in the delimitation process: one as a relevant circumstance that contributes to the drawing of the maritime boundaries, and the other as the disproportionality test, an *ex post facto* test that checks the equitableness of the delimitation result.

Disproportionality as a relevant circumstance can be triggered by three different geographical circumstances. The first concerns a significant disparity or disproportion in coastal lengths. The *Gulf of Maine* case was the first occasion in which a comparison of coastal lengths led to a

[108] *Anglo-French Arbitration* (n 1), [101].
[109] See Tanaka (n 106), 216–238.
[110] Weil (n 13), 235–236.

shift of the course of the maritime boundary. In this case, the Chamber found that:

> [A] maritime delimitation can certainly not be established by a direct division of the area in dispute proportional to the respective lengths of the coasts belonging to the parties in the relevant area, but it is equally certain that a substantial disproportion to the lengths of those coasts that resulted from a delimitation effected on a different basis would constitute a circumstance calling for an appropriate correction.[111]

The disproportion in coastal lengths is usually considered a relevant circumstance in maritime delimitation between two opposite States, which often calls for the shifting of a provisional median line towards the State with shorter coastlines. As observed in the *Jan Mayen* case, "The application of [the equidistance method] to delimitations between opposite coasts produces, in most geographical circumstances, an equitable result," but there are situations

> in which the relationship between the length of the relevant coasts and the maritime areas generated by them by application of the equidistance method, is so disproportionate that it has been found necessary to take this circumstance into account in order to ensure an equitable solution. The frequent references in the case-law to the idea of proportionality – or disproportion – confirm the importance of the proposition that an equitable delimitation must, in such circumstances, take into account the disparity between the respective coastal lengths of the relevant area.[112]

International jurisprudence has acknowledged that "it is normally only where the disparities in the lengths of the relevant coasts are substantial that an adjustment or shifting of the provisional line is called for."[113] Nevertheless, "substantial" is hardly an objective criterion, and its measurement is subject to the discretion of international courts and tribunals.[114]

The second geographical circumstance that may produce disproportionate effect is irregular coastal configuration. Commenting on the "element of a reasonable degree of proportionality" in the *North Sea* cases, the ICJ in the *Libya/Malta* case observed that "since an

[111] *The Gulf of Maine* (n 18), 323 [185].

[112] *Maritime Delimitation in the Area between Greenland and Jan Mayen (Denmark v. Norway) [1993] ICJ Rep 38*, 67 [65].

[113] *Nicaragua* v. *Colombia I* (n 4), 702 [210].

[114] See H. Thirlway, "The Law and Procedure of the International Court of Justice 1960–1989, Part Six" (1995) 65 *BYIL* 1, 60.

equidistance line is based on a principle of proximity and is therefore controlled only by salient coastal points, it may yield a disproportionate result where a coast is markedly irregular or markedly concave or convex."[115] The focus of this observation is placed on the equality of the surface areas. The consideration of proportionality came in because "coasts which are broadly comparable ought not to be treated differently because of a technical quirk of a particular method of tracing the course of a boundary line."[116] It should be noted that in this situation, the cut-off effect and disproportionate effect are in fact two lenses through which the same geographical facts are examined. While cut-off effect refers to the effect upon coastal projections, disproportionate effect refers to "an unjustifiable difference of treatment in a situation where the concave coastline of one State, all other facts being equal (or nearly equal), would seriously reduce its continental shelf area vis-à-vis its neighbours."[117]

The third geographical circumstance concerns maritime features such as islands, islets, or rocks, which may produce a distorting effect on the delimitation lines due to their relative location vis-à-vis the potential boundary.[118] The idea of distortion in respect of maritime features is "linked to a perception of what the line would otherwise be, if the island did not exist."[119] The function of disproportionality as a relevant circumstance in this respect is to correct the inequitableness of a line when a non-essential geographical feature causes the line to deviate.[120] Addressing the effect given to the Scilly Isles, the Court of Arbitration of the *Anglo-French Arbitration* stated that "[w]hat equity calls for is an appropriate abatement of the disproportionate effects of a considerable projection on to the Atlantic continental shelf of a somewhat attenuated portion of the coast of the United Kingdom."[121] In this regard, proportionality is "a criterion to assess the distorting effects of particular geographical features and the extent of the resulting inequity."[122]

115 *Libya/Malta* (n 2), 44 [56].
116 Ibid.
117 L. L. Herman, "The Court Giveth and the Court Taketh Away: An Analysis of the Tunisia-Libya Continental Shelf Case" (1984) 33 *ICLQ* 825, 848.
118 *Bangladesh/Myanmar* (n 6), 73 [265].
119 D. Bowett, "Islands, Rocks, Reefs, and Low-Tide Elevations in Maritime Boundary Delimitations," in J. I. Charney and L. M. Alexander (eds.), *International Maritime Boundaries, Volume I* (Martinus Nijhoff Publishers 1993), 144.
120 See Weil (n 13), 237.
121 *Anglo-French Arbitration* (n 1), 116 [249].
122 Ibid., 116–117 [250].

Similar to the effect produced by irregular coastal configurations, the disproportionate or distorting effect produced by a maritime feature may be referred to as "cut-off" effect as well. The distinction between the two is difficult to conceptualize,[123] and perhaps there is also no need to do this.[124] The second and third geographical circumstances will not be discussed further because they have been addressed in connection with the cut-off effect.[125]

The disproportionality test has been formulated as a distinct, and final, stage of the delimitation methodology in the *Black Sea* case, which is to confirm that "no great disproportionality of maritime areas is evident by comparison to the ratio of coastal lengths."[126] As the disproportionality test is an exercise that compares the ratios between coastal lengths and the ratios between attributed maritime areas, this use of disproportionality is what Weil called "proportionality *stricto sensu*."[127] The *Bay of Bengal* cases and the *Ghana/Côte d'Ivoire* case applied the disproportionality test after accomplishing the delimitation within and beyond 200 nm and treated the area beyond 200 nm as integral to the entire maritime area subject to delimitation.[128] Nevertheless, as discussed in Chapter 6, due to the lack of objective and scientific criteria to determine coastal lengths and the size of the relevant area, the validity of applying a

[123] For instance, when considering the effect of Fasht al Azm in the *Qatar* v. *Bahrain* case, the Court found that if treating the feature as part of the island of Sitrah, the equidistance line would "place the boundary disproportionately close to Qatar's mainland coast." Both cut-off effect and disproportionate effect were present. On the one hand, the boundary would be too close to Qatar's mainland coast, which cuts off its coastal projections. On the other hand, such a cut-off effect cannot be justified because the effect giving to the island of Sitrah is disproportionate, as "less than 20 per cent of the surface of this island is permanently above water." See *Maritime Delimitation and Territorial Questions (Qatar v. Bahrain) (Merits) [2001] ICJ Rep 40, 104* [218].

[124] Some scholars in fact do not distinguish between the two effects. According to Bowett, "Indeed, it would seem that the proportionality factor might only be applied, or be meaningful in the case of adjacent States (not 'opposite') where the existence of a markedly concave or convex coastline will produce a cut-off effect if the equidistance principle is applied," D. W. Bowett, *The Legal Regime of Islands in International Law* (Oceana Publications 1979), 164. Acikgonul also does not distinguish the cut-off effect and the disproportionate effect produced by insignificant maritime features. See Y. E. Acikgonul, "Reflections on the Principle of Non-Cut Off: A Growing Concept in Maritime Boundary Delimitation Law" (2016) 47 *ODIL* 52, 56–61.

[125] See Section II.A above.

[126] *Black Sea* (n 3), 103 [122].

[127] Weil (n 13), 236.

[128] *Bangladesh/Myanmar* (n 6), 125 [493]; *Bangladesh* v. *India* (n 7), [490]; *Ghana/Côte d'Ivoire* (n 8), [534].

disproportionality test under the three-stage approach is contentious.[129] These problems are accentuated in the delimitation of the continental shelf beyond 200 nm, for the lack of established outer limits of the continental shelf may further call into question the accuracy of the disproportionality test. For these reasons, it might be unwise to over-conceptualize the disproportionality test in the context of the continental shelf delimitation beyond 200 nm.

Accordingly, the following section will only analyze whether disproportion in coastal lengths will be a relevant circumstance in the delimitation of the continental shelf beyond 200 nm.

### *B Disproportion in Coastal Lengths in the Continental Shelf Delimitation beyond 200 NM*

Disproportion in coastal lengths would continue to be relevant in the delimitation of the continental shelf beyond 200 nm because there is conceptual and spatial continuity between the coasts and the continental shelf beyond 200 nm. Since the continental shelf "comprises the seabed and subsoil of the submarine areas that extend beyond its territorial sea throughout the natural prolongation of its land territory to the outer edge of the continental margin" under Article 76 of UNCLOS, the entitlement to the continental shelf beyond 200 nm is measured from the coast, though the substance of the continuity is to be proved through the application of Article 76(4). Moreover, from the perspective of the maritime space, the relevance of coasts in the delimitation of the continental shelf beyond 200 nm is also derived from the presence of the coasts that abut the relevant area to be delimited.[130]

State practice concerning the continental shelf beyond 200 nm confirms the relevance of disproportion in coastal lengths in the delimitation process. In the 2010 Norway–Russia agreement, it is reported that the existence of the particularly marked disparities in coastal lengths of the two States in the southern and middle parts of the Barents Sea contributed to the shift of the delimitation line to the west of Russia.[131] On the other hand, no such disparities of coastal lengths can be identified further north, and in that area the boundary line follows a median line which

[129] Chapter 6, Section II.B.1.
[130] See *Barbados* v. *Trinidad and Tobago* (n 25), [239].
[131] See Fife (n 93), 5185.

extends into the area beyond 200 nm in the Arctic Ocean.[132] Similarly, in the 2013 Denmark (Greenland)–Iceland Agreed Minutes, the disparity in the overall coastal length was to some extent a factor considered in the negotiations,[133] which might explain why the fixed ratio of the attribution of the continental shelf beyond 200 nm is 53 percent versus 47 percent in favor of Denmark/Greenland.[134] The 2006 Agreed Minutes concluded by Denmark (Faroe Islands), Iceland and Norway also took into account the disparity of the coastal lengths, at least in the area closest to Jan Mayen, even though the negotiated solution was not based on a detailed analysis of the disparities of the coastal lengths.[135]

Although it is contended that the role of proportionality in State practice is modest and not altogether clear,[136] the above-mentioned examples in State practice illustrate that coastal States do take into account the disparity in coastal lengths in the continental shelf beyond 200 nm. In fact, in the 2010 Joint Statement on Maritime Delimitation and Cooperation in the Barents Sea and the Arctic Ocean issued by Norway and Russia ("2010 Joint Statement"), the two parties confirmed that they had applied "relevant factors identified in this regard in international law," and explicitly referred to "the effect of major disparities in respective coastal lengths."[137] The consideration of the disparities of coastal lengths in the 2010 Norway–Russia agreement was clearly inspired by the settled jurisprudence of the ICJ on maritime delimitation.[138] Hence it is not exaggerated to say that coastal States find disproportion in coastal lengths not only relevant, but also a factor that should be addressed in order to achieve a mutually acceptable – equitable – solution in the continental shelf delimitation beyond 200 nm.

Although international courts and tribunals have not had opportunities to remark on the relevance of disproportion in coastal lengths in the

132 Ibid.

133 See B. M. Magnússon, "Denmark (Greenland)–Iceland, Report Number 9-22 (2)," in C. G. Lathrop (ed.), *International Maritime Boundaries, Vol. VII* (Brill Nijhoff Publishers 2016), 5264.

134 Ibid., 5270.

135 See R. E. Fife, "Denmark/The Faroes–Iceland–Norway, Report Number 9-26," in D. A. Colson and R. W. Smith (eds.), *International Maritime Boundaries, Vol.VI* (Martinus Nijhoff Publishers 2011), 4543.

136 See Y. Tanaka, "Reflections on the Concept of Proportionality in the Law of Maritime Delimitation" (2001), 16 *IJMCL* 433, 455 and 462.

137 See T. Henriksen and G. Ulfstein, "Maritime Delimitation in the Arctic: The Barents Sea Treaty" (2011) 42 *ODIL* 1, 6–7.

138 Fife (n 93), 5167.

delimitation of the continental shelf beyond 200 nm, it is reasonable to expect that such arguments would arise, if circumstances so require, and are likely to prevail. It is recalled that the ICJ commented that there cannot be question of "rendering the situation of a State with an extensive coastline similar to that of a State with a restricted coastline,"[139] an observation made in relation to a common continental shelf bordered by the coastal States and before the definition of the continental shelf under Article 76 entered into the law of the sea. In other words, where coastal States are on equal footing in the geomorphological or geological sense, the circumstances that are deemed relevant can only be found in coastal geography. As stated by the ICJ, "Proportionality is certainly intimately related both to the governing principle of equity, and to the importance of coasts in the generation of continental shelf rights."[140] This is the case regardless of the delimitation within or beyond 200 nm. Inasmuch as the coastal States have overlapping entitlements to the continental shelf beyond 200 nm, the influence of the coasts would be continuous. Suppose that State A and State B are opposite States with a distance of 500 nm apart, and the two could equally claim the continental shelf beyond 200 nm in accordance with Article 76. The coastlines of State A are significantly longer than those of State B. This scenario is essentially a variation of the geographical situation of the *Libya/Malta* case, though in the former the distance between the two States is stretched due to the existence of the overlapping entitlements to the continental shelf beyond 200 nm. Yet, if all other circumstances being equal, there is no reason why the disproportion in coastal lengths should not be a relevant circumstance that calls for the shifting of the boundary towards the country with the shorter coastlines.

Nevertheless, some scholars question the validity of shifting the provisional equidistance line between two opposite States because of disproportion in coastal lengths. Fietta and Cleverly argue that in situations such as the *Libya/Malta* case, if the relevant area is defined as a trapezium, a strict equidistance line automatically allocates a larger area to the longer State. As a result, there seems little reason to take into account the disproportion in coastal lengths.[141] Tanaka holds the same view, and suggests that there is no decisive reason to give an additional area to the State with the longer coastline, as a provisional median line has already

[139] *North Sea* (n 14), 49–50 [91].
[140] *Libya/Malta* (n 2), 43 [55].
[141] Fietta and Cleverly (n 89), 605.

reflected the difference in the maritime areas.[142] Despite the merits of this argument from the perspective of geometry, international courts and tribunals consistently hold, in a general fashion, that disproportion in coastal lengths is a relevant circumstance,[143] and on multiple occasions they have shifted and adjusted the provisional equidistance line to account for the disparities of coastal lengths.[144] Besides, in reality how the relevant area between two opposite coasts is defined is subject to specific geographical circumstances, which is not always a geometrical exercise.[145] A trapezium-shaped relevant area could be possible if the relevant area between the two opposite coasts is limited by claims of third States, but it would not correspond to the whole area of overlapping entitlements if the two States are situated in an open ocean, or if the State with the shorter coastline is an island State whose maritime entitlement is radially defined. As admitted by Fietta and Cleverly, "the extent of adjustment required of an equidistance line between opposite coasts in order to achieve a strictly 'proportionate' solution (from a mathematical perspective) will turn heavily on the precise shape and dimensions of the relevant area."[146] It should also be added that the jurisprudence does not support a strictly "proportionate" solution in maritime delimitation. As stated by the ICJ in the *Libya/Malta* case:

> [T]o use the ratio of coastal lengths as of itself determinative of the seaward reach and area of continental shelf proper to each Party, is to

[142] See Tanaka, *Predictability and Flexibility in the Law of Maritime Delimitation* (n 106), 223–224. See also *Libya/Malta* (n 2), 184–187 (Dissenting Opinion of Judge Schwebel); ibid., 121 (Dissenting Opinion of Judge Mosler).

[143] The potential relevance of a substantial difference in the lengths of the parties' respective coastlines is widely acknowledged, though not in every case where a party argued for the existence of disproportion in coastal lengths did a court or tribunal uphold such a claim. See *Land and Maritime Boundary between Cameroon and Nigeria (Cameroon v. Nigeria: Equatorial Guinea intervening) [2002] ICJ Rep 303, 446-447* [301]. Similarly, in the *Black Sea* case, the ICJ "sees no such particularly marked disparities between the relevant coasts of Ukraine and Romania that would require it to adjust the provisional equidistance line at this juncture." *Black Sea* (n 3), 117–118 [168].

[144] Examples include the *Gulf of Maine* case, the *Libya/Malta* case, the *Jan Mayen* case, the *Barbados* v. *Trinidad and Tobago* case, and the *Nicaragua* v. *Colombia I* case. See the discussion in Tanaka (n 106), 221–232.

[145] For instance, in the *Nicaragua* v. *Colombia I* case, the northern limit of the relevant area is determined by reference to the boundary between Nicaragua and Honduras decided by the ICJ in the 2007 *Nicaragua* v. *Honduras* case, and the southern limit by the agreement reached between Colombia and Costa Rica and the agreement between Colombia and Panama. See *Nicaragua* v. *Colombia I* (n 4), 686 [164–165].

[146] Fietta and Cleverly (n 89), 605.

> go far beyond the use of proportionality as a test of equity, and as a corrective of the unjustifiable difference of treatment resulting from some method of drawing the boundary line. If such a use of proportionality were right, it is difficult indeed to see what room would be left for any other consideration; for it would be at once the principle of entitlement to continental shelf rights and also the method of putting that principle into operation.[147]

Taking into account disproportion in coastal lengths in the delimitation process is subject to several qualifications. The first is that "the respective length of coasts can play no role in identifying the equidistance line which has been provisionally established."[148] Since the issue of significant disparities in coastal lengths is often a relevant circumstance in maritime delimitation between two opposite coasts, international courts and tribunals tend to construct an equidistance line before considering the impact of the marked difference in coastal length. This two-step delimitation methodology may also be followed in the delimitation of the continental shelf beyond 200 nm. In this connection, whether an equidistance line achieves an approximately equal division of the area of overlap in the first place could also be a factor that is to be balanced with the consideration of disproportion in coastal lengths.

The second qualification of addressing disproportion in coastal lengths is that only "a *substantial* difference in the lengths of the parties' respective coastlines *may* be a factor to be taken into consideration in order to adjust or shift the provisional delimitation line."[149] As mentioned earlier, whether the disparities in coastal lengths are "substantial," or "significant," or "marked" is an issue to be appreciated by international courts and tribunals, and currently there is no objectively established criteria in this respect. It does not seem that the delimitation of the continental shelf beyond 200 nm will differ on this point.

Finally, as emphasized throughout the jurisprudence, proportionality is conceptually different from apportionment.[150] Therefore, "taking

[147] *Libya/Malta* (n 2), 45–46 [58].

[148] *Black Sea* (n 3), 116 [163]; *Nicaragua* v. *Colombia I* (n 4), 702 [209].

[149] *Black Sea* (n 3), 116 [165] (emphasis in the original).

[150] *North Sea* (n 14), 21–22 [18]; *Anglo-French Arbitration* (n 1), [101]; *Guinea/Guinea-Bissau* (n 71) [120]; *Black Sea* (n 3), 100 [111]. For critiques on the distinction between proportionality and apportionment, see W. Friedmann, "The North Sea Continental Shelf Cases – A Critique" (1970) 64 *AJIL* 229, 238–239; Thirlway (n 114), 56; Y. Tanaka, "Reflections on the Territorial and Maritime Dispute between Nicaragua and Colombia before the International Court of Justice" (2013) 26 *LJIL* 909, 924.

account of the disparity of coastal lengths does not mean a direct and mathematical application of the relationship between the length of the coastal front [of the parties]."[151] These observations thus highlight that correcting the inequity of the disproportion in coastal lengths is not equivalent to pursuing a positive correlation between the ratios of coastal lengths and the ratios of surface areas. As put by the Court in the *Jan Mayen* case:

> [T]he law does not require a delimitation based upon an endeavour to share out an area of overlap on the basis of comparative figures for the length of the coastal fronts and the areas generated by them. [. . .] [T]he sharing-out of the area is therefore the consequence of the delimitation, not vice versa.[152]

To conclude, in light of the settled jurisprudence, disproportion in coastal lengths would continue to be a relevant circumstance in the continental shelf delimitation beyond 200 nm. As with the cut-off effect, the examination of disproportion in coastal lengths cannot be an isolated exercise singled out from the overall geographical framework. The actual existence of the disproportion and to what extent such disproportion calls for the shifting of the boundary line are matters to be appreciated together with other relevant circumstances in a given context.

[151] *Jan Mayen* (n 112), 69 [69]; *Nicaragua* v. *Colombia I* (n 4), 702 [210].
[152] *Jan Mayen* (n 112), 66–67 [64].

# 9

# Towards a Common Approach to Maritime Delimitation within and beyond 200 NM

## I The Unification of Relevant Circumstances within and beyond 200 NM

Chapter 7 and Chapter 8 have discussed in detail the circumstances relating to the delimitation of the continental shelf beyond 200 nautical miles (nm), and have found that this exercise does not differ from maritime delimitation within 200 nm simply because the entitlement beyond 200 nm differs. This conclusion is reached not merely because the tribunals of the *Bay of Bengal* cases and the *Ghana/Côte d'Ivoire* case declared the use of the same delimitation methodology; it is based on the continuing application of the rules and principles governing the relevant circumstances and delimitation methods in the delimitation beyond 200 nm. Specifically, geomorphological or geological factors are unlikely to bear on the delimitation process except for determining the area of overlapping entitlements, which is a matter of applying Article 76 of United Nations Convention on the Law of the Sea (UNCLOS or "the Convention"). Indeed, it is in this exercise that the possibility of the inappropriateness of a coast-to-coast delimitation might arise. Coastal geography, contrary to some hypotheses, continues to be relevant in the delimitation of the continental shelf beyond 200 nm, for the *Bay of Bengal* cases and the *Ghana/Côte d'Ivoire* case confirm that the delimitation beyond 200 nm remains committed to addressing the cut-off effect produced by irregular coastal configurations or incidental coastal features. State practice also suggests that disparities in coastal lengths may still be a relevant factor that features in negotiations of maritime agreements concerning the continental shelf beyond 200 nm. The equidistance method, when it is capable of achieving an approximate equal division of the area of overlap, seems equally applicable in the delimitation of the continental shelf beyond this distance. Taking stock, current development of the jurisprudence and State practice concerning the continental shelf beyond 200 nm appears to suggest a tendency towards a common approach to maritime delimitation within and beyond 200 nm on the basis of the unification of relevant circumstances.

One last aspect of the delimitation methodology for the continental shelf beyond 200 nm concerns a widely held proposition that delimitation of the continental shelf should differ from that of the EEZ because an equitable solution for the former might be different for the latter. In other words, should there be regime-specific circumstances that must be taken into account in the delimitation of the continental shelf beyond 200 nm, those circumstances may come into play in a "pure" continental shelf delimitation beyond 200 nm or take over the delimitation process when there is a need to extend the maritime boundary within 200 nm beyond that limit. Section II focuses on this issue and argues that international courts and tribunals would hardly resort to regime-specific circumstances in the continental shelf delimitation beyond 200 nm lest the boundary-making fall into distributive justice or a decision *ex aequo et bono*. Section III reviews the State practice concerning the continental shelf beyond 200 nm and examines the trend towards a single exercise of maritime delimitation in the jurisprudence. Section IV concludes with remarks on the prospects of delimitation of the continental shelf beyond 200 nm.

## II (Ir)Relevance of Regime-Specific Circumstances

The proposition that a continental shelf delimitation may be different from an EEZ delimitation finds its support in the separation of the regimes of the continental shelf and the EEZ. Despite the identical wording of the delimitation rules under Article 74(1) and Article 83(1) of UNCLOS, there is no legal requirement that factors or methods for the delimitation of the EEZ and the continental shelf should be the same.[1]

[1] See J. I. Charney, "Ocean Boundaries between Nations: A Theory for Progress" (1984) 78 *AJIL* 582, 601; D. J. Attard, *The Exclusive Economic Zone in International Law* (Oxford University Press 1987), 214; P. Weil, *The Law of Maritime Delimitation: Reflections* (Grotius Publications Limited 1989), 132–133; F. Orrego Vicuña, *The Exclusive Economic Zone: Regime and Legal Nature under International Law* (Cambridge University Press 1989), 196–197; H. Thirlway, *Law and Procedure of the International Court of Justice: Fifty Years of Jurisprudence, Volume II* (Oxford University Press 2013). 1385; B. M. Magnússon, *The Continental Shelf beyond 200 Nautical Miles: Delineation, Delimitation and Dispute Settlement* (Brill Nijhoff Publishers 2015), 160; Y. Tanaka, "Article 83," in Alexander Proelss (ed.), *The United Nations Convention on the Law of the Sea: A Commentary* (Hart 2017), 656.

International courts and tribunals maintain that the continental shelf and the EEZ are separate and co-exist with each other, even though the jurisprudence has been primarily developing in cases concerning single maritime delimitation.[2] Nevertheless, the International Court of Justice (ICJ or "the Court") stressed that the concept of a single maritime boundary does not stem from multilateral treaty law but from State practice, and it "finds its explanation in the wish of States to establish one uninterrupted boundary line delimiting the various – partially coincident – zones of maritime jurisdiction appertaining to them."[3] Since there is no legal requirement for a single line for the continental shelf and the EEZ, the delimitation of the continental shelf beyond 200 nm may thus consider factors that are solely relevant with the continental shelf regime.

Judicial practice that emphasizes the neutral factors in the single delimitation of the continental shelf and EEZ further reinforces the idea that a pure continental shelf delimitation beyond 200 nm may be qualitatively different. The *Gulf of Maine* case nurtured the concept of "neutral criteria," as the Chamber stated that "the criteria in question were then found equitable and appropriate for the delimitation of the continental shelf does not imply that they must automatically possess the same properties in relation to the simultaneous delimitation of the continental shelf and the superjacent fishery zone," and that "it is necessary [...] to rule out the application of any criterion found to be typically and exclusively bound up with the particular characteristics of one alone of the two natural realities that have to be delimited in conjunction."[4] International courts and tribunals not infrequently resort to the "neutrality" of the single maritime delimitation in order to exclude the relevance of certain factors advanced by the parties. To give some examples, in the *Ghana/Côte d'Ivoire* case, the Special Chamber of the International Tribunal for the Law of the Sea (ITLOS or "the Tribunal") precluded the consideration of the oil practice of the parties because "a *de facto* line or *modus vivendi* related to oil practice cannot *per se* be a relevant circumstance in the delimitation of an all-purpose maritime

[2] See *Maritime Boundary Arbitration (Barbados v. Trinidad and Tobago) (2006) XXVII RIAA 147* [226].

[3] *Maritime Delimitation and Territorial Questions (Qatar v. Bahrain) (Merits) [2001] ICJ Rep 40, 93* [173].

[4] *Delimitation of the Maritime Boundary in the Gulf of Maine Area (Canada/United States of America) [1984] ICJ Rep 246, 326-327* [192-193].

boundary with respect to superjacent water as well as the seabed and subsoil."[5] In the *Peru* v. *Chile* case, the ICJ did not find the evidence relating to the fishing activities of the parties determinative of the extent of the maritime boundary that might exist between the parties due to the all-purpose nature of that boundary.[6] In the context of territorial sea delimitation, the *Bangladesh* v. *India* case observed that:

> In delimiting the various maritime spaces, however, different considerations need to be taken into account. In the delimitation of the territorial sea, for instance, it is of considerable significance that the rights of the coastal State are not functional, but territorial, and entail sovereignty over the seabed, the superjacent waters and the air column [. . .]. Further to seaward, sovereign rights, rather than sovereignty itself, are at issue, and the relevant considerations differ.[7]

The Arbitral Tribunal thus suggested the existence of sovereignty-related circumstances that are exclusively relevant to the territorial sea delimitation, but did not explicitly mention what these circumstances could be. Potentially, the Arbitral Tribunal might have had historic title in mind,[8] which is a special circumstance acknowledged by Article 15 of UNCLOS but is unlikely to be a relevant circumstance in the delimitation of the continental shelf or the EEZ due to its very nature.[9] In addition, security and defense considerations may find more force in territorial sea delimitation than in the EEZ/continental shelf delimitation due to the short distance between the parties in the confined maritime areas of the former. Nonetheless, the Arbitral Tribunal made a general point that considerations vary in different maritime zones.

Notwithstanding the impression that a court or tribunal will resort to regime-specific considerations if they are asked to draw a maritime boundary exclusively for the continental shelf or the EEZ, upon closer

5 *Delimitation of the Maritime Boundary in the Atlantic Ocean (Ghana/Côte d'Ivoire), [2017] ITLOS Rep 4, 133* [477].

6 *Maritime Dispute (Peru v. Chile) [2014] ICJ Rep 3, 45* [111].

7 *Bay of Bengal Maritime Boundary Arbitration (Bangladesh v. India) (2014) 167 ILR 1, 68* [191].

8 Article 15 of UNCLOS.

9 The nature of historic title was touched upon by the *Anglo–Norwegian Fisheries* case, which stated that "[b]y 'historic waters' are usually meant waters which are treated as internal waters but which would not have that character were it not for the existence of an historic title,"*Fisheries case (United Kingdom v. Norway) [1951] ICJ Rep 116,* 130. The *South China Sea* Arbitration observed that historic title "is used specifically to refer to historic sovereignty to land or maritime areas," *South China Sea Arbitration (Philippines v. China) (Merits) (2016) 170 ILR 180* [225].

examination it will become apparent that none of these circumstances are likely to affect the location of the maritime boundary. The most frequently cited regime-specific circumstances are natural resources (e.g., fisheries and oil or gas resources), conduct or activities relating to the legal regime (e.g., fishing or exploitation of mineral resources), and the natural components or characteristics of the maritime zones (e.g., ecological environment of the seas and oceans or the geophysical attributes of the seabed). Jurisprudence has been reluctant to give effect to these circumstances, which is independent of the task of effecting a single maritime delimitation.

The restrictive approach to resource-related circumstances has both a conceptual and practical dimension. Conceptually, there have been variations in the perceptions of courts and tribunals of the relevance of natural resources in maritime delimitation. In the *North Sea* cases, the ICJ listed the "unity of deposits" as one relevant factor in the continental shelf delimitation, because the resources are the "very objective of the legal régime."[10] Note, however, that the Court was referring to the factors that are to be taken into account "in the course of the negotiations," therefore leaving the issue to the parties.[11] The *Tunisia/Libya* case and the *Libya/Malta* case more generally acknowledged the potential relevance of the presence of natural resources of the continental shelf in the process of weighing all relevant factors to achieve an equitable result.[12] In other decisions, however, courts and tribunals tested the equitableness of the delimitation result against resource-related circumstances. In other words, resource-related circumstances are not a relevant circumstance in

[10] *North Sea Continental Shelf Cases (Federal Republic of Germany/Denmark; Federal Republic of Germany/Netherlands) [1969] ICJ Rep 3, 51-52* [97].

[11] Ibid., 53-54 [101(D)(2)]. Judge Tanaka criticized the judgments as amounting to "the suggestion to the Parties that they settle their dispute by negotiations according to *ex aequo et bono* without any indication as to what are the 'principles and rules of international law', namely juridical principles and rules vested with obligatory power rather than considerations of expediency – factors or criteria – which are not incorporated in the legal norm and about which the Parties did not request an answer," ibid., 196 (Dissenting Opinion of Judge Tanaka).

[12] The *Tunisia/Libya* case stated that "[a]s to the presence of oil-wells in an area to be delimited, it may, depending on the facts, be an element to be taken into account in the process of weighing all relevant factors to achieve an equitable result," *Continental Shelf (Tunisia/Libyan Arab Jamahiriya) [1982] ICJ Rep 18, 77-78* [107]. The *Libya/Malta* case observed that "[t]he natural resources of the continental shelf under delimitation 'so far as known or readily ascertainable' might well constitute relevant circumstances which it would be reasonable to take into account in a delimitation,"*Continental Shelf (Libyan Arab Jamahiriya/Malta) [1985] ICJ Rep 13, 41* [50].

establishing the maritime boundaries, but are assessed as indicia of an equitable solution.[13] The Chamber in the *Gulf of Maine* case, bearing in mind that the Georges Bank "is the real subject of the dispute," decided that the circumstances and activities relating to resources were "ineligible for consideration as criteria to be applied in the delimitation process itself," though they may "be relevant to assessment of the equitable character of a delimitation first established on the basis of criteria borrowed from physical and political geography."[14] According to the Chamber, these circumstances were examined to ensure that the delimitation result would not be "radically inequitable," or "likely to entail catastrophic repercussions for the livelihood and economic well-being of the population of the countries concerned."[15]

In the practice of international courts and tribunals, however, only in the *Jan Mayen* case was the provisional delimitation line adjusted in order to ensure an "equitable access" to the fisheries located in the disputed maritime areas.[16] This is in fact exceptional in the jurisprudence.[17] As observed in the *Barbados* v. *Trinidad and Tobago* case and confirmed by subsequent judicial decisions, "[r]esource-related criteria have been treated more cautiously by the decisions of international courts and tribunals, which have not generally applied this factor as a relevant circumstance."[18]

Whether conceptually or practically, the jurisprudence hardly supports the view that the course of the maritime boundary should be drawn in a manner to accommodate the location or attribution of natural resources. The cautious attitude of the judiciary towards resource-related

[13] See M. D. Evans, "Relevant Circumstances," in A. G. Oude Elferink et al. (eds.), *Maritime Boundary Delimitation: The Case Law: Is It Consistent and Predictable?* (Cambridge University Press 2018), 256; M. Lando, *Maritime Delimitation as a Judicial Process* (Cambridge University Press 2018), 198–199; Y. Tanaka, *Predictability and Flexibility in the Law of Maritime Delimitation* (2nd ed., Hart 2019), 392–392.

[14] *The Gulf of Maine* (n 4), 278 [59] and 340 [232].

[15] Ibid., 342 [237]. See also *Delimitation of the Maritime Boundary between Guinea and Guinea-Bissau (Guinea/Guinea-Bissau) (1985) XIX RIAA 149* [121–122]. *Decision in Case concerning Delimitation of Maritime Areas (St Pierre and Miquelon), 31 ILM 1145 (1992)* [84-85].

[16] *Maritime Delimitation in the Area between Greenland and Jan Mayen (Denmark v. Norway) [1993] ICJ Rep 38, 79* [90].

[17] Tanaka (n 13), 393.

[18] *Barbados* v. *Trinidad and Tobago* (n 2), [241]. For subsequent decisions endorsing this view, see *Maritime Delimitation in the Black Sea (Romania v. Ukraine) [2009] ICJ Rep 61, 125-126* [198]; *Territorial and Maritime Dispute (Nicaragua v. Colombia) [2012] ICJ Rep 624, 706* [223]; *Bangladesh* v. *India* (n 7), 138-139 [423].

circumstances originates not from the task of effecting a single maritime delimitation, but from principles of the law of maritime delimitation. International courts and tribunals consistently hold that maritime delimitation is not about distributive justice,[19] and that it cannot be a process of apportioning natural resources.[20] These principles to a large extent preclude the possibility of delimiting the continental shelf and the EEZ differently based on resource distribution considerations. Location of or access to natural resources is often linked to economic development of one country,[21] or to economic dependency on natural resources,[22] and a court or tribunal can hardly address these considerations without falling into a decision of distributive justice or a decision *ex aequo et bono*.[23] Above all, the objective of maritime delimitation is to establish a *permanent* boundary that fixes the spatial scope of maritime jurisdiction of the relevant parties. The influence of resource-related factors on a permanent maritime boundary can rarely be objectively ascertained by the judiciary.[24] As rightly pointed out by the *Guinea/Guinea-Bissau* case,

19 See *North Sea* (n 10), 22–23 [20]; *Libya/Malta* (n 12), 39–40 [46]; *Ghana/Côte d'Ivoire* (n 5), [452].

20 The Tribunal in the *St. Pierre and Miquelon* Arbitration stated that "the Court recognizes that it has not been requested or authorized to apportion resources on the basis of need or other economic factors. Accordingly, economic dependence and needs were not taken into account in the process of delimitation," *St. Pierre and Miquelon Arbitration* (n 15), 1173 [83]. See also P. Reuter, "Une ligne unique de délimitation des espaces maritimes?, "*Mélanges Georges Perrin* (Bernard Dutoit et Etienne Grisel 1984), 257.

21 Malta in the *Libya/Malta* case argued that economic factors should be taken into account because "the relevant equitable considerations, employed not to dictate a delimitation but to contribute to assessment of the equitableness of a delimitation otherwise arrived at, include the absence of energy resources on the island of Malta, its requirements as an island developing country, and the range of its established fishing activity." The Court rejected this contention and declared that "neither the rules determining the validity of legal entitlement to the continental shelf, nor those concerning delimitation between neighbouring countries, leave room for any considerations of economic development of the States in question," *Libya/Malta* (n 12), 41 [50].

22 In the *Eritrea/Yemen* case, Eritrea argued that "the existing fisheries practices of its nationals should not be restricted or curtailed by the delimitation to be decided by the Tribunal." The Tribunal, however, found that "[i]t is not possible or necessary for the Tribunal to reach a conclusion that either Eritrea or Yemen is economically dependent on fishing to such an extent as to suggest any particular line of delimitation." See *Second Stage of the Proceedings between Eritrea and Yemen (Maritime Delimitation) (Eritrea/Yemen) (1999) XXII RIAA 335* [54] and [64].

23 *The Gulf of Maine* (n 4), 278 [59].

24 As observed in the *Tunisia/Libya* case: "[Economic considerations] are virtually extraneous factors since they are variables which unpredictable national fortune or calamity, as the case may be, might at any time cause to tilt the scale one way or the other. A country

economic problems arising out of access to natural resources cannot constitute permanent circumstances to be taken into account for the purpose of delimitation, as "the Tribunal can be concerned only with a contemporary evaluation, it would be neither just nor equitable to base a delimitation on the evaluation of data which changes in relation to factors that are sometimes uncertain."[25]

Therefore, the principles that distinguish maritime delimitation from apportionment and from distributive justice underscore the irrelevance of resource-related circumstances, regardless of the nature of the maritime zones to be delimited. It is recalled that neither the *Tunisia/Libya* case nor the *Libya/Malta* case took into account oil or gas resources, even if both cases were concerned with the continental shelf only. As a result, it is equally unlikely that a continental shelf delimitation beyond 200 nm should take into account the location or presence of resources simply because it is a "pure" continental shelf delimitation. Likewise, in a maritime delimitation within and beyond 200 nm, it would be contradictory that the delimitation of the continental shelf and the EEZ within 200 nm disregards resource-related circumstances whereas beyond that distance natural resources regain relevance, and potentially to the benefit of one party.

In a similar vein, conduct relating to the regimes of the continental shelf or the EEZ has a very limited role in the delimitation process. Fishing activities are frequently advanced as one relevant circumstance by one party to the dispute to justify a particular method for delimitation or the existence of a pre-determined maritime boundary, but international courts and tribunals tend to disregard their relevance to the delimitation process.[26] For instance, the *Barbados* v. *Trinidad and Tobago* case observed that "[d]etermining an international maritime boundary between two States on the basis of traditional fishing on the high seas by nationals of one of those States is altogether exceptional. Support for such a principle in customary and conventional international law is largely lacking."[27] As to conduct relating to the continental shelf,

might be poor today and become rich tomorrow as a result of an event such as the discovery of a valuable economic resource," *Tunisia/Libya* (n 12), 77–78 [107]. See also H. Thirlway, "The Law and Procedure of the International Court of Justice 1960–1989 Part Five" (1994) 64 *BYIL* 1, 16; Lando (n 13), 201.

25 *Guinea/Guinea-Bissau* (n 15), [122].

26 See Tanaka (n 13), 377–379.

27 *Barbados* v. *Trinidad and Tobago* (n 2), [269].

international courts and tribunals are unequivocal in restricting the relevance of oil practice. As held by the ICJ, "[o]nly if [oil concessions and oil wells] are based on express or tacit agreement between the parties may they be taken into account."[28] As a result, conduct is currently not evidence for the appropriateness of a particular delimitation method, but evidence for the existence of agreement on a maritime boundary as such.[29] Besides, the stringent criterion applies to *existing* oil practice, and it is more difficult, if not impossible, for *potential* resource-related activities to be considered in the delimitation process.[30] This latter point is highly relevant with the delimitation of the continental shelf beyond 200 nm, because it is not unusual that actual exploitation of resources is yet to take place in areas beyond 200 nm, and that the potential for such exploitation is unclear.[31] Furthermore, from the perspective of policy considerations, if the judiciary accorded weight to existing conduct of the parties, it might encourage States to seize control over the disputed maritime areas without exercising caution or prudence in undelimited maritime areas, which may be incompatible with the objective of Articles 74 and 83. As aptly put by the Special Chamber,

> To equate oil concession limits with a maritime boundary would be equivalent to penalizing a State for exercising such caution and prudence. It would be contrary to article 74, paragraph 3, and article 83, paragraph 3, of the Convention, which require States, pending agreement on delimitation, in a spirit of understanding and cooperation, not to jeopardize or hamper the reaching of the final agreement. It would also entail negative implications for the conduct of States in the area to be delimited elsewhere.[32]

[28] See *Land and Maritime Boundary between Cameroon and Nigeria (Cameroon v. Nigeria: Equatorial Guinea intervening) [2002] ICJ Rep 303, 447-448* [304].

[29] See Lando (n 13), 214.

[30] See Evans, "Relevant Circumstances" (n 13), 254–255.

[31] The Special Chamber of the *Ghana/Côte d'Ivoire* case rejected Côte d'Ivoire's argument that in the present case "access to the oil resources is sufficiently exceptional to constitute a relevant circumstance for delimitation purposes," as the Special Chamber questioned the correctness of the factual situation and noted that "[t]hose doubts are further accentuated by the fact that most of the relevant area belongs to the Ivorian basin, whose potential for the exploitation of hydrocarbon resources is not yet fully clear." Importantly, the Special Chamber emphasized that even if Côte d'Ivoire were correct in the exceptional concentration of hydrocarbon resources in the disputed area, "the Special Chamber would be bound to reiterate that the process of delimiting maritime zones is not meant to refashion nature." See *Ghana/Côte d'Ivoire* (n 5), [437–438] and [451].

[32] Ibid., [225].

Although the Special Chamber made the observation in the context of assessing the existence of a tacit agreement on a maritime boundary, it is arguable that this observation is of equal value for examining the relevance of conduct in the delimitation process.

In terms of the characteristics of maritime zones, it has been suggested that since the EEZ is mostly composed of the water column and the continental shelf is mostly composed of the seabed and subsoil, these characteristics may call for different lines for delimitation of the EEZ and the continental shelf. In the *Gulf of Maine* case, one of the boundary lines proposed by the United States focused on the "ecological aspects of the area,"[33] which was intended to support the "single-State management as justifying the award to one Party *in toto* of the resources of Georges Bank, which is the real subject of the dispute."[34] The Chamber rejected this proposal because it was "too much geared to one aspect of the present problem for it to be capable of being considered equitable in relation to the characteristics of the case."[35] Could it be that if it was a fishery zone delimitation that had been sought, the Chamber would have delimited the zone according to ecological aspects of the maritime zones? It seems unlikely, because the Chamber was surely unwilling to engage with the "uncertainty of the distribution of the fish resources of the area according to the different ecosystems identified."[36]

In this connection, it is necessary to clarify the "neutral criteria" rhetoric that has been associated with single maritime delimitation. Circumstances relating to coastal geography were regarded as neutral criteria in the *Gulf of Maine* case, but, as pointed out by Evans, there was nothing particularly "neutral" in these circumstances albeit that they were presented in this form of language, because all the circumstances deemed relevant in this case, such as proportionality, non-encroachment, and equal division of the area of overlap, were precisely those developed by the ICJ in the continental shelf delimitation cases.[37] The use of "neutral criteria" rhetoric in the jurisprudence is more akin to a strategy of the courts and tribunals to exclude those more ambitious and controversial factors advanced by the parties, such as ecological factors, or to

[33] *The Gulf of Maine* (n 4), 316 [166].

[34] Ibid., 317 [168].

[35] Ibid.

[36] Ibid.

[37] See M. D. Evans, "Delimitation and the Common Maritime Boundary" (1994) 64 *BYIL* 283, 307.

underlie the irrelevance of geological and geomorphological factors.[38] In other words, it is not that coastal geography offers "neutral criteria" for a single maritime delimitation, but that the courts and tribunals "neutralize" the factors that were originally relevant with the continental shelf delimitation and apply them to the EEZ delimitation and the single maritime delimitation as well.[39]

Hence none of the regime-specific circumstances would assume importance in the delimitation of the continental shelf beyond 200 nm. Above all, the act of delimitation is essentially an exercise that allocates maritime space, therefore, "the ultimate goals and purposes of delimitation are at variance with its underlying concepts."[40] This is consistent with the distinction made between the rules governing maritime delimitation and the rules conferring maritime rights to coastal States.[41] Maritime delimitation is essentially about the spatial division of maritime jurisdictions, thus it is the relationship of the coasts to the area to be delimited that is the key consideration in maritime delimitation.[42] Circumstances relating to coastal geography dominate the delimitation process not because they are "neutral criteria," but because they may be the only circumstances that can satisfy the "search for predictable, objectively-determined criteria for delimitation."[43] Resource-related circumstances or conduct can hardly be disassociated from economic, social, or political considerations, even though these considerations constitute the rationale for the regimes of the EEZ and the continental shelf.[44] As to geomorphology or geology of the continental shelf, or the ecological environment of the waters, they are at variance with the legal, political, constructive, and, in a word, man-made nature of maritime boundary-making.

It is on the basis of this key consideration that a common approach to maritime delimitation within and beyond 200 nm would emerge. Once the existence of the entitlement to the continental shelf beyond 200 nm is ascertained in accordance with Article 76 of UNCLOS, the measurement

[38] Ibid., 307–308, 321.

[39] Ibid., 330.

[40] See T. Cottier, *Equitable Principles of Maritime Boundary Delimitation: The Quest for Distributive Justice in International Law* (Cambridge University Press 2015), 458.

[41] See *North Sea* (n 10), 32 [46].

[42] See Evans (n 13), 260; Tanaka (n 13), 446.

[43] *Barbados* v. *Trinidad and Tobago* (n 2), [230].

[44] See D. N. Hutchinson, "The Seaward Limit to Continental Shelf Jurisdiction in Customary International Law" (1986) 56 *BYIL* 111, 111–115.

of that entitlement begins at the coasts rather than the 200 nm limit.[45] The legal, conceptual, and physical continuity of the continental shelf beyond 200 nm with the maritime area within that distance further reinforces the connection between the coasts and the maritime area beyond 200 nm. In a scenario of overlapping entitlements within and beyond 200 nm, the continental shelf beyond 200 nm cannot be singled out from the maritime area to be delimited, and the coasts exert a controlling influence in the delimitation process. This is the case between two adjacent coastal States, and the course of the complete maritime boundary line must fully appreciate the influence of coastal configuration, as the coasts constitute the common reference line for all maritime zones.[46]

Therefore, despite the intuitively persuasive nature of the proposition concerning regime-specific considerations, international jurisprudence has consistently distanced itself from considerations of such circumstances not because they are not "neutral" in a single maritime delimitation, but because they are inherently in tension with the rules and objectives of maritime delimitation. Ultimately, maritime delimitation is about the spatial division of the area of overlap, and circumstances relating to coastal geography constitute the common denominator for maritime delimitation within and beyond 200 nm.

Nonetheless, nothing in the preceding discussion is meant to diminish the freedom of States to negotiate maritime boundary agreements by focusing on the resources of the disputed areas, the ecological environment of the maritime areas, or the geophysical features of the seabed, which, as a result, may produce boundaries that are more closely attached to one regime than the other.[47] In fact, a survey of State practice shows that States usually adopt flexible approaches to accommodating resource-related factors or other circumstances of economic nature, such as inserting common deposit clauses, establishing joint development regimes, and combining a delimitation agreement with a fisheries agreement or arrangement.[48] This may well be the case in State practice concerning the delimitation of the continental shelf beyond 200 nm.[49]

[45] See L. H. Legault and B. Hankey, "From Sea to Seabed: The Single Maritime Boundary in the Gulf of Maine Case" (1985) 79 *AJIL* 961, 983.

[46] See Reuter (n 20), 261–264.

[47] See Orrego Vicuña (n 1), 204–205.

[48] See Tanaka (n 13), 380–393.

[49] For example, Annex I and Annex II to the Treaty between the Kingdom of Norway and the Russian Federation concerning maritime Delimitation and Cooperation in the Barents Sea and the Arctic Ocean (September 15, 2010, 2791 UNTS 3) provide for

## III Integration of Maritime Delimitation within and beyond 200 NM

### *A State Practice Concerning the Continental Shelf beyond 200 NM*

State practice concerning the delimitation of the continental shelf beyond 200 nm to a considerable extent confirms the tendency towards a common approach to maritime delimitation within and beyond 200 nm. There are in total 15 boundary agreements concerning the continental shelf beyond 200 nm (Appendix 4). The majority of these agreements do not distinguish the delimitation of the continental shelf beyond 200 nm from that within 200 nm, and the continental shelf delimitation beyond 200 nm is subordinate to the overall objectives of the boundary agreement. Specifically, there are four types of approaches to delimiting the continental shelf beyond 200 nm.

#### 1 Adoption of the Same Method within and beyond 200 NM

Seven boundary agreements adopt the same delimitation method within and beyond 200 nm. Equidistance is adopted by four agreements as the sole or principal delimitation method. The 1982 Australia–France agreement is comprised of two boundary lines, one between Australia and France (New Caledonia) and the other between the Australian Heard/McDonald Islands and the French Kerguelen Islands. While the former "straightened" the equidistance line for practical reasons,[50] the latter represents a simple application of the equidistance method.[51] The 1988 Australia–Solomon Islands agreement also employs equidistance throughout this "short and simple mid-ocean boundary,"[52] and it only

detailed cooperative arrangements for fisheries and transboundary hydrocarbon deposits. Article IV of the Treaty between the Government of the United States of America and the Government of the United Mexican States on the Delimitation of the Continental Shelf in the Western Gulf of Mexico beyond 200 Nautical Miles (June 9, 2000, (2001) 44 LoSB 71) creates a 10-year moratorium on commercial oil and gas exploitation in a zone which is 1.4 nm wide on each side of the boundary.

50 C. H. Park, "Australia–France (New Caledonia), Report Number 5-1," in J. I. Charney and L. M. Alexander (eds.), *International Maritime Boundaries, Vol. I* (Martinus Nijhoff Publishers 1993), 908.

51 J. R. V. Prescott, "Australia (Heard/McDonald Islands)–France (Kerguelen Islands), Report Number 6-1," in J. I. Charney and L. M. Alexander (eds.), *International Maritime Boundaries, Vol. II* (Martinus Nijhoff Publishers 1993), 1189.

52 See C. H. Park, "Australia–Solomon Islands, Report Number 5-4," in J. I. Charney and L. M. Alexander (eds.), *International Maritime Boundaries, Vol. I* (Martinus Nijhoff Publishers 1993), 979.

slightly touches upon the continental shelf beyond 200 nm. The 2009 Barbados–France (Guadeloupe and Martinique) agreement provisionally delimits the continental shelf beyond 200 nm,[53] and the equidistance method is used throughout the entire delimitation area.[54] In the 2000 Mexico–United States agreement, equidistance continues to be applied to delimit the so-called "western gap" of the Gulf of Mexico created by the 1978 Treaty.[55] As a result of the use of equidistance, the United States renounced possible claims to approximately 62 percent of the area and Mexico renounced approximately 38 percent of the area.[56] Therefore, the 2000 agreement is subject to the overall objective of delimiting the western sector of the Gulf of Mexico even if the agreement is by itself solely concerned with the continental shelf beyond 200 nm. The parties agreed that "the geography of the coastlines that would determine the boundary line was in balance based on equidistance."[57]

The 2009 Kenya–Tanzania agreement formally delimits the EEZ and the continental shelves between the two parties, which extends the territorial sea boundary defined in their 1976 agreement.[58] A parallel line of latitude constitutes the principal delimitation method, because due to the adjacent coastal relationship and the maritime features located close to the land boundary, the use of a parallel line of latitude could prevent a cut-off effect on one of the States and maximize both countries' seaward access.[59] The continuous relevance of avoiding a cut-off effect may underlie the continuous use of the same method to the continental shelf beyond 200 nm.[60]

[53] See Article 3.1 of the Agreement between the Government of Barbados and the Government of the French Republic on the Delimitation of the Maritime Space between Barbados and France (October 15, 2009, 2663 UNTS 163).

[54] C. W. Dundas, "Barbados–France (Guadeloupe and Martinique), Report Number 2-30," in D. A. Colson and R. W. Smith (eds.), *International Maritime Boundaries, Vol. V* (Brill Nijhoff Publishers 2011), 4225–4226.

[55] See R. W. Smith, "Mexico–United States, Report Number 1-5(2)," in J. I. Charney and R. W. Smith (eds.), *International Maritime Boundaries, Vol. IV* (Martinus Nijhoff Publishers 2002), 2626.

[56] Ibid., 2625.

[57] Ibid., 2623.

[58] See M. Pratt, "Kenya–Tanzania, Report Number 4-5(2)," in C. G. Lathrop (ed.), *International Maritime Boundaries, Vol. VII* (Brill Nijhoff Publishers 2016), 4781.

[59] See A. O. Adede, "Kenya–Tanzania, Report Number 4-5," in J. I. Charney and L. M. Alexander (eds.), *International Maritime Boundaries, Vol. I* (Martinus Nijhoff Publishers 1993), 877.

[60] Chapter 8, Section II.A.

The remaining two agreements, namely the 2017 France (French Guiana)–Suriname agreement and the 1990 Trinidad and Tobago–Venezuela agreement, do not specify the delimitation methods, but in both agreements the boundary lines within 200 nm extend to the continental shelf beyond 200 nm without a change of direction. Thus, the continental shelf delimitation beyond 200 nm is part and parcel of the entire delimitation process. The 1990 Trinidad and Tobago–Venezuela agreement is a settlement in favor of Venezuela because it deviates from an equidistance line in order to give Venezuela a corridor to access the Atlantic Ocean.[61] The maritime boundary has already been adjusted within 200 nm. From Point 20, the boundary line goes in a true northerly direction for 6 nm, arriving at Point 21, after which the boundary bends and extends in a northeasterly direction for 163 nm until Point 22, a point located on the approximate outer edge of the continental margin.[62] The maritime boundary in the 2017 France (French Guiana)–Suriname agreement, for its part, consists of two segments. While the first, short, segment follows an azimuth of 24.5 degrees for approximately 15 nm, the second segment follows an azimuth of 27 degrees in an open-ended fashion, which is expected to intersect with the outer limits of the continental shelf of France.[63]

### 2 Combination of Methods for an Overall Equitable Solution

Three agreements employ a flexible approach to maritime delimitation, employing a variety of methods throughout the delimitation process in order to achieve an overall equitable result.

The 1988 Ireland–United Kingdom agreement establishes two continental shelf boundaries between the two countries that extend well beyond 200 nm, and it serves the particular purpose of facilitating offshore petroleum exploration and exploitation.[64] The boundary lines are

61 K. G. Nweihed, "Trinidad and Tobago–Venezuela, Report Number 2-13(3)," in J. I. Charney and L. M. Alexander (eds.), *International Maritime Boundaries, Vol. I* (Martinus Nijhoff Publishers 1993), 681–682.

62 Ibid., 680–681.

63 See S. Benjamin, "France (French Guiana)–Suriname, Report Number 3-11," in C. G. Lathrop (ed.), *International Maritime Boundaries, Vol. VIII* (Brill Nijhoff Publishers 2019), 3.

64 The Preamble of the agreement specifies that the two parties wish "to open up further opportunities for their respective offshore petroleum and related industries." See the Agreement between the Republic of Ireland and the United Kingdom of Great Britain and Northern Ireland Concerning the Delimitation of the Continental Shelf between the Two Countries (November 7, 1988, 1765 UNTS 42).

"stepped" because they follow parallel lines of latitude and meridians of longitude so that the lines could accommodate the two governments' block systems as far as possible.[65] The stepped boundary lines extend to areas beyond 200 nm, and the termini of the boundary lines are located on the approximate outer limits of the continental shelf by applying Article 76 of UNCLOS.[66] Although the pattern and shape of the boundary lines are zigzag-like, it is suggested that the lines do not depart markedly from equidistance lines.[67] The delimitation of the continental shelf beyond 200 nm is integral to the delimitation process, and subject to the overall pragmatic methodology whose primary objective is resource-production oriented.

The 1990 United States–Soviet Union agreement produces the longest maritime boundary in the world, which is approximately 1,600 nm in length.[68] Different methods are used in different segments of the boundary, and various factors such as fisheries and hydrocarbon resources were prominent in the negotiations.[69] The boundary line delimits the continental shelf beyond 200 nm in the Arctic, North Pacific Ocean, and Bering and Chukchi Seas. No specific method was uniquely used for the continental shelf beyond 200 nm. On the contrary, the boundary line places most of the area beyond 200 nm of the Bering Sea under the jurisdiction of the United States, which demonstrates that the delimitation of the continental shelf beyond 200 nm was negotiated as part of the package.[70]

The 2010 Norway–Russia agreement also applies different methods for different segments of the boundary. As to the continental shelf beyond 200 nm, while the boundary line delimiting the continental shelf beyond 200 nm in the Arctic Ocean follows essentially an equidistance line, the other segment delimiting the Loop Hole of the Barents Sea departs significantly from an equidistance line, leaving most of the continental

[65] See D. H. Anderson, "Ireland–United Kingdom, Report Number 9-5," in J. I. Charney and L. M. Alexander (eds.), *International Maritime Boundaries, Vol. II* (Martinus Nijhoff Publishers 1993), 1770.

[66] Ibid.

[67] See D. A. Colson, "The Delimitation of the Outer Continental Shelf between Neighboring States" (2003) 97 *AJIL* 91, 95.

[68] E. G. Verville, "United States–Soviet Union, Report Number 1-6," in I. L. Charney and L. M. Alexander (eds.), *International Maritime Boundaries, Vol.I* (Martinus Nijhoff Publishers 1993), 447–448.

[69] See B. M. Magnússon, "Outer Continental Shelf Boundary Agreements" (2013) 62 *ICLQ* 345, 356.

[70] Verville (n 68), 451.

shelf beyond 200 nm in this area under the jurisdiction of Russia.[71] It is interesting to note that the shift of the equidistance line in favor of Russia in the Loop Hole is a result of taking into account the disparities in coastal lengths of the two countries.[72] Nevertheless, methods are secondary to the primary goal of equal division of the relevant area, because the delimitation achieves a division of the disputed area of 175,200 km$^2$ into two areas of a total equal size of 87,600 km$^2$ in maritime areas of the Barents Sea and the Arctic Ocean.[73]

The flexible approach to achieving an overall equitable solution can also be seen from the innovative and pragmatic approach to the "grey area" issue. All three agreements produced "grey areas" that are located beyond the 200 nm of one party, but within its side of the maritime boundary, because the relevant boundary lines are not equidistance lines. The parties to these agreements decided to exchange or transfer their EEZ rights or continental shelf rights to the other party so that each party could exercise jurisdiction in all their maritime zones within 200 nm.[74] These practices are in line with the jurisprudence that the potential creation of "grey areas" is not a relevant circumstance in the delimitation process. Instead, avoiding conflicts in the exercise of maritime jurisdictions in the "grey area" is a post-delimitation issue to be addressed through cooperation by the relevant parties.

### 3 Specific Arrangements for the Continental Shelf beyond 200 NM

In three other agreements, specific arrangements are made for the continental shelf beyond 200 nm. The 2006 Agreements between Denmark (Faroe Islands), Iceland, and Norway divide the area beyond 200 nm by sharing out the area subject to delimitation, with provisions allowing for subsequent adjustment of the provisional lines in accordance with fixed ratios assigned to the respective party.[75] The parties did not formulate a particular legal reasoning that dictated the outcome, though it has been reported that disparities in coastal lengths and maritime delimitation

71 See R. E. Fife, "Norway–Russia Federation, Report Number 9-6(3)," in C. G. Lathrop (ed.), *International Maritime Boundaries, Vol. VII* (Brill Nijhoff Publishers 2016), 5188.

72 Chapter 8, Section III.B.

73 Fife (n 71), 5185.

74 See discussion in Chapter 3, Section III.D.

75 See R. E. Fife, "Denmark/The Faroes–Iceland–Norway, Report Number 9-26," in D. A. Colson and R. W. Smith (eds.), *International Maritime Boundaries, Vol. VI* (Martinus Nijhoff Publishers 2011), 4548.

agreements within 200 nm may have contributed to assessing what could constitute an equitable solution with regard to the delimitation beyond 200 nm.[76]

The 2013 Denmark (Greenland)–Iceland Agreed Minutes provisionally delimit the continental shelf beyond 200 nm between the two countries, which connects the terminus of the single maritime boundary for the continental shelf and the fishery zone within 200 nm reached by the two parties in 1997.[77] The 2013 Denmark (Greenland)–Iceland Agreed Minutes divided the area of overlap with a fixed ration because the equidistance method previously used in the 1997 agreement can no longer accurately divide the area of overlapping entitlements to the continental shelf beyond 200 nm.[78]

The 2004 Australia–New Zealand agreement establishes maritime boundaries for the EEZ and the continental shelves. Whereas equidistance is applied to delimit the maritime zones within 200 nm, the delimitation of the continental shelf beyond 200 nm departs from equidistance lines due to the consideration of New Zealand's entitlement to the continental shelf beyond 200 nm.[79] This agreement is one of the rare occasions in State practice that geomorphological or geological factors play a decisive role in the delimitation of the continental shelf beyond 200 nm.[80]

## 4 Separate Lines for the Continental Shelves and the EEZ

The 1978 Australia–Papua New Guinea agreement and the 1997 Australia–Indonesia agreement establish separate boundaries for the continental shelves and the EEZ. The 1978 Australia–Papua New Guinea agreement deals with four types of maritime boundaries and addresses various related issues in a very difficult geographical area.[81]

[76] Ibid., 4543.

[77] See Agreement between the Government of the Kingdom of Denmark along with the Local Government of Greenland on the one hand and the Government of the Republic of Iceland on the other hand on the Delimitation of the Continental Shelf and Fishery Zone in the Area between Greenland and Iceland (November 11, 1997), (1999) 39 LoSB 35.

[78] See B. M. Magnússon, "Denmark (Greenland)–Iceland, Report Number 9-22 (2)," in C. G. Lathrop (ed.), *International Maritime Boundaries, Vol. VII* (Brill Nijhoff Publishers 2016), 5265.

[79] See N. Fyfe and G. French, "Australia–New Zealand, Report Number 5-26," in D. A. Colson and R. W. Smith (eds.), *International Maritime Boundaries, Vol. V* (Martinus Nijhoff Publishers 2005), 3764.

[80] Chapter 7, Section II.B.

[81] See Magnússon (n 69), 351.

Most of the agreement relating to the seabed does not concern the continental shelf beyond 200 nm, and only in the Coral Sea does a small segment of the maritime boundary extend beyond 200 nm.[82] As a result, it is difficult to ascertain the correlation between the delimitation methods and the continental shelf beyond 200 nm.

As to the 1997 Australia–Indonesia agreement, in the continental shelf delimitation, the western part of the seabed boundary is located along a line 60 nm seaward of the foot of the continental slope of the Australian continental margin, thus Australia acquired a continental shelf beyond 200 nm in this area even though the distance between the two parties is less than 400 nm.[83] The consideration of geophysics of the seabed in the 1997 agreement seems to be a continuation of the 1972 agreement concerning the Timor Sea and the Arafura Sea; the latter was concluded in the aftermath of the 1969 *North Sea* continental shelf cases and the impact of geomorphology and geology upon the course of the seabed boundary was strong.[84]

To sum up, a majority of maritime boundary agreements concerning the continental shelf beyond 200 nm either apply the same delimitation method throughout the delimitation within and beyond 200 nm, or employ a combination of methods that is aimed at an overall equitable solution without distinguishing the delimitation beyond 200 nm from that within 200 nm. What is common among these agreements is that the area of the continental shelf beyond 200 nm is deemed part of the entire area subject to delimitation. Even if the entitlement to the continental shelf beyond 200 nm is established differently, this fact has very limited impact on the delimitation process in the majority of cases.

Even in agreements where specific arrangements are made for the continental shelf beyond 200 nm, principles and considerations relevant in maritime delimitation within 200 nm continue to guide the delimitation beyond that distance, which is another proof of the integration of maritime delimitation within and beyond 200 nm. The delimitation lines in the 2006 Agreed Minutes between Denmark (Faroe Islands), Iceland, and Norway, to a certain degree, resemble equidistance lines,[85] whereas the 2013 Denmark (Greenland)–Iceland Agreed Minutes are settled on an approximate equal division of the area of overlap.[86]

[82] See ibid.
[83] See ibid., 357.
[84] See Tanaka (n 13), 297.
[85] Fife (n 75), 4543.
[86] Magnússon (n 78), 5270.

Although in some agreements the delimitation of the continental shelf beyond 200 nm is subject to separate considerations, this is because of the mutual agreement of the parties to assign weight to geophysical factors or to have separate lines for different maritime zones. Nevertheless, these practices are in the minority. In any event, maritime boundary agreements are outcomes of political compromises, thus one should be mindful of not inferring normative conclusions from these practices.[87]

### B *The Trend of a Single Exercise of Maritime Delimitation*

At last, there is already a strong tendency towards the unification of the law of maritime delimitation in respect of the territorial sea, the EEZ, and the continental shelf. This general background of the normative development of the law of maritime delimitation should be kept in mind in the formulation and application of the methodology for the continental shelf beyond 200 nm.

The process of unification of the law of maritime delimitation took place first through the assimilation of the legal principles and rules of maritime delimitation. As early as the *Anglo-French Arbitration*, the Court of Arbitration found a close connection between Article 6 of the 1958 Convention on the Continental Shelf (CCS) and the equitable principles under customary international law, and "in the circumstances of the present case, the rules of customary law lead to much the same result as the provisions of Article 6."[88] Moreover, the Court of Arbitration stated that "the rules of customary law are a relevant and even essential means both for interpreting and completing the provisions of Article 6."[89] Subsequently, the *Jan Mayen* case assimilated Article 6 of the CCS with customary rules governing the delimitation of the continental shelf and the fishery zone, and observed that:

[87] See Lando (n 13), 293; M. Mendelson, "On the Quasi-Normative Effect of Maritime Boundary Agreements," in N. Ando et al. (eds.), *Liber Amicorum Judge Shigeru Oda, Volume II* (Kluwer Law International 2002), 1077–1083; P. Weil, "Geographical Considerations in Maritime Delimitation," in J. I. Charney and L. M. Alexander (eds.), *International Maritime Boundaries, Volume I* (Martinus Nijhoff Publishers 1993), 123; B. M. Magnússon, "Is There a Temporal Relationship between the Delineation and the Delimitation of the Continental Shelf beyond 200 Nautical Miles?" (2013) 28 *IJMCL* 465, 471.

[88] *Delimitation of the Continental Shelf between the United Kingdom of Great Britain and Northern Ireland, and the French Republic (United Kingdom/France) (1978) 18 RIAA 3* [65].

[89] Ibid., [75].

> The fact that it is the 1958 Convention which applies to the continental shelf delimitation in this case does not mean that Article 6 thereof can be interpreted and applied either without reference to customary law on the subject, or wholly independently of the fact that a fishery zone boundary is also in question in these waters.[90]

In fact, the ICJ found that the boundary for the fishery zones (delimited on the basis of customary international law) and the boundary for the continental shelf (delimited on the basis of Article 6 of the CCS) were coincident at all points.[91] In the *Qatar* v. *Bahrain* case, the ICJ further unified the delimitation rules governing territorial sea with those governing the continental shelf and the EEZ:

> [T]he equidistance/special circumstances rule, which is applicable in particular to the delimitation of the territorial sea, and the equitable principles/relevant circumstances rule, as it has been developed since 1958 in case-law and State practice with regard to the delimitation of the continental shelf and the exclusive economic zone, are closely interrelated.[92]

In the words of President Guillaume regarding the *Qatar* v. *Bahrain* case, the Court "unified the law of maritime delimitation – whether the continental shelf, territorial sea or the exclusive economic zone – in holding that in all these cases it was necessary to first draw the line of equidistance, then adjust it to take account of relevant factors related mainly to the coastline."[93] The *Qatar* v. *Bahrain* case thus marked the unification of the law of maritime delimitation not only with respect to the governing rules, but also to the delimitation methodology.[94] In the view of Anderson, the courts and tribunals harmonized the delimitation approaches to delimiting the territorial sea, the EEZ, and the continental shelf.[95] As further summarized in the *Cameroon* v. *Nigeria* case:

> The Court has on various occasions made it clear what the applicable criteria, principles and rules of delimitation are when a line covering

90 See *Jan Mayen* (n 16), 58–59 [46].

91 See ibid., 79–81 [90–93].

92 *Qatar* v. *Bahrain* (n 3), 111 [231].

93 G. Guillaume, "The Use of Precedent by International Judges and Arbitrators" (2011) 2 *JIDS* 5, 11–12.

94 This case is particularly telling for it applied, for the first time, the corrective-equity approach in the delimitation between States with adjacent coasts. See Tanaka (n 13), 98.

95 D. Anderson, "Developments in Maritime Boundary Law and Practice," in D. A. Colson and R. W. Smith (eds.), *International Maritime Boundaries, Volume V* (Brill Nijhoff Publishers 2005), 3209.

> several zones of coincident jurisdictions is to be determined. They are expressed in the so-called equitable principles/relevant circumstances method. This method, which is very similar to the equidistance/special circumstances method applicable in delimitation of the territorial sea, involves first drawing an equidistance line, then considering whether there are factors calling for the adjustment or shifting of that line in order to achieve an "equitable result."[96]

Consequently, despite the fundamental differences in the nature of the territorial sea and the continental shelf and the EEZ, the law of maritime delimitation is unified under the corrective-equity approach.[97] Such a trend is further confirmed by the practice of a single exercise of delimiting the territorial sea, the EEZ, and the continental shelf where the parties request a single line to be drawn across these maritime zones. In the *Qatar* v. *Bahrain* case, although the ICJ distinguished the task of the territorial sea delimitation from that of the continental shelf and the EEZ delimitation, it nonetheless acknowledged "that its ultimate task is to draw a single maritime boundary that serves other purposes as well."[98] In the *Nicaragua* v. *Honduras* case, when it came to the drawing of the bisector line to be constructed from the mainland, the Court "'grouped' together the delimitation of the territorial sea with that of the continental shelf and the EEZ – thereby subsuming this part of the territorial sea delimitation under the overall, 'single' delimitation line."[99] In a more controversial move, the *Croatia/Slovenia Arbitration* transplanted the delimitation rule for the territorial sea under Article 15 of UNCLOS to the delimitation of the continental shelf and the EEZ by stating that "[i]n relation to the delimitation both of the territorial sea and of the maritime zones beyond the territorial sea, international law thus calls for the application of an equidistance line, unless another line is required by special circumstances."[100] The formulation of the methodology is debatable,[101] and it is doubtful whether the disproportionality test under the

[96] *Cameroon* v. *Nigeria* (n 28), 441 [288].

[97] See Tanaka (n 13), 168.

[98] *Qatar* v. *Bahrain* (n 3), 93 [174].

[99] D. Vidas, "The Delimitation of the Territorial Sea, the Continental Shelf, and the EEZ – A Comparative Perspective," in A. G. Oude Elferink et al. (eds.), *Maritime Boundary Delimitation: The Case Law: Is It Consistent and Predictable?* (Cambridge University Press 2018), 49.

[100] *Arbitration between Croatia and Slovenia under the Arbitration Agreement of 4 November 2009 (Croatia/Slovenia), Award of 29 June 2017* [1000].

[101] In fact, considerable uncertainties arise from the interpretation and application of Article 15 of UNCLOS, in particular with respect to whether special circumstances are

three-stage approach for the delimitation of the continental shelf and the EEZ finds a place in the territorial sea delimitation.[102] Notably, however, in the *Ghana/Côte d'Ivoire* case, while the Special Chamber stressed that "under the Convention different rules apply to the delimitation of territorial seas and the delimitation of exclusive economic zones and continental shelves,"[103] it considered it appropriate to use the same methodology for the delimitation of the parties' territorial sea, EEZ and the continental shelves within and beyond 200 nm, which was largely out of the agreement of the parties.[104]

In the light of the trend towards a unification of the law and methodology of maritime delimitation, it is not surprising that the continental shelf delimitation beyond 200 nm is increasingly subsumed in the single exercise of maritime delimitation within and beyond 200 nm. The *Bangladesh/Myanmar* case did not complete the drawing of a provisional equidistance line even within the 200 nm limits,[105] and it adjusted the provisional line to account for the concavity of the coasts of Bangladesh.[106] Therefore, when the Tribunal applied the three-stage approach to the continental shelf beyond 200 nm, it in fact extended the adjusted equidistance line to the area beyond 200 nm, a decision

exception to the use of equidistance or factors correcting a provisional equidistance line. The latter interpretation will be in line with the formulation of the two-stage or three-stage approach in delimiting the continental shelf and the EEZ. In the *Nicaragua* v. *Honduras* case, however, the ICJ suggested that "special circumstances" not only operates as a corrective element to a line already drawn, but also in itself constitutes an exception that justifies the use of an alternative method. See *Territorial and Maritime Dispute between Nicaragua and Honduras in the Caribbean Sea (Nicaragua v. Honduras) [2007] ICJ Rep 659, 733-734* [280]. For a discussion on the conceptual and practical confusion arising out of the delimitation methodology for the territorial sea, see Vidas (n 99), 47–61; M. Lando, "Judicial Uncertainties Concerning Territorial Sea Delimitation under Article 15 of the United Nations Convention on the Law of the Sea" (2017) 66 *ICLQ* 589.

102 In the *Costa Rica* v. *Nicaragua* case, the ICJ describes the delimitation methodology for the territorial sea as: "In accordance with its established jurisprudence, the Court will proceed in *two stages*: first, the Court will draw a provisional median line; second, it will consider whether any special circumstances exist which justify adjusting such a line," *Maritime Delimitation in the Caribbean Sea and the Pacific Ocean (Costa Rica v. Nicaragua) and Land Boundary in the Northern Part of Isla Portillos (Costa Rica v. Nicaragua) [2018] ICJ Rep 139, 177* [98] (emphasis added).

103 *Ghana/Côte d'Ivoire* (n 5), [260].

104 Ibid., [263].

105 See *Delimitation of the Maritime Boundary in the Bay of Bengal (Bangladesh/Myanmar) (Judgment) [2012] ITLOS Rep 4,* 189 (Separate Opinion of Judge Cot).

106 Ibid., 87–89 [323–336].

based on the application of the same delimitation methodology and the consideration of the same relevant circumstances.[107] The *Bangladesh* v. *India* case, on the contrary, applied the three-stage approach to maritime delimitation within and beyond 200 nm in a single exercise, for the Arbitral Tribunal drew a provisional equidistance line throughout the maritime areas within and beyond 200 nm, and decided the scope and manners of adjustment *after* considering the relevant circumstance (i.e., the concavity of the coast) within and beyond 200 nm.[108] The *Ghana/Côte d'Ivoire* case drew a provisional equidistance line throughout all these maritime zones until it reached the outer limits of the continental shelf beyond 200 nm.[109] Although the Special Chamber addressed the delimitation of the continental shelf beyond 200 nm separately, it succinctly decided that it was "inappropriate to make a distinction between the continental shelf within and beyond 200 nm as far as the delimitation methodology is concerned,"[110] and rejected all the relevant circumstances proposed by the parties so that the provisional line became the final boundary line.[111] Accordingly, the application of the three-stage approach in the *Bangladesh/Myanmar* case was dominated by the maritime delimitation within 200 nm, whereas the three-stage approach was applied to the maritime delimitation within and beyond 200 nm as a single exercise in the *Bangladesh* v. *India* case and the *Ghana/Côte d'Ivoire* case.

The jurisprudence thus demonstrates a strong tendency towards the unification of the delimitation methodology – whether under customary international law or treaty rules, under the CCS or UNCLOS, and regardless of whether the maritime zones to be delimited are territorial sea, continental shelf, EEZ, or a single maritime boundary for all these zones.[112] The common approach to maritime delimitation reflects the idea that maritime delimitation is an identical exercise for all maritime areas.[113] Legal principles, rules, and relevant circumstances, once developed in the continental shelf delimitation in the early jurisprudence, migrated into the single maritime delimitation that simultaneously

[107] See ibid., 117–118 [455–462].

[108] See *Bangladesh* v. *India* (n 7), [421], [460–463], and [473–475].

[109] *Ghana/Côte d'Ivoire* (n 5), [401].

[110] Ibid., [526].

[111] Ibid., [540].

[112] See J. Shi, "Maritime Delimitation in the Jurisprudence of the International Court of Justice" (2010) 9 *Chinese JIL* 271, 290–291.

[113] See Weil (n 1), 115.

divides the EEZ and the continental shelf.[114] The *Bay of Bengal* cases and the *Ghana/Côte d'Ivoire* case are the most recent examples confirming this trend in the continental shelf delimitation beyond 200 nm, at least as far as delimitation between adjacent coastal relationships is concerned. As pointed out earlier, however, such a scenario accounts for the majority of the cases where there might be overlapping entitlements to the continental shelf beyond 200 nm, which may be another factor that strengthens the unification of the common approach to maritime delimitation within and beyond 200 nm.

## IV Prospect of the Continental Shelf Delimitation beyond 200 NM

It is likely that the delimitation of the continental shelf beyond 200 nm will increasingly be a subject of interest for States, given the unexpected large number of submissions that are already made or to be made to the Commission on the Limits of the Continental Shelf (CLCS or "the Commission").[115]A consistent, coherent, and stable body of jurisprudence will therefore be desirable for encouraging coastal States to settle their disputes concerning the continental shelf beyond 200 nm through peaceful means, including through third-party dispute settlement mechanisms. At the same time, the healthy development of the law of maritime delimitation will also largely depend on how international courts and tribunals handle the delimitation of the continental shelf beyond 200 nm, which is particularly challenging due to the particularity of establishing the entitlement to the continental shelf beyond 200 nm.

The ICJ, ITLOS, and UNCLOS Annex VII tribunal have been consistent in upholding the conceptual distinction between delineation of the outer limits of the continental shelf and the delimitation of the continental shelf beyond 200 nm, which underlies the competence of international courts and tribunals to delimit the continental shelf beyond 200 nm in the absence of recommendations of the CLCS. It is expected, however, that in deciding the admissibility of a claim to delimit the continental shelf beyond 200 nm, more attention could be given to the implications of the entitlement for delineation and delimitation. Due to the fact that establishing the entitlement to the continental shelf beyond 200 nm is integral to both the delineation process and the delimitation

[114] See D. A. Colson, "The United Kingdom–France Continental Shelf Arbitration" (1978) 72 *AJIL* 95, 111.

[115] See Chapter 1, Section I.

process, a conceptual distinction between delineation and delimitation may fall short of accurately capturing the interaction between delineation and delimitation in a given context. In particular, factual certainty of the existence and/or the extent of the entitlement to the continental shelf beyond 200 nm may prove to be a key factor in the judicial decision-making process. On the one hand, international courts and tribunals may lack the capacity or incentive to engage with fact-intensive exercises in relation to establishing the entitlement to the continental shelf beyond 200 nm. On the other, where the existence of the continental shelf entitlement is debated or where the constitutive elements of the entitlement (e.g., the FOS, outer edge of the continental margin, and the outer limits of the continental shelf) must be specified for purposes of determining the area of overlap, a judicial decision on these matters may run the risk of replacing the function of the CLCS or conflicting with the findings of the CLCS, thus creating complex legal and legitimate difficulties incompatible with the institutional framework under UNCLOS.

It is recalled that ITLOS interpreted a complementary role of the CLCS and the tribunals out of the institutional arrangement of UNCLOS.[116] This complementary role is not, and cannot be, premised on neat separateness between delineation and delimitation, or between the mandate of the CLCS in establishing the outer limits and the competence of courts and tribunals to delimit the continental shelf beyond 200 nm. Rather, it arises out of the fact that, in certain circumstances, the issues falling within the mandate of one institution constitute the basis for the effective operation of the other. As maritime delimitation presupposes an area of overlapping entitlements, recommendations of the CLCS that ascertain the existence and extent of the entitlement provide the most authoritative evidence that a court or tribunal could rely on for purposes of maritime delimitation. This, however, by no means suggests that there is a temporal relationship between delineation and delimitation in principle; whether such a temporal relationship exists is a question that cannot be answered in abstract.[117] What follows is that the competence of a court or tribunal to delimit the continental shelf beyond 200 nm before the parties receive recommendations from the CLCS is also a case-specific question. In this respect, international courts and tribunals should resist the temptation to reach overly general conclusions regarding the relationship between delineation and delimitation out of

[116] See *Bangladesh/Myanmar* (n 105), 98 [373].
[117] See Chapter 3, Section II, and Chapter 4, Section III.C.3.

narrowly defined procedural and geographical frameworks. In particular, it is important to bear in mind that the circumstances that allow the *Bay of Bengal* cases and *Ghana/Côte d'Ivoire* case to delimit the continental shelf beyond 200 nm may not be present in other cases with different geographical and procedural contexts. Therefore, it is the CLCS that has a primary role to ascertain the existence and extent of the entitlement to the continental shelf beyond 200 nm, which constitutes the factual basis for a delimitation decided by a court.[118]

Another aspect of the complementary role of the CLCS and courts and tribunals that can be developed is the contribution of the judiciary to removing the obstacles in the delineation process in the work of the CLCS by settling legal disputes. It has been argued that the exclusion of legal expertise from the CLCS "makes it possible to insulate the CLCS to a large extent from (the resolution of) legal disputes and have it focus on the tasks which have been entrusted to it under the Convention."[119] This could only be possible where the legal disputes do not relate to the legal basis for the submitting State's right to establish the entitlement to the continental shelf beyond 200 nm.[120] The input of courts and tribunals can be significant in cases concerning territorial disputes, disputes concerning Article 121(3), or disputes concerning the applicability of the Statement of Understanding in regions outside the southern Bay of Bengal, because on these occasions clarification of the legal issues could remove the legal uncertainties underlying a submitting State's very entitlement to establish the outer limits of the continental shelf through the CLCS. Similarly, in a particularly challenging case such as that of *Nicaragua* v. *Colombia II*, it seems that the successful settlement of the dispute has to combine the work of the ICJ and that of the CLCS. While the CLCS has the main role of verifying the claim of Nicaragua to a continental shelf beyond 200 nm, the ICJ may undertake to clarify whether Nicaragua's alleged continental shelf beyond 200 nm could encroach on a 200 nm shelf of Colombia, a non-party to UNCLOS. To block Nicaragua's submission before the CLCS may force both tasks onto

[118] See L. D. M. Nelson, "The Continental Shelf: Interplay of Law and Science," in N. Ando et al. (eds.), *Liber Amicorum Judge Shigeru Oda, Volume II* (Kluwer Law International 2002), 1253.

[119] A. G. Oude Elferink, "The Continental Shelf beyond 200 NM: The Relationship between the CLCS and Third Party Dispute Settlement," in A. G. Oude Elferink and D. R. Rothwell (eds.), *Oceans Management in the 21st Century: Institutional Frameworks and Responses* (Martinus Nijhoff Publishers 2004), 123.

[120] Chapter 4, Section IV.

the ICJ, and the lack of a recommendation from the CLCS may prevent the Court from reaching a legally sound conclusion on the basis of accurate and comprehensive factual information.

In addition to the procedural issues, the delimitation of the continental shelf beyond 200 nm remains to be refined in terms of delimitation methodology. Here again, whether the geomorphology- or geology-based entitlement to the continental shelf beyond 200 nm introduces a new dimension to be taken into account in the delimitation methodology has been a puzzle ever since the *Libya/Malta* case excluded geomorphological or geological factors from maritime delimitation within 200 nm.[121] Essentially, it is a question that arises out of the relationship between the basis of entitlement and maritime delimitation.[122] The latter issue is, however, not a major concern of the recent jurisprudence, which has been oriented towards the formulation and application of delimitation methodology. In any event, it might be unwise to over-conceptualize their relationship because rules governing maritime entitlements and those governing maritime delimitation are discrete and have different objectives. While the former provides coastal States with the maximum seaward limits allowed under international law, the latter rather aims to divide the overlap of two or more equally valid entitlements so that the maritime entitlements could produce their effects "in a reasonable and mutually balanced way."[123] Given the spatial nature of the exercise of maritime delimitation, there is no intrinsic reason why elements constitutive of the maritime entitlement should be accounted for in this process.

That said, international courts and tribunals may still need to address the implications of the entitlement to the continental shelf beyond 200 nm in connection with the application of the three-stage approach, which is now the reference methodology. Arguments for introducing geomorphological or geological factors into the delimitation of the continental shelf beyond 200 nm will probably be put forward in connection with the adjustment of the line provisionally constructed. The *Bangladesh/Myanmar* case made clear that once the existence of

[121] *Libya/Malta* (n 12), 35 [39].

[122] See N. Marques Antunes and V. Becker-Weinberg, "Entitlement to Maritime Zones and Their Delimitation: In the Doldrums of Uncertainty and Unpredictability," in A. G. Oude Elferink et al. (eds.), *Maritime Boundary Delimitation: The Case Law: Is It Consistent and Predictable?* (Cambridge University Press 2018), 86–88.

[123] *Black Sea* (n 18), 127 [201].

overlapping entitlements to the continental shelf beyond 200 nm was ascertained, there would be no room for arguing for a larger share of the continental shelf beyond 200 nm on the basis of the so-called superiority of geology over geomorphology.[124] Whereas ITLOS prudently concluded that such argument "has no relevance *to the present case*,"[125] it is foreseeable that future cases will reach the same conclusion on the irrelevance of geomorphological or geological factors in the delimitation process, whose role is confined to the determination of the area of overlapping entitlements. Legal criteria that would support an analysis of the "relative naturalness" of continental shelf entitlements by reference to elements of Article 76 of UNCLOS are non-existent, nor are there any legal justifications for effecting a maritime delimitation on the basis of the natural components of the seabed, no matter how significant they are in geomorphological or geological terms.[126]

On the contrary, coastal geography tends to have a continuing relevance in the delimitation of the continental shelf beyond 200 nm. The principle that "the land dominates the sea" continues to govern the delimitation process, even though the maritime area to be divided lies further to the coasts. Circumstances relating to coastal geography, such as coastal configuration, substantial disparities in coastal lengths, and the existence of incidental maritime features, remain the principal relevant circumstances in the delimitation of the continental shelf beyond 200 nm, in particular in cases concerning maritime delimitation within and beyond 200 nm.

Therefore, a common approach to maritime boundary-making within and beyond 200 nm may crystalize over time. This has emerged in the *Bay of Bengal* cases and the *Ghana/Côte d'Ivoire* case through the declaration of the applicability of the same delimitation methodology (i.e., the three-stage approach) throughout the delimitation process, but this is only on the "surface." If one delves into the "depths" of the law of maritime delimitation, it will be found that the common approach to maritime delimitation within and beyond 200 nm stems from the principles and relevant circumstances that have been the fabric of the law ever since the *North Sea* cases: non-cut-off, disproportionality, "equity does not imply equality," the distinction between delimitation and apportionment, equal division of the area of overlap, etc. It is to be

[124] *Bangladesh/Myanmar* (n 105), 118 [460].
[125] Ibid. (emphasis added).
[126] Chapter 7, Section II.B. and III.A.

remembered that these principles and relevant circumstances arose out of the continental shelf delimitation in the first place. Just as international courts and tribunals "neutralized" these principles and relevant circumstances in order to delimit the fishery zone, the EEZ, and the single maritime delimitation of the EEZ and the continental shelf, it could be equally expected that the judiciary will resort to the existing concepts, principles, and relevant circumstances in the delimitation of the continental shelf beyond 200 nm, instead of basing their decision on more radical or entirely new elements advanced by the parties to the dispute. Above all, clarification of the continuing relevance of coastal geography and the irrelevance of geomorphology and geology will be the most definitive step towards the unification of the approach to maritime delimitation within and beyond 200 nm.

Finally, a word of qualification is, as always, needed. Since it is often the hard cases that end up in litigations,[127] there is good chance that a court or tribunal may deviate from an established delimitation methodology in order to address the complex factual and legal difficulties arising in a specific context.[128] As rightly observed by Weil, "The judicial fluctuations are an unavoidable fact of life, bearing witness to the vitality of the subject-matter."[129] Therefore, perhaps more patience is required before a common approach to maritime delimitation within and beyond 200 nm can take shape and stabilize.

[127] See L. Legault and B. Hankey, "Method, Oppositeness and Adjacency, and Proportionality in Maritime Boundary Delimitation," in J. I. Charney and L. M. Alexander (eds.), *International Maritime Boundaries, Volume I* (Martinus Nijhoff Publishers 1993), 205.

[128] See M. D. Evans, "Maritime Boundary Delimitation," in D. R. Rothwell et al. (eds.), *The Oxford Handbook of the Law of the Sea* (Oxford University Press 2015), 278.

[129] Weil (n 1), 11.

# Appendix 1

**Individual submissions wherein states refrain from encroaching on neighboring states' 200 nm limits**
(in chronological order by date of submission)[1]

| | Submitting State | Date of submission | Neighboring States | Methods of self-restraint |
|---|---|---|---|---|
| 1 | Australia | November 15, 2004 | Non-Australian islands (Three Kings Ridge Region) | Fixed points on the 200 nm limits of the neighboring State |
| 2 | New Zealand | June 19, 2006 | Australia, Fiji, and Tonga | Fixed points on the 200 nm limits of the neighboring State |
| 3 | Norway (North East Atlantic and the Arctic) | November 27, 2006 | Denmark (Faroes), Iceland, and Russia | Fixed points on the 200 nm limits of the neighboring State |
| 4 | France (New Caledonia) | May 22, 2007 | Australia | Fixed points on the 200 nm limits of the neighboring State |
| 5 | Japan | November 12, 2008 | Federated States of Micronesia, Palau, and the United States | Fixed points on the 200 nm limits of the neighboring State |
| 6 | United Kingdom (Hatton Rockall Area) | March 31, 2009 | Iceland | Endpoints deliberately stop short of the 200 nm limits of the neighboring State |
| 7 | The Cook Islands (Manihiki Plateau) | April 16, 2009 | Kiribati and the United States | Fixed points on the 200 nm limits of the neighboring State |
| 8 | Ghana | April 28, 2009 | Nigeria | Endpoints deliberately stop short of the 200 nm limits of the neighboring State |

[1] Information based on executive summaries of the submissions available at the CLCS website: www.un.org/Depts/los/clcs_new/commission_submissions.htm.

| | | | | |
|---|---|---|---|---|
| 9 | Iceland (Ægir Basin area and in the western and southern parts of Reykjanes Ridge) | April 29, 2009 | Norway (Jan Mayen), Denmark (Greenland), and Denmark (Faroes) | Towards Norway (Jan Mayen) and Denmark (Greenland): Fixed points on the 200 nm limits of the neighboring State<br>Towards Denmark (Faroes): endpoints deliberately stop short of the 200 nm limits of the neighboring State |
| 10 | Denmark (north of the Faroe Islands) | April 29, 2009 | Iceland and Norway (the mainland and Jan Mayen) | Fixed points on the 200 nm limits of the neighboring State |
| 11 | Pakistan | April 30, 2009 | Oman | Endpoints deliberately stop short of the 200 nm limits of the neighboring State |
| 12 | Palau | May 8, 2009 | Japan, Federated States of Micronesia, Indonesia, and the Philippines, | Fixed points on the 200 nm limits of the neighboring State |
| 13 | Sri Lanka | May 8, 2009 | India (Andaman Islands) | Fixed points on the 200 nm limits of the neighboring State |
| 14 | Portugal | May 11, 2009 | Morocco | Fixed points on the 200 nm limits of the neighboring State |
| 15 | Tonga | May 11, 2009 | New Zealand | Fixed points on the 200 nm limits of the neighboring State |
| 16 | Mozambique | July 7, 2010 | South Africa and France (Europa Island) | Fixed points on the 200 nm limits of the neighboring State |

*(cont.)*

| | Submitting State | Date of submission | Neighboring States | Methods of self-restraint |
|---|---|---|---|---|
| 17 | Maldives | July 26, 2010 | India, Sri Lanka, Chagos Archipelago[2] | Fixed points on the 200 nm limits of the neighboring State |
| 18 | Denmark (Faroe-Rockall Plateau Region) | December 2, 2010 | Iceland and Ireland | Fixed points on the 200 nm limits of the neighboring State |
| 19 | Mexico (eastern polygon in the Gulf of Mexico) | December 19, 2011 | Cuba and the United States | Endpoints deliberately stop short of the 200 nm limits of the neighboring States |
| 20 | Tanzania | January 18, 2012 | Seychelles | Fixed points on the 200 nm limits of the neighboring State |
| 21 | Denmark (Southern Continental Shelf of Greenland) | June 14, 2012 | Canada and Iceland | Fixed points on the 200 nm limits of the neighboring State |
| 22 | Federated States of Micronesia (Eauripik Rise) | August 30, 2013 | Indonesia and Papua New Guinea | Fixed points on the 200 nm limits of the neighboring State |

[2] The territorial sovereignty of Chagos Archipelago is contested between the United Kingdom and Mauritius. Maldives fixed points of its proposed outer limits of the continental shelf beyond 200 nm on the 200 nm limits of Chagos Archipelago, but did not fully depict the 200 nm limits of Chagos Archipelago. Both the United Kingdom and Mauritius raised the issue that Maldives did not take full account of Chagos Archipelago's 200 nm. This reflects an issue of overlapping entitlements of the continental shelf and the EEZ within 200 nm. See Note Verbale of the United Kingdom dated on August 9, 2010 and Note Verbale of Mauritius dated March 24, 2011.

| | | | | |
|---|---|---|---|---|
| 23 | Denmark (North-Eastern Continental Shelf of Greenland) | November 26, 2013 | Norway (Svalbard) | Fixed points on the 200 nm limits of the neighboring State |
| 24 | Canada (Atlantic Ocean) | December 6, 2013 | Denmark (Greenland) | Fixed points on the 200 nm limits of the neighboring State |
| 25 | Tonga (western part of the Lau-Colville Ridge) | April 23, 2014 | New Zealand | Fixed points on the 200 nm limits of the neighboring State |
| 26 | Somalia | July 21, 2014 | Yemen | Fixed points on the 200 nm limits of the neighboring State |
| 27 | Denmark (Northern Continental Shelf of Greenland) | December 15, 2014 | Canada, Norway, and Russia | Fixed points on the 200 nm limits of the neighboring State |
| 28 | Oman | October 26, 2017 | India | Fixed points on the 200 nm limits of the neighboring State |
| 29 | Indonesia (Eauripik Rise) | April 11, 2019 | Federated States of Micronesia and Palau | Fixed points on the 200 nm limits of the neighboring State |
| 30 | Canada (Arctic Ocean) | May 23, 2019 | Russia and the United States | Fixed points on the 200 nm limits of the neighboring State |

# Appendix 2

**Coordination between delineation and delimitation in state practice**
(in chronological order by date of submission)[3]

| | Submitting State(s) | Date of submission | Approaches | Diplomatic Notes from Interested States[4] |
|---|---|---|---|---|
| 1 | (a) Russia (Okhotsk Sea) | February 28, 2013 | | Japan: without prejudice to territorial and delimitation issues |
| | (b) Russia (Arctic Ocean) | August 3, 2015 | **No-objection agreement** (with Denmark)<br>**No-objection agreement** (with Canada)<br>**Prior delimitation** (with the United States)<br>**Prior delimitation** (with Norway) | |
| 2 | (a) Brazil (Brazilian Southern Region) | April 10, 2015 | **Self-constraint** (provisional extension of the pre-existing maritime boundary with Uruguay) | |

[3] Information based on executive summaries of the submissions and diplomatic notes sent by States available at the CLCS website, available at www.un.org/Depts/los/clcs_new/commission_submissions.htm. The following eight submissions are not included in this Appendix because they do not concern any overlapping claims to the continental shelf beyond 200 nm: the United Kingdom in respect of Ascension Island (May 9, 2008), the Philippines in respect of Benham Rise region (April 8, 2009), Norway in respect of Bovetøya (May 4, 2009), Mauritius in respect of the region of Rodrigues Island (May 6, 2009), Seychelles in respect of the Northern Plateau Region (May 7, 2009), France in respect of La Réunion Island and Saint-Paul and Amsterdam Islands (May 8, 2009), France in respect of French Polynesia (April 6, 2018), and Brazil in respect of Brazilian Oriental and Meridional Margin (December 7, 2018).

[4] Where the executive summary of the submission of a State does not include any approach identified in this Appendix, position indicated by the diplomatic notes from other interested States will be supplied.

(*cont.*)

| | Submitting State(s) | Date of submission | Approaches | Diplomatic Notes from Interested States[4] |
|---|---|---|---|---|
| | (b) Brazil (Brazilian Equatorial Margin) | September 8, 2017 | **Self-constraint** (provisional extension of the pre-existing maritime boundary with French Guiana) | |
| 3 | Australia | November 15, 2004 | **Prior delimitation** (with France: Kerguelen Islands-McDonald/ Heard Islands)<br>**Prior delimitation** (with New Zealand) | |
| 4 | Ireland (Porcupine Abyssal Plain) | May 25, 2005 | | Denmark: "without prejudice" statement<br>Iceland: "without prejudice" statement |
| 5 | New Zealand | April 19, 2006 | **Prior delimitation** (with Australia)<br>**No-objection agreement** (Fiji and Tonga) | France: Indication of potential overlap and "without prejudice statement" |
| 6 | France, Ireland, Spain and the United Kingdom (the Celtic Sea and the Bay of Biscay) | May 19, 2006 | **Joint submission** | |
| 7 | Norway (North East Atlantic and the Arctic) | November 27, 2006 | **Provisional delimitation** (with Denmark and Iceland) | |

| | | | | |
|---|---|---|---|---|
| 8 | France (French Guiana)<br>France (New Caledonia)[5] | May 22, 2007 | **Self-constraint** (provisional extension of the pre-existing maritime boundary with Brazil) | Suriname: "without prejudice" statement<br>New Zealand: "without prejudice" statement |
| 9 | Mexico (western polygon in the Gulf of Mexico) | December 13, 2007 | **Prior delimitation** (with the United States) | |
| 10 | Barbados | July 25, 2011 | **No-objection agreement** (with Suriname, Guyana, France) | Venezuela: "without prejudice" statement<br>Trinidad and Tobago: indication of disputes over the existence of the entitlement |
| 11 | Indonesia (North West of Sumatra Island) | June 16, 2008 | **Self-constraint** (extension of a provisional equidistance line with India) | |
| 12 | Japan[6] | November 12, 2008 | **No-objection agreement** (with Palau and the United States) | |
| 13 | Mauritius and Seychelles (Mascarene Plateau) | December 1, 2008 | **Joint submission** | |
| 14 | Suriname | December 5, 2008 | **No-objection agreement** (with Barbados, France, Guyana, Trinidad and Tobago, and Venezuela) | |

[5] The part concerning southeastern part of New Caledonia was objected to by Vanuatu. See Appendix 3.
[6] The part concerning Oki-no-Tori Shima was objected to by China and Korea, see Appendix 3.

(*cont.*)

| | Submitting State(s) | Date of submission | Approaches | Diplomatic Notes from Interested States[4] |
|---|---|---|---|---|
| 15 | France (French Antilles and the Kerguelen Islands) | February 5, 2009 | **No-objection agreement** (with Suriname)<br>**Prior delimitation** (with Australia: Kerguelen Islands–McDonald/Heard Islands) | |
| 16 | Uruguay | April 7, 2009 | **Self-constraint** (provisional extension of the pre-existing maritime boundary with Brazil)<br>**Self-constraint** (fixed point on a provisional equidistance line (with Argentina)) | |
| 17 | The Cook Islands (Manihiki Plauteau) | April 16, 2009 | | New Zealand: indication of potential overlap and "without prejudice" statement |
| 18 | Argentina[7] | April 21, 2009 | **Self-constraint** (provisional extension of the pre-existing maritime boundary with Uruguay) | |

[7] The parts of the submission concerning Islas Malvinas, Georgias del Sur and Sandwich del Sur were objected to by the United Kingdom. See Appendix 3.

| | | | |
|---|---|---|---|
| 19 | Ghana | April 28, 2009 | **No-objection agreement** (with ECOWAS member States) |
| 20 | Iceland (Ægir Basin area) | April 29, 2009 | **Provisional delimitation** (with Denmark and Norway) |
| 21 | Denmark (north of Faroe Islands) | April 29, 2009 | **Provisional delimitation** (with Iceland and Norway) |
| 22 | Pakistan | April 30, 2009 | **Self-constraint** (provisional equidistance line with India) |
| 23 | South Africa (mainland) | May 5, 2009 | **Self-constraint** (provisional equidistance line with Namibia and Mozambique)<br>**No-objection agreement** (with Mozambique) |
| 24 | The Federated States of Micronesia, Papua New Guinea and Solomon Islands (Ontong Java) | May 5, 2009 | **Joint submission** |
| 25 | Malaysia and Vietnam (southern part of the South China Sea)[8] | May 6, 2009 | **Joint submission** |

[8] This joint submission was objected to by China and the Philippines. See Appendix 3.

(*cont.*)

| | Submitting State(s) | Date of submission | Approaches | Diplomatic Notes from Interested States[4] |
|---|---|---|---|---|
| 26 | France and South Africa (Crozet Archipelago and the Prince Edward Islands) | May 6, 2009 | **Joint submission** | |
| 27 | Nigeria | May 7, 2009 | **No-objection agreement** (ECOWAS member States) | |
| 28 | Côte d'Ivoire | May 8, 2009 | **No-objection agreement** (ECOWAS member States) | |
| 29 | Sri Lanka | May 8, 2009 | **No-objection agreement** (with India) | Maldives: reserves its right to comment<br>Bangladesh: reserves its right to comment |
| 30 | Portugal | May 11, 2009 | | Morocco: "without prejudice" statement<br>Spain: "without prejudice" statement |
| 31 | Spain (in respect of Galicia) | May 11, 2009 | **No-objection agreement** (with Portugal) | |
| 32 | Tonga | May 11, 2009 | | New Zealand: indication of overlap and "without prejudice" statement<br>Fiji: indication of overlap and "without prejudice" statement |

| | | | | |
|---|---|---|---|---|
| 34 | Trinidad and Tobago | May 12, 2009 | **No-objection agreement** (with Guyana, Suriname, and Venezuela) | |
| 35 | Namibia | May 12, 2009 | **Self-constraint** (provisional maritime boundary with South Africa) | |
| 36 | Cuba | June 1, 2009 | | Mexico: "without prejudice" statement<br>The United States: indication of overlap and "without prejudice" statement |
| 37 | Mozambique | July 7, 2010 | **No-objection agreement** (with South Africa and Madagascar) | |
| 38 | Madagascar | April 29, 2011 | **No-objection agreement** (with Mozambique) | |
| 39 | Mexico (eastern polygon in the Gulf of Mexico) | December 19, 2011 | Acknowledgment of overlap | |
| 40 | Tanzania | January 18, 2012 | **Prior delimitation** (with Kenya)<br>**No-objection agreement** (with Seychelles) | |
| 41 | Denmark (the Southern Continental Shelf of Greenland) | June 14, 2012 | **No-objection agreement** (with Canada) | |
| 42 | Tuvalu, France and New Zealand (Tokelau) (Robbie Ridge) | December 7, 2012 | **Joint submission** | |

*(cont.)*

| | Submitting State(s) | Date of submission | Approaches | Diplomatic Notes from Interested States[4] |
|---|---|---|---|---|
| 43 | Kiribati | December 24, 2012 | | The United States: indication of overlap and "without prejudice" statement |
| 44 | Federated States of Micronesia (Eauripik Rise) | August 30, 2013 | | Indonesia: indication of overlap and "without prejudice" statement |
| 45 | Denmark (the North-Eastern of Greenland) | November 26, 2013 | **No-objection agreement** (with Norway) | |
| 46 | Canada (Atlantic Ocean)[9] | February 6, 2014 | **No-objection agreement** (with Denmark and the United States) | |
| 47 | Tonga (Lau-Colville Ridge) | April 23, 2014 | | Fiji: indication of overlap and existence of disputes concerning Article 13(2) and Article 121(3) of UNCLOS |
| 48 | Cabo Verde, The Gambia, Guinea, Guinea-Bissau, Mauritania, Senegal and Sierra Leone (Atlantic Ocean adjacent to the coast of West Africa) | September 25, 2014 | **Joint submission** | |

[9] The part concerning the Nova Scotia region was objected to by France. See Appendix 3.

| | | | | |
|---|---|---|---|---|
| 49 | Denmark (the northern continental shelf of Greenland) | December 15, 2014 | **No-objection agreement** (with Norway and Russia) | |
| 50 | Spain (Canary Islands) | December 17, 2014 | | Morocco: indication of overlap and "without prejudice" statement |
| 51 | Oman | October 26, 2017 | Acknowledgment of overlap (with Pakistan and India) | |
| 52 | Benin and Togolese Republic | September 21, 2018 | **Joint submission** | |
| 53 | Liberia | October 23, 2018 | Acknowledgment of overlap (with Sierra Leone and Côte d'Ivoire) | |
| 54 | Indonesia (Eauripik Rise) | April 11, 2019 | Acknowledgement of overlap (with Federated States of Micronesia, Palau and Papua New Guinea) | |
| 55 | Canada (Arctic Ocean) | May 23, 2019 | **No-objection agreement** (with Denmark, Russia, and the United States) | |

# Appendix 3

**Objections raised to submissions**
(in chronological order by date of submission)[10]

| | Submitting State | Date of submission | Reasons indicated for objection | States raising objections |
|---|---|---|---|---|
| 1 | France (New Caledonia) | May 22, 2007 | Territorial disputes | Vanuatu |
| 2 | Japan | November 12, 2008 | Maritime entitlement disputes (Article 121(3)) | China<br>Korea |
| 3 | Myanmar | December 16, 2008 | Maritime delimitation<br>Applicability of Statement of Understanding<br>Maritime entitlement disputes (Article 7) | Bangladesh (maritime delimitation and baselines)<br>India (Statement of Understanding) |
| 4 | Yemen (south east of Socotra Island) | March 20, 2009 | Maritime delimitation | Somalia |
| 5 | The United Kingdom (the Hatton-Rockall area) | March 31, 2009 | Maritime delimitation/maritime entitlement disputes (Article 76) | Iceland<br>Denmark |
| 6 | Ireland (the Hatton-Rockall area) | March 31, 2009 | Maritime delimitation/maritime entitlement disputes (Article 76) | Iceland<br>Denmark |
| 7 | Fiji | April 20, 2009 | Maritime delimitation | Vanuatu |

[10] Information based on executive summaries of the submissions and communications available at the CLCS website, available at www.un.org/Depts/los/clcs_new/commission_submissions.htm.

*(cont.)*

| | Submitting State | Date of submission | Reasons indicated for objection | States raising objections |
|---|---|---|---|---|
| 8 | Argentina | April 21, 2009 | Territorial disputes | The United Kingdom |
| 9 | Joint submission by Vietnam and Malaysia | May 5, 2009 | Territorial disputes<br>Maritime delimitation<br>Maritime entitlement disputes (Article 76 and/or Article 121(3)) | China<br>The Philippines |
| 10 | Kenya[11] | May 6, 2009 | Maritime delimitation | Somalia |
| 11 | Vietnam (North Area) | May 7, 2009 | Territorial disputes<br>Maritime delimitation<br>Maritime entitlement disputes (Article 76 and/or Article 121(3)) | China: territorial and maritime entitlement disputes<br>The Philippines: maritime delimitation |
| 12 | Palau[12] | May 8, 2009 | Maritime delimitation | The Philippines |
| 13 | The United Kingdom (the Falkland Islands, and of South Georgia and the South Sandwich Islands) | May 11, 2009 | Territorial disputes | Argentina |

[11] Somalia withdrew its objection in the Note Verbale dated July 7, 2015, and the CLCS determined that it was in a position to proceed with the establishment of a subcommission. "Progress of work in the Commission on the Limits of the Continental Shelf" (Thirty-eighth session, New York, July 20–September 4, 2015) (CLCS/90).

[12] Subsequently Palau submitted an amended submission on October 26, 2017, which excluded the area subject to overlapping claims with the Philippines. Since the Philippines made no objection to the amended submission, the CLCS decided to proceed to consider Palau's partial amended submission. See "Progress of work in the Commission on the Limits of the Continental Shelf" (Forty-sixth session, New York, January 29–March 16, 2018) (CLCS/103).

| | | | | |
|---|---|---|---|---|
| 14 | India[13] | May 11, 2009 | Maritime delimitation<br>Maritime entitlement disputes (Article 7) | Bangladesh<br>Myanmar |
| 15 | Maldives | July 26, 2010 | Maritime entitlement disputes (Article 56) | Mauritius |
| 16 | Denmark (the Faroe-Rockall area) | December 2, 2010 | Maritime entitlement disputes (Article 76) | Iceland |
| 17 | Bangladesh | February 25, 2011 | Maritime delimitation<br>Maritime entitlement disputes (Article 7) | Myanmar<br>India |
| 18 | Guyana | September 6, 2011 | Territorial disputes | Venezuela |
| 19 | Gabon | April 10, 2010 | Maritime delimitation | Angola |
| 20 | China | December 14, 2012 | Territorial disputes<br>Maritime delimitation<br>Maritime entitlement disputes (Article 76) | Japan |

13 The Notes Verbales of Bangladesh and Myanmar did not explicitly object to the consideration of India's submission. Nevertheless, the CLCS decided to defer further consideration of the submission "in order to take into account any further developments that might occur in the intervening period." "Progress of work in the Commission on the Limits of the Continental Shelf" (Twenty-eighth session, New York, August 1–September 9, 2011) (CLCS/72). Subsequently the CLCS decided to establish a subcommission for the consideration of India's submission. "Progress of work in the Commission on the Limits of the Continental Shelf" (Fiftieth session, New York, July 1–August 16, 2019) (CLCS/50/2), [79].

(*cont.*)

| | Submitting State | Date of submission | Reasons indicated for objection | States raising objections |
|---|---|---|---|---|
| 21 | Korea | December 26, 2012 | Maritime delimitation<br>Maritime entitlement disputes (Article 76) | Japan |
| 22 | Nicaragua | June 24, 2013 | Maritime entitlement disputes (Article 76) | Colombia, Costa Rica, and Panama |
| 23 | Angola | December 6, 2013 | Maritime entitlement disputes (Article 7 and Article 77)<br>Maritime delimitation | Democratic Republic of the Congo: maritime entitlement disputes<br>Gabon: maritime delimitation |
| 24 | Bahamas[14] | February 6, 2014 | Maritime delimitation | The United States |
| 25 | Canada (Atlantic Ocean) | February 6, 2014 | Maritime entitlement disputes (Article 76) | France |
| 26 | France (St. Pierre and Miquelon) | April 16, 2014 | Maritime entitlement disputes (Article 76) | Canada |
| 27 | Somalia[15] | July 21, 2014 | Maritime delimitation | Yemen |
| 28 | Mauritius | March 26, 2019 | Territorial disputes | The United Kingdom |
| 29 | Malaysia | December 12, 2019 | Territorial disputes<br>Maritime entitlement disputes (Article 76 and/or Article 121(3)) | China and the Philippines |

[14] The United States withdrew its objection in its Note Verbale dated August 9, 2018.
[15] Kenya withdrew its objection in the Note Verbale dated June 30, 2015.

# Appendix 4

**State practice concerning the continental shelf delimitation beyond 200 nm**

| | Parties | Coastal relationship | Maritime zone(s) | Methods in maritime zones within 200 nm | Methods beyond 200 nm | Use of geophysical factors |
|---|---|---|---|---|---|---|
| **I Adoption of the same method within and beyond 200 nm** | | | | | | |
| 1(a) | 1982 Australia (Heard/ McDonald Islands)–France (Kerguelen Islands) | Opposite | A single line | Equidistance | The same method | Determination of the terminus |
| 1(b) | 1982 Australia–France (New Caledonia) | Opposite | A single line | Equidistance with modifications | The same method | Determination of the terminus |
| 2 | 1998 Australia–Solomon Islands | Opposite | A single line | Equidistance with modifications | The same method | – |
| 3 | 2000 Mexico–United States | Hybrid | Continental shelf boundary | Equidistance | The same method | – |
| 4 | 2009 Barbados– France (Guadeloupe and Martinique) | Lateral (towards the open ocean) | A single line | Equidistance | The same method | Determination of the terminus |

| | | | | | | |
|---|---|---|---|---|---|---|
| 5 | 2009 Kenya–Tanzania | Adjacent | A single line | (Primarily) a line parallel of latitude | Extension of the boundary line | – |
| 6 | 2017 France (French Guiana)–Suriname | Adjacent | A single line | Unspecified | Extension of the boundary line | – |
| 7 | 1990 Trinidad and Tobago–Venezuela | Lateral (towards the open ocean) | A single line | Unspecified | Extension of the boundary line | Determination of the terminus |
| **II Combination of methods for an overall equitable solution** | | | | | | |
| 8 | 1988 Ireland–United Kingdom | Hybrid of opposite and lateral (towards the open ocean) | Continental shelf boundary | Stepped lines | | Determination of the terminus |
| 9 | 1990 United States–Soviet Union | Opposite | A single line | A combination of methods | | – |
| 10 | 2010 Norway–Russia | Opposite | A single line | Equal division of maritime zones | | – |
| **III Specific arrangements for the continental shelf beyond 200 nm** | | | | | | |
| 11 | 2004 Australia–New Zealand | Opposite | | Equidistance | Considerations of respective natural prolongations | Determination of the course of the boundary |

(*cont.*)

| | Parties | Coastal relationship | Maritime zone(s) | Methods in maritime zones within 200 nm | Methods beyond 200 nm | Use of geophysical factors |
|---|---|---|---|---|---|---|
| 12 | 2006 Denmark/The Faroes– Iceland–Norway Agreed Minutes | – | Continental shelf beyond 200 nm | | Sharing out the continental shelf beyond 200 nm | – |
| 13 | 2013 Denmark (Greenland)–Iceland Agreed Minutes | Opposite | Continental shelf beyond 200 nm | | Sharing out the continental shelf beyond 200 nm | – |
| **IV Separate lines for the continental shelves and the EEZ** | | | | | | |
| 14 | 1978 Australia–Papua New Guinea | Opposite | Continental shelf and fishery zone | A combination of methods | – | – |
| 15 | 1997 Australia–Indonesia | Opposite | Continental shelf and fishery zone | A combination of methods | Part of the seabed boundary line follows the outer edge of Australia's continental margin | Determination of the course of the boundary |

# BIBLIOGRAPHY

## (in alphabetical order by author)


Acikgonul, Y. E. "Reflections on the Principle of Non-Cut Off: A Growing Concept in Maritime Boundary Delimitation Law" (2016) 47 *Ocean Development & International Law* 52.

Adede, A. "Kenya–Tanzania, Report Number 4-5," in J. I. Charney and L. M. Alexander (eds.), *International Maritime Boundaries, Vol. I* (Martinus Nijhoff 1993).

Allott, P. "Power Sharing in the Law of the Sea" (1983) 77 *American Journal of International Law* 1.

Anderson, D. "Ireland–United Kingdom, Report Number 9-5," in J. I. Charney and L. M. Alexander (eds.), *International Maritime Boundaries, Vol. II* (Martinus Nijhoff 1993).

"Developments in Maritime Boundary Law and Practice," in D. A. Colson and R. W. Smith (eds.), *International Maritime Boundaries, Volume V* (Brill Nijhoff 2005).

"Scientific Evidence in Cases under Part XV of the LOSC," in M. H. Nordquist, R. Long, T. H. Heidar, and J. N. Moore(eds.), *Law, Science & Ocean Management* (Martinus Nijhoff Publishers 2007).

*Modern Law of the Sea: Selected Essays* (Martinus Nijhoff Publishers 2008).

"Recent Decisions of Courts and Tribunals in Maritime Boundary Cases," in D. A. Colson and R. W. Smith (eds.), *International Maritime Boundaries, Volume VI* (Martinus Nijhoff Publishers 2011).

"Recent Judicial Decisions Concerning Maritime Delimitation," in L. del Castillo (ed.), *Law of the Sea, From Grotius to the International Tribunal for the Law of the Sea, Liber Amicorum Judge Hugo Caminos* (Brill Nijhoff 2015).

"Ireland–United Kingdom, Report Number 9-5(3)," in C. G. Lathrop (ed.), *International Maritime Boundaries, Vol. VII* (Brill Nijhoff 2016).

"Some Recent Developments in the Law Relating to the Continental Shelf," (1988) 6 *Journal of Energy & Natural Resources Law* 95.

"Delimitation of the Maritime Boundary in the Bay of Bengal (Bangladesh/Myanmar) – Case No. 16" (2012) 106 *American Journal of International Law* 817.

Apollis, G. *Les Frontières Maritimes en Droit International: Mutations et Perspectives* (Faculté de droit et des sciences économiques 1979).

Arbour, J.-M. "Les fondements du titre de l'Etat sur les espaces maritimes et ses rapports avec l'opération de delimitation," in D. Pharand and U. Leanza (eds.), *The Continental Shelf and the Exclusive Economic Zone/Le Plateau continental et la zone économique exclusive* (Martinus Nijhoff Publishers 1993).

Armas-Pfirter, F. M. "Submissions on the Outer Limit of the Continental Shelf: Practice to Date and Some Issues of Debate," in D. Vidas (ed.), *Law, Technology and Science for Oceans in Globalisation: IUU Fishing, Oil Pollution, Bioprospecting, Outer Continental Shelf* (Martinus Nijhoff Publishers 2010).

Attard, D. J. *The Exclusive Economic Zone in International Law* (Oxford University Press 1987).

Beazley, P. "Technical Aspects of Maritime Boundary Delimitation" (1994) 1 *Maritime Briefing* 1.

Beigzadeh, E. "La Commission des Limites du Plateau Continental" (2000) 5 *Annuaire du Droit de la Mer* 71.

Benjamin, S. "France (French Guiana)–Suriname, Report Number 3-11," in C. G. Lathrop (ed.), *International Maritime Boundaries, Vol. VIII* (Brill Nijhoff 2019).

Benzing, M. "Evidentiary Issues," in A. Zimmermann, C. Tomuschat, K. Oellers-Frahm, and C. J. Tams (eds.), *The Statute of the International Court of Justice: A Commentary* (2nd ed., Oxford University Press 2012).

Bowett, D. "Islands, Rocks, Reefs, and Low-Tide Elevations in Maritime Boundary Delimitations," in J. I. Charney and L. M. Alexander (eds.), *International Maritime Boundaries, Volume I* (Martinus Nijhoff Publishers 1993).

*The Legal Regime of Islands in International Law* (Oceana Publications, Inc. 1979).

Brekke, H. "*Defining and Recognizing the Outer Limits of the Continental Shelf in the Polar Regions*," in R. C. Powell and K. Dodds (eds.), *Polar Geopolitics? Knowledges, Resources and Legal Regimes* (Edward Elgar Publishing Limited 2014).

Brekke, H. and Symonds, P. "Submarine Ridges and Elevations of Article 76 in Light of Published Summaries of Recommendations of the Commission on the Limits of the Continental Shelf" (2011) 42 *Ocean Development & International Law* 289.

Brown, E. D. *The Legal Regime of Hydrospace* (Stevens & Sons 1971).

"The Anglo-French Continental Shelf Case" (1978) 16 *San Diego Law Review* 461.

*Sea-Bed Energy and Minerals: The International Legal Regime* (Martinus Nijhoff Publishers 1992).

Brownlie, I. *Principles of Public International Law* (7th ed., Oxford University Press 2008).

Busch, S. V. *Establishing Continental Shelf Limits beyond 200 Nautical Miles by the Coastal State: A Right of Involvement for Other States?* (Brill Nijhoff 2016).

"The Delimitation of the Continental Shelf Beyond 200 Nm: Procedural Issues," in Alex G. Oude Elferink, Tore Henriksen and Signe Veierud Busch (eds.), *Maritime Boundary Delimitation: The Case Law: Is It Consistent and Predictable?* (Cambridge University Press 2018).

Caflisch, L. "Les zones maritimes sous juridiction nationale, leurs limites et leur delimitation," in D. Bardonnet and M. Virally (eds.), *Le nouveau droit international de la mer* (Pedone 1983).

"The Peaceful Settlement of Disputes on Maritime Delimitation," in J. Basedow, U. Magnus, and R. Wolfrum (eds.), *The Hamburg Lectures on Maritime Affairs 2009 & 2010* (Springer Berlin Heidelberg 2012).

Carleton, C. M. "Delimitation Issues," in P. J. Cook and C. M. Carleton (eds.), *Continental Shelf Limits: The Scientific and Legal Interface* (Oxford University Press 2000).

Carleton, C. M., Shipman, S., Monahan, D., and Parson, L. "The Practical Realisation of the Continental Shelf Limit," in P. J. Cook and C. M. Carleton (eds), *Continental Shelf Limits: The Scientific and Legal Interface* (Oxford University Press 2000).

Carleton, C. M., Gautier, P., Golitsyn, M., Lodge, W., and Yanai, S. "Current Issues Regarding the Delimitation of the Outer Continental Shelf: A Panel Discussion in the International Tribunal for the Law of the Sea (30 September 2012)," in Jürgen Basedow, Ulrich Magnus and Rüdiger Wolfrum (eds.), *The Hamburg Lectures on Maritime Affairs 2011-2013* (Springer, Berlin, Heidelberg 2015).

Charney, J. I. "The United States and the Law of the Sea After UNCLOS III – The Impact of General International Law" (1983) 46 *Law and Contemporary Problems* 37.

"Ocean Boundaries between Nations: A Theory for Progress" (1984) 78 *American Journal of International Law* 582

"The Exclusive Economic Zone and Public International Law" (1985) 15 *Ocean Development & International Law* 233.

"Progress in International Maritime Boundary Delimitation Law" (1994) 88 *American Journal of International Law* 227.

"International Maritime Boundaries for the Continental Shelf: The Relevance of Natural Prolongation," in N. Ando, E. McWhinney, and R. Wolfrum (eds.), *Liber Amicorum Judge Shigeru Oda, Volume II* (Kluwer Law International 2002).

Charney, J. I. and Alexander, L. M. (eds.) *International Maritime Boundaries, Volume II* (Martinus Nijhoff Publishers 1993).

Churchill, R. "Dispute Settlement under the UN Convention on the Law of the Sea: Survey for 2006" (2007) 22 *International Journal of Marine and Coastal Law* 463.

"Bangladesh/Myanmar Case: Continuity and Novelty in the Law of Maritime Boundary Delimitation" (2012) 1 *Cambridge Journal of International and Comparative Law* 137.

Churchill R. and Lowe A. *The Law of the Sea* (3rd ed., Manchester University Press 1999).

Colson, D. "The Delimitation of the Outer Continental Shelf between Neighboring States" (2003) 97 *American Journal of International Law* 91.

"The United Kingdom - France Continental Shelf Arbitration" (1978) 72 *American Journal of International Law* 95.

Cottier, T. *Equitable Principles of Maritime Boundary Delimitation: The Quest for Distributive Justice in International Law* (Cambridge University Press 2015).

Crawford, J. *Change, Order, Chance: The Course of International Law*, Vol. 365 (Martinus Nijhoff Publishers 2013).

de La Fayette, L. "The Award in the Canada–France Maritime Boundary Arbitration" (1993) 8 *International Journal of Marine and Coastal Law* 77.

de Marffy, Mantuano A. "La Fixation des Dernières Limites Maritimes: La Rôle de la Commission des Limites du Plateau Continental," in V. Coussirat-Coustère (ed.), *La mer et son droit: mélanges offerts à Laurent Lucchini et Jean-Pierre Quéneudec* (Éditions A Pedone 2003).

Delabie, L. "The Role of Equity, Equitable Principles, and the Equitable Solution in Maritime Delimitation," in A. G. Oude Elferink, T. Henriksen, and S. V. Busch (eds.), *Maritime Boundary Delimitation: The Case Law: Is It Consistent and Predictable?* (Cambridge University Press 2018).

Dundas, C. "Barbados–France (Guadeloupe and Martinique), Report Number 2-30," in D. A. Colson and R. W. Smith (eds.), *International Maritime Boundaries, Vol. V* (Brill Nijhoff 2011).

Eiriksson, G. "The Case of Disagreement between the Coastal State and the Commission on the Limits of the Continental Shelf," in M. H. Nordquist, J. N. Moore, and T. H. Heidar (eds.), *Legal and Scientific Aspects of Continental Shelf Limits* (Martinus Nijhoff Publishers 2004).

Emery, K. O. "Geological Limits of the Continental Shelf" (1981) 10 *Ocean Development & International Law* 1.

Evans, M. D. *Relevant Circumstances and Maritime Delimitation* (Oxford University Press 1989)

"Maritime Delimitation and Expanding Categories of Relevant Circumstances" (1991) 40 *International and Comparative Law Quarterly* 1.

"Less than an Ocean Apart: The St Pierre and Miquelon and Jan Mayen Islands and the Delimitation of Maritime Zones" (1994) 43 *International and Comparative Law Quarterly* 678.

"Delimitation and the Common Maritime Boundary" (1994) 64 *British Yearbook of International Law* 283.

"Maritime Boundary Delimitation: Where Do We Go From Here?," in D. Freestone, R. Barnes and D. Ong (eds.), *The Law of the Sea: Progress and Prospects* (Oxford University Press 2006).

"Maritime Boundary Delimitation," in D. R. Rothwell, A. G. Oude Elferink, K. N. Scott, and T. Stephens (eds.), *The Oxford Handbook of the Law of the Sea* (Oxford University Press 2015).

"Maritime Boundary Delimitation: Whatever Next?," in J. Barrett and R. Barnes (eds.), *Law of the Sea: UNCLOS as a Living Treaty* (British Institute of International and Comparative Law 2016).

"Relevant Circumstances," in A. G. Oude Elferink, T. Henriksen, and S. V. Busch (eds.), *Maritime Boundary Delimitation: The Case Law: Is It Consistent and Predictable?* (Cambridge University Press 2018).

Feldman M. B. "The Tunisia–Libya Continental Shelf Case: Geographic Justice or Judicial Compromise?" (1983) 77 *American Journal of International Law* 219.

Fietta, S. and Cleverly, R., *A Practitioner's Guide to Maritime Boundary Delimitation* (Oxford University Press 2016).

Fife, R. "Denmark/The Faroes–Iceland–Norway, Report Number 9-26," in D. A. Colson and R. W. Smith (eds.), *International Maritime Boundaries, Vol. VI* (Martinus Nijhoff 2011).

"Norway-Russia Federation, Report Number 9-6(3)," in C. G. Lathrop (ed.), *International Maritime Boundaries, Vol. VII* (Brill Nijhoff 2016).

Fitzmaurice, G. G. "*Some Problems Regarding the Formal Sources of International Law*", *Symbolae Verzijl* (Martinus Nijhoff Publishers 1958).

Friedmann, W. "The North Sea Continental Shelf Cases – A Critique" (1970) 64 *American Journal of International Law* 229.

Fyfe, N. and French, G. "Australia–New Zealand, Report Number 5-26," in D. A. Colson and R. W. Smith (eds.), *International Maritime Boundaries, Vol. V* (Martinus Nijhoff 2005).

Gao, J. "The Okinawa Trough Issue in the Continental Shelf Delimitation Disputes within the East China Sea" (2010) 9 *Chinese Journal of International Law* 143.

"The Seafloor High Issue in Article 76 of the LOS Convention: Some Views from the Perspective of Legal Interpretation" (2012) 43 *Ocean Development & International Law* 119.

Gau, M.-S. "Third Party Intervention in the Commission on the Limits of the Continental Shelf Regarding a Submission Involving a Dispute" (2009) 40 *Ocean Development & International Law* 61.

"The Commission on the Limits of the Continental Shelf as a Mechanism to Prevent Encroachment upon the Area" (2011) 10 *Chinese Journal of International Law* 3.

"Recent Decisions by the Commission on the Limits of the Continental Shelf on Japan's Submission for Outer Continental Shelf" (2012) 11 *Chinese Journal of International Law* 487.

Guillaume, G. "The Use of Precedent by International Judges and Arbitrators" (2011) 2 *Journal of International Dispute Settlement* 5.

Hayashi, M. "Sea Level Rise and the Law of the Sea: How Can the Affected States Be Better Protected?," in C. Schofield, S. Lee, and M.-S. Kwon (eds.), *The Limits of Maritime Jurisdiction* (Martinus Nijhoff Publishers 2014).

Hedberg, H. D. "*Ocean Floor Boundaries*" (1979) *204 Science* (American Association for the Advancement of Science) 135.

Heidar, T. H. "Legal Aspects of Continental Shelf Limits," in M. H. Nordquist, J. N. Moore and T. H. Heidar (eds.), *Legal and Scientific Aspects of Continental Shelf Limits* (Martinus Nijhoff Publishers 2004).

"Delimitation of the Continental Shelf and Determination of the Outer Limits of the Continental Shelf beyond 200 Nautical Miles in Areas of Overlapping Claims: The Nordic Model," in M. W. Lodge and M. H. Nordquist (eds.), *Peaceful Order in the World's Oceans: Essays in Honor of Satya N. Nandan* (Brill Nijhoff 2014).

Henriksen, T. and Ulfstein, G. "Maritime Delimitation in the Arctic: The Barents Sea Treaty" (2011) 42 *Ocean Development & International Law* 1.

Herman, L. L. "The Court Giveth and the Court Taketh Away: An Analysis of the Tunisia–Libya Continental Shelf Case" (1984) 33 *International and Comparative Law Quarterly* 825.

Higgins, R. *Problems and Process: International Law and How We Use It* (Reprinted, Oxford University Press 2010).

Highet, K. "Whatever Became of Natural Prolongation?," in D. Dorinda and L. de Vorsey (eds.), *Rights to Oceanic Resources: Deciding and Drawing Maritime Boundaries* (Martinus Nijhoff Publishers 1989).

"The Use of Geophysical Factors in the Delimitation of Maritime Boundaries," in J. I. Charney and L. M. Alexander (eds.), *International Maritime Boundaries, Volume I* (Martinus Nijhoff Publishers 1993).

Hutchinson, D. N. "The Concept of Natural Prolongation in the Jurisprudence Concerning Delimitation of Continental Shelf Areas" (1985) 55 *British Yearbook of International Law* 133.

"The Seaward Limit to Continental Shelf Jurisdiction in Customary International Law" (1986) 56 *British Yearbook of International Law* 111.

Ida, R. "The Role of Proportionality in Maritime Delimitation Revisited: The Origin and Meaning of the Principle from the Early Decisions of the Court," in N. Ando, E. McWhinney, and R. Wolfrum (eds.), *Liber Amicorum Judge Shigeru Oda, Volume II* (Kluwer Law International 2002).

International Law Association, "Preliminary Report of the Committee on Legal Issues of the Outer Continental Shelf," *Report of the Seventieth Conference* (New Delhi, 2002).

Jarmache, E. "A propos de la Commission des Limites du Plateau Continental" (2006) XI *Annuaire du Droit de la Mer* 51.

"La pratique de la Commission des Limites du Plateau Continental" (2008) 54 *Annuaire français de droit international* 429.

Jennings, R. Y. "The Limits of Continental Shelf Jurisdiction: Some Possible Implications of the North Sea Case Judgment" (1969) 18 *International & Comparative Law Quarterly* 819.

"The Principles Governing Maritime Boundaries," in K. Hailbronner (ed.), *Staat und Völkerrechtsordnung, Festschrift für Karl Doehring* (Springer 1989).

Jensen, Ø. *The Commission on the Limits of the Continental Shelf: Law and Legitimacy* (Martinus Nijhoff 2014).

"Maritime Boundary Delimitation Beyond 200 Nautical Miles: The International Judiciary and the Commission on the Limits of the Continental Shelf" (2015) 84 *Nordic Journal of International Law* 580.

"The Delimitation of the Continental Shelf beyond 200 Nm: Substantive Issues," in A. G. Oude Elferink, T. Henriksen, and S. V. Busch (eds.), *Maritime Boundary Delimitation: The Case Law: Is It Consistent and Predictable?* (Cambridge University Press 2018).

Kamto, M. "Considérations Actuelles sur la Méthode de Délimitation Maritime devant la Cour Internationale de Justice: de Charybde en Scylla?," in J. Crawford, A. Koroma, S. Mahmoudi, and A. Pellet (eds.), *The International Legal Order: Current Needs and Possible Responses* (Brill Nijhoff 2017).

Karagiannis, S. "Observations sur la Commission des Limites du Plateau Continental" (1994) 8 *Espaces et ressources maritimes* 163.

Kaye, S. "The Use of Multiple Boundaries in Maritime Boundary Delimitation: Law and Practice" (1998) 19 *Australian Year Book of International Law* 49.

Kim, H.-J. "La délimitation de la frontière maritime dans le golfe du Bengale: courir deux lièvres à la fois avec succès dans le règlement de la délimitation maritime" (2012) 58 *Annuaire Français de Droit International* 443.

Kim, H."Natural Prolongation: A Living Myth in the Regime of the Continental Shelf?" (2014) 45 *Ocean Development & International Law* 374.

Kolb, R. *Case Law on Equitable Maritime Delimitation: Digest and Commentaries* (Martinus Nijhoff Publishers 2003).

Kunoy, B. "A Geometric Variable Scope of Delimitations: The Impact of a Geological and Geomorphologic Title to the Outer Continental Shelf" (2006) 11 *Austrian Review of International and European Law* 49.

"Admissibility of a Plea to an International Adjudicative Forum to Delimit the Outer Continental Shelf Prior to the Adoption of Final Recommendations by the Commission on the Limits of the Continental Shelf" (2010) 25 *International Journal of Marine and Coastal Law* 237.

"The Terms of Reference of the Commission on the Limits of the Continental Shelf: A Creeping Legal Mandate" (2012) 25 *Leiden Journal of International Law* 109.

"The Delimitation of an Indicative Area of Overlapping Entitlement to the Outer Continental Shelf" (2013) 83 *British Yearbook of International Law* 61.

"Agreed Minutes on the Delimitation of the Continental Shelf beyond 200 Nautical Miles between Greenland and Iceland in the Irminger Sea" (2013) 12 *Chinese Journal of International Law* 125.

"Assertions of Entitlement to the Outer Continental Shelf in the Central Arctic Ocean" (2017) 66 *International & Comparative Law Quarterly* 367.

Kunoy, B., Heinesen, M. V., and Mørk, F. "Appraisal of Applicable Depth Constraint for the Purpose of Establishing the Outer Limits of the Continental Shelf" (2010) 41 *Ocean Development & International Law* 357.

Kwiatkowska, B. *The 200 Mile Exclusive Economic Zone in the New Law of the Sea* (Martinus Nijhoff Publishers 1989).

"The 2006 Barbados/Trinidad and Tobago Award: A Landmark in Compulsory Jurisdiction and Equitable Maritime Boundary Delimitation" (2007) 22 *International Journal of Marine and Coastal Law* 7.

Lando, M. "Delimiting the Continental Shelf Beyond 200 Nautical Miles at the International Court of Justice: The Nicaragua v. Colombia Cases" (2017) 16 *Chinese Journal of International Law* 137.

"Judicial Uncertainties Concerning Territorial Sea Delimitation under Article 15 of the United Nations Convention on the Law of the Sea" (2017) 66 *International and Comparative Law Quarterly* 589.

*Maritime Delimitation as a Judicial Process* (Cambridge University Press 2018).

Lathrop, C. G. "Continental Shelf Delimitation Beyond 200 Nautical Miles: Approaches Taken by Coastal States before the Commission on the Limits of the Continental Shelf," in R. W. Smith and D. A. Colson (eds.), *International Maritime Boundaries, Volume VI* (Martinus Nijhoff Publishers 2011).

Lathrop, C. (ed.), *International Maritime Boundaries, Volume VII* (Brill Nijhoff 2016).

Lathrop, C. "The Provisional Equidistance Line: Charting a Course Between Objectivity and Subjectivity?," in A. G. Oude Elferink, T. Henriksen, and S. V. Busch (eds.), *Maritime Boundary Delimitation: The Case Law: Is It Consistent and Predictable?* (Cambridge University Press 2018).

Lauterpacht, E. "Equity, Evasion, Equivocation and Evolution in International Law," *Proceedings and Committee Reports of the American Branch of the International Law Association* (1977).

Lauterpacht, H. "De l'Interpretation des Traités: Rapport" (1950) 43 *Annuaire de l'Institut de Droit International* 366.

"Sovereignty over Submarine Areas" (1950) 27 *British Yearbook of International Law* 376.

Lee, K. B. "Should the Invocation of Paragraph 5(a) of Annex I to the CLCS Rules of Procedure Result in an Automatic Deferral of the Consideration of a Submission?" (2014) 13 *Chinese Journal of International Law* 605.

Legault, L. and Hankey, B. "Method, Oppositeness and Adjacency, and Proportionality in Maritime Boundary Delimitation," in J. I. Charney and L. M. Alexander (eds.), *International Maritime Boundaries, Volume I* (Martinus Nijhoff Publishers 1993).

Legault, L. H. and Hankey, B. "From Sea to Seabed: The Single Maritime Boundary in the Gulf of Maine Case" (1985) 79 *American Journal of International Law* 961.

Liao, X. "Evaluation of Scientific Evidence by International Courts and Tribunals in the Continental Shelf Delimitation Cases" (2017) 48 *Ocean Development & International Law* 136.

"The Timor Sea Conciliation under Article 298 and Annex V of UNCLOS: A Critique" (2019) 18 *Chinese Journal of International Law* 281.

Lilje-Jensen, J. and Thamsborg, M. "The Role of Natural Prolongation in Relation to Shelf Delimitation beyond 200 Nautical Miles" (1995) 64 *Nordic Journal of International Law* 619.

Lloyd, S. "Natural Prolongation: Have the Rumours Its Demise Been Greatly Exaggerated" (1991) 3 *African Journal of International and Comparative Law* 558.

Lucchini, L. "La délimitation des frontières maritimes dans la jurisprudence international: vue d'ensemble," in R. Lagoni and D. Vignes (eds.), *Maritime Delimitation* (Martinus Nijhoff Publishers 2006).

Lucchini, L. and Voelckel, M. *Droit de La Mer, Tome II, Délimitation* (Pedone 1996).

Lucky, A. "The Issues Concerning the Continental Shelf: Reflections" (2015) 17 *International Community Law Review* 95.

Macnab, R. "Initial Assessment," in P. J. Cook and C. M. Carleton (eds.), *Continental Shelf Limits: The Scientific and Legal Interface* (Oxford University Press 2000).

"The Case for Transparency in the Delimitation of the Outer Continental Shelf in Accordance with UNCLOS Article 76" (2004) 35 *Ocean Development & International Law* 1.

Maggio, A. "Article 77," in A Proelss (ed.), *The United Nations Convention on the Law of the Sea: A Commentary* (Hart 2017).

Magnússon, B. M. "Denmark (Greenland)–Iceland, Report Number 9-22 (2)," in C. G. Lathrop (ed.), *International Maritime Boundaries, Vol. VII* (Brill Nijhoff 2016).

Magnússon, B. *The Continental Shelf beyond 200 Nautical Miles: Delineation, Delimitation and Dispute Settlement* (Brill Nijhoff 2015).

"Is There a Temporal Relationship between the Delineation and the Delimitation of the Continental Shelf beyond 200 Nautical Miles?" (2013) 28 *International Journal of Marine and Coastal Law* 465.

"Outer Continental Shelf Boundary Agreements" (2013) 62 *International and Comparative Law Quarterly* 345.

"The Rejection of a Theoretical Beauty: The Foot of the Continental Slope in Maritime Boundary Delimitations beyond 200 Nautical Miles" (2014) 45 *Ocean Development & International Law* 41.

Marques, Antunes N. *Towards the Conceptualisation of Maritime Delimitation: Legal and Technical Aspects of a Political Process* (Martinus Nijhoff Publishers 2003).

Marques, Antunes N. and Becker-Weinberg, V. "Entitlement to Maritime Zones and Their Delimitation: In the Doldrums of Uncertainty and Unpredictability," in A. G. Oude Elferink, T. Henriksen, and S. V. Busch (eds.), *Maritime Boundary Delimitation: The Case Law: Is It Consistent and Predictable?* (Cambridge University Press 2018).

Mayer, L. "The Continental Shelf and Changing Sea Level," in M. H. Nordquist and J. N. Moore (eds.), *Maritime Border Diplomacy* (Martinus Nijhoff Publishers 2012).

Mbengue, M. M. "Scientific Fact-Finding by International Courts and Tribunals" (2012) 3 *Journal of International Dispute Settlement* 509.

McDorman, T. L. "The Entry into Force of the 1982 LOS Convention and the Article 76 Outer Continental Shelf Regime" (1995) 10 *International Journal of Marine and Coastal Law* 165.

"The Role of the Commission on the Limits of the Continental Shelf: A Technical Body in a Political World" (2002) 17 *International Journal of Marine and Coastal Law* 301.

"The Continental Shelf beyond 200 NM: A First Look at the Bay of Bengal (Bangladesh/Myanmar) Case," in M. H. Nordquist, J. N. Moore, A. Chircop, and R. Long (eds.), *The Regulation of Continental Shelf Development: Rethinking International Standards* (Martinus Nijhoff Publishers 2013).

"The Continental Shelf," in D. R. Rothwell, A. G. Oude Elferink, K. N. Scott, and T. Stephens (eds.), *The Oxford Handbook of the Law of the Sea* (Oxford University Press 2015).

"Revisiting the Commission on the Limits of the Continental Shelf: 'A Technical Body in a Political World,'" in M. H. Nordquist, J. N. Moore, and R. Long (eds.), *Legal Order in the World's Oceans: UN Convention on the Law of the Sea* (Brill Nijhoff 2017).

McRae, D. "The Applicable Law: The Geneva Convention on the Continental Shelf, the LOSC, and Customary International Law," in A. G. Oude

Elferink, T. Henriksen, and S. V. Busch (eds.), *Maritime Boundary Delimitation: The Case Law: Is It Consistent and Predictable?* (Cambridge University Press 2018).

"Delimitation of the Continental Shelf between the United Kingdom and France: The Channel Arbitration" (1977) 15 *Canadian Yearbook of International Law* 173.

Mendelson, M. "On the Quasi-Normative Effect of Maritime Boundary Agreements," in N. Ando, E. McWhinney, and R. Wolfrum (eds.), *Liber Amicorum Judge Shigeru Oda*, Volume *II* (Kluwer Law International 2002).

Mensah, T. A. "Delimitation of the Continental Shelf: The Methodology," in J. Carlos Sainz-Borgo, H. Guomundsdottir, G. D. Guomundsdottir, J. M. Amaya-Castro, M. Kanade, Y. Saab, and H. Sipalla (eds.), *Liber Amicorum: In Honour of a Modern Renaissance Man His Excellency Guomundur* (Universal Law Publishing 2017).

Mørk, F. "Identification of the Base of the Continental Slope on Sedimentary Fans" (2016) 47 *Ocean Development & International Law* 131.

Mouton, M. "The Continental Shelf" (1954) 85 *Recueil des Cours* 345.

Murphy, S. "International Law Relating to Islands" (2016) 386 *Recueil des Cours* 9.

Namountougou, M. A. "La Commission des Limites du Plateau Continental: Problèmes de Statut Juridique et Attributions" (2008) *Revue Belge de Droit International* 292.

Nandan, SN and Rosenne, S (eds.), *United Nations Convention on the Law of the Sea 1982: A Commentary, Volume II* (Martinus Nijhoff Publishers 1993).

(eds.), *United Nations Convention on the Law of the Sea 1982: A Commentary, Volume III* (Martinus Nijhoff Publishers 1995).

Nelson, L. D. M. "Claims to the Continental Shelf Beyond the 200-Mile Limit," in C. Philipp (ed.), *Liber amicorum Günther Jaenicke - Zum 85. Geburtstag* (Springer 1998).

"The Continental Shelf: Interplay of Law and Science," in N. Ando, E. McWhinney, and R. Wolfrum (eds.), *Liber Amicorum Judge Shigeru Oda, Volume II* (Kluwer Law International 2002).

"The Settlement of Disputes Arising from Conflicting Outer Continental Shelf Claims" (2009) 24 *International Journal of Marine and Coastal Law* 409.

"The Commission on the Limits of the Continental Shelf and Coastal States' Submissions," in H. P. Hestermeyer, D. König and N. Matz-Lück (eds.), *Coexistence, Cooperation and Solidarity: Liber Amicorum Rüdiger Wolfrum, Volume II* (Martinus Nijhoff Publishers 2012).

Noyes, J. E. "Judicial and Arbitral Proceedings and the Outer Limits of the Continental Shelf" (2009) 42 *Vanderbilt Journal of Transnational Law* 1211.

Nweihed, K. "Trinidad and Tobago–Venezuela, Report Number 2-13(3)," in J. I. Charney and LM Alexander (eds.), *International Maritime Boundaries, Vol. I* (Martinus Nijhoff 1993).

O'Connell, D. P. *The International Law of the Sea, Volume I* (I. A. Shearer ed., Oxford University Press 1982).

Oda, S. "Proposals for Revising the Convention on the Continental Shelf", *Fifty Years of the Law of the Sea: with a special section on the International Court of Justice: Selected Writings* (Kluwer Law International 2003).

"The Continental Shelf[1955]", *Fifty Years of the Law of the Sea: with a special section on the International Court of Justice: Selected Writings* (Kluwer Law International 2003).

Ong, D. M. "*Delimitation of the Outer Continental Shelf and Prospects for Revenue Sharing Between States and the International Community*," in J. Barrett and R. Barnes (eds.), *Law of the Sea: UNCLOS as a Living Treaty* (British Institute of International and Comparative Law 2016).

Orrego Vicuña, F. *The Exclusive Economic Zone: Regime and Legal Nature under International Law* (Cambridge University Press 1989).

"La Limite Intérieure de La Limite Extérieure: Le Chevauchement de Revendications et La Délimitation Du Plateau Continental Étendu," in R. Casado Raigón and G. Cataldi (eds.), *L'évolution et l'état actuel du droit international de la mer: mélanges de droit de la mer offerts à Daniel Vignes* (Bruylant 2009).

Oude Elferink, A. G. "Does Undisputed Title to a Maritime Zone Always Exclude Its Delimitation: The Grey Area Issue" (1998) 13 *International Journal of Marine and Coastal Law* 143.

"The Impact of the Law of the Sea Convention on the Delimitation of Maritime Boundaries," in D. Vidas and W. Østreng (eds.), *Order for the Oceans at the Turn of the Century* (Kluwer Law International 1999).

"Submissions of Coastal States to the CLCS in Cases of Unresolved Land or Maritime Disputes," in M. H. Nordquist. J. N. Moore and T. H. Heidar (eds.), *Legal and Scientific Aspects of Continental Shelf Limits* (Martinus Nijhoff Publishers 2004).

"The Continental Shelf beyond 200 NM: The Relationship between the CLCS and Third Party Dispute Settlement," in A. G. Oude Elferink and D. R. Rothwell (eds.), *Oceans Management in the 21st Century: Institutional Frameworks and Responses* (Martinus Nijhoff Publishers 2004).

"Article 76 of the LOSC on the Definition of the Continental Shelf: Questions Concerning Its Interpretation from a Legal Perspective" (2006) 21 *International Journal of Marine and Coastal Law* 269.

"The Establishment of Outer Limits of the Continental Shelf beyond 200 Nautical Miles by the Coastal State: The Possibilities of Other States to Have an Impact on the Process" (2009) 24 *International Journal of Marine and Coastal Law* 535.

*The Delimitation of the Continental Shelf between Denmark, Germany and the Netherlands: Arguing Law, Practicing Politics?* (Cambridge University Press 2013).

"International Law and Negotiated and Adjudicated Maritime Boundaries: A Complex Relationship" (2015) 58 *German Yearbook of International Law* 231.

"ITLOS's Approach to the Delimitation of the Continental Shelf Beyond 200 Nautical Miles in the Bangladesh/Myanmar Case: Theoretical and Practical Difficulties," in R. Wolfrum, M. Seršić, and T. Šošić (eds.), *Contemporary Developments in International Law: Essays in Honour of Budislav Vukas* (Brill 2015).

"The Delimitation of the Continental Shelf Beyond 200 Nautical Miles in the Arctic Ocean: Recent Developments, Applicable Law and Possible Outcomes," in R. Long, J. N. Moore, and M. H. Nordquist (eds.), *Challenges of the Changing Arctic* (Brill 2016).

"Paragraph 5(a) of Annex I to the Rules of Procedure of the Commission on the Limits of the Continental Shelf: Solution to a Problem or Problem without a Solution?," in M. H. Nordquist, J. N. Moore, and R. Long (eds.), *Legal Order in the World's Oceans: UN Convention on the Law of the Sea* (Brill Nijhoff 2017).

"Relevant Coasts and Relevant Area - The Difficulty of Developing General Concepts in a Case-Specific Context," in A. G. Oude Elferink, T. Henriksen, and S. V. Busch (eds.), *Maritime Boundary Delimitation: The Case Law: Is It Consistent and Predictable?* (Cambridge University Press 2018).

Oude Elferink, A. G. and Johnson, C. "Outer Limits of the Continental Shelf and "Disputed Areas": State Practice Concerning Article 76(10) of the LOS Convention" (2006) 21 *International Journal of Marine and Coastal Law* 461.

Oude Elferink, A. G. Henriksen, T. and Busch, S. V. "Conclusions," in Alex G. Oude Elferink, Tore Henriksen and Signe Veierud Busch (eds.), *Maritime Boundary Delimitation: The Case Law: Is It Consistent and Predictable?* (Cambridge University Press 2018).

"The Judiciary and the Law of Maritime Delimitation: Setting the Stage," in Alex G. Oude Elferink, Tore Henriksen and Signe Veierud Busch (eds.), *Maritime Boundary Delimitation: The Case Law: Is It Consistent and Predictable?* (Cambridge University Press 2018).

Oxman, B. H. "Political, Strategic, and Historical Considerations," in J. I. Charney and L. M. Alexander (eds.), *International Maritime Boundaries, Volume I* (Martinus Nijhoff Publishers 1993).

"The Territorial Temptation: A Siren Song at Sea" (2006) 100 *American Journal of International Law* 830.

Paik, J.-H. "The Role of Proportionality in Maritime Delimitation: State of Jurisprudence," in H. P. Hestermeyer, D. König, N. Matz-Lück, V. Röben, A. Seibert-Fohr, P.-T. Stoll, and S. Vöneky (eds.), *Coexistence, Cooperation and Solidarity: Liber Amicorum Rüdiger Wolfrum, Volume I* (Martinus Nijhoff Publishers 2012).

"The Origin of the Principle of Natural Prolongation: North Sea Continental Shelf Cases Revisited," in L. del Castillo (ed.), *Law of the Sea, From Grotius to the International Tribunal for the Law of the Sea: Liber Amicorum Judge Hugo Caminos* (Brill Nijhoff 2015).

Park, C.-H. "Australia–France (New Caledonia), Report Number 5-1," in J. I. Charney and L. M. Alexander (eds.), *International Maritime Boundaries, Vol. I* (Martinus Nijhoff 1993).

"Australia–Papua New Guinea, Report Number 5-3," in J. I. Charney and L. M. Alexander (eds.), *International Maritime Boundaries, Vol. I* (Martinus Nijhoff 1993).

"Australia–Solomon Islands, Report Number 5-4," in J. I. Charney and L. M. Alexander (eds.), *International Maritime Boundaries, Vol. I* (Martinus Nijhoff 1993).

"Papua New Guinea–Solomon Islands, Report Number 5-16," in J. I. Charney and L. M. Alexander (eds.), *International Maritime Boundaries, Vol. I* (Martinus Nijhoff 1993).

Parson, L. "Observations on the Article 76 Process: Coastal States" Submissions and the Work Outstanding for the Commission on the Limits of the Continental Shelf," in J. Barrett and R. Barnes (eds.), *Law of the Sea: UNCLOS as a Living Treaty* (British Institute of International & Comparative Law 2016).

"Article 76," in A. Proelss (ed.), *The United Nations Convention on the Law of the Sea: A Commentary* (Hart 2017).

Phillips, J. C. "The Exclusive Economic Zone as a Concept in International Law" (1977) 26 *International and Comparative Law Quarterly* 585.

Platzöder, R. (ed.), Third United Nations Conference on the Law of the Sea: Documents, Volume I (Oceana Publications, Inc. 1982).

(ed.), Third United Nations Conference on the Law of the Sea: Documents, Volume II (Oceana Publications, Inc. 1982).

(ed.), Third United Nations Conference on the Law of the Sea: Documents, Volume III (Oceana Publications, Inc. 1982).

(ed.), Third United Nations Conference on the Law of the Sea: Documents, Volume IV (Oceana Publications, Inc. 1982).

(ed.), Third United Nations Conference on the Law of the Sea: Documents, Volume V (Oceana Publications, Inc. 1982).

(ed.), Third United Nations Conference on the Law of the Sea: Documents, Volume XI (Oceana Publications, Inc. 1982).

Pratt, M. "Kenya–Tanzania, Report Number 4-5(2)," in C. G. Lathrop (ed.), *International Maritime Boundaries, Vol. VII* (Brill Nijhoff 2016).

Prescott, V. "Australia–Indonesia (Timor and Arafura Seas), Report Number 6-2 (2)," in J. I. Charney and Lewis M. Alexander (eds.), *International Maritime Boundaries, Vol. I* (Martinus Nijhoff 1993).

"Australia (Heard/McDonald Islands)–France (Kerguelen Islands), Report Number 6-1," in J. I. Charney and L. M. Alexander (eds.), *International Maritime Boundaries, Vol. II* (Martinus Nijhoff 1993).

"Australia–Indonesia, Report Number 6-2(6)," in J. I. Charney and R. W. Smith (eds.), *International Maritime Boundaries, Vol. IV* (Martinus Nijhoff 2002).

"Resources of the Continental Margin and International Law," in P. J. Cook and C. M. Carleton (eds.), *Continental Shelf Limits: The Scientific and Legal Interface* (Oxford University Press 2000).

Prescott, V. and Schofield, C. H. *The Maritime Political Boundaries of the World* (2nd ed., Martinus Nijhoff Publishers 2005).

Prescott, V. and Triggs, G. "Mauritius–Syechelles, Report Number 6-22," in D. A. Colson and R. W. Smith (eds.), *International Maritime Boundaries, Vol. VI* (Martinus Nijhoff 2011).

Proelss, A. "Article 56," in A. Proelss (ed.), *The United Nations Convention on the Law of the Sea: A Commentary* (Hart 2017).

Pulvenis, J.-F. "The Continental Shelf Definition and Rules Applicable to Resources," in R.-J. Dupuy and D. Vignes (eds.), *A Handbook on the New Law of the Sea* (Martinus Nijhoff Publishers 1991).

Reuter, P. J.-M. "Une ligne unique de délimitation des espaces maritimes?", *Mélanges Georges Perrin* (Bernard Dutoit et Etienne Grisel 1984).

Riddell, A. "Evidence, Fact-Finding, and Experts," in C. P. R Romano, K. J. Alter, and Y. Shany (eds.), *The Oxford Handbook of International Adjudication* (Oxford University Press 2013).

Rosenne, S. *The Law and Practice of the International Court* (A W Sijthoff-Leyden 1965).

"The Position of the International Court of Justice on the Foundations of the Principle of Equity in International Law," in A. Bloed and P. van Dijk (eds.), *Forty Years International Court of Justice: Jurisdiction, Equity and Equality* (Europa Instituut 1988).

Roughton, D. and Trehearne, C. "The Continental Shelf" in D. Attard, M. Fitzmaurice, and N. A. Martinez Gutierrez (eds.), *The IMLI Manual on International Maritime Law, Volume I: The Law of the Sea* (Oxford University Press 2014).

Sbolci, L. "Supplementary Means of Interpretation," in E. Cannizzaro (ed.), *The Law of Treaties Beyond the Vienna Convention* (Oxford University Press 2011).

Schachter, O. "Linking Equity and Law in Maritime Delimitation," in N. Ando, E. McWhinney, and R. Wolfrum (eds.), *Liber Amicorum Judge Shigeru Oda, Volume II* (Kluwer Law International 2002).

Schofield, C. Telesetsky, A. and Lee, S. "A Tribunal Navigating Complex Waters: Implications of the Bay of Bengal Case" (2013) 44 *Ocean Development & International Law* 363.

Scofield, C. and Arsana, I. "Indonesia–Philippines, Report Number 5-41," in C. G. Lathrop (ed.), *International Maritime Boundaries, Vol. VII* (Brill Nijhoff 2016).

Scovazzi, T. "Where the Judge Approaches the Legislator: Some Cases Relating to Law of the Sea," in N. Boschiero, T. Scovazzi, C. Pitea, and C. Ragni (eds.), *International Courts and the Development of International Law: Essays in Honour of Tullio Treves* (TMC Asser Press 2013).

Serdy, A. "The Commission on the Limits of the Continental Shelf and Its Disturbing Propensity to Legislate" (2011) 26 *International Journal of Marine and Coastal Law* 355.

"Interpretation of UNCLOS Article 76 and the Negative Recommendation of the Commission on the Limits of the Continental Shelf on Ascension Island: Is the United Kingdom Stuck with It?" (2013) 2 *Cambridge Journal of International and Comparative Law* 591.

"Delineation of the Outer Limits of Canada's Arctic Ocean Continental Shelf and Its Delimitation with Neighboring States: Does It Matter Which Comes First?," in S. Lalonde and T. L. McDorman (eds.), *International Law and Politics of the Arctic Ocean: Essays in Honor of Donat Pharand* (Brill Nijhoff 2015).

Shi, J. "Maritime Delimitation in the Jurisprudence of the International Court of Justice" (2010) 9 *Chinese Journal of International Law* 271.

Simma, B. "The International Court of Justice and Scientific Expertise" (2012) 106 *Proceedings of the Annual Meeting* (American Society of International Law) 230.

Smith, R. W. "Mexico–United States, Report Number 1-5(2)," in J. I. Charney and R. W. Smith (eds.), *International Maritime Boundaries, Vol. IV* (Martinus Nijhoff 2002).

Smith, R. "Geographic Considerations in Maritime Boundary Delimitations," in D. G. Dallmeyer and L. DeVorsey, Jr. (eds.), *Rights to Oceanic Resources* (Martinus Nijhoff Publishers 1989).

Smith, R. W. and Taft, G. "Legal Aspects of the Continental Shelf," in P. J. Cook and C. M. Carleton (eds.), *Continental Shelf Limits: The Scientific and Legal Interface* (Oxford University Press 2000).

Suarez, S. V. *The Outer Limits of the Continental Shelf: Legal Aspects of Their Establishment* (Springer 2008).

Subedi, S. P. "Problems and Prospects for the Commission on the Limits of the Continental Shelf in Dealing with Submissions by Coastal States in Relation to the Ocean Territory beyond 200 Nautical Miles," (2011) 26 *International Journal of Marine and Coastal Law* 413.

Taft, G. "Applying the Law of the Sea Convention and the Role of the Scientific Community Relating to Establishing the Outer Limits of the Continental Shelf Where It Extends Beyond the 200 Mile Limit," in M. H. Nordquist, R. Long, T. H. Heidar, and J. N. Moore (eds.), *Law, Science & Ocean Management* (Martinus Nijhoff Publishers 2007).

"The United Nations Convention on the Law of the Sea: The Commission on the Limits of the Continental Shelf – A Force for Enhancing Stability in the Oceans (or Not)" (2010) 24 *Ocean Yearbook* 151.

Talmon, S. "Determining Customary International Law: The ICJ's Methodology between Induction, Deduction and Assertion" (2015) 26 *European Journal of International Law* 417.

Tams, C. J. "Article 50," in A. Zimmermann, C. Tomuschat, K. Oellers-Frahm, and C. J. Tam (eds.), *The Statute of the International Court of Justice: A Commentary* (2nd ed., Oxford University Press 2012).

Tanaka, Y. "Reflections on the Concept of Proportionality in the Law of Maritime Delimitation" (2001) 16 *International Journal of Marine and Coastal Law* 433.

"Reflections on Arctic Maritime Delimitations: A Comparative Analysis between the Case Law and State Practice" (2011) 80 *Nordic Journal of International Law* 459.

*The International Law of the Sea* (Cambridge University Press 2012).

"Reflections on the Territorial and Maritime Dispute between Nicaragua and Colombia before the International Court of Justice" (2013) 26 *Leiden Journal of International Law* 909.

"Article 83," in Alexander Proelss (ed.), *The United Nations Convention on the Law of the Sea: A Commentary* (Hart 2017).

"The Disproportionality Test in the Law of Maritime Delimitation," in Alex G. Oude Elferink, Tore Henriksen and Signe Veierud Busch (eds.), *Maritime Boundary Delimitation: The Case Law: Is It Consistent and Predictable?* (Cambridge University Press 2018).

*Predictability and Flexibility in the Law of Maritime Delimitation* (2nd ed., Hart 2019).

Tanja, G. J. *The Legal Determination of International Maritime Boundaries: The Progressive Development of Continental Shelf, EFZ and EEZ Law* (Kluwer Law and Taxation Publishers 1990).

Tassin, V. J. M. *Les défis de l'extension du plateau continental: La consécration d'un nouveau rapport de l'État à son territoire* (Pedone 2013).

Thirlway, H. "The Law and Procedure of the International Court of Justice 1960-1989: Part One" (1990) 60 *British Yearbook of International Law* 1.

"The Law and Procedure of the International Court of Justice 1960–1989 Part Five" (1994) 64 *British Yearbook of International Law* 1.

"The Law and Procedure of the International Court of Justice 1960–1989, Part Six" (1995) 65 *British Yearbook of International Law* 1.

"Article 30," in A. Zimmermann, C. Tomuschat, K. Oellers-Frahm, and J. Tams (eds.), *The Statute of the International Court of Justice: A Commentary* (2nd ed., Oxford University Press 2012).

*Law and Procedure of the International Court of Justice: Fifty Years of Jurisprudence, Volume I* (Oxford University Press 2013).

*Law and Procedure of the International Court of Justice: Fifty Years of Jurisprudence, Volume II* (Oxford University Press 2013).

*The International Court of Justice* (Oxford University Press 2016)

Thor Gudlaugsson, S. "Natural Prolongation and the Concept of the Continental Margin for the Purposes of Article 76," in M. H. Nordquist, J.N. Moore, and T. H. Heidar (eds.), *Legal and Scientific Aspects of Continental Shelf Limits* (Martinus Nijhoff Publishers 2004).

Tomka, P. "Custom and the International Court of Justice" (2013) 12 *Law and Practice of International Courts and Tribunals* 195.

Tomuschat, C. "Article 36," in A. Zimmermann, C. Tomuschat, K. Oellers-Frahm, and C. J. Tams (eds.), *The Statute of the International Court of Justice: A Commentary* (3rd ed., Oxford University Press 2019).

Treves, T. "La limite extérieure du plateau continental: Evolution récente de la pratique" (1989) 35 *Annuaire français de droit international* 724.

"Remarks on Submissions to the Commission on the Limits of the Continental Shelf in Response to Judge Marotta's Report" (2006) 21 *International Journal of Marine and Coastal Law* 363.

"Law and Science in the Interpretation of the Law of the Sea Convention: Article 76 Between the Law of the Sea Tribunal and the Commission on the Limits of the Continental Shelf" (2012) 3 *Journal of International Dispute Settlement* 483.

"Law and Science in the Jurisprudence of the International Tribunal for the Law of the Sea," in Harry N. Scheiber, James Kraska and Kwon (eds.), *Science, Technology, and New Challenges to Ocean Law* (Brill Nijhoff 2015).

"UNCLOS and Non-Party States before the International Court of Justice," in Carlo Espósito, J. Kraska, H. N. Scheiber, and M.-S. Kwon (eds.), *Oceans Law and Policy: 20 Years under UNCLOS* (Brill Nijhoff 2016).

Thygesen, K. and Baker, E. *The Shelf Programme: A Decade of Successfully Helping to Secure the Maritime Rights of Developing Coastal States* (GRID–Arendal 2015).

United Nations (ed.), *Laws and Regulations on the Regime of the High Seas* (United Nations 1951).

(ed.), *The Law of the Sea: National Legislation on the Continental Shelf* (United Nations 1989).

*The Law of the Sea: Definition of the Continental Shelf* (United Nations 1993).

Van Pay, B. J. "Disputed Areas Beyond 200 Nautical Miles: How Many and Will Geophysical Characteristics Matter in Their Resolution?," in M. H. Nordquist and J. N. Moore (eds.), *Maritime Border Diplomacy* (Martinus Nijhoff Publishers 2012).

Vega-Barbosa, G. "The Admissibility of Outer Continental Shelf Delimitation Claims Before the ICJ Absent a Recommendation by the CLCS" (2018) 49 *Ocean Development & International Law* 103.

Verville, E. "United States-Soviet Union, Report Number 1-6," in I. L. Charney and L. M. Alexander (eds.), *International Maritime Boundaries, Vol. I* (Martinus Nijhoff 1993).

Vidas, D. "Consolidation or Deviation? On Trends and Challenges in the Settlement of Maritime Delimitation Disputes by International Courts and Tribunals," in N. Boschiero, T. Scovazzi, C. Pitea, and C. Ragni (eds.), *International Courts and the Development of International Law: Essays in Honour of Tullio Treves* (T M C Asser Press 2013).

"The Delimitation of the Territorial Sea, the Continental Shelf, and the EEZ - A Comparative Perspective," in A. G. Oude Elferink, T. Henriksen, and S. V. Busch (eds.), *Maritime Boundary Delimitation: The Case Law: Is It Consistent and Predictable?* (Cambridge University Press 2018).

Villiger, M. E. *Customary International Law and Treaties: A Study of Their Interactions and Interrelations with Special Consideration of the 1969 Vienna Convention on the Law of Treaties* (Martinus Nijhoff Publishers 1985).

Volterra, R. "Problems Arising from Submissions by States to the CLCS in Relation to Disputed Areas: A Selective Survey of State Practice to Date," in C. R. Symmons (ed.), *Selected Contemporary Issues in the Law of the Sea* (Martinus Nijhoff Publishers 2011).

Waldock, C. H. M. "The Legal Basis of Claims to the Continental Shelf" (1950) 36 *Transactions of the Grotius Society* 115.

Weil, P. "Délimitation Maritime et Délimitation Terrestre," in M. Tabory and Y. Dinstein (eds.), *International Law at a Time of Perplexity: Essays in Honour of Shabtai Rosenne* (Martinus Nijhoff Publishers 1989).

*The Law of Maritime Delimitation: Reflections* (Grotius Publications Limited 1989).

"Geographical Considerations in Maritime Delimitation," in J. I. Charney and L. M. Alexander (eds.), *International Maritime Boundaries, Volume I* (Martinus Nijhoff Publishers 1993).

"A propos du droit coutumier en matière de délimitation maritime", *Écrits de droit international* (Presses Universitaires de France 2000).

Wolfrum, R. "The Role of International Dispute Settlement Institutions in the Delimitation of the Outer Continental Shelf," in R. Lagoni and D. Vignes (eds.), *Maritime Delimitation* (Martinus Nijhoff Publishers 2006).

"The Delimitation of the Outer Continental Shelf: Procedural Considerations", *liber amicorum Jean-Pierre Cot: Le procès international.* (Bruylant 2009).

Yanai, S. "International Law Concerning Maritime Boundary Delimitation," in D. Attard, M. Fitzmaurice, and N. A. Martinez Gutierrez (eds.), *The IMLI Manual on International Maritime Law, Volume I: The Law of the Sea* (Oxford University Press 2014).

# INDEX

For EU product safety concerns, contact us at Calle de José Abascal, 56–1°,
28003 Madrid, Spain or eugpsr@cambridge.org.

www.ingramcontent.com/pod-product-compliance
Ingram Content Group UK Ltd.
Pitfield, Milton Keynes, MK11 3LW, UK
UKHW022313240426
470365UK00021B/615
* 9 7 8 1 1 0 8 8 2 1 6 5 0 *